THE REMINISCENCES OF
Vice Admiral David C. Richardson
U.S. Navy (Retired)

INTERVIEWED BY
Paul Stillwell

U.S. Naval Institute • Annapolis, Maryland

Copyright © 1998

Preface

Through much of the oral history that follows, Admiral Richardson demonstrates himself as an individual who was not easily satisfied with the status quo. As a midshipman and junior officer, he felt restless at what he considered the Navy's often stifling ways of operating and training to operate. Naval aviation appealed to him because it was forward-looking and because aviators seemed to have a more open-minded approach than surface officers. He was a fighter pilot during the last days of peace prior to World War II and in the wearisome Guadalcanal campaign in late 1942.

Back in the States he had training billets that enabled him to pass on to new pilots what he had learned in the Pacific theater of war. Time and again, as he subsequently moved up the ladder of seniority, both at sea and ashore, Richardson sought to bring a rational approach to naval warfare and instill improvements as appropriate. In the late 1940s he was involved at the Naval War College in analytical studies of World War II operations and commanded a carrier air group. In the 1950s he was on the Joint Staff, was executive officer of an escort carrier in the Korean War, and served in OpNav. He had two tours involving NATO, then later commanded the aged oiler <u>Cimarron</u> and the aircraft carrier <u>Hornet</u>.

During much of the latter part of Admiral Richardson's career, his particular emphasis was on the merging of intelligence and operations. The transcript returns to this theme time and again when he discusses his tours of duty as Commander Task Force 77, Commander Sixth Fleet, and as a consultant following retirement from active service. Of particular note was the careful study of bombing results in North Vietnam to increase effectiveness and the creation in Sixth Fleet of the Ocean Surveillance Information System. He provides numerous examples to illustrate his point that operational commanders need timely, accurate information on which to base decisions.

In the course of moving from the initial raw transcript of the oral interviews to this final version, both Admiral Richardson and I have done considerable editing in the interests of accuracy, smoothness, and clarity. Some sections have been rearranged in sequence in order to facilitate a chronological approach to his career. In addition, I have inserted footnotes to provide further information for readers who use the volume. In going through the entire process of editing and footnoting, Admiral Richardson has been most cooperative. The result is a final version that has been considerably enhanced over that in the raw initial transcripts.

Ms. Ann Hassinger of the Naval Institute's history division has made a significant contribution through her diligence in the overall process of printing, proofreading, and overseeing the binding of the completed volumes.

Paul Stillwell
Director, History Division
U.S. Naval Institute
January 1998

VICE ADMIRAL DAVID CHARLES RICHARDSON
UNITED STATES NAVY (RETIRED)

David Charles Richardson was born in Meridian, Mississippi, on 8 April 1914, son of Mr. I. W. Richardson and Mrs. Anne Kate Schamber Richardson. He attended Meridian High School and Marion (Alabama) Institute before entering the U.S. Naval Academy, Annapolis, Maryland, on 27 June 1932. Graduated with the degree of bachelor of science and commissioned ensign in the U.S. Navy on 4 June 1936, he subsequently progressed in rank to that of vice admiral, to date from 14 August 1968.

After graduation from the Naval Academy in June 1936, he was assigned for two years to the battleship Tennessee (BB-43). When detached, he joined the destroyer Downes (DD-375) as communication officer and served in that capacity until February 1939, when he reported to the Naval Air Station, Pensacola, Florida, for flight training. He was designated a naval aviator in April 1940 and was ordered to Fighting Squadron Five. He served in that squadron, after the outbreak of World War II, until December 1942. He participated in combat operations in both the Atlantic and Pacific oceans, including the assault on Guadalcanal and in its subsequent defense. He was awarded the Distinguished Flying Cross and is credited with shooting down four enemy aircraft.

During the period January 1943 to September 1944, he was flight officer in fighter operational training units in Jacksonville and Sanford, Florida, and subsequently in command of fighter training units in Vero Beach and Daytona Beach, Florida. He was next assigned to Fighter Squadron One as commanding Officer. In January 1945 he joined the staff of Commander Air Force Pacific Fleet and served throughout that year as assistant force training officer. He was awarded the Bronze Star Medal "for meritorious achievement [in that capacity] in connection with operations against enemy Japanese forces in the Pacific War Area from March 3 to September 2, 1945 . . . "

From January to June 1946, he was a student at the Royal Navy Staff College, London, England. Upon his return to the United States, he reported to the Naval War College, where he was student for a year, then served a year on the staff of the college for preparation of analyses of naval actions of World War II. In September 1948 he became Commander Air Group 13 and deployed to the Western Pacific on board the carrier Princeton (CV-37). When detached from that assignment in September 1949, he was ordered to the Joint Staff, Joint Chiefs of Staff, Washington, D.C., where he was assigned to the Joint Strategic Plans Group with the element designated cognizance of North Atlantic Treaty Organization affairs. His team was involved in the transition from NATO planning groups to a command structure, and with the establishment of military plans and policies at the outset of the NATO organization. He next had sea duty from April 1952 until August 1953 as executive officer of the escort carrier Badoeng Strait (CVE-116). In that capacity he saw further combat duty in Korean waters under the United Nations Command.

After a year's service as war plans officer on the staff of Commander Air Force Pacific Fleet, he reported to the Navy Department, Washington, D.C., for duty in the Office of the Chief of Naval Operations (Air Weapons Analysis), from August 1954 until June 1957. He then joined the staff of Commander Striking and Support Force, Southern Europe, as plans, operations, and intelligence officer. In September 1959 he assumed command of the oiler Cimarron (AO-22). Upon completion of that assignment he became commanding officer of the antisubmarine carrier Hornet (CVS-12). During his tour as commanding officer, the Hornet won four of the five major awards for this class ship in the Pacific, including the Battle Efficiency E. In November 1961 he reported to the Office of the Chief of Naval Operations. There he served as assistant for Joint Chiefs Matters to the Director, Strategic Plans Division.

In February 1964 he became Commander Fleet Air Norfolk/Commander Naval Air Bases Fourth and Fifth Naval Districts, with headquarters at the Naval Air Station, Norfolk, Virginia. In February 1966 he assumed command of Carrier Division Seven and in August of that year transferred to command of Task Force 77 of the Seventh Fleet, which consisted of five attack carriers and about 24 destroyers and cruisers. This force was engaged in combat operations against North Vietnam. He was awarded the Distinguished Service Medal "for exceptionally meritorious service from July 1966 to May 1967 . . . " He is also entitled to the ribbon for and a facsimile of the Navy United Commendation awarded his flagships during this period.

On 5 July 1967 he reported as Assistant Deputy Chief of Naval Operations (Air), Navy Department, and in August 1968 assumed command of the Sixth Fleet, with additional duty as Commander Naval Striking and Support Forces, Southern Europe. "For exceptionally meritorious service" in the latter, assignment, he was awarded a gold star in lieu of a second Distinguished Service Medal. He became deputy Commander in Chief U.S. Pacific Fleet and Chief of Staff to the Commander in Chief Pacific Fleet in September 1970. He was awarded a gold star in lieu of a third Distinguished Service Medal and was cited in part as follows: "Because of his rare ability to synthesize all information flowing into Headquarters and to make exact and timely recommendations to the Commander, [he] made a most significant contribution to the Pacific Fleet readiness . . . " On 1 July 1972 he was transferred to the retired list of the U.S. Navy.

Dates of Rank:

27 June 1932	Midshipman
4 June 1936	Ensign
4 June 1939	Lieutenant (junior grade)
1 January 1942	Lieutenant
30 March 1943	Lieutenant Commander
15 March 1944	Commander
1 January 1955	Captain
1 June 1964	Rear Admiral
14 August 1968	Vice Admiral

Chronological Record of Service:

June 1936 to June 1938	USS Tennessee (BB-43)
June 1938 to January 1939	USS Downes (DD-375)
January 1939 to April 1940	Instruction at Naval Air Station, Pensacola, Florida
April 1940 to December 1942	Fighting Squadron Five
December 1942 to May 1943	Naval Air Operational Training Naval Air Station, Jacksonville, Florida
May 1943 to August 1943	Naval Air Station, Jacksonville, Florida
August 1943 to January 1944	Naval Air Station, Sanford, Florida
January 1944 to March 1944	Naval Air Station, Vero Beach, Florida
September 1944 to January 1945	Commanding Officer, Fighting Squadron One
January 1945 to December 1945	Staff, Commander Air Force Pacific Fleet
January 1946 to June 1946	Student at the Royal Naval Staff College, London, England
June 1946 to June 1947	Student, Naval War College, Newport, Rhode Island
June 1947 to May 1948	Staff, Naval War College
May 1948 to July 1948	Instruction at Naval Air Station, Jacksonville, Florida
August 1948 to September 1949	Commander Carrier Air Group 13
September 1949 to March 1952	Joint Strategic Plans Group, the Joint Staff
April 1952 to July 1953	Executive Office, USS Badoeng Strait (CVE-116)
July 1953 to August 1954	War Plans Officer, Staff, Commander Air Force Pacific Fleet
August 1954 to June 1957	Head, Sea Based Air Striking Forces, office of the Deputy Chief of Naval Operations (Air)
June 1957 to August 1959	Assistant Chief of Staff for Plans, Operations, and Intelligence, headquarters Naval Striking and Support Forces, Southern Europe
August 1959 to September 1959	Student, Naval Schools Command, Treasure Island, San Francisco
September 1959 to September 1960	Commanding Officer, USS Cimarron (AO-22)
September 1960 to October 1961	Commanding Officer, USS Hornet (CVS-12)
October 1961 to February 1964	Assistant to the Director of the Strategic Plans Division for JCS Matters, Office of the Chief of Naval Operations
February 1964 to February 1966	Commander Fleet Air Norfolk/ Commander Naval Air Bases, Fourth and Fifth Naval Districts
February 1966 to August 1966	Commander Carrier Division Seven
August 1966 to May 1967	Commander Carrier Division Five/Commander Task Force 77
July 1967 to August 1968	Assistant Deputy Chief of Naval Operations (Air), Office of the Chief of Naval Operations
August 1968 to August 1970	Commander Sixth Fleet/Commander Striking and Support Forces, Southern Europe

August 1970 to June 1972   Deputy Commander in Chief Pacific Fleet

Medals and Awards

Distinguished Service Medal with two gold stars in lieu of second and third awards
Distinguished Flying Cross
Bronze Star Medal
Purple Heart
President Unit Citation awarded to the First Marine Division, Reinforced
Navy Unit Commendation awarded to the USS Constellation (CVA-64)
Navy Unit Commendation awarded to the USS Oriskany (CVA-34)
Navy Unit Commendation awarded to the USS Kitty Hawk (CVA-63)
American Defense Service Medal with Fleet Clasp
American Campaign Medal
World War II Victory Medal
Navy Occupation Service Medal with Asia Clasp
China Service Medal
National Defense Service Medal with one bronze star in lieu of second award
Korean Service Medal
United Nations Service Medal
Vietnam Service Medal with one bronze star
Republic of Vietnam Campaign Medal with Device
Korean Presidential Unit Citation Badge

Personal Data

Wife: Jeanne McHugh Simonds Richardson
Children: David Wilson Richardson, born 30 December 1943
           Suzanne Caprice Simonds (stepdaughter), born 11 January 1948
           Robert M. Richardson, born 14 July 1950
           Ruthanne Richardson, born 15 February 1956
           Jeanne Schamber Richardson, born 14 May 1958
           Samuel Bristol Richardson, born 3 September 1961

Authorization

The U.S. Naval Institute is hereby authorized to make available to individuals, libraries, and other repositories of its choosing the transcripts of three oral history interviews concerning the life and naval career of the undersigned. The interviews were recorded on 29 March 1992, 30 March 1992, and 2 April 1992 in collaboration with Paul Stillwell for the U.S. Naval Institute.

The undersigned does hereby release and assign to the U.S. Naval Institute the rights and title to these interviews, with the exception that the undersigned retains the right to use the material for his own purposes, as he sees fit. The copyright in both the oral and transcribed versions shall be the sole property of the U.S. Naval Institute. The tape recordings of the interviews are and will remain the property of the U.S. Naval Institute.

Signed and sealed this 27th day of October 1997.

David C. Richardson
Vice Admiral, U.S. Navy (Retired)

David C. Richardson #1 - 1

Interview Number 1 with Vice Admiral David C. Richardson, U.S. Navy (Retired)

Place: Admiral Richardson's in-town home, Coronado, California

Date: Sunday, 29 March 1992

Interviewer: Paul Stillwell

Q: Admiral, just to begin at the beginning, could you please start with when and where you were born and something about your parents and your ancestors.

Admiral Richardson: I was born in Meridian, Mississippi, on April 8, 1914. My father was of English and Welsh descent. His antecedents came to this country in the late 1600s. The earliest record we have is about a Welshman by the name of John Ap Evan and his wife, Barbara, from Tregerif. One of their daughters, Elizabeth Bevan, married Samuel Richardson, and that was ten generations back from me. My mother's family is German--Schambers and Schweikers. They came to Mississippi and Indiana in the early 1800s from southwestern Germany.

I attended high school in Meridian, Mississippi, prepped for the Naval Academy at Marion Military Institute, entered the Naval Academy in the summer of 1932, graduating with the class of '36.

Q: I'd be interested in a little more detail on your boyhood. What do you remember about growing up in Mississippi?

Admiral Richardson: Well, it was a rural community, lots of sports--baseball, kids, football, things of that nature. I was too small to be effective in sports. Very pleasant, wonderful childhood.

Q: What sort of subjects did you do best in in school?

Admiral Richardson: Chemistry was my best subject. I did fairly well in all of my subjects, except language, and I might add that I was a horrible disappointment to my Spanish teacher at the Naval Academy. I've forgotten his name. He was a little short fellow.*

Q: He'd been there almost from the time of the Spanish-American War, I believe.

Admiral Richardson: I think he had. He came over one day with his little notebook when I was reciting something. He looked down at his book, then he looked up at me, and then back down to his book. He shook his head in disbelief and walked away. [Laughter]

Q: What sort of work was your father in?

Admiral Richardson: He was a lumberman and had been with the railroad before he moved south from Indiana. He was born in Kentucky. In 1937 he died of a stroke at age 57. My mother lived on in Mississippi and later moved to Long Beach, California. Then she lived here in Coronado in this house--508 Ninth Street--in her later years. She died in 1974.

When I commanded Sixth Fleet--August of '68 to the end of August '70--Ike Kidd had First Fleet.† My mother had cancer. Ike would send a car and driver over, pick her up, take her to the hospital for her treatment, and bring her home.

Q: He was very thoughtful in that regard.

Admiral Richardson: Yes.

Q: As a boy did you have any hobbies or interests other than the scholastic ones?

---

* Professor Arturo Fernandez taught in the modern languages department of the Naval Academy from 1905 to 1938.
† Vice Admiral Isaac C. Kidd, Jr., USN, served as Commander First Fleet from September 1969 to August 1970.

Admiral Richardson: Well, at the Naval Academy, I boxed for three years, but I decided getting my head punched wasn't such a good idea.

Q: What do you remember about the racial climate in Mississippi as you grew up? That, of course, is Deep South.

Admiral Richardson: We really had no problems that we as youngsters were aware of. There were occasional brushes on sidewalks when groups of blacks and groups of whites would come toward each other, and there would be a struggle about who would move off the sidewalk. Nothing of significance at that time.

My uncle lived in Meridian until his death in '79. I was back to visit with him many times through the mid- and late-'70s because he was in ill health. While I was there, one night he wanted me to get him a bottle of whiskey at a shopping center up the street several blocks, so I drove. It was 8:00 or 9:00 at night. There was one light on in the entire shopping center, the one in the liquor store. I walked into the place. There was a young woman, maybe 19 or 20 years old, tending the cash register. She was the only person in the entire square. I got my bottle of liquor and paid her. As I started out, I said, "Aren't you afraid of being here?"

She said, "No, no problem."

I think blacks and whites there respected one another, in general.

Q: What motivated you to seek an appointment to the Naval Academy?

Admiral Richardson: I suspected my dad thought a naval officer would spend his life reclining in a comfortable deck chair on a battleship, living a very pleasant life, perhaps with a whiskey sour in his hand. He thought that would be great for him, hence for me.

Q: Was it something you sought for yourself?

Admiral Richardson: No, it wasn't, although when I was perhaps 12 to 15 years old, in that range, Stick Sutherland, naval aviator, came to an Easter party at our house.* He was dressed in whites. He was a very good-looking man, anyway, and I took one look at him, and I said, "That's for me."

Q: The Marion Institute had quite a reputation as a feeder school for the Naval Academy.†

Admiral Richardson: Yes.

Q: How did that arrangement work out in your case?

Admiral Richardson: Very well.

Q: What do you remember specifically about the system that was used there?

Admiral Richardson: The main thing was that they made you work hard. You were on a strict time schedule, and you were expected to move right along in your studies. Their instruction was of good quality, and the discipline was good. I thought it was a very fine school. In fact, I later sent two of my sons there for a couple of years each.

Q: Some of the prep schools used the method of teaching from old entrance exams. Did Marion do that?

Admiral Richardson: Yes, they did, but not exclusively that. But if one also studied the old entrance exams, there was just about every aspect of English and mathematics that one could expect to meet. I took the long exam. I don't remember the details now, but there were four or five different subjects. Geometry was one.

---

* Ensign William A. Sutherland, Jr., USN, who eventually retired as a rear admiral in 1967.
† Marion Military Institute is in Marion, Alabama, which is on the west side of the state, relatively close to Meridian, on the east side of Mississippi.

Q: Your father must have been reasonably prosperous to send you to the school during the Depression.*

Admiral Richardson: No, he and his partner went broke in 1935. They were shipping lumber out to Chicago and the central U.S. on the Illinois Central Railroad. When the carloads of lumber would get there, the recipients were always finding something wrong. Then the lumber had to be sold at auction. Buyers were able to get carload lots at $21.00 to $23.00 per 1,000 board feet that way. But Dad and his partner sold only the amount of lumber that they had to sell in order to keep liquid. You can do that for only so long, because it was going below cost. So they closed down in '34 or '35. Then he opened up a couple of service stations, which he then ran until he suffered a stroke in 1936.

Q: That was at a time you were already a midshipman, so he evidently was able to afford it before then.

Admiral Richardson: Yes. The costs weren't all that stiff. As I recall, it was $1,500, and I had that much in my savings account. That was a lot of money in those days.

Q: Yes, indeed, it was. It's probably more than you made as an ensign, or close to it.

Admiral Richardson: My base pay was $125.00 a month as an ensign.

Q: What sort of political maneuvering went into getting your appointment to the Naval Academy?

Admiral Richardson: The head of the major bank in Meridian was a very close friend of the

---

* Following the crash of the New York Stock Exchange in late October 1929, the United States was plunged into the Great Depression, from which it did not recover until the nation geared up for World War II at the beginning of the 1940s. The Depression was marked by high unemployment and many business failures.

family. Ross Collins was the congressman from the area.* He had promised me an appointment several years earlier, but when the Depression came and Congress cut back on the number of people who were entering, Collins lost that appointment. He offered me an appointment to West Point instead.

The president of the bank, a man by the name of Paul Brown, went to Collins and gave him the Dutch uncle treatment: "You promised, and you come through." So Collins traded the West Point appointment with a congressman from Pennsylvania for one for me. I was appointed from western Pennsylvania, so my accent was suspicious, to say the least. But you can imagine this, "Where are you from?" I was asked on reporting in.

[Imitating southern accent] "I'm frum Pennsylvania, suh." [Laughter]

Q: I'll bet you got some interesting reactions.

Admiral Richardson: Yes.

Q: What do you recall about arriving in Annapolis and beginning the process of being a plebe?†

Admiral Richardson: Nothing that's noteworthy. I followed my nose. That's about all there was to it. I was paired with a very fine young man by the name of Bill Kaufman, William M. Kaufman.‡ He and I roomed together the rest of our time at the Naval Academy. We had two more roommates that joined us. After graduation, all four of us went out to the battleship <u>Tennessee</u> together. Two of our four roommates are dead now. One, Vice Admiral Jim O'Grady, died about three or four years ago.§ The other, Warfield

---

* Ross A. Collins (Democrat-Mississippi) served in the U.S. House of Representatives from 1921 to 1935 and from 1937 to 1943. Collins hailed from Meridian, the same town in which the Richardsons lived.
† A midshipman in his first year is called a plebe; second year, youngster or third classman; third year, second classman; fourth year, first classman.
‡ Midshipman William M. Kaufman, USN, stood 17th of the 261 graduates in the class of 1936. He eventually retired as a captain in 1966.
§ Vice Admiral James W. O'Grady, USN (Ret.), died 13 October 1986.

Bennett, from Kentucky, died three years ago of Lou Gehrig's disease.* Bill Kaufman lives in the San Francisco area now, and we are in close touch.

Q: People have memories of the hazing--or whatever you might want to call it--as part of the indoctrination process. What are your recollections?

Admiral Richardson: My first classman was a Jewish man named Coleman, who came from the Bronx. I haven't thought of it in a long time. He was absolutely filthy. The clothes he wore were all stamped "Do not send to the laundry." All that was left of his shirts was the collar and surrounding cloth, but that's all that shows anyway outside his uniform. I'd have to make his bed up every Saturday night. He had no spare linen. He expected me to go to my classmates and "borrow" their linen to give him a clean bed. I wouldn't do it. I'd just pull the old dirty linen and put it back on his bed again. After many weeks of that, he lit into me. Dirty shirts--the same thing with that. But one time he signed up for going out early to the local Roman Catholic church service, then lied about it and got kicked out of the Naval Academy. The authorities were waiting for him to make a mistake.

My first class year, he came down to see me. I was a three-striper.† He gave me a long lecture on how to behave at the Naval Academy. [Laughter] He'd already given me a perfect lesson on how not to behave. But I was amused at the change that took place in him when he really had to realize how he'd blown it, and for nothing more than sleeping in.

Q: How had he survived so long with that habit of filth? That's uncharacteristic of a midshipman.

Admiral Richardson: I don't know. In fact, the officers were laying for him. They'd had their eyes on him for some time, I'm sure, and they just could never quite catch him, because they knew they didn't want him. And so that's not strange. His roommate was really no better.

---

* Captain Warfield C. Bennett, Jr., USN (Ret.), died 30 June 1988.
† In the first-class or senior year, midshipmen in positions of leadership are identified by the number of stripes.

Q: Was that because of his Jewishness or his personal habits?

Admiral Richardson: No, it wasn't because of his Jewishness at all; it was because of his personal habits. There was no problem with that. We had no blacks there at that time.* That could have been a problem then had there been some.

Q: What do you remember about the business of having to memorize vast quantities of information and square corners and drill and do errands and all that?

Admiral Richardson: That didn't bother me. It was routine, and it really wasn't all bad, because you had young men coming in from all walks of life. Some of my classmates were poor as church mice. Others had well-to-do parents. The process of hazing had a beneficial effect on their young egos. It resulted in a feeling toward one's classmates that really wouldn't be there if we had not all endured a certain common experience. So the problem with hazing, in my view, is not the "damage" that's alleged to be inflicted on the plebes; it's the damage that it sometimes inflicts on those who do the hazing. It revealed more about the character of those who hazed.

Q: Damaged in what sense?

Admiral Richardson: Well, I'm not sure just how to put it, but it's an emotional thing. A little power can be a good thing, but sometimes--and in immature minds--it can be a bad thing. These young men, with considerably more power over their youngsters two to three years behind them, can damage themselves. The ones I have known who exploited hazing never got anywhere later in the service. I don't know one that I came to think of as a jerk who went anywhere in the service later.

---

* Midshipman George Joseph Trivers, USN, lasted three weeks after his arrival in 1937, the year after Richardson graduated. The first black graduate was Wesley A. Brown in the class of 1949. His oral history is in the Naval Institute collection. See R. L. Field, "The Black Midshipman at the Naval Academy," U.S. Naval Institute Proceedings, April 1973, page 31.

Q: Do you remember examples of this misuse of power?

Admiral Richardson: Well, yes. Overbearing.

Q: Physical punishment?

Admiral Richardson: No, no, it wasn't physical. I don't think the physical side of it really bothered people very much. Besides, that's something you can react to. It's an emotional condition, one where they're browbeating you.

Q: Intimidation.

Admiral Richardson: Intimidation and browbeating. That's the sort of thing that some do, and it's very unfortunate.

Q: That's like this fellow you mentioned who served best as a bad example. It showed you not how to develop. [Laughter]

Admiral Richardson: [Laughter] That's right.

Q: What do you recall about the academic side of the Naval Academy?

Admiral Richardson: I didn't think highly of it. It was unimaginative. It did not teach us to think. It did teach us to memorize. We spent a lot of time memorizing. We did silly things. For example, we wasted a lot of time learning how to disassemble and assemble a Mark 21 torpedo so that we could do it in the dark, as if it made a bit of difference. Thank goodness that the Naval Academy has radically changed its approach to instruction.

Back on my 50th anniversary, in 1986, we were briefed by the captain, then dean of academics. After listening to all the technology and very impressive alternatives available for instruction, I asked him if they were instructing anything in intelligence. He said, no, that they didn't want to handle classified matter. I explained that it has nothing to do with classification; it has everything to do with the process of thinking. I said, "After all, the objective of midshipmen is to be leaders and solve problems, and you solve problems by first analyzing the hell out of what the problem is."

Q: In your reflection back, do you have any explanation for that system that was used back in the 1930s?

Admiral Richardson: No, I don't. There were both professors and professional naval officers there. The better instructors were the naval officers who had had a tough time when they were midshipmen. They were able to explain things more carefully. I don't know. I've never known how one can instruct to greater advantage. But everyone was moved along at the same rate, and much seemed to have been skipped over in order to carry you through a designated distance in a short time. Somehow we never quite understood the processes that were fundamental in electrical engineering, mechanical engineering, and so forth. We never really did come to an understanding of why things worked the way they did.

Q: You talked about how the process of hazing solidified your class, drew you together. Was there something about the academy experience that made leaders of those who went through?

Admiral Richardson: I think so. The counterpart to the hazing, of course, is the fact that the first class is given considerable authority over the three younger classes, and they're held accountable. A fundamental to developing leadership is to be out in a leading position in some way. Yes, it is definitely a help.

Q: What do you remember about your time as a three-striper? What did that involve?

Admiral Richardson: I was company commander. That simply put me in charge of one of the two companies in the third battalion at the Naval Academy. At that time, we had four battalions, two companies in each. There would be a three-striper company commander the first third of the year, another the second third, etc. I had it in one of those three times.

Q: You talked about how that taught accountability. Are there any examples of that that you recall?

Admiral Richardson: No, I don't recall any specific examples.

Q: I suppose it was a matter of having your people where they were supposed to be at the right time.

Admiral Richardson: Yes. The company commander had battalion duties, company duties, within the confines of the building, and you marched the company to class and back. At the time, everybody went in parade formation to class. In addition, you were responsible for the conduct and appearance of your company--the areas other than their academics.

It was an intermediary position between the commissioned officer company commander and battalion commander and the midshipmen themselves. So you were sitting there with some considerable understanding about what was going on amongst the troops. As long as it didn't get out of hand or create a problem in the front office, why, you sort of went along with everything.

Q: Did you view part of the process of the Naval Academy as a weeding-out of those who should not be naval officers?

Admiral Richardson: A number of people who came to the Naval Academy left plebe year simply because they didn't want to take the regimentation and discipline. Whether they might have made good naval officers, who knows? But it was a tough four years, and to a young man, four years were an eternity. So those who were fainthearted dropped out. Every class, I would suppose, has maybe 5% who drop by the wayside at the outset.

Q: Did you enjoy being a midshipman?

Admiral Richardson: I can't say I did especially, no. It was hard work and almost no liberty.

Q: It was something to be gotten through.

Admiral Richardson: That is right. I was glad when it was all behind me.

Q: Most Naval Academy graduates recall experiences with duty officers who were especially officious in enforcing their duties. Do you recall such people?

Admiral Richardson: Not that I was directly involved with, no. I didn't run into any officers who gave me a hard time. There was a game that was played between some duty officers whom we suspected had, in their day, played the midshipman game at the outer edges. That is, they had Frenched out and done all the other things that one could think of.[*] When they came back as company officers, they were very clever in the various ways they would catch the current crop of midshipmen.

Q: Because they knew those ways themselves. [Laughter]

Admiral Richardson: They knew those ways. That's right. We knew who they were, so it became a game.

---

[*] "French out" is midshipman slang for leaving the Naval Academy without authorization.

Q: Were there any members either of the Bancroft Hall organization or the faculty whom you saw as especially good role models?*

Admiral Richardson: No, I don't recall anyone in particular that I looked up to as a role model. There were a number of people that I liked, admired, and respected. But as a role model, I would look for someone who was most outstanding, a Tom Hamilton type. I don't recall anyone quite like that.

Q: He, of course, was the football coach.† What do you remember about attending athletic events, and particularly the Army-Navy games?

Admiral Richardson: I guess I remember Slade Cutter in the class of '35 and Bush Bringle in the class of '37.‡ We had a very, very good team that year, including Dick Burns and others.§

Q: Anything you recall of the pageantry of going to those games?

Admiral Richardson: I don't know anything that I would single out as noteworthy. We enjoyed going. We certainly liked it when Navy beat Army, and never more so than when we were plebes and got to carry on until Christmas.

Q: What was included in "carrying on"?

---

* Bancroft Hall is the large multi-wing dormitory that houses Naval Academy midshipmen. It also contains the offices of members of the executive department, including the commandant, executive officer, and battalion and company officers.
† Lieutenant (junior grade) Thomas J. Hamilton, USN, was the Naval Academy's head football coach from 1934 to 1936, when he compiled a record of 19-8-0. The oral history of Hamilton, who retired as a rear admiral, is in the Naval Institute collection.
‡ Midshipman Slade D. Cutter, USN, kicked the field goal in Navy's 3-0 victory over Army in the 1934 game. The oral history of Cutter, who retired as a captain, is in the Naval Institute collection. Midshipman William F. Bringle, USN. Bringle eventually retired as a four-star admiral.
§ Midshipman Richard H. Burns, USN, graduated in the class of 1935. He retired as a captain.

Admiral Richardson: Well, it just meant that you were not being hazed--no more square corners, no more reciting the menus, no more reporting in to your first classman before the evening meal--that sort of things. Spooning was the other thing, of course.* A number of upperclassmen would spoon on you, particularly if they happened to be from your home state.

Q: Do you recall any who spooned on you?

Admiral Richardson: Oh, yes. There were quite a few from Mississippi, and they all spooned on me: Claude Bailey, Bob Canon, Walker Ethridge.† Walker Ethridge was from my home town. He was a naval aviator, and he was killed in the final year of World War II. He was a very fine, very fine officer who would have gone way up had he survived. Claude Bailey was originally appointed to the Naval Academy in 1927. He would have graduated in '31. He bilged out, as I recall, plebe year. He was reappointed and bilged out a second time youngster year. He was again reappointed and graduated with the class of '34. He, Canon, Walker Ethridge, and one other were probably the champion bridge players at the academy.

Q: What sort of a sense of loyalty and affection did you develop toward the Naval Academy during that experience?

Admiral Richardson: Well, I guess it's sort of like a family. There is a strong sense of loyalty to the institution. I don't think that that comment inhibits one from criticizing. I certainly hope it doesn't, because there were many things that needed to be done better. If I were there as a commandant of midshipmen, I would pay special attention on the upperclassmen and their hazing, because I'd want to make sure they weren't corrupted by that process.

---

* "Spoon" is midshipman slang for the practice of recognizing a junior midshipman and extending a hand of friendship.
† Midshipman Claude F. Bailey, USN; Midshipman Robert H. Canon, USN; Midshipman Walker Ethridge, USN; all were in the class of 1934.

I wouldn't worry so much about plebes. They do very well. Plebe year is really made more tolerant by the affinities that you develop with your upperclassmen, and they help you when things get tough. So it's a process you go through, and it usually evolves into a close relationship as you go along. Many a midshipman and his first classman are very close. When I was a first classman, we had an enormous number of plebes.* It got to where we'd dare not raise a broom to beat them, because there were 12 of them to 4 of us. The situation sometimes got out of hand in a hurry if we turned on them physically. [Laughter] We had a good relationship.

Q: What do you recall about the training cruises during the summers? Your first would have been in the summer of 1933.

Admiral Richardson: Yes. We had a short, two-month cruise, because of the financial situation, generally. It was on the Wyoming.† Hammocks, alternated navigating, OD-type thing, and engineering and gunnery.‡

Of course, the big guns--the 14-inch and 16-inch--in those days were what the Navy was all about, and there still was no institutional comprehension that this stuff was becoming pretty ancient as a strategic weapon. So we were busy learning things that weren't looking ahead; they were looking back to World War I.

Our cruise first class year was a very nice cruise to Norway, Denmark, and into Germany--a Northern European cruise. We went somewhere in England, probably Plymouth, and it was a much more enjoyable cruise. But other than the topside work and navigational work, and the engineering, that was good, because that was certainly what we worked with the first three or four years in the fleet.

---

* The class of 1939 had 581 graduates and 220 non-graduates.
† USS Wyoming (BB-32) was commissioned as a battleship in 1912 and served in that role until being demilitarized as a result of the 1930 London Treaty on the limitation of naval armaments. She was redesignated AG-17 in 1931 and thereafter served into the mid-1940s as a training ship for gunnery and for midshipman cruises.
‡ OD--officer of the deck.

Q: I think it would have been useful just to be able to apply these things that you had been learning in classes all along.

Admiral Richardson: Well, what you learn in class is theoretical, and what you learn on the cruise itself is the real-life thing. I guess the problem basically was that we were learning facts and not processes in class, as a general rule. There were, of course, exceptions. Navigation was an exception. We learned the processes of navigation. I don't know of any way that might have been taught better, but not so in electronics. Then I reported in to a battleship that had electric drive, and certainly the application of what I was supposed to have learned was there. Part of the time I was in engineering. Of course, by the time we came through each of the three junior officer rotational assignments, we really did know what went with that. They were gunnery, engineering, and officer of the deck.

Q: Anything else to finish up about the Naval Academy?

Admiral Richardson: I can't think of anything. I never requested nor wanted to go back there for duty, which was a surprise to many people, including my wife. Basically, I felt that at least while I was there I was too constrained. You know this business about--how does that saying go? Oh, these are the rules of the Navy. And he that is wise will observe them. It's about being careful what you speak of your seniors and that sort of thing. It's one thing to read about it and be mindful of it, but to actually be indoctrinated by some of those so-called rules, I thought was pretty stupid, and still think so.

Q: What do you remember about the graduation itself, when your class left Annapolis?

Admiral Richardson: The ceremony itself was, of course, a delight.[*] All of a sudden the chains that had locked us down were let loose. I looked at classmates in their first few years out in the fleet, and some of them became something akin to wild men, compared to their time in the Naval Academy, where they were so constrained. There we didn't even go

---

[*] The graduation was on 4 June 1936. Richardson stood 119 of the 261 graduates in the class.

out but what? Twice a year as a plebe and once a quarter or once a month as a youngster. First class had a little bit of freedom. But when these young classmates hit the fleet in the summer of '36, a number became quite wild, drank too much, chased around too much. That was brought on by the extent of the constraint that they endured. That was bad.

It's one of those things that you live through, but I lost several classmates through misbehaving, classmates who could have been very fine naval officers, and one who was. He was kicked out. He was on the Nevada. The Nevada was a ship with a particularly bad reputation because of the young '36ers and maybe some others who misbehaved while ashore in Long Beach. The skipper clamped down on them, and several were thrown out of the Navy. At least one came back into the Navy during World War II. One classmate, named Hutchins, served with great distinction in the war as the skipper of a destroyer.[*]

We lost people we shouldn't have lost had they really been brought up properly as young men at the Naval Academy. The line of instruction was too hidebound, and I mean by that not the technical instruction, but I mean the character instruction--"Now, these are the laws of the Navy and he that is wise will obey them." That, as far as I am concerned, is absolutely full of the wrong stuff.

Q: Because it is so restrictive?

Admiral Richardson: Well, I look for redeeming qualities in the thoughts in there, and I don't find them. There's something called--what's the word?

Q: Moderation? Common sense?

Admiral Richardson: Yes, common sense would certainly cover it, but you should be diplomatic. You certainly don't want to be outrageous to your commanding officer. You

---

[*] Ensign Charles H. Hutchins, USN, reported to the battleship Nevada (BB-36) following graduation from the Naval Academy. As a Naval Reserve lieutenant commander, he was the skipper of the destroyer Borie (DD-215) when she rammed and sank the surfaced German submarine U-405 on 1 November 1943. The Borie also sank as a result of the action.

certainly don't want to go around bad-mouthing him, because the walls do tell on you. My example is only symptomatic.

That whole mental attitude of our naval officers, and I'm referring to the broad general average in all the ships--the battleships in particular; the destroyers were a little different--was characterized by constraints in the '30s, and that lasted into the war itself. That's what led to the disaster at Savo Island--the loss of those three cruisers off Florida Island.[*] It was a way of thinking that didn't survive combat.

Q: Just to go back a bit, one aspect of your midshipman time we haven't talked about at all is the social life. How active were you in that?

Admiral Richardson: Well, I guess my greatest disappointment was when I accommodated a classmate from Mississippi whose cousin was coming up for second class summer. He wanted me to date her for all of that second class June Week, and I said I would. But then I immediately started getting other people to sign up on her card for certain nights so that I wouldn't be stuck with her the whole time. Well, I went to meet her, and she was a living doll. [Laughter] I went around trying to collect all of these signups back again. I don't think I succeeded in a single one. The minute I walked in, they knew damn well what was going on. So I think I had my one dance with her one evening, and that was it.

Q: I think that's known as poetic justice. [Laughter]

Admiral Richardson: [Laughter] And there were other occasions that I dated different girls. No steady, until my first class year. I met a young woman I was very enamored of, and we went together all first class year, and then I went to the West Coast. Her mother and father came out on a vacation and visited with me for a while. He was a high official in Haverty Furniture Store. It just seemed to me that we were oceans apart, and so I deliberately broke that up, simply because I couldn't see how that situation could work out.

---

[*] On the night of 8-9 August 1942, between Guadalcanal and nearby Savo Island, a Japanese surface force surprised Allied forces and sank four cruisers, the USS Astoria (CA-34), USS Quincy (CA-39), USS Vincennes (CA-44), and HMAS Canberra.

If I had known that I could go to flight training, I wouldn't have broken up. But not knowing that and seeing the future as it looked to me in 1936, I canceled.

Q: One final question on the Naval Academy before we move on. How much awareness did you get then of aviation? Was that made appealing at all?

Admiral Richardson: No. We had aviation second class summer a little bit. I think we may have ridden in a plane, but nothing noteworthy at all. It had no effect on me. I knew I wanted aviation way before that, and that didn't change it at all.

Q: How was it that these four midshipmen who had been so close were all able to go to the same ship, the Tennessee, for first duty?[*]

Admiral Richardson: Well, the executive officer at the Naval Academy, Oscar Badger, was very fond of our class president, Griff Sexton.[†] Griff and his two roommates and my three roommates and I were often at his house. Oscar Badger wanted Griff and his roommates to go to his cruiser. He was to be the XO of a cruiser.

Q: The Indianapolis.

Admiral Richardson: And he wanted those three to go with him. But we had set up amongst ourselves that we all were going to request the same ship. And so Griff told him what the plan was. Griff said he appreciated the proposal, but he did want to stick with our group. Oscar Badger said, "That's fine." We were able to do it. It worked out. I don't quite know how it happened, but it did.

---

[*] USS Tennessee (BB-43) was commissioned 3 June 1920. She had a standard displacement of 32,300 tons, was 624 feet long and 97 feet in the beam. Her top speed was 21 knots. As of the mid-1930s she was armed with 12 14-inch guns, 12 5-inch broadside guns, and eight 5-inch antiaircraft guns. She served throughout World War II and was eventually decommissioned in 1947.
[†] Commander Oscar C. Badger, USN. Midshipman Ormond Griffith Sexton III, USN.

Then, of course, we frequently saw Oscar. He lived in Long Beach. They had a house in Long Beach, and I guess the seven of us--in groups of two, three, or four--went to his place time and time again in the years '36 to '38.

Q: What was your initial duty in the Tennessee?

Admiral Richardson: Assistant division officer, second division, which had number-two turret. And I looked at my lieutenant division officer, Brim Campbell out of the class of '22, and here we were, 14 years later, and he was a lieutenant division officer.[*] I thought, "There's got to be more to life than this." It just seemed to me that other than the communicators and one or two specialties--a few jobs like that, where you had to perform to something--the rest would become child's play. And to see talents being wasted, that's the way I looked at it.

Q: You saw it as a stagnant system.

Admiral Richardson: A very stagnant system.

Q: What specifically do you recall about being in that gunnery department role?

Admiral Richardson: Spot two and then spot one. Spot two the first year. And I must have spent a good bit of time in turret two, but mostly I functioned as spot two.

Q: How important was the airplane in spotting during those years?

Admiral Richardson: Well, it was very important. We'd launch them, and they'd get out halfway and they could see a hell of a lot better than we could, particularly the distance of misses, how far beyond or close. They could do a much better job of spotting than we could.

---

[*] Lieutenant William S. Campbell, USN.

Q: What do you remember about the ship's antiaircraft capability?

Admiral Richardson: Oh, it was not enough to mention. When World War II came along, we strapped guns all over the place, and even then, it takes heavy caliber guns to be effective in time. But in '36 it was rudimentary to the point of being practically useless.

Q: I understand that with the optical range finder system for the 5-inch/25s, maybe a level bomber could be tracked, but it was almost hopeless against a dive bomber.

Admiral Richardson: Yes. I don't remember those details. I was never on the AA battery, actually, so I didn't try to work that problem.

Q: Would it be fair to say that those series of gunnery exercises that were held back then were as stilted in their way as the instruction was at the Naval Academy?

Admiral Richardson: No, I don't think so. I think that given the fact that there were hostile battleships and there was a general anticipation . . . [Telephone interruption. Tape recorder turned off]

Q: On these gunnery exercises, though, there was not a whole lot of imagination. There was a lot of rote procedure in those.

Admiral Richardson: Well, it was a question of accuracy, and the battle efficiency pennant winner had to be very good in all aspects of gunnery. That was the measure, really, of effectiveness. The major measure of effectiveness of a commanding officer was how well his ship performed in gunnery, and it was a time thing.

One of the things that I remember in particular was the great care that went into instructing people on how to handle the powder in those turrets. The book seemed to be made up of analyses of incidents in the past where terrible things had happened. It is a dangerous thing when you've got that much powder flying around that is susceptible to sparks. We were all made to realize that. Handling procedures, safety precautions were a major factor in the whole thing, and that's certainly real life.

The actual firing involved working the Ford rangekeeper, which was an early computer. It was a mechanical computer, but it predicted. It took the pattern of the recent past--as accurately as you could discern it from a distance--and projected it into the future, which is exactly what a computer does in modeling. So that entire process was impressive and real life and would have been more useful had not the aeronautical industry exploded in its technological development.

Q: Certainly the building of teamwork was one of the important results of that incessant drilling--getting the ammunition up from down below, bringing in the inputs from the plot and the range finder and so forth.

Admiral Richardson: Yes, it was indeed. It cut time.

Q: Another important factor was to make sure the gas ejection air was working on these turrets to clear out the barrel after each round.

Admiral Richardson: The entire process, the entire procedure was crucial.

Q: What do you recall about the camaraderie in the JO mess?

Admiral Richardson: Well, it was very good. I thought that certainly was so in our ship, and I think in most ships, it was very, very fine.

We had an incident. The Tennessee went to the shipyard in early '37 for an overhaul, an overhaul which, incidentally, was shortened somewhat because of the high danger of Japanese surprise attack at that time. It's intriguing that this went back as far as at least 1937, to my personal knowledge. But when we came out of the shipyard, we had a brand-new skipper.* The chief engineer was moved up to navigator. The assistant navigator was out of the class of '34 and was on leave. One of my academy roommates, Jim O'Grady, was topside engineer in the engineering plant when we came into San Francisco Bay. I remember a man by the name of Smith, a lieutenant who was maybe the number-two engineer.† I think the number-one engineer was a brand-new man.

So as we stood looking at Oakland, we noticed a ring of mud moving out from the hull. We must be aground!‡ Indeed, we were aground. Jim O'Grady, when he began to lose vacuum, shut down the plant and saved the ship from having to renew all of the innards of the condensers. Baked clay would have kept the water from going through. We were able to clean out the engineering plant in just a few days' time. But we had to off-load fuel and ammunition, then get pulled off.

What happened was that the "engineer" navigator was taking a sequence of bearings but not making fixes. He wasn't getting simultaneous bearings for fixes, so we were out of position. The skipper was new and didn't check him, and so we were aground.

Q: There was a picture of it in Life magazine, which must have been embarrassing.§

Admiral Richardson: In 1937, we'd gone in for the opening of the Golden Gate Bridge. I thought of all the care that goes into managing a turret. Then, somehow, a sequence of events occurs that culminates in disaster. Certainly, if the assistant navigator hadn't been on leave, this wouldn't have happened. And had the navigator been in his job long enough to navigate properly. God knows what he did all the years before then. In those days, you were sort of brain dead by the time you'd reached a more important position.

Q: What do you mean by that--"brain dead?"

---

* Captain John T. G. Stapler, USN, commanded the Tennessee from 8 May 1937 to 24 July 1937.
† Lieutenant James M. Smith, USN.
‡ The grounding occurred on 11 June 1937.
§ Life, 28 June 1937, page 26, shows a picture of the ship aground with barges alongside to off-load fuel and ammunition.

Admiral Richardson: Because you had not been challenged in so many years, you were doing things by rote, nothing new, nothing different, and "brain dead" is about a good way to put it. This man, who must have at some point in time had to have known something of navigation, didn't even know to take simultaneous bearings. They cashiered him and the skipper; their careers ended. But the engineering department got a big kudo for functioning properly.

Q: What was the reaction throughout the ship?

Admiral Richardson: Incredibility, I guess. Also we missed a lot of liberty time. [Laughter]

Q: Well, if you could compare it to that turret situation, perhaps the reason for the brain-deadness was that it wasn't life-threatening, so he wasn't as alert as he should have been.

Admiral Richardson: A new skipper, a new navigator, the complete changeover of everything that had to do with safe navigation of that ship should have been ringing bells, yet it was allowed to happen. To some extent, it was an institutional failure. It was an individual failure, but it was also an institutional failure. The skipper should not have allowed those departures unless he had an awful lot of confidence in himself. While we were off-loading ammunition, I was officer of the deck. The skipper put his arm around my shoulder and ruminated about how quickly a career can come to an end.*

Q: Was it a matter of being set off course by current?

Admiral Richardson: Well, the currents are there in San Francisco anyway. It was a matter of getting on that mud flat because he was out of position. He should have known exactly

---

* Captain Stapler was relieved of command on 24 July 1937 by Captain Edwin A. Wolleson, USN. Stapler retired as a captain in June 1941.

where that ship was, and he didn't. Of course, he drifted. So, yes, currents, but it was a predictable drift. It was well known. Anytime you go into Bremerton, for example, why, it's downright exciting, the water's moving so fast.* Taking a carrier in and out of that place is nothing less than thrilling.

Q: On those JO messes, one characterization I've heard is that they were enjoyable because they were so much more relaxed than the wardroom.†

Admiral Richardson: That's very true.

Q: Even at some point, almost like a fraternity house atmosphere. I'm wondering how it was in your JO mess.

Admiral Richardson: That's a good description. It was fun. There was the poker game going on and things like that. You could walk in and out. But the camaraderie was very good, I think, for both ensigns and jaygees. When you became a lieutenant, you moved up. We were a lot more fun.

Q: What sorts of things did you do on liberty?

Admiral Richardson: Well, Long Beach wasn't too good a liberty town, but we went to the beach. We had dates. We went up to L.A., and we'd take our girls to nightclubs and things like that. Nothing very startling.

Q: What do you recall about the business of running boats between ship and shore?

Admiral Richardson: Well, it was a pain in the neck having to wait, and then there were occasional instances where an accident would occur. Not very often. The coxswains were

---

* Puget Sound Navy Yard, Bremerton, Washington.
† JO--junior officer.

very good as a group. They were very sharp. And, of course, in those days a good many of the coxswains of boats had been first class and were busted down once or twice for getting drunk ashore or whatever, so there were a lot of old-timers around who had a lot of experience, and whatever it was they were supposed to do, they did quite well.

Q: Any other observations on the Tennessee's enlisted men?

Admiral Richardson: No. They were a very good lot. The chiefs, the people, in general, knew every aspect of that ship. Looking back on the degree of knowledge that our engineers had in particular, when I was skipper of the Cimarron and the Hornet, I would love to have had the level of knowledge available that our chiefs and first class then had. We were rich in competence at those levels, because the people so involved knew every detail of the system from one end to the other, every valve, everything else. That wasn't the case later, and it hasn't been the case since.

Q: One phenomenon from those years, particularly in engineering, was a man who would stay in the same ship for years and years and years, so he really knew that plant. Any experiences you recall from standing engineering watches?

Admiral Richardson: No.

Q: What about bridge watches?

Admiral Richardson: Well, we used a stadimeter. We were generally gauged by how accurately we kept our ship in position on that stadimeter--up a turn, down a turn.

We had an aviator aboard by the name of Cecil B. Gill.[*] He died just about a month ago here in Coronado. I didn't know he was here until I read his obituary, or I would have been around to see him. He made captain. But he was, to my way of thinking, an ideal officer of the deck. He let the junior officers run the deck, and he didn't get all

---

[*] Lieutenant Cecil B. Gill, USN.

excited, as some did, if you got 10 or 15 feet out of position. [Laughter] Your sole criterion seemed to be your ability to anticipate half a turn on a prop. He required you to be reasonably in place, but he had you do everything. And his general demeanor and attitude was far more relaxed. I remember him as an OD because it seemed to me that his attitude, his outlook was good, and that's what I wanted to see in my ODs later--someone that was interested in the real issues and not wrapped up over some stupid detail of little consequence.

Q: I talked to Admiral Arleigh Burke last year about this ship handling and the fetish on station keeping and turning in the wake and so forth.* He said it wasn't so important for tactical value, but it was something that could be measured, and the idea was that if an officer did well in something that could be measured, he would do well in other things, also.

Admiral Richardson: Well, yes, that's true, but it depends upon what your scale of measurement is. Naval aviators at the end of World War II began screening all captains for command of a ship. A screening board looked at the performance of the new aviator captains, their backgrounds, how well they had handled their jobs in command of squadrons, and what was said about them in detail--in other words, their leadership qualities, as evidenced in earlier commands. The board then said they could be relied on to be assigned as skipper of a ship. Well, that was pre-selection. There was at first opposition to it, particularly among the 1100s, the blackshoes.† But pretty soon they came around and did the same thing. I think they're all doing that now.

    I remember when Arleigh Burke was CNO and the head aviator at that time, the DCNO (Air), had gotten approval to assign aviators to surface ships other than carriers--a

---

* Admiral Arleigh A. Burke, USN, served as Chief of Naval Operations from 17 August 1955 to 1 August 1961. His oral history is in the Naval Institute collection.
† In the early days of naval aviation, the aviators wore brown shoes with their khaki uniforms and green uniforms. They thus acquired the nickname "brown shoes" to distinguish them from the traditional surface ship officers, who were known as "black shoes." The designator 1100 applied to general unrestricted line officers--for the most part, those in surface ships--from the 1950s to the 1970s, at which time a separate surface warfare designator was created.

make-you-learn thing.* This happened in about '60, '61. As an example, I went to an oiler, the Cimarron. I think practically all oilers were commanded by aviators and may still be. But he went to Arleigh Burke, and he said, "I want you to know, you're getting the finest naval aviators we have to command these support ships."

Arleigh Burke said, "I don't want your finest. I want your luckiest."

Q: What do you remember about the Marines on board the Tennessee?

Admiral Richardson: Nothing in particular. They were there.

Q: You said you had officer of the deck duties when the Tennessee was aground. What did that consist of?

Admiral Richardson: That was in-port duty. It wasn't underway duty.

Q: Did you stand it on the bridge?

Admiral Richardson: No. You stood that on the quarterdeck.

Q: So the captain came around to the quarterdeck to consult?

Admiral Richardson: The captain was walking the decks, and I was there. He put his arm on my shoulder as we walked along and philosophized about the finger of fate.

Q: How did the ship get refloated?

---

* Vice Admiral Robert B. Pirie, Jr., USN, served as Deputy Chief of Naval Operations (Air) from 26 May 1958 to 1 November 1962. His oral history is in the Naval Institute collection.

Admiral Richardson: We off-loaded ammunition, and when the tide got higher, tugs came and pulled and pulled and pulled. It took quite a while to get it off. We had to lighten the ship because we were high and dry. We were way up.

Q: Anything else you remember about Bremerton overhauls, other than that one getting cut short?

Admiral Richardson: Well, yes. One thing that I remember there was shore patrol and the very large number of whorehouses in that place. There must have been 20 of them, and on shore patrol we'd make the rounds. We were interested in assuring that there was no raucous behavior. I never envisioned so doggone many places like that. There are always some around.

I had another shore patrol duty when I was going through flight training. I was then a jaygee. The Marines normally had shore patrol in Pensacola, but the night of the Marine ball, I caught shore patrol. The white-haired chief, an old hand, went around with me. He knew the places. I didn't. I just trotted along behind him and watched him kick open the doors of motels. These weren't high-class motels; these were crummy places. He would kick open the door and look in to see if a sailor was in there. There might be other people there but, Good Lord, this was the way it was. [Laughter]

Q: Was the shore patrol essentially sanctioning these places?

Admiral Richardson: It wasn't a question of sanctioning or non-sanctioning. The shore patrol had nothing to do with them. But they did have to do with the behavior of the sailors ashore. So if there were a ruckus anywhere, then the shore patrol would be called right away to come in. We would meander around and, by being around, make sure trouble did not erupt.

Q: Was prostitution legal in Bremerton?

Admiral Richardson: Well, yes. If it was not legal, it was not constrained in any way.

Q: It existed.

Admiral Richardson: It existed, and obviously so. The other and more useful thing that I remember up there was how much you could get done by being pleasant to the workmen, like having coffee available and doing minor things to ease their way. They really were glad to do a good job for you. But the mental attitude, in general, was one that was combative. If you met them halfway, or maybe a little beyond halfway, they did wonders for you. But if you were adamant and domineering, you didn't get a damn thing.

Q: So it was kind of a self-fulfilling prophecy. If you view them as bad and treat them that way, they will be bad.

Admiral Richardson: That's exactly right. But it was amazing how much you could get done for a pound of coffee--little things like that. If you tie in with them, show an interest, and go down to where they were working and have them explain it to you, you became part of the solution, not just something else that had to be dealt with. There were other anecdotes of various types that came along, none of them really noteworthy.

Q: If you remember any examples, that would be useful.

Admiral Richardson: One thing that bothered me, I knew we were getting ripped off by one of the local merchants. Meat was being shorted. I was the treasurer of the mess at the time, so I decided to check everything myself. So when the order was delivered, I went and weighed this stuff myself. But instead of complaining, I just made a record of it, and then at the end of the month, I deducted from the bill the amount for the underweight.

So this guy went to the executive officer, and I got called in. [Laughter] I told him, "There just didn't seem to me to be any point to complain on a case-by-case basis. I wanted the problem solved, and the only way I could see the problem solved is just to do it this way."

The XO said, "Well, you just can't do it that way. You have to complain at the time." So that's the way it was.

Q: You got his attention.

Admiral Richardson: Yes. And I'm sure the executive officer had to laugh over it. But it wasn't considered the legal way to do things. You had to meet it at the point in time, and that probably is legalistically correct today.

Q: What do you remember about trying to satisfy the tastes of hungry ensigns and jaygees?[*]

Admiral Richardson: I don't know. I think our mess bill was $15.00 a month. It wasn't very much. There were very few complaints, for a very good reason. He who complained would be the next mess treasurer. [Laughter]

Q: What do you remember about the role of the blacks in serving as mess attendants and steward's mates?

Admiral Richardson: I don't remember anything in particular at that point in time. We did later have blacks serving when I was in Fighting Five.

Q: What do you remember about inspections and the whole business of spit and polish and protocol in a battleship?

Admiral Richardson: Nothing in particular. Well, I don't think it was any different then from now. The protocols, I thought, were good. The business of calling and that sort of

---

[*] Jaygee--lieutenant (junior grade).

thing was a structured thing, but it made a lot of sense, the practical solution to a problem that, if not structured, meant that a lot of people would never get to know one another.*

Q: It allowed people to get more of the sense of the personality of the boss instead of just the official demeanor.

Admiral Richardson: That's very true. Of course, you got more of that in parties than you did in an official call. On the calls at least you met his wife, saw his family and home, and you do definitely get a feel from that. But you get a better feel for individuals when you're at a party, and the way people are at parties. The fellowship on Tennessee was absolutely superb, up and down. I've never seen it better. I've never experienced it better.

Q: How would you explain that?

Admiral Richardson: Well, it's a funny thing. A ship seems to develop a certain character, and I suppose someone comes along who has a very attractive personality and creates a mood that somehow the ship seems to absorb. Then others who come seem to fit into that. But it does persevere, and I'm sure a bad mood perseveres too. That's one of the aspects of group behavior.

Q: Any of the skippers that you remember specifically from Tennessee?

Admiral Richardson: Yes, Captain Wolleson. His personality created in his crew the desire to do all they could to make Tennessee number one.

Q: What about the fleet problems, which were an application of all the individual training you'd done before then?

---

* It was expected that officers newly reporting for duty would make brief calls at the homes of senior officers to become better acquainted.

Admiral Richardson: I can't comment on that because I wasn't familiar enough with it. Yes, we had them, but the things that went on in the general area of wide-area surveillance and operational reaction, I had no way of knowing what that was. These exercises were thoroughly written up and analyzed afterward, and I have learned since that what took place at Pearl Harbor in '41 had been foretold in fleet exercises. But I wouldn't have known that from what we were doing. No, at my level we had pretty much a worm's-eye view of things at that point in time.

Q: More and more during the '30s the idea was coming along that the carrier could be an offensive weapon instead of just a scout.

Admiral Richardson: Yes, that's right. That's right. There were patrol planes operating. There were problems due to rudimentary instrumentation when they flew in low-visibility weather. One night in Tennessee we were engaged in a rescue off the coast. We searched for a downed patrol plane. I don't know that anybody who was in the plane survived. At that point in time, aviation was coming along, but flight instrumentation was still rudimentary.

This whole thing began to change rapidly starting about '37 or so, but the impact of it was being felt in '41 and '42 and particularly in '43. But back in earlier times, that was not apparent.

Q: That fleet problem in '37 went out to Hawaii. Do you have any recollections of being out there?

Admiral Richardson: We went out in July or August of '36. I don't recall we ever went out in '37. We may have.

Q: What are your recollections of Hawaii from that period?

Admiral Richardson: Oh, it was a lovely, elegant, easy-living area. The Royal Hawaiian, with all its open space and elegance, and the area adjacent where people rented little cottages and so forth.* We had a lot of fun out there that summer. One of the seven of us who went together to the Tennessee was engaged to a young woman who lived in Honolulu. His father was a naval officer, a Commander Crutchfield, and our shipmate was Jack Crutchfield.† He was lost in a submarine in 1943. But he married the girl he was dating there at that time, Barbara. Through Barbara we met a lot of the young women there. I dated George Patton's daughter.‡ She had a photographic memory. She talked constantly, never stopped.

Q: Any other details you remember about Patton's daughter?

Admiral Richardson: She said she was always the life of the party. People invited her to parties because she was super-active. She married a man out of the class of '35, West Point.§ She talked so constantly that he once put her out of the car when they were dating and made her run along behind the car. [Laughter] This, she told me.

Q: And she still married him? [Laughter]

Admiral Richardson: She married him. She told me a story one time about her dad, then Lieutenant Colonel George Patton. It was her mother's birthday. There were two sisters.** Came her mother's birthday. Nobody said a word to her. They went through the day into the evening with not one word of remembrance. While having their evening meal in the

---
* The Royal Hawaiian is a luxury hotel, still in business on Waikiki Beach all these years later.
† Commander James A. Crutchfield, USN, was then the executive officer of the heavy cruiser San Francisco (CA-38). Ensign Jack R. Crutchfield, USN, served in the Tennessee.
‡ George S. Patton, Jr., became famous as an Army officer in World War II, leading the U.S. Third Army across Europe following the D-Day invasion in 1944. At the time of his death in late 1945 he was a four-star general. In the mid-1930s, as a lieutenant colonel, he was stationed with the Army's Hawaiian Department at Fort Shafter on Oahu.
§ Patton's younger daughter, Ruth Ellen, was married in 1940 to First Lieutenant James W. Totten, USA, who had graduated from the Military Academy in 1935. Totten eventually retired as a major general in 1967. For photos of the weddings of both of Patton's daughters, see Martin Blumenson, Patton: The Man Behind the Legend (New York: Morrow, 1985).
** Ruth Ellen's older sister was Beatrice, who also married a West Pointer.

dining room, again no one said a word about her birthday. Finally, she broke down and started crying and raising Cain because nobody remembered her birthday. So Colonel Patton got very stern with her, saying, "You're carrying on." He got up, seemingly in disgust, and marched out.

Two or three minutes later, there was a loud clonk, clonk, clonk. Into the dining room, through the kitchen, came George Patton pulling a horse that was her present. When he got into the dining room, he said, "Now will you shut up?" [Laughter] They concocted that whole thing, every one of them.

Q: Did the Tennessee get down to the Caribbean at all?

Admiral Richardson: The Tennessee, no. It was in the Pacific. I left it in the summer of '38 and went to the Downes, and I left the Downes in the Panama Canal, going through to the fleet exercise that took place in the Atlantic in early '39. I entered flight training in February of '39.

Q: Please tell me about your service in the Downes.

Admiral Richardson: The Downes was a relatively new 1,500-tonner.[*] As communicator I was also the permanent deck watch stander in the training exercises, day and night. Anytime when we went to GQ, I became the officer of the deck.[†] I got to where I was a damn good ship handler. The XO, the chief engineer, the gunnery officer, and one other officer would all go to their specific duty stations in gunnery or engineering and whatnot.[‡] So I was the one who was always ship handler in the exercises. Incidentally, the XO was Bob Cronin, fine guy.[§] I never saw him after that time.

---

[*] USS Downes (DD-375), a Farragut-class destroyer, was commissioned 15 January 1937. She had a standard displacement of 1,500 tons, was 341 feet long, and 35 feet in the beam. Her design speed was 36 knots. She was armed with five 5-inch guns and twelve 21-inch torpedo tubes. She and the Cassin (DD-372) were badly damaged in dry dock when the Japanese attacked Pearl Harbor in 1941. Both were eventually rebuilt and returned to service.
[†] GQ--general quarters.
[‡] XO--executive officer.
[§] Lieutenant Robert E. Cronin, USN.

The skipper became unhappy with the performance of ship handling on the part of some of the other officers when not in exercises, so he took me off full time and made the others come and brush up on ship handling. But I always enjoyed the exercises that we ran. They were sheer delight--just great fun. Of course, you stayed awake all the time. It seemed you never slept. During a fleet exercise of eight, ten days, if you got two or three hours' sleep a night, you were fortunate.

Q: How can you remain effective on that little sleep?

Admiral Richardson: Well, I'm sure you aren't as effective as you might otherwise be, but you do it. How do the SEALs do it?* How do the Spetsnaz do it?† One of the things they train for is enduring long times without sleep.

Q: I guess there's a natural selection process. Those who can't do it drop out of the program.

Admiral Richardson: They do quickly in either SEALs or Spetsnaz.

Q: What do you remember just about making the transition from a battleship to a destroyer psychologically? It's a far different environment.

Admiral Richardson: Well, much different. A destroyer is much more enjoyable because you have responsibility, and on the big ships you don't really matter. School doesn't keep or not depending upon you.

Q: You can have much more of an impact also.

---

* SEALs--Navy personnel trained for sea, air, and land operations. In previous years similar individuals were designated as part of underwater demolition teams (UDTs). In addition to that specialty, the SEALs have a broader mission that includes commando-type operations ashore.
† Spetsnaz was the designation for the Soviet Union's special forces; included were both naval and ground forces.

Admiral Richardson: That's right. You have a lot impact on a small ship.

Q: Those ships built in that era were known as the "gold-platers."* Were they looked up to by the four-stacker types?

Admiral Richardson: I guess they were. In any destroyer, you're hanging on for dear life all the time.

Q: Any specifics you remember in that regard?

Admiral Richardson: Well, only that when you're maneuvering at high speed and when you've got a few waves out there of six or eight feet or higher, you're plunging and you're having to hold on every place you go all the time.

Q: What sort of missions did the ship carry out during your time on board?

Admiral Richardson: Torpedo attack and gunnery. Mostly torpedo attacks, and that's why the maneuvering came in, because you were clearing to fire all the broadside torpedoes. That was what it all about, and that lasted on up into World War II. Both Japanese and our people were doing that.

Q: How would you assess yourself as a ship handler?

Admiral Richardson: I was good. There are only two categories--good or disastrous. If you weren't good, you weren't tolerated, because you were moving fast, you were maneuvering, and you were only 300 yards apart. I think that was it. The distance was 700 yards between battleships; DDs were much closer. It looked awfully close.

---

* The first of the "gold-platers," the modern destroyers designed in the 1930s, was the USS Farragut (DD-348), commissioned 18 June 1934. They replaced the four-stackers as the front-line destroyers in the U.S. Fleet.

Q: Did the destroyers fuel under way in those days?

Admiral Richardson: I don't recall we did.

Q: What do you remember about the capabilities of those communications that you were running?

Admiral Richardson: Communications were pretty rudimentary. We had codes and an electronic cipher machine. Encoding and decoding, that's what kept you awake so much of the time. When not on watch, the communicator was working the communication side. A lot of that in a fleet problem was encoding and decoding the traffic. And, of course, there were signal flags for close-in operations.

But the functioning of radar and signal technology and the impact of the atmosphere, that was not understood. We knew little about it. If messages didn't get through, we had only the roughest idea as to why they didn't. We did know about daylight and nighttime frequency choices, as I recall. That, of course, affected reception at distances. There is also the ground wave effect, which goes out several hundred miles. We were given instructions on what frequencies to use day or night to maximize our signal strength, but as I recall, that was the extent of the guidance then available to us.

Q: There was probably something of an art that an experienced radioman could get pretty good at.

Admiral Richardson: I imagine so, yes. They would have a much better understanding because they were working it, and they would probably be way ahead of the rest of us.

Q: Did you do much ship-to-ship communication by voice?

Admiral Richardson: I don't remember. I think not.

Q: Certainly, CW was the primary mode for radio communications.*

Admiral Richardson: And we had signal flags, which were used for almost all close-in work. All of our turns were executed by visual signals. And at night, blinking light. I don't recall that we used voice at that time.

Q: What specifics do you recall about where the ship went while you were on board?

Admiral Richardson: We operated off Southern California. I reported in maybe July of '38. And then we practiced for the fleet exercise and the transit to the East Coast. Right after the first of the year, we started down toward the Panama Canal as part of the fleet in exercises all of the way and transited into the Atlantic. I don't recall that we left the Southern California area until then.

Q: Did you work with carriers at all?

Admiral Richardson: I don't recall that we did. We may have.

Q: Anything you remember about the tactical doctrine for destroyers at that time?

Admiral Richardson: No. The focus was on torpedo firing, and the trick, of course, was to get in and turn--all in unison--and fire your torpedoes in spreads. The torpedoes weren't capable of long-distance runs, so if you got in, not having had heavy shellfire, you were very fortunate.

Q: What was it about aviation that particularly appealed to you during that period?

---

* CW, or continuous wave, referred to a type of radio wave interrupted into the dots and dashes of the Morse code for the purpose of communication.

Admiral Richardson: Well, I don't know that I had any contact really with aviation. I used to see the carrier planes. I remember the bumblebee look of the F3F.* That's what we had in Fighting Squadron Five when I reported in. For the first year, we were flying the F3Fs. But nothing in particular, other than during fleet exercises we'd see them flying overhead, going somewhere for some reason.

Q: Some aviators have talked of having this desire to fly since they were boys. How did the desire come about in you?

Admiral Richardson: Oh, I don't know. I didn't have that particular motivation that has people flying model airplanes as youths, that sort of thing. I never got caught up with that, maybe because I was never exposed to it.

I had wanted to go into aviation from the time I was at the Naval Academy, but the thing that really came home to me out in the fleet was what I saw in the attitude and outlook of aviators. It was an openness. What I saw within the surface community was a tight, constrained atmosphere that I liked not at all. So the general demeanor of the aviation community appealed to me. But that was about it.

Q: So it wasn't a love for flying, per se. It was more an attitude.

Admiral Richardson: That's right. That's exactly right. I had no real basis for liking the flying side of it.

Q: This would also go along with what you described as the attitude at the academy, where everything was so rigid, and this was an escape from that.

Admiral Richardson: Yes. In terms of escaping, I had originally felt that I would be leaving the Navy after a few years. I had wanted to go into aviation, and I was told on graduation I

---

* Grumman F3F fighters first entered fleet squadrons in 1936. The F3F-3 was 23 feet, 2 inches long; wing span of 32 feet; gross weight of 4,795 pounds; and top speed of 264 miles per hour. It was the last biplane fighter in any of the U.S. armed services.

couldn't, because my eyes were 19/20. After I had been spot one on the Tennessee for my second year, my eyes recovered. As it turned out, after I reported in to the Downes I took a physical exam just to find out if I could go into aviation. I took it here at NAS North Island and passed it.[*]

Unbeknown to me, they sent the exam report in to the Bureau of Navigation.[†] I went on leave after taking the exam. When I got back to the ship, my skipper, Lieutenant Commander Paré, asked me why had I not told him of my "request" for flight training.[‡] I replied that I had not made one. He said, "You better go down to your desk and read the traffic."

So I went down, and on my desk was a message, "The Bureau of Navigation to skipper of the Downes. Why has not Ensign Richardson's request for flight training been forwarded?"

The answer went back, "Because he hasn't submitted it. If and when he does, I'll forward it." [Laughter]

Then the next message said, "If he submits prior to a certain date [which was almost immediately], he will be appointed to the February class. Appointment June class problematic."

So I went up to see the skipper and I told him what had happened. I wanted to know if I was physically qualified, but I had not gone behind his back. He said, "Well, is your insurance paid up?"

I said, "What there is, yes."

He said, "Well, if you want to do this, you better get your request in." So I did.

I did not want to leave the ship prior to the East Coast battle exercises. I thought it would leave him in the hole. But he said, "No, you do what you want to do," so I did. I was put in class 123 in February of 1939.

---

[*] North Island Naval Air Station is on the end of the Coronado peninsula, across the harbor from San Diego. It is close to the house in which this interview was taking place.
[†] Prior to World War II, assignments of naval officers were made by the Bureau of Navigation. On 13 May 1942, it became the Bureau of Naval Personnel (BuPers), a title that better described its function.
[‡] Lieutenant Commander Edward E. Paré, USN.

Q: Your skipper in the Downes really sounds atypical, because I've heard so many who would squash those requests or turn them back.

Admiral Richardson: Well, he was a good guy but didn't progress in the war.[*] I lost contact with him.

Q: Anything more to mention on the Downes before we move on to flight training?

Admiral Richardson: No, I think not.

Q: How did it go once you got to Pensacola?

Admiral Richardson: It went fine. I enjoyed every minute of the time there. I liked the way people looked at things, the way people thought. Of course, ground school was quite easy for us because of having the Naval Academy behind us. At this point in time I was about to become jaygee. The morning I was scheduled to fly for the first time--and this was maybe three weeks after we arrived there--I came down with a painful ache in my side. So I turned in to the hospital. They took my appendix out immediately. I spent the next ten days in the hospital, then home, and so I missed out on flying. I wasn't allowed to fly for three months.

I did attend the ground school classes and got all of that out of the way. I went through flight training with three or four other Naval Academy classmates who for different reasons had fallen back. That gave me half a day to have fun: fish, build a boat, those sorts of things.

On my first flight I failed to buckle my safety belt--or if I buckled it, it wasn't done properly--and it fell apart. We took off. There was a mirror on a strut by the pilot in the front seat so he could observe me in the back seat. He had me take off. That seemed a bit premature to me, never having even flown a plane before.

---

[*] As a captain in World War II, Paré commanded the At Sea Logistics Service Group that provided underway replenishment services to the combatant ships.

I had ridden once, back when I maybe was 12, 13 years old. I had forgotten about this. At a fairground, Art Davis, who was an early aviator, in a beautiful little airplane, was working the fairground circuit, taking people up for rides. I went to him and said, "Why don't you let me clean your plane for you?" So I cleaned his plane after flights. In return for that, he gave me a ride. That was my first ride in an airplane, and I thoroughly enjoyed it. We flew 10 or 15 minutes.

I think I flew once at the Naval Academy. It probably was in a patrol plane with half a dozen other midshipmen. Then here, for the first time, I was instructed to make the takeoff.

Q: Were you in an N3N?

Admiral Richardson: Yes, an N3N on floats.* So I started my takeoff. Well, of course, my idea of getting off the water was that you heave the stick back, and the plane goes up. And it did--pretty steeply. The pilot kicked the stick forward. When he did, I began to lift out of my seat. I was looking at myself in the mirror, wondering when this seat belt was going to catch me. I finally decided it wasn't, so I grabbed the gunwales and held on. As I was looking in the mirror, I saw the horrified look of my instructor in the front seat. It was a God-awful look, scared to death. [Laughter] He jerked the stick back, and I banged back down into the cockpit.

Q: And fastened your seat belt.

Admiral Richardson: And I fastened my seat belt. You're damned right I did.

Things went perfectly normally through the rest of training. Then, when I was in the Squadron Three several months later, flying with a very experienced lieutenant aviator, we were coming in to land at the main field. It was clear to me that he was a little low. We wouldn't make it over the trees. As we got right about where the trees were at the edge of

---

* "Yellow Peril" was the nickname for the yellow-painted N3N trainer, a biplane equipped with a centerline pontoon. It was 26 feet long, had a wing span of 34 feet, gross weight of 2,792 pounds, and a top speed of 126 miles per hour.

the field, I came back a bit on that stick. He was flying, not me, but I corrected, and we tipped up and went over the treetops. So when we got out, he turned around, and I prepared for a chewing-out. Instead, he said, "Well, even the best of us make mistakes." But not many--not in airplanes.

Q: True enough.

Admiral Richardson: That was damn small consolation. I was grateful I had pulled that stick back. I didn't like the looks of it.

Flight training was fun. I thoroughly enjoyed every bit of it. We went through five squadrons. Two, three, and five were land planes. One and four were seaplanes. In four we went to the big boats, and they were fun. They were fun when you were flying them but not fun to ride in. Then in five we were in fighters--formation flying and that sort of thing. It just was a great delight.

Q: I've heard that big boats call for a great deal of physical exertion.

Admiral Richardson: Yes. You manhandled them getting them off the water; that's right.

Q: Did you get a sense of exhilaration from flying?

Admiral Richardson: Yes, I suppose so. I enjoyed it. I loved it. You can call that exhilaration if you want. It's not a sudden thrill that you get. But it's not so much a thrill as a sense of enjoyment. My youngest son is an instructor in Top Gun now.[*] He went through Pensacola, and he had more flight time than anybody else in his squadron. He had more flight time than anybody because he was always around when there was the likelihood of a fight. He loves to fly.

---

[*] "Top Gun" is the generally applied nickname for the Navy's fighter combat school. At the time of the interview it was based at Miramar Naval Air Station, 13 miles north of San Diego. The son is Samuel Bristol Richardson, a lieutenant at the time of the interview.

Q: So he must have inherited that one.

Admiral Richardson: Maybe so. [Laughter] But I never felt that flying was an end in itself, and I've been critical of naval aviators who extol flying to the extent of their larger duty as naval officers. That, to me, is something where they will persist in staying in aviation and avoiding any other type of duty for love of flying, love of aviation. But they let down their fellow aviators, because we have to have people at the top who are competent in aviation, and we don't always have that.

Q: One advantage of the old system of going to a surface ship first was that a man became a naval officer before he became an aviator.

Admiral Richardson: Yes, that's true, and I don't know that that's bad. It depends a great deal upon the relevance of the ship to the jobs ahead.

Q: And the other part of it is that he learns how to work with subordinates instead of just handling a machine.

Admiral Richardson: Yes, that's true, but times change. For example, when the Missouri put Tomahawk aboard, in my view a very wise thing to do.[*] Tomahawk opens new visions for surface ships.[†] Then, of course, surface-to-air capability of the various missiles is extremely important, and one has to wonder how long air attack in the classic version can last against surface-to-air missilery. We saw the Israeli Air Force decimated in the October '73 War. Had to be reconstituted with U.S. Air Force F-4s because of hostile surface-to-air capability, and that capability is growing.

---

[*] In the 1980s the Missouri (BB-63) and the other Iowa-class battleships were recommissioned after being modernized by the addition of Tomahawk cruise missiles. The Missouri was decommissioned a few days after this interview.
[†] Tomahawk is a long-range cruise missile that entered the fleet in the early 1980s, capable of delivering either conventional or nuclear warheads. Originally conceived to have both antiship and land-attack versions, the antiship type is no longer in service. For details see Miles A. Libbey III, "Tomahawk," U.S. Naval Institute Proceedings, May 1984, pages 150-163.

Q: How much do you remember about tactical training as part of your becoming a naval aviator?

Admiral Richardson: Well, it had a good bit to do with maneuvers, with individual accuracy in gunnery and in dropping bombs. And in night flying. There were group tactics, formation flying. We had rudimentary radios. But it wasn't really until World War II that we encountered really up-to-date thinking in terms of using multiple airplanes to mutual advantage, as with the Thach Weave.[*]

Q: He was an operational genius.

Admiral Richardson: Yes, Jimmy Thach. You might say this whole business about Top Gun is neither more nor less than an extension of what I believe started with him. Now, maybe others did, and there are always unsung heroes who found solutions before the problems were known, and it was never acknowledged until the right circumstances came along later. As far as I know, it was Jimmy Thach.

Q: He said in his oral history that he did that right here at Coronado. He worked that out with kitchen matches on his table at home.

Admiral Richardson: I knew him, liked him, admired him. Another whom I admired was Norm Ellis, my skipper in Fighting Five, the fighter squadron I went to after flight training.[†] He was a lieutenant commander and had an enormous effect on my life subsequently. He was a top-flight leader. A later skipper of the squadron was Wallace Beakley, who went on to be a vice admiral.[‡]

---

[*] The Thach Weave was developed shortly before World War II by Lieutenant Commander John S. Thach, USN, commanding officer of Fighting Squadron Three. It was a means of enabling the F4F Wildcat to counter the better-performing Japanese Zero fighter. Thach, who retired as a four-star admiral, described the origin of the maneuver in his Naval Institute oral history.
[†] Lieutenant Commander Norman W. Ellis, USN.
[‡] Lieutenant Commander Wallace M. Beakley, USN.

Q: Well, there were so few carriers then that they really had the cream of the crop available for those jobs.

Admiral Richardson: Yes.

Q: How did you get into that squadron? How were you picked for fighters?

Admiral Richardson: I have no idea. I requested fighters. Stick Sutherland, I mentioned him earlier, was in a senior position in the training command at the time when I went through.* I thought the patrol planes were the thing of the future, and I put in for that. He called and said, "Unh-unh, don't. Put in for carrier aviation." So I changed it. That's the specific reason. So then I ended up going to Fighting Five.

Q: It turned out he gave you great advice.

Admiral Richardson: He sure did.

Q: What do you recall from your time in the Yorktown?†

Admiral Richardson: Well, the Yorktown was a very good ship. The skippers were good, the performance of the air wing, none better. The Enterprise was our competition in that, and we were quite certain we were better than they were.

Q: What skippers did you have in the Yorktown then?

---

* Lieutenant William A. Sutherland, Jr., USN.
† The USS Yorktown (CV-5) was commissioned 30 September 1937. She had a standard displacement of 19,800 tons, was 810 feet long, 83 feet in the beam, and had an extreme width of 114 feet. Her top speed was 32.5 knots. She had eight 5-inch guns and could accommodate approximately 90-100 aircraft.

Admiral Richardson: I don't remember their names. But the ones that I knew on the Yorktown were all the kind of people who really knew what was going on all over their ship. They worked with their squadrons. They didn't journey solely between in-port cabin, sea cabin, and the bridge. They were down through the ship. And they knew their people. They involved themselves in the functioning of the ship. I've seen a lot of that. Whenever you see a good ship, a characteristic is that the skipper is interested in all his departments and their functioning. They are the ones who win battle efficiency E's.[*] I joined the Yorktown in April of '40, and left her on the East Coast in the summer of '41.

Q: How much of a feeling did you have during that period of the inevitability of war?

Admiral Richardson: I don't know that we really thought quite that way. We certainly felt it was coming, and we knew what we had to do. We did not have great respect for the Japanese, which was our mistake. We learned differently in a hurry.

Q: What was that based on, would you say?

Admiral Richardson: Well, it was ideas that they copied everything and that they couldn't see, their glasses were that thick. Oh, that's old stuff, all pure hokum.

Q: Lack of knowledge, really.

Admiral Richardson: Lack of knowledge. We had no appreciation of their operational competence, and that was a great intelligence failure.

Q: Do you remember the secret transit through the Panama Canal?[†]

---

[*] An "E" is generally awarded to a ship or component of a ship as a result of top performance in competition with other ships during a given time period.
[†] This event was on the night of 6-7 May 1941 as the Yorktown was shifted to the Atlantic Fleet to strengthen it in the face of the threat from the German Navy.

Admiral Richardson: [Laughter] With "Wasp" painted on the back. Indeed, I do. Everybody laughing on the dockside, "There goes the Yorktown."

"Why have they got 'Wasp' painted on it?" You could see Yorktown beneath Wasp.

Q: Any other details of that canal transit?

Admiral Richardson: No. Awful hot. I don't recall anything else.

Q: Was your squadron based at North Island before that?

Admiral Richardson: Yes. And then, of course, the year of '40, we were in Honolulu the whole time, except for a week or ten days when Admiral Richardson, who's no kin to me, brought the fleet back.[*]

One morning in April 1941, I drove to Pearl Harbor and parked my car dockside. We thought we were going out for a day's operations. Instead, we came through the canal three weeks later. The wives asked, "Where are the car keys?" and so forth, "Where are you?" all of that. They started getting letters, "Why don't you visit your Uncle Jim? Why don't this or that?" All of "this or that" centered on Norfolk, so they figured we must be in Norfolk. That's how they knew where we were.

Q: Admiral, in making the transition to the squadron, we didn't discuss your marriage. How did you meet your future wife?

Admiral Richardson: I met her through friends in Long Beach. It must have been in late '37 when I was in the Tennessee.

---

[*] Admiral James O. Richardson, USN, served as Commander in Chief U.S. Fleet from 6 January 1940 to 1 February 1941. Fleet Problem XXI took place in the Hawaiian area in the spring of 1940. When it was completed, President Franklin D. Roosevelt directed that the fleet remain at Pearl Harbor rather than return to its bases on the West Coast. The idea was that leaving the fleet in Hawaii would serve as a deterrent to Japanese aggression in the Far East.

Q: What was her name?

Admiral Richardson: Dorothy House. She and her mother and a younger brother, who had died at an earlier time, came from Lincoln, Nebraska. She had a number of brothers and sisters who lived in Lincoln, but I never saw any of them. Her mother was on bad terms with the rest of the family. I don't know why that was. I never pried into that. But there was no contact between her and her husband or her other children. She had 11 or 12 children, and that's reason enough.

Dorothy and I went together over a year. We were married in the fall of 1939. She became ill a year later in Honolulu. She had schizophrenia and was hospitalized once in Honolulu. I knew that she had been hospitalized with a nervous breakdown before I'd ever met her, but that meant nothing to me. At that time, in 1940, the doctor in Honolulu told me, "Get a divorce. As she goes through life, this will occur more often, more seriously, and it'll just continue that way."

That upset me a great deal. I went to see my skipper, Norm Ellis. Norm knew the skipper of the Navy hospital in Honolulu, and he said that this doctor was a psychiatrist. So Ellis got in touch with him. The hospital skipper went out and talked with my wife. She was incarcerated in town in a section where her activities were controlled, along with others. This doctor said the advice I was given was totally wrong, and he said, "No, just don't do what that dumb-dumb said."

Only years later did I actually come to learn that the first doctor's advice was accurate. As we went through the years, this thing did become more often. When I was working on the Joint Staff--very busy, very intense--our oldest son, David, was seven years old. He was born in December 1943. Now he's a naval aviator. He went through the Naval Academy, class of '66. Then he left active duty and went into the reserves; he's a computer whiz now. But back when David was seven--this would have been in late 1950--we had a baby named Robert who was about six months old. My wife was feeding the baby a bottle, and the baby was screaming mightily. I was fixing dinner, but I went over to find out what the trouble was. The baby's bottle was extremely hot. I got so angry that I lost control of myself. I snatched the baby away from her, laid him down, then I left the house, went out and walked around the block to get control of myself.

And I thought, "This is absurd. We've been through this so many times." When Dorothy was good, she was great. She even knew when she was getting into these conditions. She understood the process as well as anyone, maybe better. But I thought, "This has got to stop." And so I put her in the Catholic hospital in Baltimore--Seton--and she was there for a year or so, I guess. My mother was living in Long Beach, California. She came and took care of the kids.

Earlier, when I was at the Naval War College from mid-'46 to mid-'48, Dorothy was in a hospital in Providence two or three times for as much as three months at a time. When I had Air Group 13 in 1949, down in Jacksonville, she was under psychiatric care and in a hospital a couple of times for three or four days. It was been a nearly continuous thing after 1946. She wasn't ill through the war. I thank God for that. So I just decided that I had to start thinking about the rest of the family, so I decided to divorce her.

I was told at Seton in 1951 that she would never come out of a mental hospital. If she did, by any chance, she should never have any emotional strain placed on her. I brought her out West, and she was placed in Patton in San Bernardino by court order. She was in Patton for a good many years. Finally she did come out and stayed with friends in Long Beach for two or three years. She died about 20 years ago.

I remarried in '55, and I've joked and said my wife and I had three kids before we were married. She had one, a girl, and I had two boys when we started out. Then we had two girls and a son together. They came two years apart. Our son is out at Miramar as an instructor in Top Gun. This girl you just met is the younger of the two daughters we had together. She and her husband David just got married here two years ago.[*]

Q: So you have five children altogether?

---

[*] Lieutenant David Courtney, USN, a SEAL.

Admiral Richardson: I have five blood children and one stepchild, a daughter.[*] Now, my wife's first husband was Bruce Simonds, who was a squadron commander during the Korean War.[†] He was on the Kearsarge as an attack squadron commander. He was attending MIT when the war broke out.[‡] He and John Kirk and Mike Michaelis were in the same class and close friends.[§] They applied for flight assignments. Bruce took off from the Kearsarge on a bombing run into North Korea. My Naval Academy roommate, Jim O'Grady, was XO of the Kearsarge.[**] Years later, Jim described what happened. Bruce lost power right after takeoff and went into the drink. I had photographs given me by Jim that I never showed my wife for years, then finally did.

Bruce was in the Naval Academy class of '41. He was a very, very talented gent. He was a gymnast on the parallel bar. He was the leader of the team on the parallel bar as a midshipman. But down he went into the soup after taking off from Kearsarge. He certainly was physically able to survive that wreck, but obviously his chute or something he wore got caught in the fuselage of that plane. The pictures show him swimming outside the cockpit, but by the time the helicopter got there, the plane and Bruce were both down, so he drowned. He was pulled down.

Q: I think you told me that your present wife was a Navy junior.[††]

Admiral Richardson: Yes. Her dad was William Bristol McHugh.[‡‡] He's out of the class of '21. He died in late 1988. His widow, Ruth, lives here in San Diego. Jeanne's mother will have her 89th birthday this December, and she's in good health. We were all down at Le

---

[*] David Wilson Richardson, born 30 December 1943; Suzanne Caprice Simonds, born 12 Janaury 1948; Robert M. Richardson, born 14 July 1950; Ruthanne Richardson, born 15 February 1956; Jeanne Schamber Richardson (married to David Courtney), born 14 May 1958; Samuel Bristol Richardson, born 3 September 1961.
[†] Commander Bruce T. Simonds, USN, was killed on 16 October 1952 while commanding Attack Squadron 702, which flew AD-4 Skyraiders.
[‡] MIT--Massachusetts Institute of Technology.
[§] Lieutenant Commander John E. Kirk, USN; Lieutenant Commander Frederick H. Michaelis, USN. The oral history of Michaelis, who retired as a four-star admiral, is in the Naval Institute collection.
[**] O'Grady was then a commander.
[††] Her maiden name was Jeanne McHugh.
[‡‡] McHugh retired as a captain in 1951.

Meridien for brunch today. I was sorry I didn't know how to reach you to get you to join us. It was a beautiful brunch.

Q: Probably a lot of things I don't need and shouldn't eat anyway. [Laughter]

Well, going back to VF-5, what do you remember about Lieutenant Commander Ellis as a teacher in molding the squadron?

Admiral Richardson: Well, he was casual and offhand, but he gave a lot of instruction on proper group flying techniques and things like that. In his manner, he was a very cheerful sort of a fellow.

Norm kept the idea of the objective always in the forefront. Never mind all the folderol, provided it was not unsafe. When we would fly in Fighting Five, when he first saw the Cast flag go up, he started judging when he was going to land on board that ship.[*] As the carrier turned into the wind, he started down. Now, he might be anywhere within sight of the carrier. He just went down like that, and his wingman opened out on him like that [demonstration with hands], and down he went. He'd slow down by working the problem far enough away from the carrier so that he could get into proper speed before landing aboard.

The objective was to land aboard the minute that carrier got into the wind and Cast went up. Now, if he was too soon, he went on by, and number two landed. Let me say that the first plane would land within five seconds--and certainly within ten seconds--of two-blocking Cast, which meant "commence landing." But I always remember that sense of the objective. When I had an air group, I'd do the same thing the minute that ship got into the wind. I had a torpedo squadron commander who used to go through the entire sequence, and I used to press on him to try to get him to cut short the procedures when he was flight leader. I said, "Let's get results." It didn't work. He was a longtime friend of mine, but I couldn't make him cut the routine when the deck was ready and waiting.

---

[*] "Cast" stood for the letter C in the phonetic alphabet of the time.

Q: For the benefit of those who will eventually read this in transcript form, I should say that you have been talking with your hands and illustrating these maneuvers, which is the sure sign of a true fighter pilot.

Admiral Richardson: I won't argue that. [Laughter]

Q: What do you recall of your first carrier landing?

Admiral Richardson: Well, it was difficult at first in the F3F. The plane handled beautifully, but the visibility was terrible, and it took me at least 20 landings before I got to be reasonably good at it.

On one occasion a year later, when I was landing on the Ranger, East Coast, I came in and things weren't right. My right wing dropped at the ramp, and I decided that I couldn't make it. I poured the soup on and pulled the F3F up sharply and went off to the starboard of the Ranger like this and went around for another approach. I got down to the wardroom after landing aboard and heard a couple of ship's company officers say, "Did you see that plane out there? I was on the gun mount. That plane wasn't five feet from me." [Laughter]

I thought, "My God, was I that close?" I must have been slipping to the right in the first place, so I pulled it up and went around.

Q: I'm sure that was a surprise to those on board.

Admiral Richardson: It was a shocker.

Q: Was the Ranger the ship you first landed on?

Admiral Richardson: No, Yorktown. We were on the Yorktown for over a year. Then when we came to the East Coast, we were on the Ranger when she first came out for practice landings, and we may have made a short cruise on her.

Then our squadron transitioned to F4F-3s.* I was in a flight of four F3F-3s that we flew to San Diego for disposal in the spring of 1941. We landed in a small town in Utah for the night, our second stopover. While in a restaurant, we heard the radio announcing the German invasion of Russia.†

We got our new planes operational in a hurry. We had a very experienced squadron--a lot of old-timers in it. Three-quarters of our squadron pilots had over 1,000 hours each. So we went aboard the Wasp, and we were aboard the Wasp in the fall of '41, during October, November, December.‡ VF-5 went in place of VF-71. That was the proper Wasp squadron, but they made no special effort to get ready. So ComAirLant broke that squadron up, fired the skipper, transitioned a number of the people to other squadrons, and turned some out of aviation.§ They broke up the squadron because of its lack of drive. Then the reformed squadron relieved us on Wasp on the 17th of February 1942. We'd been up in Argentia, Newfoundland, and were approaching Boston Harbor when they came out. We took off, and the newly formed squadron landed aboard.

Prior to that, the Wasp was on Atlantic patrol during the fall of '41. The other squadrons with us were VS-7, VB-7, and VT-7.** We were in Bermuda the weekend that Pearl Harbor was hit, and when the message came in, it was about 6:00 o'clock our time.†† We were just about ready for the evening meal when in came that message that we've seen many times since then, "This is no drill. Pearl Harbor is under attack. This is no drill."

We then got under way the next morning and headed down toward the Caribbean. We were directed to attack French ships, including a carrier in Martinique. What happened, though, was that they came over to the Free French. But we didn't know that when we started out. The attack didn't occur. But we went down there in readiness to attack the ships that were there.

---

* Grumman F4F Wildcat fighters first entered fleet squadrons in late 1940. The F4F-4 model was 28 feet, 9 inches long; wing span of 38 feet; gross weight of 7,952 pounds; and top speed of 318 miles per hour.
† The German attack on the Soviet Union began on 22 June 1941.
‡ The USS Wasp (CV-7) was commissioned 25 April 1940. She had a standard displacement of 14,700 tons, was 741 feet long, 81 feet in the beam, and extreme width of 109 feet. She had a top speed of 29.5 knots and could accommodate approximately 80 aircraft.
§ ComAirLant--Commander Aircraft, Atlantic Fleet--the type commander for aircraft and aircraft carriers.
** VS-7--Scouting Seven; VB-7--Bombing Seven; VT-7--Torpedo Seven.
†† Japanese carrier-based planes attacked Pacific Fleet ships in Pearl Harbor, Hawaii, on the morning of 7 December 1941.

Then we came back into Norfolk to have a radar put aboard. Wasp had no radar until then. We took off and went into the North Atlantic right after New Year's and headed for Argentia, escorting a number of merchant ships. The skipper of the Wasp was Black Jack Reeves.* He was . . .

Q: Unforgettable.

Admiral Richardson: . . . unforgettable. And I'll never forgive the man. He was so dictatorial. He had everybody scared to death--the XO and everybody on the ship.

Q: Do you recall examples of his behavior?

Admiral Richardson: Yes. J. J. Southerland was a classmate of mine who was killed in '49 when he was CAG on Midway.† Wallace Beakley, who was the air group commander at this particular point in time when I was on the Wasp, was the skipper of the Midway when Southerland was killed. An ensign flying a Corsair took off at night on the signal that was being given Southerland.‡ The ensign's propeller chewed the tail off Southerland's plane. Southerland went into the drink and was lost.

But back to the Wasp and Reeves. The squadron played baseball against the ship's officers. Pug Southerland was referee at first base. The skipper got a hit and got thrown out at first base in a very close call. Pug said, "Out!"

The skipper said, "It was not out."

"Out!" said Pug. Reeves burned, but "out" it was.

Our skipper, Wallace Beakley, gave us a lecture after that. [Laughter] He said, "Now, look here. That's all right. I can understand that. But you know what I've got to do now? I've got to play golf with that SOB for the next week to make up for it." [Laughter] That was his comment. But he was chuckling unto himself. We weren't pushovers.

---

* Captain John W. Reeves, Jr., USN, commanded the aircraft carrier Wasp (CV-7) from her commissioning on 25 April 1940 to 31 May 1942.
† Commander James J. Southerland II, USN, was killed 12 October 1949. CAG--air group commander.
‡ The Vought F4U Corsair was a fighter plane used in carriers in the 1940s and 1950s.

Q: What kind of a guy was Beakley?

Admiral Richardson: Beakley was a fine guy, well-balanced, good humor, very courageous. He stood up to the skipper, and the skipper respected him. Beakley became Commander Seventh Fleet years later.* In about 1969 he and his wife came into Lisbon on a cruise. I was then in Lisbon as Commander Sixth Fleet on Little Rock. My wife and I went over and called on them, then made my car and driver available to them for their stay.

But back in the war, we had a flight of scout planes out, and they came back at sunset to land aboard Wasp. That was when they were supposed to be back and land. But Reeves was taking a nap, and he would not let planes land while he napped. The officer of the deck was afraid to wake him, so these planes orbited overhead for an added hour on a windy, black night, miserable weather, no horizon, drizzling rain. Finally, when the skipper got up, they were brought aboard. Well, hell, they couldn't even find the carrier. One plane made an approach on one of the merchant vessels and almost flew into that.

There was a young aviator out of '37 piloting one of the planes. His approach was bad. Reeves yelled out, "What plane was that?" The pilot was taking a wave-off as he flew by. The signal bridge shone a light on his plane in order to get his side number and answer the skipper's question. The pilot, blinded by the damn light, flew up ahead, and I saw him turn to the left and lose altitude. He dragged his left wing into the ocean.

Q: Was he recovered?

Admiral Richardson: No. That was the end of him. It was miserable weather, choppy seas, cold, submarine-infested waters, just miserable, short of a storm but black as pitch. I'm trying to remember that fellow's name.

Q: That wave-off cost him his life.

---

* As a vice admiral, Beakley served as Commander Seventh Fleet from January 1957 to September 1958.

Admiral Richardson: That wave-off cost him his life. That wave-off with this signal light, flashed on his side to answer the skipper's question, cost him his life.

On another occasion, when coming down the coast, the Wasp had a collision with a destroyer.

Q: The Stack.*

Admiral Richardson: You know of that incident.

Q: I talked to the officer who was the OOD in the Wasp.†

Admiral Richardson: Well, they were yelling up, "Stop the goddamn ship!" Finally, they got the word up to the bridge. Black Jack Reeves is not my kind of man. I despise him and the kind of an attitude that he had.

Q: Did you have a job within the squadron--maintenance or whatever?

Admiral Richardson: I had all of them as time went on. When we left the Wasp, we went to Oceana.‡ We shifted to F4F-4s. And then we were there about a month. Of course, Oceana at that time was just a mud field with a few shacks and a triangle runway structure, all quite short. Then we were ordered to go to the West Coast and out to Honolulu. So some drove and others flew across the country. We had six fairly new pilots that we had with us on the Wasp. We were loaded aboard tankers, planes covered with paralquetone.§

---

* The destroyer Stack (DD-406) collided with the aircraft carrier Wasp (CV-7) at 0550 on the morning of 17 March 1942. The ships were part of a task group steaming from Casco Bay, Maine, to Norfolk, Virginia.
† This is in the Naval Institute oral history of Vice Admiral Thomas R. Weschler, USN (Ret.). For the perspective of an officer then in the Stack, see the Naval Institute oral hisory of Admiral Harold E. Shear, USN (Ret.).
‡ Oceana Naval Air Station, Virginia Beach, Virginia.
§ Paralquetone was a coating to prevent salt water damage.

When we got there, we learned we were to go aboard "Sara."[*]

"Sara" had been torpedoed and was back in the Navy shipyard getting repairs.[†] Then in May she came down the coast and went out to Pearl in early June, but not in time to get in the Battle of Midway.[‡] She was two days late for the battle. We were to be the fighter squadron aboard Saratoga when she got to Pearl. So we got all set to go, cleaned up the planes, and were practicing in Honolulu and ready to go.

We'd heard at that time that there was code-breaking taking place. It's a funny thing. It made the rounds in Pearl, and we thought we knew that we had the inside dope on the coming Battle of Midway. I'm fairly sure we had this as a rumor before the battle. I could be wrong. It's been a long time, and I can't quite swear to it. But certainly during and after the battle, we had a lot of knowledge about how that all came to be from code-breaking.

Q: Just sort of common knowledge, you're suggesting.

Admiral Richardson: Yes, it was within our squadron, and I suspect broadly, because our skipper talked about it. He had picked up some of the stories about it. I think we knew that this battle was coming off and that we were setting a trap, as it were, and I think we knew that beforehand.

But when Saratoga got there, the battle was over. The other carriers were leaving, or had gone. We didn't make it.

So then, a month later, we went south on her and were in the invasion of Guadalcanal.[§] We flew combat air patrols over Guadalcanal on August 7 and 8. Frank

---

[*] USS Saratoga (CV-3) was commissioned 16 November 1927. She had a standard displacement of 33,000 tons, was 888 feet long, 106 feet in the beam, an extreme width of 130 feet on the flight deck, and had a draft of 24 feet. She had a top speed of 33.5 knots and could accommodate approximately 60-70 aircraft. She was originally armed with eight 8-inch guns that were later removed in World War II.

[†] On 11 January 1942, a Japanese submarine torpedoed the Saratoga when she was 500 miles southwest of Oahu, Hawaii. Six of the aircraft carrier's crew members were killed.

[‡] From 4 to 6 June 1942, U.S. and Japanese naval forces fought a battle northwest of Midway Island in the Pacific. After Japanese bombers had struck the island, carrier-based U.S. dive-bombers attacked and sank the Japanese carriers Hiryu, Soryu, Kaga, and Akagi and the cruiser Mikuma. U.S. ships lost were the carrier Yorktown (CV-5) and the destroyer Hammann (DD-412). The battle was both a tactical and strategic victory for U.S. forces.

[§] The invasion took place on 7 August 1942.

Jack Fletcher was our task force commander.* Leigh Noyes was our carrier commander.† It was quite apparent to us that Frank Jack Fletcher was a man of great indecision. We'd be given our flight schedules. We would then be told to man the planes. We'd man, we'd get ready to take off, then be told by radio, "Taxi forward." Our comment was, "We're wearing our equipment out going up and down the flight deck."

Of course, I know a lot more about what happened since that time than I knew at the time itself. Cryptolog, if you've read it, has a very detailed story about Frank Jack Fletcher and his behavior in the Coral Sea battle.‡ And, you know, they're having a conference in Pensacola very soon. Bill Leonard, a rear admiral, is talking about the Coral Sea battle.§ When I saw that program, I took my copies of Cryptolog written by the individual who was Fletcher's radio intelligence man.

Q: Forrest Biard.**

Admiral Richardson: Biard, yes. And I sent copies to Bill Leonard in case he didn't know any of that. Evidently he didn't, because in his letter back he was very thankful for receiving that information.

Q: Well, there are some skeptics of Biard's version.

Admiral Richardson: There may be. There may be. The only thing I can say is that Biard's version is completely consistent with what I saw in the campaign later. Of course, on August 8 Fletcher just left Kelly Turner, turned south and said, "I'm leaving."††

It was right at that time we had an experience you know very well, the Battle of Savo Island, where three of our cruisers, the Astoria, Quincy, and Vincennes went down.

---

* Vice Admiral Frank Jack Fletcher, USN, embarked in the Saratoga, was the overall task force commander for the Guadalcanal operation.
† Rear Admiral Leigh Noyes, USN, embarked in the Wasp.
‡ Cryptolog is a quarterly newspaper published by the Naval Cryptologic Veterans Association.
§ Rear Admiral William N. Leonard, USN (Ret.).
** Lieutenant Forrest R. Biard, USN, had been a Japanese language student before the war.
†† Rear Admiral Richmond Kelly Turner, USN, was the amphibious task force commander for the invasion of Guadalcanal.

The skipper of one of the cruisers was Sammy Moore.* His daughter married Don Griffin. Admiral Don Griffin lives in Washington now.† He's a four-star. But Moore's daughter and my roommate dated second class year. Sammy Moore was my navigation instructor at the Naval Academy.‡

Daddy Greenman had another one of the three cruisers.§ He had been my battalion officer at the Naval Academy. The command duty officers in both ships pleaded with the captains over the phone to let them open fire, but their response was, "No, wait till I get to the bridge. I want to be sure we aren't shooting up our own forces." There was, of course, good reason for believing that was a possibility. But the delays were deadly.

Q: That's an excellent illustration of your earlier point that initiative was not taken freely.

Admiral Richardson: That's right. We'd been in the war ten months, and still we were inhibited in allowing the watch to initiate action.

After the initial invasion, then the Saratoga transited back and forth well south of Guadalcanal. We were just creating a damn groove in the water, and that seemed stupid to all of us, the whole squadron--skipper Roy Simpler, Pug Southerland, myself.** Chick Harmer was the XO.†† I was flight officer.

Q: Did Simpler relieve Ellis?

Admiral Richardson: Beakley had relieved Ellis and then Simpler, who was XO, fleeted up when Beakley became CAG on Wasp. That would have been right about that time when we came off of Wasp. Beakley was kept aboard by Reeves, and Simpler relieved him. So Simpler was skipper for the rest of my time in Fighting Five. Then there was Kenny Craig,

---

* Captain Samuel N. Moore, USN, was commanding officer of the heavy cruiser Quincy (CA-39) when she was sunk. The destroyer Samuel N. Moore (DD-747) was named in his honor.
† Admiral Charles D. Griffin, USN (Ret.), has a two-volume oral history in the Naval Institute collection.
‡ Moore was a commander while at the Naval Academy in the mid-1930s.
§ Captain William G. Greenman, USN, was commanding officer of the heavy cruiser Astoria (CA-34) when she was sunk.
** Lieutenant Commander Leroy C. Simpler, USN.
†† Lieutenant Richard E. Harmer, USN.

who was XO in 1940.* Kenny is the class president of the Naval Academy class of '26.† You see his name in the Shipmate.‡ He was mainly a big boat pilot. He was a hell of a fine guy. I don't recall any special competence as a fighter pilot, but I know he flew the four-engine Mars seaplane. He was a longtime aviator, but I'm not sure that very much of it was in carrier aviation.

Q: Simpler had been one of those Sparrowhawk pilots in the dirigibles.§

Admiral Richardson: That's right, yes.

Q: What do you recall about him?

Admiral Richardson: Well, Roy was a delightful guy. He's dead now. He died about a year or so ago. He was just made a Golden Eagle two years ago.** I've been one about five or six years--early and pioneer naval aviators. At our meeting in Pensacola, my wife and I went out to see him and visited. I enjoyed him very much.

At one point in time when we were on Guadalcanal, everybody in our squadron had at least one shoot-down except Roy Simpler, the skipper. He didn't have any, and some had three or four. Altogether we got 95 down there. We never really got credit for very much, because--lacking an office--our record keeping was disastrous. The Marines were set up. They had to be for planning and operations. Turner Caldwell and his scout bombers worked with the Marines.†† They were scheduled by Marines for scouting missions and for attack. Theirs was written up, along with the Marines, but we were only supposed to take

---

* Lieutenant Kenneth Craig, USN.
† Craig retired in 1961 as a rear admiral.
‡ Shipmate is the monthly magazine of the Naval Academy Alumni Association.
§ The F9C Sparrowhawk fighter operated in the early 1930s from the rigid airships Akron (ZRS-4) and Macon (ZRS-5).
** The Golden Eagles is an organization limited to 200 people. It was formed following the commissioning of the USS Forrestal (CVA-59) in 1955 to honor early and pioneer naval aviators.
†† Lieutenant Turner F. Caldwell, USN, was in Scouting Five, a squadron of SBD Dauntless dive-bombers that moved ashore to Guadalcanal from the carrier Enterprise (CV-6).

off on signal and shoot down planes over the field, and there wasn't very much written up about it.

But, anyway, Roy kept assigning himself to the most likely time that we would encounter hostile planes so that he could get a shoot-down. And he finally got one, but other squadron members had a number more. I had four--three of them on Guadalcanal.

I was shot down my second day there, September 12, by a plane I never saw. An explosive bullet hit right behind the seat and exploded in the cockpit. It hit the oil line between two oil coolers, one of which was in each wing. It severed that line. The engine rotation had to be cut way back, and I had to make a power-off approach coming back into Henderson Field.* But in the meantime, my calves froze on me; in fact, I still have probably 100 tiny bits of metal in the calves. I could not work the pedals to brake. I was sent to the hospital on Efate for about three weeks.†

I came back up to Guadalcanal and was there for a week before the squadron was pulled out. By then we had lost all the planes we started with. We were reinforced one time up there by pilots from VF-72, and they came up with about 12 planes. We must have lost some 40 planes that were burned out or destroyed in air combat or ship shelling there.

I got two on one bombing run on October 12. I had just come back from the hospital. Hayden Jensen led the strike.‡ We were up to 28,000 feet when the Bettys came over.§ As soon as I opened fire, my target flamed. I was number four, with three ahead of me. I saw three planes burned. And then I opened fire. I was a good gunner, and zapped the wing tank and it went into flames. I had time to kick up and open fire on a second plane, and did. Those bullets just played hell out of the six .50-caliber guns. The one thing that F4F-4s had was a hell of a lot of firepower, and if you got anywhere near them, you were going to kill them. We shot down five of eight Bettys, although Japanese records don't confirm this. I wonder if their records of losses were just inaccurate or maybe "cooked." I saw them diving down aflame.

---

* Henderson Field was the U.S. Navy-Marine Corps airstrip on Guadalcanal. It was named in honor of Major Lofton R. Henderson, USMC, who was lost in action during the Battle of Midway.
† Efate, an island in the New Hebrides chain, became the site of a U.S. base in March 1942.
‡ Lieutenant (junior grade) Hayden M. Jensen, USN.
§ The Japanese G4M (known by the Allied code name Betty) was a Mitsubishi Type 1 two-engine, land-based torpedo bomber.

Q: Did you aim for the wing root?

Admiral Richardson: Well, you're aiming well ahead of the plane, because you've got relative motion going.

Q: You're talking about a deflection shot, then.

Admiral Richardson: Yes, it's called a high-side approach, because they're coming toward you, and you're coming down on them like that. So I flamed the second one, and they both were in flames, so there's no question but that they went in. I didn't see them hit because we were too high.

Then I flew our last plane maybe a couple days later in another raid. I was on the tail of a Zero.[*] This was up around 26,000-27,000 feet. I was trying to kick my plane into position to open fire, and was just about in position, when that guy looked around and saw me. And when he did, he pulled up in a loop--at that altitude! All I could do was just hang there. The difference in performance was enormous. I thought, "This is no place for me now." I pushed over and went straight down. Well, when I did, I saw the Zero coming across my path below. I had only to make a minor correction to open fire. He flew through one hell of a lot of bullets.

Q: He never saw you, maybe.

Admiral Richardson: He probably never saw me. He didn't try to avoid. I saw pieces flying from his plane, and there was enough of it to where it had to have broken up. But I went by, diving vertically and turning.

Q: When was your first shoot-down?

---

[*] The Mitsubishi-built A6M Zero was the best-known fighter plane in the Japanese Navy in World War II. The standard A6M2 had a top speed of 317 miles per hour and was armed with two 7.7-millimeter machine guns and two 20-millimeter cannons.

Admiral Richardson: August 24. It was the initial combat action in the Battle of the Eastern Solomons. I was launched with my division about noon for combat air patrol. My former wingman, now section leader, Frank Green, led the second section.[*] Intercept control directed us to close a bogey at 20,000 feet.[†] We were at 15,000. I tally-hoed a large seaplane.[‡] It commenced a full-speed descent to the south. We chased it for 55 miles before closing to shooting range. I closed straight in from astern. Green flew out to the left to close from the beam.

The rear gunner in the four-engine plane opened fire. I could see his tracer shots falling well short of me as I closed. I selected the starboard inboard engine as my aim point and opened fire with six .50-caliber guns. The engine broke out in a long trailing fire immediately. I pulled up, then rolled over to my left side to see what happened. The seaplane, which had been flying only a few feet above the surface, had crashed and burned. A large fire burned on the ocean surface. It was <u>Saratoga</u>'s first shoot-down, nine months into the war.

Q: This is where we really need videotape to record your hand movements. [Laughter] Well, back to mid-September. You were making a forced landing.

Admiral Richardson: Well, I landed. I couldn't control the brakes of the plane, so it ran off the side of the runway. But at that point in time it was so slow, it didn't do any damage. There were potholes all over the place, shell holes. Out came a Jeep. They leaped up on the plane--no prop rotation. They had to pull me out of the cockpit, because I couldn't get out, and they took me to the little hospital there on the field.

That night, we were three deep, and I was in the bottom bunk. There was a fellow in the bunk right above me complaining because the fellow in the top bunk was urinating on him. There were maybe 12 or 18 spaces in this "hospital." Finally he got one of the corpsmen over. The corpsman said, "Urinating, hell. He's hemorrhaging."

---

[*] Ensign Frank O. Green, USNR.
[†] "Bogey" is a term used to designate an unidentified air contact.
[‡] Tally-ho is the term used when a fighter pilot sights a designated target aircraft.

The next day, I was put aboard a DC-3 that flew out in the evening for the hospital on the island of Efate.*

Q: Did you have trouble getting out of the plane because you were wounded?

Admiral Richardson: Yes. My feet and legs were just paralyzed from the knees down. I could move my leg around like that, but I couldn't control my feet.

Q: Do you think the torpedoing of the Saratoga was because of this predictable pattern of steaming back and forth?†

Admiral Richardson: No, I didn't mean it that way. What I meant by that was it was an open invitation because they kept plowing up and down the same path day in, day out, and if they kept that up long enough, we were going to dig a groove in the ocean. They didn't seem to think that some submarine would finally wise up and find them.

Q: It sounds like we're saying essentially the same thing.

Admiral Richardson: Yes. When the torpedo hit the "Sara," I was going up a ladder and the ship started shaking and vibrating in a rhythmic fashion. That was after the battle on the 24th of August. The torpedo hit the starboard side aft and ruptured a fuel tank. An enormous column of oil went up into the air, landed on the flight deck, washed a man standing on the flight deck into the gun pit, and broke his leg. That was the one casualty.

We then manned our planes after a period of time, with minimum gear, and were launched to the airstrip prepared by Seabees in Efate.‡ From there we went up to

---

* In World War II the DC-3, which had already been successful as a commercial aircraft, carried the Navy designation of R4D and the Army Air Forces designation C-47.
† On 31 August 1942, the Japanese submarine I-26 torpedoed and damaged the aircraft carrier Sartaoga (CV-3) while she was operating in the Solomons.
‡ Seabees is the name universally applied to members of the Navy's mobile construction battalions (CBs).

Guadalcanal, about 11 September, to reinforce the Marines. We had maybe 30 enlisted men from our squadron with us. I don't know how we got them in, but somehow we did.

In the Battle of the Eastern Solomons, after my shoot-down, we were directed to land on Enterprise. Then I reported in to the ops officer on the Enterprise, who was John Crommelin.[*]

Q: Why to the Enterprise?

Admiral Richardson: Well, because the Saratoga was busy launching and couldn't accommodate us, so we were landed on the Enterprise. Then the Enterprise rearmed us and flew us off when the Japanese were coming in. As one learns from reading the account of that battle, you know there was a great deal of confusion about where the Japs were. Our response was not well managed at all. The problem was interpreting the radar's indication of altitude.

I was not launched with my division but instead with three other pilots--Dufilho, Haynes, and another fellow whom I'd flown with once.[†] They were transplants to Fighting Five. And I had been upset earlier with Dick Gray, their normal leader, because his wingmen didn't stay close in.[‡] They spread out a lot. And he said, "Don't you worry. Whenever there's combat, they get right in there close, but they take it easy the rest of the time." But they didn't.

Anyway, the four of us took off, and I was the division leader, and we were climbing, headed due west. I spotted planes up to the right coming in--they were the Japs--so I made a sharp turn to the right to close. I looked around, and these guys were way behind me. They hadn't closed up on me. I figured, "Well, I'll cut across. They'll close on me." Well, two of them were shot down. The fourth one survived. He said that right after I made that turn, they encountered a flight of Zeros that came in head on from above. If I hadn't turned, why, I would have been right in that thing too. Well, I never saw them. I

---

[*] Commander John G. Crommelin, Jr., USN.
[†] Lieutenant (junior grade) Marion W. Dufilho, USN; Ensign Leon W. Haynes, Jr., USNR.
[‡] Lieutenant (junior grade) Richard Gray, USN.

never knew they were there. And so we lost two of the pilots. I couldn't close the planes up to the north before they dove. So I turned and tried to get at planes in the dive itself.

Q: All by yourself? No wingman?

Admiral Richardson: All by myself now. I looked around, still searching for one of my squadron mates, to see where the hell they were. Then I saw a plane closing from behind, and it looked like an SBD.* It probably took five seconds or so--and he wasn't very far behind me--when I said to myself, "Hey, wait, that's a Jap." So I banked sharply right then left. This guy went sailing right past me. I was looking at him, not 50 feet away, off my left wingtip. I could recognize all the features of his face. He was in a Jap Zero, and he just went sailing by me and climbing. So down I went, straight, and then went to "Sara" to get aboard and get reconstituted.

Q: Anything you remember about your encounter with Crommelin?

Admiral Richardson: Well, yes. Thumbing through the book, we were trying to decide what sort of a plane I had shot down, because we hadn't seen it previously. It was their new large, long-distance seaplane that had a high speed. We could just barely overtake it. We were coming down from 15,000 feet, and he'd been up about 20,000. So that was one fast boat, remarkable for a seaplane.

Q: What do you remember about Don Felt as the CAG in the Saratoga?†

Admiral Richardson: I know Don to this day, and I've always had a wonderful rapport with him. I knew him better than most. I liked him as the CAG. I enjoyed him. He had an adamant manner about him, as you well know.

---

* The Douglas-built SBD was the U.S. Navy's foremost dive-bomber at the time.
† Commander Harry Don Felt, USN, was Commander Air Group Three in the Saratoga. The oral history of Felt, who retired as a four-star admiral, is in the Naval Institute's collection.

David C. Richardson #1 - 69

Q: He was not completely enjoyed by everybody.

Admiral Richardson: No, he wasn't. He was not enjoyed by anybody that he could buffalo. But I never had that problem with him. Because I flew with him in <u>Saratoga</u>, we got along fine. [Chuckles]

Q: What can you say about the evolution of fighter tactics and doctrine in that period from 1940 up to '42, when you were actually using it?

Admiral Richardson: As far as I know, the indoctrination came after the war started, when the Thach Weave came. It must have made its entry, I'd say, in February, March, or April of '42, right in that time frame, and we were indoctrinated in that and trained in that. But I don't recall any other type of tactical training that went in at that time. There were, of course, group tactics and maintaining the integrity of large strike forces and mutual support and all that sort of thing. But as far as the section, division, and squadron versus section, division, and squadron in counter combat--nothing more.

Q: Before, I think it had been three-plane sections, hadn't it, and then you went to two pairs?

Admiral Richardson: Yes. Back when we had the F3Fs, it was three-plane sections, and then we went to two-plane sections. But there were also two-plane sections. I know in flying in flight training in Pensacola in Squadron Five, we went out as a division of four. Not three or not six, but a division of four, two and two, and that wingman stuff was all the thing then.

Q: How would you compare the F3F and the F4F?

Admiral Richardson: No comparison. The F3F was a delightful plane to fly if you didn't mind cranking the wheels up. Of course, in the early F4Fs you cranked them up too. But it

David C. Richardson #1 - 70

was a fun plane, and you could just do anything with it. The F4F-3 was good; the F4F-4 was too heavy.

Q: Going back to the Saratoga, she was a much older ship than the Wasp and the Yorktown. What sort of living conditions did you encounter on board?

Admiral Richardson: Well, they certainly were adequate. The Saratoga's strength was its awkwardness, and that was because it was highly compartmented. That made it difficult to get around. The ready rooms were quite small. But it was a good ship to be on.

Q: In what sense was it a good ship?

Admiral Richardson: High speed, stable, steady, secure, and it operated the air group well. But you can't blame the ship for the weaknesses of its top commanders--Fletcher and Leigh Noyes.

Q: I interviewed one of the enlisted men who served in the Saratoga during the war, and he said that the head arrangements, for example, were literally out of another era.[*] They were much less modern than in the typical World War II ships.

Admiral Richardson: They probably were. I just don't remember. Certainly the Yorktown was a more pleasant and easier place. But the "Sara," other than its high degree of compartmentation, was okay,. We sure missed it when we were on Guadalcanal--especially its compartmentation.

Q: So that made it difficult to get from one place to another?

Admiral Richardson: Yes.

---

[*] This is in the Naval Institute oral history of Roger L. Bond.

Q: What were the living conditions like on Guadalcanal?

Admiral Richardson: Very interesting. We heard complaints here in Desert Storm about the inability of the intelligence people to predict how the Iraqis would behave when Desert Storm came around, but that's because nobody asked anyone who had been through Guadalcanal. When you've been shelled night after night, there isn't any spunk left in you.

During that period in October, the 12th to the 15th or 16th of October, the shelling was at its highest level. There were two 14-inch battleships and a number of cruisers. They would come down in the evening and turn, and from about 2200 to 2230, they'd shell the area, and then they'd turn around. There would be about a 15-minute respite around, say, midnight or a little afterward, and then about 2:30 it would be over and they'd be getting the hell away before dawn permitted the aircraft to launch.

We were in little dugouts, and there was no water. I mean, you just picked yourself out a hole somewhere. We had quarter-inch or three-eighths-inch steel plate over the tops of our holes in the ground that were deep enough to where you could sit and bend over like this sitting in the ground. They probably were about two and a half feet deep, and you had to crawl when you went in and out. We'd go out to urinate, then come back in. Well, on one occasion I went out, and it was all wet when I came back in. Somebody in our little hole didn't have guts enough to go out, so he urinated in the entrance. That was the sort of thing you ran into.

There was a corpsman that probably wasn't over 17 or 18 years old in that dugout with me. There were maybe five or six of us in this one hole. The corpsman was shaking with such an amplitude, just like this, vibrating his whole body, and I laid on top of him to try to calm him down or constrain the magnitude of his shakes.

I had a close friend, classmate, company mate, platoon mate at the academy. His name was Dick Wallace, and he went into the Marine Corps.[*] There was a Lieutenant Colonel Luckey who had what they then called the Special Weapons Battalion, which was made up of a few 3-inch guns that he'd haul down to the beach to battle the battleships and

---

[*] Captain Richard W. Wallace, USMC.

cruisers.* But he had a luxurious dugout. It was a hole with coconut logs across the top, and you could stand up in it. Once or twice before the shelling, I went down and spent the night with Dick because there was a cot in the place.

One morning after one of the shellings, Dick and I went out, and there were four 8-inch shells around this dugout, none of which exploded and none of them were over 10, 12 feet away. That's about how far out they were--spaced like the symbols on a 5 card, with our dugout in the middle. They probably wouldn't have hurt us if they'd exploded, but they sure would have given us a thrill. Anyway, it was comfortable sleeping there for the one or two times I was able to get down there.

Then after several days of shelling in our area, we said, "The hell with this. Let's get out." We went in different directions, but four or five of us in Fighting Five went up with the 7th Marines to the southwest of the field and up along the ridge line. We dug ourselves little foxholes, on the leeward side, and that's where we would stay. We stayed up there for maybe three nights.

On one occasion, there was a Japanese night attack up the ridge on the other side. The Japs were yelling, and a number of the Marines turned and ran. The colonel said, "The ones who run one night are the ones who stand the next." Courage is a funny thing. It has as much to do with whether you had a good night's sleep or a reasonable night's sleep and some food as with anything else. Courage is a variable.

Enough stayed to hold, and so when we left, I had four pistols that I had brought up. As it turned out, we didn't need them. I had them, so I kept these four pistols in my bag. When we were about to leave, we asked the Marines, "Well, what do you want?" Mostly they wanted those pistols. They took three of them, and I kept my fourth one. We left everything else, as I said, all of our spare underwear, socks, you name it, everything except what we wore. Then we left.

Well, a heavy shelling just takes the substance out of a person. Yes, you can still perform, but your proficiency is way down. If we had endured what the Iraqis were made to endure in Desert Storm--without support of any sort and no apparent effort being made to relieve them--then you just are not effective. I would have been surprised had they been.

---

* Lieutenant Colonel Robert B. Luckey, USMC.

I was surprised that the loss of life was so very light, but I wasn't at all surprised that they were a pushover, because if you've endured bombing and shelling for a long time, it saps your resolve.

Q: Did you ever get outside where you could see these shells coming in?

Admiral Richardson: No. We were always underground to avoid flying shrapnel and debris.

Q: I suspect that that steel plate you described was to protect you against fragments, because a direct hit wouldn't have been stopped.

Admiral Richardson: That plate wouldn't have done anything at all. No, this was all Jap construction. They had dug the holes. They put the steel plates in place; they left those. And we subsisted, as well as survived, off of what they left behind. The food we had up there for a long time was canned tuna and other things that the Japs left.

Q: How adequate was the diet? Or was it adequate?

Admiral Richardson: We had heart of palm salad when I was down with the Marines. [Laughter] And canned tuna the rest of the time.

Q: Did you have any interaction with the Marine fighter pilots there?

Admiral Richardson: No, none at all.

Q: Who ran your operation?

Admiral Richardson: Well, Roy Simpler was our skipper, and he ran the operation. He was in contact with Roy Geiger, who was in charge of air operations.* But the planning by Geiger on had to do basically with search and attack. Air defense was an automatic thing. You just launched everything you had whenever you had word that something was coming, and then you tried to reach enough altitude to do battle.

There were few records of our performance up there until after Roy Simpler was able to put them together much later. I had no awards of any sort until 1944. I couldn't get a hotel room in '43 or '44, whereas some Air Force second lieutenant who had flown five missions over the Atlantic would have an air medal, and they'd give him a room right away.† [Laughter]

For a long time, I refused to wear any ribbons at all. I'd been denied them when they could have been so useful. [Laughter] Finally, when I was at the war college, a commodore stopped me one day and said, "You're out of uniform."

I said, "Well, how's that?"

He said, "You haven't any ribbons."

I decided, hell, it isn't worth going through the story with him, and why should I beat that old horse at this point in time, and so I put on my ribbons.

Q: What awards did you get?

Admiral Richardson: Distinguished Flying Cross for three official shoot-downs (I had a fourth by my count); Air Medals, Bronze Star, Purple Heart, a lot of theater medals. Then subsequently I was awarded three Distinguished Service Medals in my later duties.

Q: What was your mission when you were flying from that field, as opposed to what it had been on board the ship?

Admiral Richardson: Well, it was to shoot down incoming Japanese airplanes.

---

* Major General Roy S. Geiger, USMC, Commanding General, First Marine Air Wing.
† On 20 June 1941 the U.S. Army Air Corps was officially redesignated the U.S. Army Air Forces. In 1947 it became a separate service, the U.S. Air Force.

Q: Were these warnings from coast watchers?

Admiral Richardson: Some were from coast watchers. We may have had a radar capability about that time, I'm not sure. With ships in the bay, certainly we would have had whatever radar capability we had operating. In fact, it was a failure of the surface radar functioning that let the Japs get in when they sank the <u>Canberra</u>, <u>Astoria</u>, <u>Quincy</u>, and <u>Vincennes</u>. Two destroyers were out as pickets.

So I'm sure they were using radar, but I wasn't aware of any of that. All I knew was we were being launched. The Japs were expected at such and such a time. We'd launch as soon as we could, because those planes were so slow, 500 feet a minute would be the top rate of climb, once you got above about 15,000-16,000 feet. So if you hadn't had 30 minutes' warning time, you might as well not have gone, other than to not be on the field when they were dropping bombs.

Q: That's an interesting observation.

Admiral Richardson: Well, it took a long time to get up to altitude. You didn't want to be on the field. We flew off to get off the field at times when we knew we hadn't time to get up. We flew away, out over the water somewhere, and came back 20 minutes later.

Q: I would think that having ships there was rather an infrequent thing, because they were highly vulnerable.

Admiral Richardson: We had a number of ships that were coming in throughout that time. If you were to go back through the history of that, my recollection is that almost every day a destroyer was coming in bringing aviation fuel which they'd dump off. There were a number of ships that were coming in. And it wasn't all that hazardous, because a pattern of operations developed, and there were times when you could come in and get away fairly safely. You didn't have to stay there. In fact, when we left, we flew out, as I recall it was the 16th of October that the squadron was taken off.

Now, a lot of our enlisted personnel--and Roy Simpler stayed with the enlisted personnel--went aboard a destroyer to come out that night. That destroyer was hit and some of our men killed. The greatest loss we had in our enlisted personnel was when that destroyer was hit. All of that I have in the Fighting Five war diary submissions. I searched them out of the Naval Gun Factory a couple of years ago.[*]

Q: Did you have any radar-controlled intercepts, or was it always a matter of them coming in the same direction?

Admiral Richardson: They were always coming in the same direction. You just had to get up there. I don't recall that we ever had any instructions on where to go, but we knew where they were coming from.

Q: So your effectiveness was directly related to how much warning you had and, thus, your altitude capabilities.

Admiral Richardson: That's exactly right. If we'd have been in F4F-3s, instead of F4F-4s, we'd have made that thing so costly for the Japanese that it would have been pitiful. But with the 4s, we couldn't do it.

Q: Why was the 4 version heavier? More armor?

Admiral Richardson: It had two more .50-caliber guns in the wings, making six. It had less ammunition. The 4s had 400 rounds. Earlier, the F4F-3, with four .50-calibers, had 400 rounds per gun. With six, it was 280 per gun, still plenty.

---

[*] The Naval Historical Center is in the Washington Navy Yard, which was previously known as the Naval Gun Factory. In the mid-1990s, subsequent to this interview, the Navy's operational records for World War II were transferred to the National Archives.

But the thing that ran the weight up was the wing-folding device that they put in because you get more of them aboard ship. That made them almost 1,000 pounds heavier, and that 1,000 pounds just made all the difference. The F4F-4 struggled to climb 800 feet a minute at low altitude versus 1,500, 1,600 in the F4F-3. It's an enormous difference. We'd have been better off without it. Fewer planes, but with the 3s, we'd have had a lot better chance.

Q: And the irony is when you were ashore, the wing-folding device didn't make any difference.

Admiral Richardson: No good at all, no. But our planes could reach altitude above the Bettys at 22,000 to 25,000 feet. We had Air Force planes up there, P-39s, P-38s. I was told that their maximum altitude was 18,000 feet, and they had no superchargers. They couldn't even get in the air battle.

Q: I know the P-39 couldn't go very high. I didn't realize the P-38 had that problem.

Admiral Richardson: I don't think either one could get up anywhere near combat altitude. They had to be up 25,000 to 28,000 feet to attack the enemy, and the Zeros were up above that.

Q: How capable were the Japanese pilots you tangled with?

Admiral Richardson: Well, I didn't see any real capability. It seemed mostly that air combat was a melee. You take their bomber pilots. They just maintained formation and kept going. And finally when they were nearly all gone, the others flew back. The next day some more came. They kept nice closed-in formations. The skill of their individual pilots was best measured in their carrier attacks against our ships, and I never really saw a lot of that. On August 24, they hit the Enterprise. Enterprise and Saratoga were the two there that day.

The Enterprise left that day, and "Sara" stayed and maybe the Hornet. I don't think that the Hornet was in the immediate vicinity on the 24th. She may have been refueling. I was back in the States when the Hornet was sunk.[*]

Q: Please describe the process of coming back to the States.

Admiral Richardson: When we came out of Guadalcanal, four of us from Fighting Five--Hayden Jensen, Wally Clarke, Frank Green, and myself--were the first ones to come back to the States, and we were really the first Navy people out.[†] So we landed in Honolulu, having been through Noumea, then up. We were in a Mariner flying boat, as I recall. And we had nothing, no change of clothes, no pay records, nothing at all. So we were put into the BOQ on Ford Island in Pearl Harbor, and we were invited to a cocktail party at the O-club that night.[‡] So we bathed and brushed our only clothes off. But when we arrived, we were still wearing beards and looked like street people. We went to the party, the four returning "heroes." The admiral took one look at us and said, "Get those four clowns out of here." So we were invited back to the BOQ. There were women at the party. We looked disgraceful. This wouldn't have happened a year or two later, nor with other admirals.

As I recall, Bob Pirie was the gent who invited us to the party.[§] Of course, he was outraged. But he was a lieutenant commander, so there wasn't much he could do. We were invited out, so we left.

Well, it wasn't until we got back to San Diego, to ComFAir West Coast, that they put together some records and gave us some money.[**] Maybe some people had earlier loaned or given us some khakis. I was housed temporarily in the Hotel del Coronado while awaiting what would be our pay records. But when we came out of Guadalcanal, I brought only my .45 pistol. I left all my underwear and khakis, such as they were, for the Marines.

---

[*] The carrier Hornet (CV-8) was sunk 27 October 1942 as a result of damage inflicted the previous day by Japanese aircraft in the Battle of Santa Cruz Islands.
[†] Lieutenant (junior grade) Hayden M. Jensen, USN; Ensign Walter E. Clarke, USNR; Ensign Frank O. Green, USNR.
[‡] BOQ--bachelor officers' quarters; O-club--officers' club.
[§] Lieutenant Commander Robert B. Pirie, USN, was then on the staff of Vice Admiral John H. Towers, USN, Commander Air Force Pacific Fleet.
[**] ComFAir--Commander Fleet Air.

That's what they wanted and needed, so we left what little we had. We left for them every bit of it that we weren't actually wearing.

Q: What happened after that?

Admiral Richardson: After getting ourselves put back together, the four of us were all ordered to the Operational Training Command. We started a fighter training unit there for advanced training. At that point in time, they were bringing back pilots from the war and putting them there. Well, the four of us were all together, and we stayed together. Three or four others from our squadron joined us. In January of '43 we were the first fighter training unit at Cecil Field.[*]

Then we went down to Lee Field.[†] We were expanding the fighter training. Our unit kept its integrity. The Fighting Five group of eight or nine of us, along with some East Coasters and others, started the fighter training unit at Lee Field. Months later we were moved to Sanford, still as a group, to start up that fighter training unit. Some of our squadrons were transferred to open up every fighter training unit except the one at Melbourne, Florida.

Q: What do you remember about the specifics of this training program? Did you have a syllabus to start with or did you have to develop that?

Admiral Richardson: We developed the syllabus in early 1943. We had these young people about four months. They came from earlier training with about 240 hours' flight time in training types of aircraft.

Q: Did they have their wings when they got to you?

---

[*] Cecil Field is part of Naval Air Station Jacksonville, Florida.
[†] Lee Field was at Naval Air Station Green Cove Springs, Florida.

Admiral Richardson: Oh, yes, yes, they had their wings, but they had not been into the specific operational type plane that they were now going into. And so when they came, they went through training in the type planes they would fly in combat. We trained them in tactics and gunnery. We had Corsairs and Wildcats, then later the F6Fs.[*]

In fact, I flew the first Corsair that came into operational training. I was told Lindbergh flew it down to Jacksonville. I went over to pick it up.[†] Well, he wasn't there when I got there, I'm sorry to say. But he had a lot to do with the designing of that cockpit. He was tall, and when I got in that cockpit, I sank below the gunwales. It was up here. I couldn't see out. I could see up. In order to fly that thing, I had to put stacks of cushions beneath me and back of me, and I could barely reach the pedals at that.

Q: I think John Hyland had the same problem.[‡]

Admiral Richardson: Yes. The Corsair had a nose that went way out there. I was told to not land that plane three point. Instead, I should land wheels first. I was warned, "About halfway in your run-out, that right wing will drop." Sure enough, it did, and it would throw you into a ground loop if you weren't aware of it. You'd think that you were looping and you'd correct. Then you'd really throw yourself into a ground loop. In later models they improved that deficiency and also made it so ordinary-sized people could fly it.

We had with each group of students a combat-experienced instructor, usually a lieutenant, occasionally a lieutenant commander, and an assistant instructor who was a turnaround student who had just been through the course. We kept him to become the division leader in that second group. The eight of them worked together--eight people, eight planes. They did gunnery, navigation, familiarization, tactics. We had about 100

---

[*] Grumman F6F Hellcat fighters first entered fleet squadrons in early 1943. The most commonly employed version of the airplane was the F6F-5, which was 34 feet long, wing span of 43 feet, gross weight of 15,413 pounds, and top speed of 380 miles per hour. The Vought F4U Corsair first entered fleet squadrons in 1942. The F4U-1 was 33 feet, 4 inches long; wing span of 41 feet; gross weight of 14,000 pounds; and top speed of 417 miles per hour.

[†] Charles A. Lindbergh, who had captured the public's attention with his solo flight across the Atlantic in 1927, was an Army reservist who was not granted an active commission because of his isolationist activities prior to the war. He did, however, do some unofficial flying during the war.

[‡] The oral history of Admiral John J. Hyland, USN (Ret.), is also in the Naval Institute collection.

flight hours in the syllabus. We operated under the Commander Operational Training Command, a rear admiral.

These teams would then go and be used to form a new squadron, or as replacements in an existing squadron. In the latter case, four people would go as a unit to a squadron that had lost pilots, and they'd fill it up to complement. Instead of sending singles, we'd send divisions of four who would fight together. It was a good setup.

One thing I learned--and it is one of those things that defies normal logic--when more and more ships were being commissioned, more squadrons were forming up, more and more of our key enlisted people were being pulled, and we were having less and less talent at the top, and having to stretch out our talent for engine overhauls and other technical work.

Q: So you're talking about the maintenance area.

Admiral Richardson: Yes, I'm talking about maintenance now. I did what seemed logical. I concentrated what little talent we had left in the hangars to do the major work, such as engine checks and assemblies. We tried to get along that way.

Well, along came a Navy captain who took over the training unit at Sanford, and he said, "This is conceptually wrong." What he did was assign his planes in squadrons, say, 12 planes in a "squadron" with eight pilots in training. Then he'd put one experienced engine maintenance man in charge, with a bunch of nearly new enlisted men assigned to each. The Sanford skipper's availability went way up, while ours continued plunging. So I copied what he did, and our availability then started going up. What he did was decentralize, and decentralization--in business, in squadrons, in anything, generally--is the way to get results. With guidance and willing but inexperienced workers, the results are great.

Q: Who was this organizational genius?

Admiral Richardson: Oh, God. I once knew his name, but I can't remember it. He was quite senior to the rest of us in similar positions when he was put in charge at Sanford. He must have been out of about '30, '31, somewhere in there.

Q: Well, if he was a captain, he might have been even more senior than that.

Admiral Richardson: He may have been. He was there, I'd say, from about February or March of '44 through probably most of the rest of that year, in charge of the fighter training unit at Sanford, Florida. I wish I knew his name, because he sure taught me a lesson: you provide leadership, and the guys whose hearts are in the right place pick up and learn in a hurry. They can do all sorts of things under supervision that you wouldn't dare let them get near otherwise.

Q: What was included in this program that you ran down in Florida?

Admiral Richardson: Well, besides familiarization and group tactics, which is what you started out with, you went into a lot of gunnery. There were six major gunnery approaches, and we worked out over the Atlantic, using towed sleeves for targets in gunnery. They did high side and low side and front and up above and coming in like this, approaches from all angles. Lots of gunnery. That was basically it.

Q: What about the business of maneuvering and dogfighting? Was that part of it?

Admiral Richardson: Yes. That was done earlier in the tactical phase, where they worked together as divisions in squadrons. They worked as groups, and they also broke into basic fighting units, which is the two-plane unit, for some of their work. They had eight or ten hours of flying their planes singly, which included stunts and things like that to get the feel. So the syllabus probably ran about three to four months and took roughly 100 to 120 hours to complete the course. The weak ones were weeded out and ordered to squadrons other than fighters and, in some cases, to other than carrier based.

Q: How much flying did you do yourself during this?

Admiral Richardson: Not a great deal. I lectured all of the students. One of the things I did was investigate accidents. In very nearly every case, the individual killed himself while doing something foolish. So I lectured every group of students on accident prevention. And I was responsible for the instructors' performance and duty assignments. I investigated every accident and came back with the story. Then, when necessary, I made changes in the syllabus.

I would fly probably 12, 15 hours a month, not a lot. I didn't fly with the individual groups--at least not after the first six months. I ran the schedules and managed the flight program. I just really didn't have time to fly with students. This was a seven-day work week and went from sunup to after sundown. I would often get home at 8:00 or 9:00 or 10:00 at night. But whatever went on in flight was my personal responsibility. It absorbed all my time.

We went to Cecil Field in mid-January. In early February, we had a little quick storm, not a tornado, but not unlike one. It was a small, intense storm. We were just getting ready for inspection Saturday morning. The skipper was there. I was the number-two. Damned if this storm didn't hit our planes on the line and flipped a half a dozen of them over. It put an SBD up on the roof of the hangar. We had a real problem on our hands with wrecked airplanes. So I broke off the inspection, got the guys out and started right away working, disassembling the damaged planes, taking the wings off if it was on its back.

What struck the skipper was that I moved out immediately on the thing. The funny thing about it is that one of the training officers at that time was Dave McDonald. He was in the headquarters at Operational Training Command, and he knew about that.[*] My skipper was very praiseworthy that somebody moved right away on the damn thing.

---

[*] Lieutenant Commander David L. McDonald, USN, later Chief of Naval Operations, 1963-67.

David C. Richardson #1 - 84

Q: When was that chronologically, do you remember?

Admiral Richardson: That was in, I'd say, early to mid-February of 1943. But in those early days in the training command, Dave McDonald came to know me, and this had something to do with my assignment as Commander Task Force 77, years later when McDonald was CNO.[*]

Q: I especially remember something from Jimmy Thach's oral history about when he had VF-3 before the war. He said he had a little black book, and just looking at his individual pilots' proficiency, he made some predictions on which ones would get killed first, and it came true. He threw away the book at that point. But did you see people in the Operational Training Command that you didn't think would be adequate fighter pilots and get rid of them for their own protection?

Admiral Richardson: Yes, we did. I say "we" because this generally started with the lieutenant in charge of these groups. We saw certain people who had dangerous tendencies, irresponsible tendencies, and, yes, we would get rid of them.

Now, an incident of exceptional interest. Raleigh Kirkpatrick was still skipper at Sanford in early '44.[†] Raleigh was out of the class of '35. One of the top men in the Naval Academy class of '41, whose name I've long since forgotten, was going through training there, and Raleigh decided he was a danger to himself and to others and should be gotten out. He went up to Operational Training Command headquarters and said he wanted this pilot's wings removed.

They said, "No. He can damn well hack it." There was a general idea at the top of the Operational Training Command that you either hack it or your time is over. No outs. They would not agree with Raleigh to turn this man out of flying.

So one day an accident occurred south of Daytona Beach. I went to investigate and soon found a hole in a marshy area, a hole in the ground, and the tail of an F6F poking

---

[*] This assignment came about in 1966 and is discussed later in the oral history.
[†] Lieutenant Commander Raleigh C. Kirkpatrick, Jr., USN.

up in the debris. It turned out not to be one of our planes. It was a plane from Sanford, and you know who was piloting that plane. So he was killed. And that's when Raleigh told me, "I did my damndest to get him turned out. He just simply wasn't a safe aviator." It wasn't a question of him being chicken and wanting out. He just wasn't a natural flier. It is something I still get angry over.

That wasn't the case, though, with others who had no Naval Academy background. I don't recall we had any problem getting rid of anybody else that we wanted to. I had always set as my own standard that if any of my instructors said, "You've got no business being an aviator," I'd accept it, because I didn't see any point in screwing up and breaking my neck and possibly others.

Q: Some other people, though, it may have been such a matter of pride that they would not do that voluntarily.

Admiral Richardson: I suppose so. I'm sure that that's true. But I don't know. My belief about others is, in some degree, guided by my attitude toward myself.

Q: But not everybody is like you.

Admiral Richardson: No, we're all different. That's true.

Q: Did you have any opportunities to relax during this extended period in the training command?

Admiral Richardson: Lord, no. It was seven days a week, 52 weeks a year. It was all-consuming. I never went anywhere on leave.

Q: You lose your freshness and your sharpness after that.

Admiral Richardson: Well, maybe. But, like a Boston marathon runner, you just keep going. There was a war out there.

Q: You weren't given any options, evidently.

Admiral Richardson: I don't think it even occurred to me. No, I didn't feel that I ever needed a vacation. I don't think I took a single day off for two years, all of '43 and all of '44, until I left to go out to the West Coast. But, no, there just was a big job still to be done, and you just kept going.

Q: Any other specifics to mention from the time in Florida?

Admiral Richardson: No.

Q: Did you feel any frustration that the war was going on without you at this point?

Admiral Richardson: I guess I didn't. I knew I had certainly done my part in it. I had an awful lot of Guadalcanal still in me at that time, and it wasn't something you relish. No, I didn't have an itch to get back into it. I was glad when I later got orders to skipper Fighting One, but if they had sent a call through, "We're looking for volunteers to go out," I probably wouldn't have volunteered.

Q: Did you get any inputs from people like Jimmy Thach and Jimmy Flatley while you were going along with this course?[*]

Admiral Richardson: No. That sort of stuff made the rounds, and so I'd say that we were certainly up on the power curve in tactical experiments. One way we were up was because we had a constant flow of pilots coming out of the war, and so whatever they were doing, we knew. They were coming back and becoming our instructors as lieutenants.

---

[*] Commander James H. Flatley, Jr., USN, was also a noted fighter tactician of the period.

Of course, I went from lieutenant to lieutenant commander in about March or April of '43. The following year, in about April, I moved up to commander. At that point in time, you were shooting up in rank. Then I stayed a commander for 11 years.

Q: Please tell me about the F6F compared with the F4F-4.

Admiral Richardson: Much improved effectiveness came with the introduction of F6Fs and F4Us. The F6F was an aviator's dream. It was an easy plane to fly. It had good performance and excellent visibility. It had powerful climb--1,500 to 1,800 feet a minute, 2,500 feet down at lower altitudes. It was a dream airplane compared with the F4F, but it was heavy. It couldn't be compared with the later F8F Bearcat.

After I had been at Sanford, Florida, for a while, another fighting unit was set up in Vero Beach, and I was sent down as the skipper of that one. That was to be a Marine-Navy organization, 100 Navy planes and 50 Marine planes. But in the course of the first two months, the training command increased the Marines to 100 and reduced the Navy to 50. I was offered the new unit being started up in Daytona Beach. I then took charge of that.

I moved up there in February 1944, as that was converted from a bomber base to a fighter base. I led that effort and was the training officer. There was a skipper of the base, and then the training officer was in charge of the 150-plane training unit. I started that unit up, and I was up there from late January to October.

Then I was ordered out to Fighting One as skipper. The squadron went from 36 to 72 planes. I took the squadron to Fallon, Nevada, where we trained. I had a CAG whom I never saw. Then they decided to break up that enormous squadron, which was four-fifths of the wing. It made sense. I had taken with me from Daytona Beach as my XO an ex-AP, now a lieutenant commander, by the name of Boogie Hoffman.[*] He'd had a lot of experience, and he was a real gung-ho guy. He was my gunnery officer at Daytona. He took over one of the two squadrons, and I had the other one.

---

[*] Naval aviation pilots (APs) were enlisted men trained and qualified to fly aircraft. Lieutenant Commander Melvin C. Hoffman, USN, had been designated as an AP in 1929 and as a naval aviator in 1940. He commanded the squadron during its deployment on board the carrier Bennington (CV-20).

Then they pulled me and sent me out to Honolulu to be the carrier type training officer on the staff of Commander Air Force Pacific Fleet. There I worked with Tom Hamilton.[*] So there I was, very disappointed at not being permitted to keep my squadron. I was there in Honolulu that last year of the war, working with Tom Hamilton in carrier training.

My squadron went through Honolulu in about May of '45. They went forward at the tail end of the war. In the air group was Dick Crommelin.[†] Later, when I had Air Group 13 in '48 to '49, his kid brother, Quentin Crommelin, was the skipper of one of my three fighter squadrons.[‡]

Q: That was quite a family.

Admiral Richardson: Yes, sure is. Still is.

Q: Did you get to do any flying yourself in that billet?

Admiral Richardson: Yes, and I had an opportunity to fly the F8F, which was an absolute delight to fly.[§] You could do anything in that airplane. It came along in mid-1945.

Q: It was a little too late to really be useful.

Admiral Richardson: It came into the war in the summer of 1945, Air Group 19. At one time that year, I was flying in an F8F about sunset, and there was an Air Force patrol in their P-47 Thunderbolts, back from the European theater. They ran dawn and dusk patrols. So those guys spotted me and started a mock attack. I was climbing, so I poured the soup

---

[*] Captain Thomas J. Hamilton, USN. Hamilton had been the football coach at the Naval Academy when Richardson was a midshipman.
[†] Lieutenant Commander Richard G. Crommelin, USN.
[‡] Lieutenant Commander Quentin C. Crommelin, USN.
[§] Grumman F8F Bearcat fighters first entered fleet squadrons in 1945. The F8F-1 version was 28 feet long, wing span of 35 feet, gross weight of 12,947 pounds, and top speed of 421 miles per hour. It was one of the best piston-engine planes ever to serve the U.S. Navy but had a short operational life because of the advent of jet fighters.

to it, and they came right on down. When they got behind me, I just did a split-S and pulled back. I was at 14,000 feet, doing 200 knots, and I reversed myself and dropped maybe 2,000 feet. These guys turned like this, and I looked back at them and I thought, "Oh, my God, I've killed them."

Q: They were going straight down?

Admiral Richardson: They were going straight down, and those heavy P-47s don't pull through, you know. At that altitude, there was no way they could have pulled through. And I thought, "I hope to God they've got sense enough to roll out." And that's what they did; they rolled out. The Thunderbolt was just nothing compared to the F8F, which had so much maneuverability. Those P-47s were clunkers.

Q: That was a heavy airplane.

Admiral Richardson: Very heavy airplane.

Q: Please tell me more about your duties there in Hawaii.

Admiral Richardson: As the type training officer for carriers, I did all the schedules of the air groups going forward. I observed their practices and, in effect, had to certify their readiness for forward movement to Tom Hamilton, who was the force training officer. I was his deputy. That's when I first served with him and came to realize that this man was the epitome of what leadership should be. I used to watch people from coxswains to flags come in seeking his counsel or his help, and it was a parade. Every day, two, three, or more people came in--ensigns, admirals, seamen, you name it, He always responded to everyone, and he always tried to give them whatever it was they wanted. But if anyone ever let him down . . .

Q: It was all over for that person.

Admiral Richardson: All over. But he just would break his heart to help. Once I went down to the base at Kahului on Maui, checking on two of the air groups there. The CAG complained that their living conditions were unsanitary, that the jaygee communicators for the base had all the Jeeps. The CAGs had maybe a set of wheels, but no squadron commander had anything. The shower facilities were a mess. Practically everybody had athlete's foot. They were very unhappy. Then I learned that a substantial amount of money was being spent on the commanding officer's quarters, a Captain Cotton.[*] He had been out of the Navy, then recalled during the war and made skipper of the air base there. He was spending the available funds fixing his quarters.

So I went to Tom Hamilton with the story. He set up an administrative inspection. Three or four days later, we descended on the base, about eight or ten of us, and went through the various departments and really checked the base out thoroughly. When we came back with that report, the admiral fired Cotton, got a new skipper in, and cleaned things up. You got results with that man. When he went to the admiral, he got results.

Q: What admiral was that?

Admiral Richardson: I don't remember the name of the admiral. Sorry.

Q: I gather that Hamilton was a very pleasant person to deal with--very friendly.

Admiral Richardson: Very friendly, pleasant, but with enormous energy and a powerful intellect. He was a very warm-hearted gent. He was very fond of Bush Bringle, one of his favorite people, and I got along with him awfully well.[†] His wife once told me that Bush and I were his favorite people. Of that I was very proud.

Q: What else do you recall about being out in Hawaii?

---

[*] Captain Clement F. Cotton, USN.
[†] Lieutenant Commander William F. Bringle, USN, later a four-star admiral.

Admiral Richardson: Well, I flew a lot. I flew down to the airfield at Hilo, Hawaii, and to Puunene and Kahului, and I was out on the carriers a good bit. I not only scheduled the various operations, but I observed them and scheduled them onto the various bombing ranges--things like that. I spent a lot of time observing their proficiency. I knew the CAGs and the squadron commanders. When they had beefs, why, I was the guy who they beefed to, and I did what I could to alleviate whatever kind of problems they had.

Q: So now you were dealing with full-fledged operational units instead of nuggets just out of the training command.

Admiral Richardson: Yes, now these were air groups. But, you see, they started out on the East Coast or West Coast, and they went aboard ship. Then, coming through Pearl, they went through a period of four to six weeks where they got their carrier type training. They had done all of the earlier levels of work--squadron work and all that. They'd done all their practicing and gunnery and bomb dropping, and now they were doing their carrier-based strike operations.

They were based ashore because of the type of operations and the fact that they were building up carrier landings. A lot of the work was carrier landing work, building up their competence. The pilots were having to get 20 to 30 carrier landings each. They had just lifted the planes aboard, then out they went, and some of the pilots may never have made a carrier landing. So there was a lot of preliminary work that they were doing, as well as group work. They ended up running group gropes. The whole thing was in a four- to six-week period. If they were not up to acceptable standards, then we held them back a week or two for more training.

Sometimes we had problems. One carrier came through, and Joe Clifton was the XO.[*] The ship had a poisonous mood due to the commanding officer. He had done a number of things that soured him with his crew and air group, so Joe Clifton came to see Tom Hamilton about it.

---

[*] Commander Joseph C. Clifton, USN, served as executive officer of the carrier Wasp (CV-18) in 1945.

Q: Essentially putting his boss on report.

Admiral Richardson: He sure was. Joe had told Tom what the problems were. Tom took it in to the admiral, who immediately removed the skipper. He shipped him back to the States and put a new skipper aboard. Clifton was in charge while the ship was tied up right outside our headquarters awaiting a new skipper. In a day or so, the whole crew was in the hangar deck playing basketball. It was a totally different mood. Before that, the ship was quiet, no activity, everybody glum. The new skipper came, and the entire attitude of that ship changed. Well, Joe was right. Of course, he put his neck on the line in doing that. But whose wasn't in those days?

Q: You bet he did. Clifton was very results-oriented.

Admiral Richardson: He was indeed, that's right. But Hamilton knew Clifton well enough to accept his assessment. The admiral probably had a pretty good feel for that skipper before he came out there. I'm sure that any skipper of a carrier was pretty well known to most of the flags that were aviators, so he had no trouble arriving at that decision.

Q: The question is, how did he get the command in the first place?

Admiral Richardson: Well, that's right. That was done back in Washington. But thereafter the theater commanders ran things.

Q: Clifton was a man with a very colorful personality. What else do you remember about him?

Admiral Richardson: [Chuckles] Well, when I had the Cimarron, Joe Clifton was the flag officer of a carrier out in WestPac at the time.* I remember we had a radio on board, but it really was not near as good as booming Joe Clifton. You'd hear his voice so far out over the ocean. [Laughter]

Q: Did you work primarily with the air group commanders? Was that your point of contact?

Admiral Richardson: The air group commanders were my point of contact, and I worked with squadron commanders as well as the CAG, but it was always through the CAG. He was the boss man.

Q: Any of those individuals you especially remember, the CAGs?

Admiral Richardson: One was Scoofer Coffin, who then had the first F8F outfit, but he didn't really get into the war.† His group came through in about June of 1945. They got out forward, but I don't think any action occurred after they got there. Of course, he had the most capable air group in the world at that time with all his F8Fs. I don't remember individuals now. It's been too long.

Q: You said when you were back in the Tennessee that ships had personalities. Could you see that in these carriers as they came through?

Admiral Richardson: No, I couldn't, not in the carriers. I wasn't that intimate with them. You could see it a bit in the air groups. You could see it a lot in the air groups. The mood of people is quite obvious early. Not in the carriers, because I really wasn't aboard the carriers the carriers that much. I was airborne when I was watching them. But if there were a problem, we heard about it from the CAG and squadron commanders.

---

* In 1960-61 Rear Admiral Clifton served as Commander Carrier Division Seven. WestPac--Western Pacific.
† Commander Albert P. Coffin, USN.

Q: Did you see any sense of impatience on their part that the war would be over before they got a chance?

Admiral Richardson: No, I didn't see that.

Q: Probably not, because at that point the expectation was still that the war would go on into '46.

Admiral Richardson: Well, we were also working on the invasion plans for Kyushu.* The thought of all of us who were involved in that was this invasion had to be the stupidest thing ever. We thought it was dumb to land people in the Japanese homeland and to fight the kind of battles that we'd been fighting on Iwo Jima and elsewhere. Why don't we just declare the war over unilaterally, then keep our submarines around the Jap islands, to keep them totally isolated from the outside world until they get tired of living that way . . .

We really seriously said, "You know, there isn't any point in this. All we have to do is let submarines sink every damn ship that tries to leave or come into that place and then forget 'em." We all knew that that invasion, and the idea of fighting up through the islands had to be a stupid thing. My God, millions of people would have been killed, both Japanese and American--just incredible carnage. We knew that, because we'd already seen it.

Q: How much, if any, did the arrival of the kamikazes play a part in your training?

Admiral Richardson: Well, it didn't. It didn't play any part in the work we were doing. It was another airplane that you shot down. We weren't strategizing. All of this had to do with strategizing, and that was up to Mitscher.† Have you ever read Marc Mitscher, the story of his life?

---

* Operation Olympic was the code name for the Allied invasion of the Japanese island of Kyushu, scheduled for 1 November 1945.
† Vice Admiral Marc A. Mitscher, USN, served as Commander Task Force 58, the fast carrier task force, in 1944-45.

Q: Yes.

Admiral Richardson: It's fabulous. I got a copy for my son to read. And McCain.[*]

Q: What part did IFF play?[†]

Admiral Richardson: We went through procedures in returning. We'd approach and we'd make a 90-degree turn and then we'd make another turn, do things like that, rather than use electronic devices, which we didn't have.

Q: What about the business of radar control of the CAP and so forth?[‡] Was that part of your training, or was that something at another level?

Admiral Richardson: No, it was not. The effectiveness of radar increased radically, and the intercept controller, as you saw here, got better and better. The older radars had bedspring antennas. That thing was kept so secret, and for a long time we didn't know just what it was. They were under high security--a secret weapon. But it became common knowledge during the summer and fall of '42.

Q: How long did you stay in that job?

Admiral Richardson: I left in November of 1945 with orders to something I couldn't even decipher--ALUSNA London.[§] I hadn't the remotest idea what the hell I was supposed to do. I was to report in London about the second or third of January, 1946. So I was home

---

[*] Vice Admiral John S. McCain, USN, was Commander Task Force 38, the fast carrier task force, during the closing months of World War II.
[†] IFF--identification, friend or foe. This was an electronic feature that allowed friendly aircraft to have an additional identifying signature when they showed up on radar screens.
[‡] CAP--combat air patrol.
[§] ALUSNA--American Legation, United States Naval Attaché.

the month of December, and I left right after Christmas to get to New York and get overseas.

Q: Where were you when the war ended?

Admiral Richardson: In Honolulu.

Q: What do you remember about that experience?

Admiral Richardson: We knew it was coming. I don't remember how or why, but for several weeks we were expecting it momentarily. When it came, people went out shooting pistols into the air, and it was just one hell of a noisy town. An enormous sense of relief was all over.

We then had the problem of getting people home, and that was a busy, busy thing. One thing distressed me, and I tried to do something about it, but it was a total waste of time. We had started barging new airplanes out into the Pacific Ocean off Honolulu and pushing them overboard. I figured, "My God, let's at least get the engines and save those." Nope. They just started cleaning house of all of the older and newer planes, some brand new.

Then we had the problem of sending 100 cows out to Guam. Somebody had said, "We'll send them out on a carrier," and I had the job of picking out the carrier.

I said, "Well, what else? Let's use the Cowpens." [Laughter]

Q: [Laughter] I've never heard that one.

Admiral Richardson: The Cowpens got stuck with hauling 100 head of cattle out to Guam. [Laughter]

Q: How did you come to get this duty in England?

Admiral Richardson: I don't know how it happened. All I know is that I was ordered to the Royal Navy Staff College. That's the way it ended up. I went to London, and that's where I first learned what it was to be. The naval attaché was Bob Hickey, captain, and he assigned me a Jeep to use.[*] There was a Navy captain--I was a commander--who also was already there, Harry Hummer, and Harry didn't have a vehicle.[†] He went through the attaché, not the naval aviator attaché. He and I together were down at the Royal Navy Staff College in Greenwich.

It was a six-month tour, and I enjoyed it very much, except the Brits went home on Thursday afternoon, and we had Friday, Saturday, Sunday, and Monday to do things. Well, I ended up taking an apartment in London, because I was down in the college only about three days a week.

We spent two weeks in the tactical school. In the tactical school we were given a battle problem in which Soviet aircraft carriers were coming out of the Med to assault an island. My job was to run the carrier aircraft charged with defending the troops on the land. I had the only carrier force. So when in the problem those Soviet carriers were coming out, I diverted and attacked the carriers, because I couldn't defend the troops if I were sunk. And if I didn't take care of the carriers, all would be lost. [Chuckles]

Well, the head of the tactical school gave me hell. Oh, he lit into me because I disobeyed my orders. A Royal Navy commander who had been through the war made raucous remarks in my defense. The school solution, he said, was an example of hidebound Royal Navy thinking. I went to the head of my school, and he was part of the force that caught the German cruiser Graf Spee down off Uruguay.[‡]

Q: Harwood?[§]

---

[*] Captain Robert F. Hickey, USN.
[†] Captain Harry R. Hummer, Jr., USN.
[‡] In December 1939 a squadron of three cruisers--Ajax, Achilles, and Exeter--damaged the pocket battleship Admiral Graf Spee in a gun battle off Uruguay's River Plate. The German ship went into the port of Montevideo to repair damage. The German skipper, Captain Hans Langsdorff, believed a superior force awaited him if he returned to sea, so he removed the crew and ordered the Admiral Graf Spee scuttled on 17 December. He then committed suicide.
[§] Commodore Henry Harwood, RN, was commander of the British South American Station in the late 1930s.

Admiral Richardson: No, it wasn't Harwood. I forget his name. He was a ship skipper and a very fine gentleman. I said, "I guess I played hell at tactical."

He said, "No, you were absolutely right. Don't be concerned."

It had caused such a ruckus by my sticking to my guns that I felt I ought to apologize. Yes, my orders were to support the landing, and they had a pretty detailed op order. Then there came a need for a change, but I didn't get a change, so I did it anyway.

Q: It wasn't the school's solution.

Admiral Richardson: No, it was not. And I have to say that it would have been absurd to have continued sending planes in to run combat air patrol over the troops ashore. It was nutty.

Q: That seems like a really curious change of pace to go to a British staff college after all you had been through at that point.

Admiral Richardson: Yes. It was very informative, and I've learned to love the "Mr. Minister" series. If you've ever seen them, they're incredible. They come up on PBS from time to time.* It's a spoof at the civil service in Britain, and it's most humorous.

Anyway, when the civil service was briefing us, boy, those British officers really lit into them: "You guys turn our money off. You're the ones who do this or that." They figured they were slaves to their civil service, not at all were things the way the civil service told it.

Later, when I had Sixth Fleet, I learned that one of my classmates at the Royal Navy Staff College was then the four-star Brit admiral in charge of Gibraltar. I paid a visit with Little Rock, the Sixth Fleet flagship. We had a wonderful time revisiting our past. [Laughter]

---

* PBS--Public Broadcasting System.

Q: What kinds of things would you say you learned from that course?

Admiral Richardson: Well, I got a good feel for the British, and I saw the deprivations that they had suffered in the war. When I say I got a good feel for them, I saw two kinds of mentalities. One, the kind I just described that was very hidebound and unimaginative; and the other, which was very creative, very responsive to changing situations. They're smart as a whip. If you have the right one, then he does what's needed. You get the Nelsons among them, as opposed to the ones who have this total allegiance to some plan that's been laid out a day or a week or a month ahead of time.[*] Then I've seen lots of them, met them in different ways in the NATO setup, Sixth Fleet, Strike Force South.[†]

Q: What do you remember about living on the British economy? The country had really been ravaged by the war.

Admiral Richardson: Yes. Well, I used to go to Chinese restaurants to get enough food to eat. Of course, that doesn't stay with you very long, but . . .

Q: Was your family with you?

Admiral Richardson: No. I was by myself. At that point in time, there really was no way to transport them. And then I left in June and came to our Naval War College. I was there two years, my second year on the staff in the analytical section, doing analyses of recent combat actions.

In those days, in having been through what so many of us had been through, we weren't slaves to protocol or necessarily inclined toward pleasing somebody. We damned well did what we thought was right and wanted to do at that time. If somebody didn't like it, that was too bad.

---

[*] Lord Horatio Viscount Nelson (1758-1805), British naval hero of the Battle of Cape St. Vincent, 1797, Battle of the Nile, 1798, Trafalgar, 1805. He developed a reputation for doing things his own way, sometimes defying the wishes of his seniors.
[†] NATO--North Atlantic Treaty Organization.

Q: Are there any manifestations of that attitude you could suggest?

Admiral Richardson: I don't think so now. Certainly at that time we weren't particularly impressed by anybody, which is a fair way of putting it.

Q: Well, I take it you weren't rude to your British hosts.

Admiral Richardson: No. I'm now referring to the instructors at our war college then; many of them were also hidebound. We were uninhibited in our approach to things in general. If something seemed stupid, we called it that, and quickly so, and weren't particularly bothered by the fact that Naval War College staffers might not like it. That isn't strange, given what we'd been through.

Q: What could you suggest about substantive knowledge that you got from that course in Britain?

Admiral Richardson: Well, they're very good at estimate of the situation. First, be sure you know the problem. Our war college does the same thing. And that has to do with thoroughly thinking through what you're going to do in the context of what you know about the nature of the job ahead. The Brits are good at that.

The Brits have at one end of their scheme of things a mentality that's very dogged. At the other end, they're brilliant. It really is a strange thing to see this disparity between the good-thinking Brits and the bad-thinking Brits. There's quite a gulf.

Q: Do you think you could give examples of each?

Admiral Richardson: No, not really, because that comes through in lots of ways. It's just when you're with them for quite some time that you see these characteristics, and some you respect highly; others are dodos.

Q: You got to the U.S. War College. What comparison would you draw between that and the British one you'd just been through?

Admiral Richardson: I think that the U.S. Naval War College is quite different. They have as a basic philosophy that each individual is there to improve himself. One, there is no staff solution, because even an apparently stupid thing may turn out, in retrospect, to have been the right thing--simply because the other guy didn't act the way you thought he would. So don't condemn thinking. Mistakes are instructive, if admitted. There is no staff solution. But if you have used good sense and imagination and have shown an appreciation for the nature of the problem, always probing into what really is the problem, then that's great. And then there were lecturers who were top-rank people from various walks of life. The course is, in my view, effective, very good.

But one thing they did not have at the war college for so many years, despite the fact that we literally won the war in the Pacific by exploiting cryptology, was instruction in the art of exploiting intelligence. A facility for handling special intelligence was not put in there until 1971.

Q: The president of the U.S. Naval War College when you were there was the august Raymond Spruance.[*] What do you recall of him?

Admiral Richardson: A great deal. He was a very unassuming man and a very thoughtful man, and he was certainly a man guided by logic. He was very much admired by everyone. Of course, who can argue with success?[†]

During my second year at the Naval War College I was in the analytical section on the staff, making analyses of actions of World War II. This was part of the postwar work

---

[*] Admiral Raymond A. Spruance, USN, served as president of the Naval War College from 1 March 1946 to 1 July 1948.
[†] Spruance had commanded the Fifth Fleet during the victorious Central Pacific campaign of World War II. Included were his command of the amphibious operations against the Gilbert Islands, Marshalls, Marianas, Iwo Jima, and Okinawa.

done by Rafe Bates.[*] I did all of the original work on researching the latter part of the Battle of Midway and all of the Savo Island battle.[†] Thanks to Samuel Eliot Morison and his translator, Roger Pineau, we had Japanese combat diaries.[‡]

It was interesting to me that when we finished the analysis of the Battle of Midway, with its criticisms of the functioning of command, Rafe Bates had taken it upon himself to rewrite some of the history in order to extol Spruance all the more, Spruance rejected it. The three of us who were working there--two captains and myself, a commander--were very upset and objected strenuously to the final version.

Bates took it up to Spruance. Spruance went through it and sent it back, saying "If there's any one real hero in this battle, his name is Wade McClusky."[§] He made Rafe Bates revise the work by removing fancied thinking and explanations.

I did the analysis of the air activity. I was very disappointed in the effectiveness of my classmate, Jim Gray, the <u>Enterprise</u> fighter squadron commander.[**] He was thought to be cowardly, but--knowing Jim Gray--I knew that was not so. Poor thinking in the circumstances, yes; cowardly, no. Jim Gray is not cowardly.

Q: He certainly didn't have his fighters where they needed to be.

Admiral Richardson: Well, that's right. He stayed up at high altitude when the combat was going on down way below. But we'd all had preached to us to keep our altitude in order to dogfight effectively.

---

[*] Following World War II, Commodore Richard W. Bates, USN (Ret.), did a series of exhaustive analyses of World War II operations on behalf of the Naval War College.
[†] As a rear admiral in June 1942, Spruance had been pressed into service to command a carrier task force in the Battle of Midway. He did so in place of Vice Admiral William F. Halsey, Jr., USN, had to leave to receive medical treatment.
[‡] Rear Admiral Samuel Eliot Morison, USNR, was a noted civilian historian who received a Naval Reserve commission in order to collect material for what eventually became the 15-volume <u>History of United States Naval Operations in World War II</u>. Lieutenant Roger Pineau, USNR, had been a student of the Japanese language during World War II and was involved afterward in the interrogation of Japanese naval officers.
[§] On 4 June 1942, in the Battle of Midway, Lieutenant Commander C. Wade McClusky, USN, was the commander of the air group from the carrier <u>Enterprise</u> (CV-6). McClusky trailed a Japanese destroyer from the air and thus led the American strike force to the Japanese carriers.
[**] Lieutenant James S. Gray, USN, commanding officer of Fighting Six in June 1942.

Q: What basis did you have for that judgment of Gray that he was not cowardly?

Admiral Richardson: Well, I'd known him. I knew him at the Naval Academy, and I knew that--whatever you might say about him--he was just simply not cowardly. He did not do what he did out of a fear of getting tangled up in combat. That's totally out of character with him.

Q: In what way was Bates writing the report?

Admiral Richardson: He was being very critical of all sorts of actions by people in command other than Spruance--unwarranted criticisms. He was inclined to be critical anyway; it was an ego thing. If he could find a little bit of a reason for criticism, and in almost anything that anybody does there's room for some criticism, then he would condemn. But he extolled Spruance enormously, and he ran down other people. It was very unfair. It wasn't based on good evidence. There was often nothing to support his criticisms.

Having learned how Bates would try to browbeat all the time, I'd go in late in the afternoon and I'd say, "Well, Captain, I'll be flying tomorrow."

He said, "Well, I want you to look this over."

I said, "Yes, sir, I'll be happy to look it over. But my driving squad's waiting now, and I'll look it over later." Then I'd just walk out. But that's the way you had to handle him. But if he could get anything on you, he'd just drive you nuts.

Q: What do you mean "if he could get anything on you"? Like what?

Admiral Richardson: If he could succeed in putting a squeeze on you, he would exploit that. Some years later, he was missing a document. It was a copy of the Midway analysis before Bates reworked it. He rewrote it, but the original submission still existed. I was in charge of the archives. One of the two captains--I don't remember which one--told me to put that book away where Rafe Bates wouldn't get it. It would be our defense, because when this version by Rafe Bates got published, there would be a lot of damn sore people, and properly so.

So I gave it to the head civilian in the archives and said, "Commodore Bates is going to want this. [They all knew him very well]. It's to be put away and kept there. Don't give it to him!"

Months later, I was out on the <u>Princeton</u> in Tsingtao. I got a very commendatory letter from Bates, saying, "How we miss you." He could lay it on. Then, "By the way, would you please let me know where the draft Midway battle analysis is. Did you by any chance take it with you?" [Laughter]

I wrote him back and said, "No, sir. Sorry, but I did not take it. Thank you very much for your very kind remarks. I did not take this book with me."

Q: And you didn't tell him where it was.

Admiral Richardson: I didn't tell him where it was, no. So then I got another letter, and now it was threatening. "This is a very serious matter. Will you tell me where that book is?"

I wrote him back and I said, "What I told you is absolutely true. I don't have it."

He said, "I'm sure if you look, you will find it somewhere."

I said, "I do not have it. I did not take it."

Well, that was the end of it. The final version was the one Bates had redone and which then had numerous additional changes directed by Spruance.

But I liked Bates. I admired him, parts of him. Sometimes he was fabulous, and sometimes he was just an egotistical ass. The next time I went to see him, I was a rear admiral. [Laughter]

Q: This must have been much later.

Admiral Richardson: This probably was in '67. I had commanded Task Force 77 in the Gulf of Tonkin the previous year and was sent to the war college to brief the students. Boy, he just couldn't do enough to please me.

I recall one time, in the 1947-48 period, when the Duchess of Windsor was coming to Newport.* And Bates had friends in high society there. He was always finagling some sort of an invitation here or there. Somebody called him, and I took the call. The caller wanted him to come to dinner on a certain day. He accepted. Then he learned of the Duchess of Windsor's coming. She was going to be at somebody else's place, and he was trying to get out of the first invitation. He stewed over this thing, talking with me about how he could work it. I just sat there tickled to death to watch him struggle over that thing. I don't know what eventually happened. All I remember is the struggle he was having with himself.

But he had a lot of very good qualities. He was damn good thinker when he wasn't slave to his own ego. I've heard some of his intimate stories of his crucial roles in battles and seen tears coming in his eye.

Q: Did he have battle experience?

Admiral Richardson: Yes. He was chief of staff to some admiral when the Japs were coming through in the Philippines.† Bates recalled, "The admiral said, 'We will turn back,' and I said to the admiral, 'No, sir. We will persist.'" There were tears; the man hungered for glory.

Q: I've heard he was an extremely methodical man, which was both a blessing and a curse in that kind of situation.

---

* The Duchess of Windsor, the former Wallis Warfield Simpson, married Britain's Duke of Windsor in 1937. He had been King Edward VIII until he abdicated in 1936 in order to marry the American divorcee.
† Captain Bates served as chief of staff to Vice Admiral Jesse B. Oldendorf, USN, who was Commander Task Group 77.2, the Bombardment and Fire Support Group for the invasion of Lingayen Gulf on the island of Luzon in January 1945. Earlier--July 1943 to May 1944--Bates had been commanding officer of the heavy cruiser Minneapolis (CA-36).

Admiral Richardson: Yes. He was a lot like Spruance in his devotion to logic. He was very logical. If he could only have kept his outlandish ego out of the equation, he'd have been great. He was out of the Naval Academy class of '15 and was a classmate of Eisenhower, he said, who was then in West Point.*

Q: Was Commodore Bates well suited for that job?

Admiral Richardson: Well, I don't think anyone is well suited for a job when he is unduly egotistical, so, no. He was prevented from doing a lot of damage, which he could have done, by Spruance and by others. And those analyses were good analyses.

Q: And, of course, with the enormous benefit of hindsight.

Admiral Richardson: Well, of course. Exactly. But the piercing logic of situations was his field, and when it came to what the war college called the estimate of the situation or sound military decision, there was nobody superior to him working that problem. No, I respected him, but I knew him for what he was.

Q: One of the stories I've heard about him is that he was a commodore in the daytime and he was a rear admiral at night.

Admiral Richardson: No doubt. [Laughter]

Q: Because he had a tombstone promotion to rear admiral, and so when he was on the job, he was still a commodore, but then he could change uniforms at night.† [Laughter]

---

* General of the Army Dwight D. Eisenhower, USA, was the Supreme Allied Commander in Europe in 1944-45. He graduated from the Military Academy at West Point 1915.
† In the years after World War II, officers who had received combat decorations received a one-grade honorary promotion widely referred to as a "tombstone promotion." Although the individual still received the retired pay of his actual rank, he was authorized to assume the title of the higher grade. The practice ended in 1959.

Admiral Richardson: Well, he was a funny man. One time he had to go somewhere by plane, and it was snowing. It was a miserable day, and he was in an uproar. He had to go to Providence, and I said, "I'll drive you up." He was so grateful. I don't think anybody ever did anything for him. I said, "I'll be glad to drive you up. Snow? No problem."

So we started out and crossed that bridge north of the war college. We stopped at the gate to pay a toll. The man looked at us, and away we went. After I dropped off Bates, I came back over the bridge again. The man stopped me, and he said, "Who was that very important man that you had in this car when you came over?" [Laughter]

I said, "That's Commodore Bates at the Naval War College. He heads up their analytical section."

Q: What gave him the impression this was a very important man?

Admiral Richardson: Just general appearance and how he conducted himself. He was good at looking important. [Laughter]

Q: What you say about Spruance's reaction makes me admire him all the more.

Admiral Richardson: He wouldn't have any part of Bates's glorification of him. What a contrast!

Q: What do you recall about the usefulness of the war college curriculum when you went through as a student?

Admiral Richardson: Well, it was good. There may have been too much emphasis on detailed logistical planning, but that's a questionable thing. If you are building an actual amphibious plan, you've got to know boat capacities and everything right down to the last feature. But to my thinking, the war college should deal more broadly with concepts and with recognition of the importance of details--without having to work all the details. The really substantive issues have to do with the general strategy and tactical concepts.

Strategy comes in levels. There is the broader strategy, then a strategy within your tactical problem area. So I would say that concept formulation depends on a thorough analysis of the nature of the problem, plus a clear and complete identification of character of the responses that you would be making toward solving the problem. That should be where the focus is.

Now, there's nothing wrong with working details. They have a logistical course there, and the gentleman who headed it up has been highly extolled since, a very capable and dedicated gentleman.

Q: Henry Eccles.[*]

Admiral Richardson: Yes, that's right. He was there at the time, and he taught logistics. There's nothing wrong with working logistical problems, but I think when you mix up the detail logistics in a broad battle problem, you're wasting time.

Q: He felt logistics were all-important.

Admiral Richardson: They are reality. They are absolutely all-important. It's like intelligence. Anyone who develops his plans with an inadequate attention to the intelligence or to logistics is going to suffer. Even if he wins, he will have suffered needlessly.

Q: Did that course make you a better naval officer?

Admiral Richardson: Oh, I think definitely so, yes. I'm a very strong supporter of the war college.

Q: What memories do you have of distinguished visiting speakers at the Naval War College.?

---

[*] Upon retirement from active duty in 1952, Rear Admiral Henry E. Eccles, USN, began a 25-year second career as head of the logistics department of the Naval War College; he was a prolific author.

Admiral Richardson: George Kennan came up.* Cat Brown came up.† The Secretary of the Navy was upset with the effectiveness of the war college. He thought that--and he was quite right--that there was a counterrevolution of sorts going on that was getting back toward the battleship mind-set and that that needed to be stopped, and so Cat Brown came up. He was a very dynamic speaker. He talked about the role of aircraft in the war.

There were commodores up there who were blackshoe types who continued to pontificate on 1938 techniques and strategies--too much of that. So a specific effort initiated by the Secretary of the Navy was set up to correct that, and I think they did. I don't know that that was all that bad for us, because the students, almost without exception, had been through the war, and they knew firsthand a lot of this stuff. They weren't easily fooled or suckered into older beliefs. But anyway, that was a major problem in the eyes of the Secretary of the Navy.

Q: It's surprising that you'd still have reactionaries around who were not convinced by the war.

Admiral Richardson: Well, I guess that's right. But a lot of them weren't in the war, either, for Lord knows what reasons.

Q: Was there any question then about what was the mission of the Navy? At that point, there was no significant naval threat on the horizon.

Admiral Richardson: No. I'd have to say that we were still fighting the battles of 1944 and '45. I don't think we were looking ahead.

---

* George F. Kennan, who served on the State Department's policy-planning staff in the immediate post-World War II period, is credited with developing the U.S. policy of "containment" toward Communism.
† Captain Charles R. Brown, USN, had been commanding officer of the aircraft carrier Hornet (CV-12) at the end of World War II. In the 1950s he served as Commander Sixth Fleet and Commander in Chief Allied Forces Southern Europe.

Q: Of course, our capabilities were rapidly diminishing at the same time.

Admiral Richardson: Well, they did a few years later in '48, when we cut way back. Then along came the Korean War.* But I'm thinking of that period '46 to '48 or before then.

Q: There was a substantial demobilization in that period too.

Admiral Richardson: Indeed there was, yes. We didn't really drop below needs until the fall of '49. That's when we were actually closing out air groups, shifting squadrons around, saving one or two here and creating new groups, cutting from, I think, 14 to 8 carriers, with further cuts to six indicated. And along came the Korean War.

Q: One of the things that a number of people have mentioned from their war college experience is that they made useful contacts then that were important to know later in their careers. Was that the case for you?

Admiral Richardson: No. I don't know that I'd use the word "useful" in describing them. I met and knew lots of people that I worked with for a long time, but I can't quite find the word "useful." That implies seniority that helps you along your way. As regards war college classmates, yes.

Q: Well, not so much that as that you're able to deal with somebody in another command on an easier basis if you've met them before than if you're going in cold.

Admiral Richardson: Absolutely. No question about that.

Q: Did you have a role in instruction during your year on the staff in addition to this work with Commodore Bates?

---

* The Korean War began on 25 June 1950 when North Korean forces invaded South Korea.

Admiral Richardson: No.

Q: That would have been a fascinating thing to be part of. I envy you that opportunity.

Admiral Richardson: [Laughter] I know. As a historian, you certainly would.

Q: Did you factor in the results that were coming in from the strategic bombing surveys, the interrogation of the enemy people?

Admiral Richardson: No, but certainly the interrogation of the enemy. At that time, we were getting Japanese translations, and, as I said, Roger Pineau was handling that. He was providing them to Morison. Morison was frequently down with Rafe Bates. Pineau was also getting material for us, because I'd send in a request which would sit, and my feeling was that if Morison and we had the same general requirement, that he'd pull it out, because it was very difficult to, one, get at this stuff and then translate it.

Yes, I used Japanese translations extensively in that Savo Island effort. As a result of plotting and trying to figure how in hell this thing happened, it suddenly dawned on me that the Japanese suddenly saw there were in a head-on collision situation with the Chicago, Canberra, and the southern group, and they had to turn. They fired their torpedoes in turning because they were combat-ready, but that had they been somewhere other than in an actual head-on collision position, then it might have been a totally different battle.

Q: That's intriguing.

Admiral Richardson: But if you go into the details of what the Japanese said, the bearings, the reports, and what you know about where the Chicago group was, a head-on collision was building. At the last minute they turned, then fired torpedoes, then opened fire at the cruisers up to the north. Then, instead of going on in to sink the transports, they turned and got out. The Japanese faked out a number of times in that war. They seemed to lose their nerve or sense of purpose at the last minute.

Q: Their strategic objective was the transports, and they went untouched.

Admiral Richardson: That's right. And why they didn't continue on, I don't know. I mean, after all, that's the kamikaze mind, for God's sake, and yet that mentality wasn't present on numerous occasions in Japanese force commanders' mental structure. Even with Pearl Harbor some were pleading for more attacks, and they wouldn't do it.[*]

Q: The skipper of the Chicago was a man named Bode, and he did not pass the warning on after he'd been attacked.[†] He subsequently went down to Panama for duty, and an investigation team went down there checking into this, and he killed himself at that point.

Admiral Richardson: Yes, I think I heard that. I'd forgotten it, but that's right. And it's unfortunate, because if one saw how both sides were completely surprised by the near collision, he'd understand. I wouldn't want to speculate.

Q: And there were two destroyers patrolling the mouth, and neither of them saw the Japanese force coming in.

Admiral Richardson: They were at the outer edge of their stations when the Japanese came down. It's just sheer luck that the Japanese didn't run into one them. And, of course, everybody was dead tired. They'd been at general quarters for days and just weren't functioning properly. The destroyers' surface radars didn't detect them.

Q: And the support force commander was off conferring with Admiral Turner.

---

[*] Vice Admiral Chuichi Nagumo, IJN, was commander of the carrier striking force that hit Pearl Harbor in December 1941. The plan was to attack the combatant ships in the harbor, which the first and second waves accomplished effectively. Nagumo's subordinates urged him to send additional planes to attack the shore-based facilities of Pearl Harbor, but he rejected their advice and withdrew the carrier force.
[†] Captain Howard D. Bode, USN.

Admiral Richardson: Yes.

Q: The U.S. Navy learned lessons on damage control in that battle too. For example, the ships had built up layer after layer of paint in the prewar period, and it just caught fire. It turned into conflagrations.

Admiral Richardson: Yes. Those lessons we learn and forget. Probably you'll find more paint now. Also, the fuel in the scout aircraft burned after being released by shrapnel.

Q: Anything else to recall about that period with the war college?

Admiral Richardson: No, I don't recall anything specific. I think we've pretty well covered it.

Q: It must have been satisfying to get back to sea again after a long hiatus.

Admiral Richardson: Two and a half years ashore. I left Newport with orders to be Commander Air Group 13. Journeyed to Jacksonville, Florida, and then because the Princeton was leaving quite soon, I had a shortened course there. I think I was there maybe a month, just sort of getting the feel, and in Corsairs. Then I went out to the West Coast to join up with the Princeton and transition to F8F Bearcats.[*]

The ships departed before I was even carrier-qualified. We had F8Fs, and that's what I flew. My wingman was Rear Admiral Bill Harris, then an ensign.[†] He lives right here in Coronado. Whenever I see him, I signal [demonstrates], which means join up. So I

---

[*] USS Princeton (CV-37) was an Essex-class aircraft carrier, commissioned 18 November 1945. She had a standard displacement of 33,000 tons, was 888 feet long, 93 feet in the beam, and had an extreme width of 148 feet. Her top speed was 33 knots. She had 12 5-inch guns and could accommodate approximately 90 aircraft. Later in her career she served as an antisubmarine warfare carrier (CVS-37) and still later as an amphibious assault ship (LPH-5).
[†] Rear Admiral William H. Harris, USN.

had to qualify as we were headed west. Bush Bringle had the air group on the Tarawa--Air Group One.*

Q: I've heard a lot of praise for that man.

Admiral Richardson: He's a terrific gent, just wonderful. Yes, I'm very strong on Bush Bringle. He and I are close. He's getting his knees operated on now. Football wrecked them.

Anyway, we were headed west, and there were perhaps eight or ten people who needed more carrier landings. Some of them needed five or six and others two or three. I needed all 20. So we went through the exercise steaming to Honolulu. I ended up being the only one in the circle, and so I took off. I pulled the little F8F up like this, came around, landed, just flew it right around and landed, and the air officer sounded off, "The CAG just had a 55-second interval on himself." [Laughter] I landed, took off, and was back on deck in 55 seconds. Thanks, Norm Ellis.

Q: That must be the record.

Admiral Richardson: That was a record. You couldn't do it with any plane except the F8F. You could do almost anything with that. So my flying reputation was made with the other pilots by that maneuver. They had wondered what this war college "jerk" would do!

Q: Please tell me more about the F8F.

Admiral Richardson: Well, it was just a honey of a plane--extremely maneuverable, powerful. Hammerhead stalls. You could come straight down backwards and flip it. It was the nicest thing that had come along by far. But then we moved to the jets. A year

---

* Commander William F. Bringle, USN, Commander Carrier Air Group One.

later, we were getting them in Air Group Five. Pete Aurand and others were introducing the jets.*

Q: Did the F8F have as long an endurance as the F6F?

Admiral Richardson: Well, you had belly tanks, and it had so much power. I remember being very tempted to fly one to the West Coast from Honolulu. I figured out that if I didn't run into adverse wind conditions, I could make it using two belly tanks and at a cruise speed of about 180 knots. I don't know. It didn't quite develop, and I never really sold myself on the fact that I could reach the coast. But it was certainly within the ballpark.

Now, in late '48, when we headed west to Tsingtao, we put a carrier at 700 miles, another at 1,400 miles, and Bringle and a division of Corsairs left the coast, landed on the first carrier, took off within an hour or so, landed on the second carrier, took off, and landed in Honolulu. Their legs were only 700 miles, and Bush was complaining about his tailbone.

Q: I'll bet. [Laughter]

Admiral Richardson: It was, indeed, understandably sore, because that's a good three and a half hours for each leg of that flight.

Q: What was the point of that exercise?

Admiral Richardson: Well, I think it had to do with . . .

Q: Interservice rivalry?

---

* In March 1948, Commander Evan P. Aurand, USN, and Lieutenant Commander Robert M. Elder, USN, of VF-5A did carrier suitability tests on board the USS Boxer (CV-21) with the FJ-1 Fury jet fighter.

Admiral Richardson: Maybe, but I suppose it was mainly to plant ideas in the minds of congressmen that you could fly these planes great distances before the time of air-to-air refueling, but you had to have a ship out there. I suppose it was budget-driven.

Q: That's the same era when Tom Davies flew the Truculent Turtle all the way back from Australia.[*]

Admiral Richardson: Yes.

Q: What was the job of an air group commander?

Admiral Richardson: Well, the air group commander is in charge of the airborne air operations, and he's the one who is the interface between the air group and the admiral. The admiral and his staff run the air group if an admiral is embarked in the ship. Otherwise, the captain does. But when there's a flag aboard, the flag really runs the air group, and the air group commander is the one who is the interface.

Now, in the Navy, the air group commander has a great deal to say in planning. That's not so in the Air Force. But in the Navy, the air group commander's advice is desired, and his requests are listened to carefully. That's why they went to super CAG, i.e., to give this air group commander a six months' orientation into intelligence to know what was available and where he could get it if he needed.[†] The first of those are, I think, doing very well. Zlatoper, one of the first two, became CinCPacFlt.[‡]

Carlos Johnson is the name of another.[§] He later ran a program out at the Naval Intelligence Support Center in Suitland, Maryland. It provided intelligence for aviation air

---

[*] Between 29 September and 1 October 1946, a Navy crew headed by Commander Thomas D. Davies, USN, flew a P2V Neptune nicknamed "The Truculent Turtle" from Perth, Australia, to Columbus, Ohio. Their flight lasted 55 hours and 17 minutes and covered 11,235.6 miles. They established a world's record for distance in an unrefueled flight.
[†] The super CAG concept was initiated in aircraft carriers in the mid-1980s.
[‡] Admiral Ronald J. Zlatoper, USN, served as Commander in Chief Pacific Fleet from August 1994 to November 1996.
[§] Commander John Michael Johnson, USN, as of the late 1980s. He was on the fiscal year 1997 selection list as a rear admiral (lower half).

strike planning that provided tailored information in easily absorbed formats. It closed the gap between operations and intelligence. He was in charge of that effort. He was a super CAG with this intelligence education behind him, and his analysts, with the exception of one intelligence specialist, were all operational, mostly aviators.

Well, the CAG really is the expert airman that the flag relies on, or the skipper, if he's operating alone, and the squadrons function under him. The squadron skippers answer to the CAG. He's in charge, and if he's dissatisfied with them and makes his case, he removes them.

Q: What was the makeup of your air group?

Admiral Richardson: We had three F8F fighter squadrons, a Corsair squadron, which we later lost to Bush Bringle, and a torpedo squadron. Eventually, I ended up with two torpedo squadrons and three fighter squadrons. Bringle ended up with three fighter squadrons and two Corsair attack squadrons. The torpedo squadrons were flying the TBFs/TBMs.*

Q: You still had them?

Admiral Richardson: Yes. They put both torpedo squadrons in my air group. They took the two bombing squadrons and combined them in the other ship.

Q: Was the idea that those two carriers would have to operate together?

---

* The Grumman-built TBF Avenger was the U.S. Navy's standard carrier-based torpedo plane during the latter part of World War II. The TBf-1 model had a wing span of 54 feet, length of 40 feet, gross eight of 15,905 pounds, and top speed of 271 miles per hour. It was armed with one .30-caliber machine gun (two .50 caliber in the TBF-1C). The first TBF-1s reached the fleet in the spring of 1942. The General Motors-built version of the Avenger was designated TBM.

Admiral Richardson: Well, we were expected to operate together when we went out. When we got out there, we knew that Chiang Kai-shek was in deep trouble.[*] We went to Tsingtao. When we left Tsingtao, Si Ginder was our admiral.[†] He got everyone on the hangar deck, all the crew that wasn't on watch, and he gave us a pep talk: "We have been sent out here on a very important mission in our national strategic interest. We don't know when we're going to return," etc. etc.

The presidential election followed a few days later, and Dewey didn't win.[‡] The Navy had sent these carriers west with the idea, obviously, to try to save China.[§] In the politics of that time, Republicans were very critical of the Democrats over China, and so this was driven by that political objective, which fell in the drink when Truman defeated Dewey. Two weeks after the election, we headed first to Japan, then Guam, and back home by the 23rd of December.[**] But the Tarawa was sent around the world to Jacksonville.

I mentioned previously that some of my classmates and I had gotten acquainted with Oscar Badger at the Naval Academy and on the West Coast when we were ensigns. The next time I saw him, he was the flag officer in charge of the Navy's remnant force there in Tsingtao.[††] I always admired him. He was the right man in that job.

Q: I've just been interviewing a man, Fred Edwards in the class of '23, who was a department head under Badger in the North Carolina early in World War II. Edwards had no use at all for Badger, so I'd be interested in your recollections why you admired him.[‡‡]

---

[*] Generalissimo Chiang Kai-shek served as President of Nationalist China on the mainland from 1943 to 1949 and as President of the Republic of China on Taiwan from 1950 until his death in 1975.
[†] Rear Admiral Samuel P. Ginder, USN, served as Commander Carrier Division Two from January 1948 to June 1949.
[‡] On 2 November 1948, President Harry S. Truman, a Democrat, defeated his Republican challenger, Thomas E. Dewey.
[§] The Nationalist government of China, headed by Generalissimo Chiang Kai-shek, was in power at the time. I was overcome the following year by Communist forces led by Mai Tse-tung and backed by the Soviet bloc. The nationalists were then expelled to Taiwan, and the Maoists established a new government on the mainland, the People's Republic of China, on 1 October 1949.
[**] The Princeton got under way from Tsingtao on 16 November and steamed to Yokosuka, Japan.
[††] As a vice admiral, Badger served as Commander Naval Forces Western Pacific (later Seventh Task Fleet) in 1948-49.
[‡‡] Captain Frederick A. Edwards, Sr., USN (Ret.), whose oral history is in the Naval Institute collection.

Admiral Richardson: I can't tell you. I don't know any particular feature or circumstances that drives that. He certainly was, in my view, a fair man. Now, when he was a vice admiral, I admired him because he ran his show. Some admirals function as judges of staff initiatives.

There was a flag officer in Guam who came up to Tsingtao while we were there. One of the people that I had worked with in the analytical section under Rafe Bates at the Naval War College was on Badger's staff. I learned through him that this rear admiral who flew up from Guam took up with a white Russian who was a known Commie. Oscar Badger called him in, shipped him back to Guam, and I guess probably closed out his career because he was indiscreet, to say the least.

Then Oscar Badger took the Chinese remnants of Chiang Kai-shek's people out of Tsingtao and down to Taiwan when they had to surrender Tsingtao. But this was long after I had established in my mind his character. From what I saw of him, I liked him. I think when people have an antipathy towards somebody, it generally has its roots in a particular situation where there were things that may have been misunderstood.

Q: This man's view of Badger was that he always wanted to be in charge, and he always thought he knew more than everybody else.

Admiral Richardson: Well, I don't know. Never had to gauge that quality. Maybe he did.

Q: Did the Princeton and Tarawa do anything in the China area at all during that period?

Admiral Richardson: No, we didn't do anything. We went in to Tsingtao and spent a lot of time ashore in the next three weeks. Then we came out and went to Japan. We were in Yokosuka for several days, then to Guam. Instead of doing whatever else was planned, we went to Guam instead, then home.

Q: Did you do flight ops all the way over and back?

Admiral Richardson: Well, yes, going over. We were constrained. We were only allowed to operate out to 100 miles from our ship. I was worried by that, so I went to see the chief of staff and said, "We're teaching these people that's as far as they can go. We should go out further. Let us go out further ahead of the ship instead of to the stern so that you don't have to turn around and come back if we have a downed plane. Let's go out 200 miles ahead in the forward quadrants."

He went to the admiral with it, and the admiral said no. So we went 150 out ahead. He was constrained to not losing planes and time-constrained. What was driving the timing, I have no idea. That was held in sealed orders, or whatever he had. I can't even imagine what the general plan may have provided for when we got there. But we did know we were not allowed to create a situation that would delay the ship's SOA.[*]

Q: It's really curious that you would have torpedo squadrons. I don't know what they would be expected to operate against.

Admiral Richardson: Nor can I. They could drop bombs too. Paul Lovelace was the skipper of VA-135, one of the torpedo squadrons.[†]

Q: What other skippers do you remember from the group?

Admiral Richardson: Bud Frazier, VF-131; Quentin Crommelin, VF-132; I don't remember the name of the VF-133 skipper. That's over 40 years ago, and I haven't had occasion to recall it.[‡]

Q: I've been amazed by all these other things you've been pulling out. Who was the ship's skipper?

---

[*] SOA--speed of advance.
[†] Lieutenant Commander Paul C. Lovelace, USN, commanding officer of Attack Squadron 135.
[‡] The other squadrons in Air Group 13 were VA-134 and VC-130.

Admiral Richardson: Murr Arnold was the skipper.*

Q: What do you recall of him?

Admiral Richardson: He collided with the oiler. We were refueling. The carrier touched the side of the oiler, and one of the oil hose booms fell on the flight deck of the Princeton and wrecked one of our torpedo planes.

Murr Arnold and Si Ginder decided not to file the required report to CNO.† Arnold was up for admiral, and the selection board was in session. Lovelace, however, released a message reporting one destroyed aircraft--cause: collision of Princeton during refueling.

Well, off that went. In damn short order, I got hauled in by the chief of staff and thoroughly chewed out. The admiral was more than unhappy with that message being sent. But my squadron commander, Paul Lovelace, was required to report his damaged airplane to the CNO.

Q: Which was an honest report.

Admiral Richardson: Which was honest--A, B, C, D--the cause of the thing, collision between the Princeton and this oiler. [Laughter] When Ginder and Arnold saw that their whole scheme was exposed, boy, were they burned up. I then got orders that absolutely no message was ever to leave that ship without being cleared by the ship's skipper. We were independent commands, but that was the way it was going to be from then on.

Q: But Arnold got selected for admiral, anyway.

---

* Captain Murr E. Arnold, USN, commanded the USS Princeton (CV-37) from January 1948 to January 1949.
† CNO--Chief of Naval Operations.

Admiral Richardson: He was selected, anyway, because the selection board didn't learn of the collision. I had said, "This goes to an outfit in BuAer, and really nobody in OpNav is ever going to pick this up." But, boy, I had a real hot potato in my hand.

Q: Had you known Arnold back in the Yorktown?

Admiral Richardson: Yes, he was the skipper of one of the attack squadrons, but I had no feel for him.

Q: What do you recall about him as a naval officer?

Admiral Richardson: Well, he was a gruff sort of an individual, but I thought he was fine. He was skipper of Bombing Five when I was in Fighting Five. I knew him then. I had no connection with him that would enable me to judge him as a naval officer. My work on the Princeton was with the staff and a little bit with him, but not much. With his ops officer, Jim Reedy, yes, and a lot with his air officer, Pat Rooney, but not with him.*

Q: What do you remember about those two?

Admiral Richardson: Well, Rooney was a very weak aviator. I had known him from earlier days. He was one of the people in VF-71, the squadron that was broken up in the Wasp back in 1941. But Pat was Irish and attractive in many ways, and he survived that situation. He was not competent or experienced in flying. He came into the game way late, pretty senior, which I think was a handicap to him. But at this particular time, he was air officer. He didn't know how we should be operating, and he was instructing our people about the ship, how to operate about the ship and so forth.

    I was in Quentin Crommelin's ready room during a debrief when Rooney lectured the squadron. The guys in the back row were disdainful. So he finished and left, and then

---

* Commander Carl W. Rooney, USN. Commander James R. Reedy, USN. Reedy was later a rear admiral and Richardson's predecessor as Commander Task Force 77 in the Gulf of Tonkin.

Quentin really lit into those guys. He said, "Damn well treat him with respect." He said, "It's not a question of whether he was right or wrong. He's entitled to your respect, and if you want to stay in this squadron, you will so conduct yourself."

I went to Jim Reedy, who was the ship's ops officer, and said, "I don't ever want Rooney to come in our ready rooms again."

Frank Nuessle was the XO.[*] He was a fine officer. So we never suffered Pat after that. They all knew Rooney's limitations as an operator. Delightful guy, a lot of fun. He was out of '34. Reedy was '33, Nuessle was '32.

Q: But if you've got an incompetent air officer, you've got a big problem as the CAG. So how did you solve that problem?

Admiral Richardson: Well, the problem pretty much disappeared, because the operations officer plans air operations. The air officer runs his flight and hangar deck, launching and landing aboard. The air officer, if he does things in the proper sequence, that's all he has to worry about. He can be good and helpful, or he can be a mess, and he can screw you up in the area of maintenance of aircraft.

Q: What about his people on the flight deck and the hangar deck and so forth?

Admiral Richardson: They worked and did what they were supposed to do. Those routines were pretty standard.

Q: That is the ultimate flying job for a carrier pilot--running an air group.

Admiral Richardson: That's right.

Q: What are the satisfactions that come from that kind of job?

---

[*] Commander Francis E. Nuessle, USN.

Admiral Richardson: Well, I think being a squadron commander is the most satisfactory of all, because he is in direct contact with his people, enlisted and officer. CAG is next, because he's in direct contact with the skipper, to some degree with the other pilots, but not with support personnel in general. That's the squadron commander's province and prerogatives, and so you normally have no business in there. But those two jobs are by far the best.

The CAG is a hard job to beat, because if you are engaged in combat, as we will go into later in discussing the Vietnam War, the CAG has an enormous amount to say about how operations go. Air Force exchange officers were astonished at the influence that naval aviators in command roles have over what they do compared to the situation in the Air Force.

Q: Did you have a staff in that job?

Admiral Richardson: Yes, a small staff. I had an assistant and a first class or second class yeoman. Sometimes you have a chief.

Q: What do you remember about the ship itself? The Princeton was far more sophisticated than these other carriers you had been in.

Admiral Richardson: I don't remember anything noteworthy.

Q: It was just there.

Admiral Richardson: It was there.

Q: What other operations were you involved in besides this trip to China?

Admiral Richardson: We came back to the coast. We operated in North Island. We got back the 23rd of December, then operated here January, February, March, maybe. At that point in time, we were turning in all our planes. The squadrons were being reformed, and we were starting over with newly assigned pilots.

Then in the spring, about May, we were ordered to Jacksonville. I took a month's leave, came back, finished this house. I started it in early '49, and came back after flying the air group to Jacksonville. Then we were in Jax about three or four months when we got the orders to disband. I was ordered to the Joint Strategic Plans group of the Joint Staff of the Joint Chiefs of Staff. I reported there about early October.

Q: And that, I presume, was the point at which the Princeton went into mothballs.*

Admiral Richardson: Probably.

Q: What do you recall about the Joint Staff?

Admiral Richardson: I recall a lot about it. I reported in in the fall of '49, and as I walked into the building, I saw people coming out in civilian clothes, briefcases in hand. I noticed this intense appearance they all seemed to have as they left the building, and I thought, "My God, what's going on back here? I hope I don't become like that." I had the very distinct impression that these people were leaving that building each evening with the weight of the world on their shoulders. And nothing's changed my mind since. I've been on duty in the Pentagon four times now, and that's the way it was and is.

Q: Bradley was the chairman back then. What do recall about him?†

Admiral Richardson: He was a wonderful man. There were two smart men, Joint Chiefs--Bradley and Sherman.‡ The Air Force chief was Vandenberg.§ I forget the Army.** They weren't impressive.

---

* The Princeton was decommissioned 21 June 1949 at the Puget Sound Naval Shipyard. Because of the subsequent advent of the Korean War, she was recommissioned 28 August 1950.
† General of the Army Omar N. Bradley, USA, served as Chairman of the Joint Chiefs of Staff from 16 August 1949 to 14 August 1953.

Q: Denfeld was there at the outset.[*] Depending on what time of year you reported.

Admiral Richardson: Yes. This is in the late fall of '49.

Q: That's about the time he got fired.

Admiral Richardson: Yes, and Sherman came on very soon after that.

Anyway, I was on the Joint Staff until April of '52, and Sherman was the one most of that time. He and Bradley were both very capable. Vandenberg and the Army chief were not very good. That was the reputation that they had throughout the Joint Staff, not just with me.

I had been there maybe three weeks when my team got our first problem. It had to do with a recommendation that General Mark Clark had sent in for turning over equipment to the newly created Austrian Army.[†] Austria was about to be free, and the idea was to get into custody of the Austrian Army sufficient equipment capability so that the Soviets couldn't spark an uprising and take over that country.

Frank Street was my Army roommate and teammate on the Silver Team.[‡] He had been with me at the war college my first year there, just across the hall, so I knew him and liked him very much. The Air Force fellow was Colonel Jerry Culver, out of West Point '35.[§] We had a very good relationship together. So these two guys decided I was going to be the one to go in and brief General Bradley on this list of equipment that Mark Clark had sent in.

[†] Admiral Forrest P. Sherman, USN, served as Chief of Naval Operations from 2 November 1949 until his death on 22 July 1951.
[§] General Hoyt S. Vandenberg, USAF, served as Air Force Chief of Staff from 30 April 1948 to 29 June 1953.
[**] General J. Lawton Collins, USA, served as Army Chief of Staff from 16 August 1949 to 15 August 1953.
[*] Admiral Louis E. Denfeld, USN, served as Chief of Naval Operations from 15 December 1947 to 2 November 1949.
[†] General Mark W. Clark, USA, was appointed in 1945 as Commander in Chief of U.S. Occupation Forces in Austria and U.S. High Commissioner; as such, he was the supreme administrative authority in the country.
[‡] Lieutenant Colonel Frank L. Street, USA.
[§] Colonel German P. Culver, USAF.

So I went in to brief in my blue uniform--a commander. There may have been a dozen people in the room. We were going through the JCS agenda for that day. Bradley was sitting, listening, and questioning the various people who briefed him. He came to me, and I gave him a brief canned thing that my Army teammate had written up. He listened and looked, and then he said, "Commander, why does General Clark want so many 105-millimeter Howitzers instead of 155 Howitzers?"

I said, "I don't know, General. As a matter of fact, I don't know what a 155- or a 105-millimeter Howitzer looks like." [Laughter]

We went right on around, and he never cracked a smile or said anything else. But he was teasing me. He was having fun. He saw this naval officer come in there, and he knew I was brand new.

I came to know him and see him often. I used to travel with him to NATO meetings.[*] I think I attended at least three of them with him, and was with him at dinner on one of them. I was with him one evening. We were guests of the ambassador in The Hague during a NATO meeting.[†] Harriman was seated at the end of the table.[‡] Bradley was near me. There was a woman with a Belgian-lace blouse, an absolutely gorgeous blouse, and a gorgeous woman, and Omar Bradley was thoroughly enjoying a conversation with her. It was a fun affair. Somebody at the table had been in some little town when he came charging through during the war. He had, I think, eight brothers, and they constituted, at one time, a baseball team in his hometown, and she knew about that. He stopped his tank, came over, and they had a chat. Now she was reminding him of that occasion. He was being jolly, good company, thoroughly enjoying it.

The head of ISA, who was kind of a creep, and Harriman, also overly serious, were at the other end of the table.[§] They didn't enter into the pleasantness. This fellow kept whispering in Harriman's ear, and they continued conducting business the entire meal. What a waste!

---

[*] NATO--North Atlantic Treaty Organization.
[†] The Hague is in the Netherlands.
[‡] W. Averell Harriman, who served as U.S. ambassador to the Soviet Union during World War II, was serving as U.S. Representative in Europe under the Economic Cooperative Act of 1948.
[§] ISA--International Security Affairs, a branch of the Department of Defense.

Q: What was it about Bradley that impressed you?

Admiral Richardson: He was down to earth and he was full of common sense. He was genuine, real-life, very competent, no airs. He had humility. I do know that when you find a gentleman in high command who doesn't have humility, you've got real problems.

Q: Does that apply in all situations?

Admiral Richardson: In my view, yes. You damn well better have somebody who's got some humility in his system so that he doesn't make horrible mistakes, and Bradley had that. In one of the meetings, Bradley told me that Sherman was to be his relief. Then Sherman had his heart attack. I think it was to take place in a December, and it probably was December of '50.

Q: He died in the summer of '51.

Admiral Richardson: Was it? Well, whenever it was he had his heart attack. So Bradley stayed on.

Q: Was Bradley a friendly man?

Admiral Richardson: Yes. He was earthy. He was a common man, an uncommon common man. He was a very fine individual. He never put on airs, and he was never above anybody else. He was comfortable to be around. He had a lot of common sense.

Our team had a great deal to do with setting up the NATO command structure, and we worked in close connection with the Standing Group. The American team in the Standing Group was the Silver Team that preceded the three of us. When NATO was formed, the then-Silver Team became the American part of the Standing Group. They worked with the French and the Brits, so these three groups of nine people in all were the staff of the Standing Group of the NATO command structure here in Washington. At that time, there were regional planning groups. This was before the command structure came into being.

Our team set about defining the authority of a Supreme Allied Commander Europe. We knew that if Eisenhower would accept the job, that whatever we wrote would be acceptable. If he wouldn't, then we'd have to write an authorization with all sorts of constraints in it.[*] We were subsequently engaged in the creation of the other NATO command structures when NATO shifted from regional planning groups to a command structure.

But when the Korean War broke out, we sometimes had a finger in that. We had special projects from time to time. One Saturday morning I went into work and was greeted by the secretary of the Joint Staff plans group with a message, urgent, from the President. The President was on the Williamsburg down river.[†] I was to work on the answer. We were pretty near concluding the negotiations at Panmunjom at that point in time, or so we thought. Admiral Turner Joy was the chief negotiator.[‡] This would have been in early '52, so the war had more to go.

But the negotiations had progressed to the point where there were some stick points. One, we were insisting that the North Koreans not be allowed to rebuild their airfields and recreate their aircraft strength, and they were saying, "Hell, no." They weren't willing to agree to that.

And so this message came back from Truman. Obviously the Joint Chiefs--and I hadn't known this--had sent Truman a message and recommended that we acquiesce on that point. He said, "I do not understand why we should grant them this. We have defeated them at a cost of much blood and money, and I don't see any reason why we should allow them to reconstitute."

---

[*] General of the Army Dwight D. Eisenhower, USA, served during World War II as Supreme Commander of the Allied Expeditionary Force for the invasion of Europe. In the early 1950s, as a five-star general, he served as Supreme Allied Commander in Europe when the military portion of the North Atlantic Treaty Organization (NATO) was established.
[†] USS Williamsburg (AGC-369) was the presidential yacht from 5 November 1945 to 30 June 1953.
[‡] Vice Admiral C. Turner Joy, USN, served as Commander U.S. Naval Forces Far East from 27 August 1949 to 4 June 1952.

I thought, "My God, he thinks we've won this war. We haven't won this war." I was astonished, and I have always wondered how General Bradley and the Joint Chiefs conducted themselves with the President about this war. He was misinformed, as made evident in that message that he sent back.

So then about this time in came one of the war plans teams that had primary responsibility, so I passed the buck to them. But the President wanted to know why we had to give in on this point.

Q: Did we acquiesce on that?

Admiral Richardson: Yes, we did. We did, because we'd not go to war later to enforce it. My recollection is my astonishment that the President thought we had won and were in a position to dictate terms.

Q: What do you recall about the firing of MacArthur?[*]

Admiral Richardson: Well, I was terribly disappointed at the time, but I could see it. None of the Joint Chiefs had faith in him; they didn't trust him. In everything that went out to him--and I saw all this stuff--there was always a great deal of deference. From talking with other staff people there who were actually working these problems, we knew that the Joint Chiefs weren't inclined to cross him up at all, but weren't at all inclined to support him, either. So there was a distinct distrust in the minds of the Joint Chiefs where MacArthur was concerned--shared, I'm sure.

Q: Were you surprised that he got fired.

Admiral Richardson: Yes, but his getting fired was for something quite different. He was fired for what Truman considered to be insubordination. MacArthur's conduct during the

---

[*] General of the Army Douglas MacArthur, USA, was serving as Commander in Chief of U.S. Forces in the Far East and was the United Nations Commander for the war in Korea. In April 1951 President Harry S. Truman relieved him of his commands because the President considered him insubordinate.

Pacific war, in my view, was not spectacular. His management of postwar Japan was incredible, absolutely incredible. Then in the Korean War, I'm not so sure but that had he had his way, we would have been better off.

Q: Do you mean in going beyond the Yalu River?

Admiral Richardson: Well, no. What he wanted to do was to destroy the bridges before the water in the Yalu froze over, after which destroying the bridges made no difference.[*] He wanted to use a nuclear weapon to do that. I think we now know--I'm not sure of this--that the Chinese were very reluctant in this matter, very, very reluctant, and finally did go into it, but just a little bit of resolve might have turned them off. Had we dropped a nuclear weapon on that bridge, that probably would have terminated whatever thought they had of moving in. It was their entering that Chosin Reservoir and all of that came about after they came into that war. I think MacArthur was right. Now, whether, in the larger sense, using a nuclear weapon was a satisfactory answer, that's another matter.

Q: We'll never know on that one.

Admiral Richardson: We'll never know. Another thing that we always have to remember is that nuclear weapons' capabilities today and what they were then are so totally different. They were then very dirty. They're not that way today, or need not be. The technology was quite different then. And in the context of that time, MacArthur probably didn't know much about nuclear weapons, and the Joint Chiefs certainly had the resources back here know. They knew. I can't say that their decision was bad in the larger sense.

Q: How much association did you have with Sherman?

Admiral Richardson: Almost none. Very little. Just mostly by reputation I knew him.

---

[*] The Yalu River separates North Korea from Communist China. The rules of engagement prevented offensive action across the Yalu, because President Truman did not want to risk setting off a still wider war.

Q: He certainly had that reputation widely of being a brilliant man.

Admiral Richardson: Very capable, very sharp man. The Spaniards loved him. Of course, he opened Spain to the West.

Q: He was on that trip when he died. Apparently, he really overextended himself.

Admiral Richardson: Maybe so. Did he die immediately after his heart attack or was there a period?

Q: I think he died right away.

Admiral Richardson: So it was a sudden, complete thing.

Q: Oh, yes. It was very shocking. I think he had been involved in all those negotiations with Spain, and then he went to France after that.[*]

Admiral Richardson: Has there ever been a biography written of him?

Q: No, just a chapter in the book on CNOs, that I know about, and it's very praiseworthy.[†]
Do you want to resume this tomorrow? We're right at the end of the tape.

Admiral Richardson: Fine.

---

[*] Sherman arrived in Paris on 21 July 1951 after a tiring week of negotiations in Spain and Italy. At 10:40 the following morning he had a mild heart attack, then died at 1:05 that afternoon after two more heart attacks.

[†] See Clark G. Reynolds, "Forrest Percival Sherman," pages 208-232 in Robert William Love, Jr., The Chiefs of Naval Operations (Annapolis: Naval Institute Press, 1980).

David C. Richardson #2 - 133

Interview Number 2 with Vice Admiral David C. Richardson, U.S. Navy (Retired)

Place: Admiral Richardson's country home in Julian, California

Date: Monday, 30 March 1992

Interviewer: Paul Stillwell

Q: Admiral, when we broke off last night, you were talking about your service on the Joint Staff around the time of the Korean War. What do you remember during that period of the NSC 68 study and the whole policy of containment of Communism?

Admiral Richardson: We were certainly appreciative of the magnitude of the Soviet threat. We saw Soviet handiwork in the Korean incident. During those years, our primary endeavor had to do with strengthening the North Atlantic Treaty Organization, and very nearly all of my efforts during my Joint Staff tour, as I indicated earlier, were in the European area, with only an occasional exposure to operations in the Pacific.

One thing I remember in particular. Without going into the organization within the Joint Staff Strategic Plans Group, suffice to say that under the director there were three assistants--one Navy, one Army, and one Air Force. The Army assistant, an Army colonel, later became head of the 10th Corps in Korea as a lieutenant general. He remarked to me one day that it looked to him like the only ones fighting in Korea were the Marines and the Turks. This was in the early part of that invasion, when our troops had been forced back into the Pusan Peninsula. And I said, "Well, how do you make a judgment about that sitting back here?"

He said, "It's easy. You look at the list of killed, wounded, and missing. Where the list shows a number of killed and wounded, but a much greater number of missing, they're not fighting. Where you see a few killed, a number wounded, and very few missing, you know they're fighting."

Q: What do you remember specifically about NSC 68 and the role of George Kennan?[*]

Admiral Richardson: Well, I knew that George Kennan was on the State Department policy planning staff, and I knew that he had been the central architect of the policy of containment. The document itself, which is described in literature now, was a comprehensive effort to contain Communism. The line of thinking that it represented, of course, put us in the Korean War and later had a great deal to do, in my opinion, with our attitude toward North Vietnam. That line of thinking drove, as well, the emphasis that we placed on the defense of Western Europe in the Marshall Plan and in building up the NATO organization and, in particular, in establishing a command structure and developing plans that could be quickly implemented.[†]

A point that has sometimes confused people regarding NATO had to do with the treaty itself. Articles 3 and 5 in that treaty provided that if the borders of a nation were breached, then the foreign ministers would meet, and transfers of earmarked national forces would be made to the NATO command to repel those who came across the border. Well, that was unrealistic, and, of course, everyone knew that. Time doesn't permit responses that are that delayed, and so forces were contingently contributed and were in place, which then permitted an almost instantaneous response in the event of an attack.

Another feature that wasn't understood was that the United States specifically discouraged any involvement of NATO in affairs outside of NATO. There was a desire at the political level, and certainly concurred in by the military, that U.S. interests in other areas were significant and should remain within the province of U.S. policy and not have U.S. policy subordinated to NATO political policies in areas such as the Middle East and elsewhere. NATO was constrained entirely to the areas within Western Europe by our reasoning. Today, we forget that.

---

[*] NSC 68 was a National Security Council paper developed in the spring of 1950, during the administration of President Harry S Truman. It recognized the international threat posed by the Soviet Union and called for the United States to devote significantly more resources than it was to strengthening its defense posture. Its cental idea was that Communism contained the seeds of its own destruction that would flourish if expansion of territory was denied--thus containment.

[†] At the Harvard University commencement in 1947, Secretary of State George C. Marshall made an address in which he outlined a plan for the economic rebuilding of war-ravaged Europe. Congress passed the European Recovery Act, and the program of American support came to be known as the Marshall Plan.

Q: Korea is a perfect example of that. That wasn't a NATO operation.

Admiral Richardson: That's right.

Q: What was involved in your day-to-day role going about getting this NATO setup going?

Admiral Richardson: I'm not sure I know how to answer that. The main time spent was in exploring thoughts and ideas about what would work, what wouldn't work. There were personal consultations, between my Air Force teammate and Air Force plans and policy, my Army teammate and his counterparts in the Army, Department of the Army, and I had a close relationship with people in OpNav, who were concerned in general, and we put together papers based sometimes on guidance received.

Once the outlines of a policy are identified and a general direction of movement is indicated, then the fleshing-out of all of this is something that's done at the action officer level on the Joint Staff and with the involvement of the services firsthand in that preparation process, and so things evolve.

When an item has been sufficiently prepared for the Joint Chiefs' consideration, it then goes to the "Planners." On any given issue, the Air Force, Army, Navy, and Joint Staff each have one individual who meet. If the Planners are in agreement, and if the issue is not one of substantial significance that the Planners think should be referred to the Joint Chiefs, then they have the authority to "red-stripe" papers--a red stripe indicating JCS approval.

On a number of occasions, when the Planners were in agreement--and I was Navy Planner several years later--we would send a paper to the Joint Chiefs anyway. It might be something they should be aware of, should be up to date on, so they would get it. It is a process of discussion and interrogation, consolidation of views, ideas, and so forth.

Q: Was the Chairman or the Joint Staff the customer for the product that you were putting together?

Admiral Richardson: The specific customer was the Joint Chiefs. The first decisions were at the intermediate level of the Planners, so called, then at the top level of the JCS. Now, if the Chairman asserted himself in a specific way--directed something be done that way--then we did it that way.

The services were not bound by that. We, as individuals, were not bound by that. We weren't constrained in any way in stating our personal opposition and reasons therefore to our service counterparts. But that seldom happened, and when it did happen, it most often was the result of a JCS decision. Having discussed it amongst themselves, they said, "This is what we'll do." And so what they decided they would do would be given to us to work up. For that matter, if we chose to take exception to it, we were perfectly free to do so, but we would do it as a group, with our reasons, and if those reasons were persuasive, okay.

Q: Did your group draw up the charters for SACLant and SACEur?[*]

Admiral Richardson: Yes, we did. We worked in conjunction with the Standing Group. The Standing Group--that is, the French team, the British team, and the American team, working together--actually developed the charters. But they were each working in close association with their counterparts in their home countries. We, the Silver Team, were the American counterpart. So we worked hand in glove in that development, because when it was developed, it had to go up through our Joint Chiefs for their approval, and, of course, that was true for the others. But if the Standing Group, for instance, were to take off in a direction that we knew our chiefs would not approve, and we were opposed to, we had reconciliations to work out.

Q: Do you remember any of the substantive items or any of the points of disagreement?

---

[*] SACLant--Supreme Allied Commander Atlantic. SACEur--Supreme Allied Commander Europe. Both of these are multinational NATO commands, in both cases headed by U.S. officers.

Admiral Richardson: No. I mentioned yesterday that in drawing up the charter for SACEur that it would be an easy task if General Eisenhower were to be designated, and it would be an impossible task if he weren't. As it turned out, it was an easy task.

Q: He made it possible.

Admiral Richardson: He made it possible.

Q: How big a factor was the Sixth Fleet at that time in your planning for NATO?

Admiral Richardson: The Sixth Fleet was a major factor, because it was contingently committed to the defense of Southern Europe. There is in the southern region an antipathy, well known, between Greece and Turkey. But those countries are separated by water, and from an army viewpoint they are not geographically able to coordinate in direct contact. The Greeks and the Turks have their own problems that go back for many, many centuries. So the Sixth Fleet was really the glue in that whole thing--not forgetting Italy, France, and Spain--and it made a coherent integration of the forces in that region a possibility.

Q: I think an indication of how important the United States considered that commitment was that it had the newest carriers, the Midway class, and the newest cruisers, the Salem class, in the Mediterranean, even though there was a war going on in the Pacific at the time.

Admiral Richardson: Mmm--

Q: Back in the early '50s, when this structure was being drawn up, did the United States have substantially more clout than other nations because it was making the biggest contribution?

Admiral Richardson: Yes, indeed. The other countries were just simply essentially ineffective, except the Brits, and had to be reconstituted, and that, of course, took time.

I really haven't answered the question that you put to me. One thing that has been of enormous significance, and will continue to be, is that by virtue of NATO, the military leaders in Greece, Turkey, France, and Italy have all served together. Over the 40 years of service, many friendships have been created amongst the military in these various nations, and that has broadened to such a point that it is now a major factor in policy development in Turkey, Greece, and Italy.

On one occasion when the Greeks were very upset politically with the Turks and drew all of their military out of Izmir, several months later they returned. Their homes had not been ransacked. They'd been placed under Turkish Army guard. The Greeks moved back in. Everything was just like they left. Things like that have had an ameliorating influence on the political exigencies amongst these various nations. That's the glue that is NATO. It has paid off enormously in that respect.

Another serious argument took place at the outset of NATO. I was present at the meeting, and General Bradley was there. The secretaries of defense of various nations were taking the position that they couldn't see their troops defending Germany without the Germans defending themselves.

Q: A reasonable position.

Admiral Richardson: Yes, but the French were adamant against German rearmament at that point in time, and they produced a plan that provided for an integrated force of French, British, and Germans at the squad level, platoon level, and so forth. That wouldn't have worked out. The Dutch SecDef said that if the French persisted in their position, his nation would reconsider its policies toward France. Over time the French relented.

Q: How much did nuclear weapons planning play a part in this early structure of NATO?

Admiral Richardson: I'm not aware that it played any part, any vocal part. Certainly it did, but the security that surrounded nuclear weaponry, characteristics of the weapons, all of that, was so closely held at that time that its impact was not discussed in normal staff channels.

Q: Do you know at what point nuclear weapons started to be regularly deployed on Sixth Fleet ships?

Admiral Richardson: Were they regularly deployed?

Q: At some point certainly they have been. I don't know when it started.

Admiral Richardson: Well, I don't know either.

Q: You're neither confirming nor denying.

Admiral Richardson: Right.

Q: You were talking about the French reluctance to see a rearmed Germany at that point. Was that part of the rationale for a large standing U.S. force in Germany?

Admiral Richardson: At that particular point in time, 1950-51, the French adamancy was countered by the Belgian adamancy in the other direction. I mentioned that at one crucial point in the discussion--and these are the defense secretaries of the respective NATO countries--I remember the Belgian defense minister addressing the French defense minister, stating that his country would have to reexamine its position vis-à-vis France because of French opposition to German rearmament. They were very strong words. But those things settled down and sorted out, and the Germans were rearmed. They did keep the integrity of the national units, and the French accommodated. Things moved along slowly toward the end that we all know they reached.

Q: Why was Belgium supporting German rearmament?

Admiral Richardson: I can't answer that. I really don't know. All of the countries in NATO, other than the French, favored German rearmament. The British were strongly in favor of it. We were. The Belgian happened to take a bellicose view toward it--was actually belligerent at that point--and then settled down. But it took place in one of our meetings. General Bradley was sitting there as the military adviser to our SecDef when it happened, and my team was seated behind him.

Q: Was it a distraction to you to be planning for NATO when you had the Korean War on the other side of the world?

Admiral Richardson: No, no, not at that point in time.

Q: You were focused specifically on that role, then?

Admiral Richardson: On the NATO role, yes.

Q: Anything else to mention about that tour? Did you get involved or witness the "revolt of the admirals" during that period?[*]

Admiral Richardson: No. That was pretty well finished before I got there. It took place in '49. It's quite interesting to read Arthur Radford's account of that. It goes on for about ten pages in his memoirs and reads all the world like the B-2 presentations today.[†] It's almost, the entire scenario, everything about it, is almost identical to the B-2 today.[‡] [Interruption]

---

[*] The Navy and Air Force were involved in an acrimonious struggle in 1949 over the future of U.S. military aviation. See Paul Schratz, "The Admirals' Revolt," U.S. Naval Institute Proceedings, pages 64-71.
[†] See Stephen Jurika, editor, From Pearl Harbor to Vietnam: the Memoirs of Admiral Arthur W. Radford (Stanford, California: Hoover Institution Press, 1980), pages 159-195.
[‡] In recent years there have been extensive debates about the advisability of purchasing the expensive B-2 manned bomber for the Air Force.

Q: Just to wrap up the NATO discussion on sort of a light note, you were mentioning when the machine was off how you were trying to derive a name and a set of initials for the headquarters. If you could recount that, please.

Admiral Richardson: SHAEF was the name that applied during World War II.[*] Something close to that was desired. We finally ended up on SHAPE, S-H-A-P-E, but in the course of those discussions, in our lighter moments, I had suggested Supreme Headquarters International Team.[†] It was not adopted.

Q: I'm not surprised.

Well, you went from that high-level strategic-type job back into the working Navy in the Badoeng Strait.[‡] How did that assignment come about?

Admiral Richardson: Well, it just happened. I don't know any of the details. I wasn't asked for. It just came normally, sea duty following shore duty.

Q: The escort carriers were pretty much on their way out by then, weren't they?

Admiral Richardson: Yes, they were. They were being used in ASW, but also when the Korean War broke out, they were used in the Yellow Sea, to the west of the Korean Peninsula.[§]

Q: They were used for close air support.

Admiral Richardson: For close air support.

---

[*] SHAEF--Supreme Headquarters Allied Expeditionary Force.
[†] SHAPE--Supreme Headquarters Allied Powers Europe.
[‡] USS Badoeng Strait (CVE-116), a Commencement Bay-class escort carrier, was commissioned 14 November 1945. She had a standard displacement of 10,330 tons, was 557 feet long, 75 feet in the beam, and had an extreme width of 105 feet. Her top speed was 19.1 knots. The ship was originally armed with two 5-inch guns and could accommodate approximately 33 aircraft. She was eventually decommissioned in 1957.
[§] ASW--antisubmarine warfare.

Q: Where was she when you reported aboard?

Admiral Richardson: In San Diego. And we sailed very shortly after I reported in. Went to Honolulu and then into Japan and operated out of Yokosuka, running antisubmarine warfare patrols for about three months. Then the next three months we were based in Sasebo, and we had aboard the Marine Checkerboard Squadron, VMF-312.

We alternated with the British carrier in the Yellow Sea at the west end of the front line. The Marines provided close air support using Corsair aircraft. That would have been in December, January, February, the very coldest period of time.

Q: This is early '53?

Admiral Richardson: In early '53. Then there would be an overlap of a day, sometimes two days, in Sasebo with the Brits. We would go to their ship and have cocktails. They'd come to our ship and eat steaks. It was quite an intense operating period--very interesting.

Q: I've heard the British get kind of rowdy sometimes in those occasions. Did you see that?

Admiral Richardson: No, not really. Their "rowdiness" generally manifests itself with their pushing martinis on their guests. It's difficult to avoid getting too much when, if your glass is down a quarter or a half an inch, somebody immediately fills it to the top again. It's quite a trick outwitting them on how much you take aboard.

Q: How would you compare the air operations in a ship like that with a big carrier?

Admiral Richardson: Well, there was nowhere near the punch that we had in the large carriers. We had, as I recall, 24-plane squadrons. We were operating Corsairs with a maximum of 24 planes in the group. Of course, a large carrier could have three times that many and operate the same type aircraft. So it's just a question of carrying capacity.

Another aspect, of course, is that aboard the big carriers the intelligence support is much better. That isn't too critical in the particular situation where we were, because we were providing aircraft in patrol areas, and they were directed from there to their specific targets.

Q: And forward air controllers would presumably take over.

Admiral Richardson: They had local air controllers, forward air controllers, that were actually putting them on their targets.

Q: How capable were those Marine pilots?

Admiral Richardson: They were great. The squadron stayed out. The personnel in the squadron rotated. They were proficient, very proficient. But I never, of course, was able to see any of the work they actually did. In their operations around the carrier, everything that I saw was first rate. They've always been carrier-qualified and were certainly adaptable to carrier use.

Q: Jimmy Thach had a squadron on board the Sicily right at the beginning of the war. He said that they were really very proficient because there were a lot of World War II veterans in the group. Who was your skipper?

Admiral Richardson: Roy Johnson was the first skipper.* I'd been aboard maybe two months, and just immediately before we deployed forward, the new skipper came, Joey Ray.† He now lives in Winter Park.

---

* Captain Roy L. Johnson, USN, commanded the Badoeng Strait from November 1951 to July 1952. The oral history of Johnson, who retired as a four-star admiral, is in the Naval Institute collection.
† Captain Herman L. Ray, USN.

Q: What do you remember about each of those men?

Admiral Richardson: Roy had incredible stamina. He took his position on the bridge, and it didn't seem to me he ever left. We'd go through an ASW exercise, and he would literally keep himself on duty for four to five days on end. I'm sure he had to nap from time to time, but he did so in his bridge chair, and he invariably was keeping right on top of any and everything that went on. When he left, he said to me, "Now you'll be the experienced one aboard, short though that be."

Joey Ray was quite different in that regard. He delegated a great deal. It was easier working for Joey, and all of us had more responsibility working for him and didn't have the skipper watching so intently over us.

Q: It's more satisfying, too, if the skipper's not there all the time, because it implies a sense of trust and confidence.

Admiral Richardson: Yes, that's right.

Q: What was the job for you as the XO--how much operational, how much administrative?

Admiral Richardson: It was heavily administrative, and there was operation whenever I wanted to. When Joey was there, he and I alternated. He'd run the show for 12 hours at night, and then I'd run it for 12 hours. ASW philosophy at that time was hunt to exhaustion, and it was an around-the-clock operation that went on for several days against diesel-electric subs at that time. So we just simply alternated in command of an operation.

The Yellow Sea operation was different. It was a daylight operation, and you settled down for the night and things were normal.

Q: What kind of an air group did you have for ASW?

Admiral Richardson: We had the AF, a derivative of the torpedo plane that was used late in the war.* It was a turkey, but it operated okay off the ship. It was a huge thing, and it would use depth bombs as its ASW weaponry and, of course, sonobuoys.

Q: What kind of tactics did they use? Did they coordinate with the destroyer group and helicopters?

Admiral Richardson: No. We didn't have helicopters assigned to antisubmarine warfare. We didn't have destroyers accompanying us, other than maybe one or two, and there was not much of an interaction between the aircraft and the destroyers. I'm pretty hazy about how we did do that then. That was '52, '53. Actually, it was in late '52 that we were doing this. That's 40 years ago.

Q: Was it in the sense of an offensive hunter-killer group, or would it be an escort for some other unit?

Admiral Richardson: It was offensive hunter-killer. Whenever a submarine was reported, why, we went to the area and prosecuted. That was the idea.

Q: That capability upgraded dramatically, because later in the decade they came along with the Task Force Alfa and so forth.

Admiral Richardson: That's right.

Q: That had a number of destroyers with it and a big carrier and helicopters.

---

* Grumman's AF Guardian was conceived as a torpedo bomber replacement for the successful TBF Avenger. Subsequently the AF was modified to be an antisubmarine warfare aircraft with two configurations that operated in hunter-killer pairs: the radar-equipped AF-2W and the weapon-carrying AF-2S. Deliveries of the AF-2 to fleet squadrons began in October 1950. The AF-2S version was 43 feet long, wing span of 61 feet, gross weight of 25,500 pounds, and top speed of 317 miles per hour.

Admiral Richardson: That's true. That was all a good bit later, very close to ten years later. Sonobuoys became more effective and were used to much greater advantage at that time. We began to run patterns to work that problem.

Q: Did you coordinate with land-based patrol planes?

Admiral Richardson: I don't remember that we did. A part of the problem was that there were few submarines available for our training exercises. While we ran training exercises in '52, it was extremely difficult to get a submarine to work against. So we were a pretty much a standby insofar as ASW was concerned. Really, we were treading water, maintaining efficiency as best we could without actually working against live submarines.

Q: It would be hard to motivate a crew or keep it motivated under that circumstance.

Admiral Richardson: That's right.

Q: Probably that problem solved itself once you got with the Corsairs and were doing real missions.

Admiral Richardson: That's true. Then there was a reality to everything we did. That was not the case with ASW. Skill in night flying and night carrier landings--those were the principal features of operational effectiveness at that time. It was maintaining skill. And if an occasion came along to work a submarine, then we did have some capability, not significant.

Q: How did the command structure work? Did you work for a cardiv commander who set up the operation plan?

Admiral Richardson: Yes.

Q: Whom did you report to, then, when you were in the Yellow Sea?

Admiral Richardson: We were under Com7thFlt in some form.* The command structure was defined by the United Nations command.

Q: What do you remember about liberty stops and logistic support in Japan?

Admiral Richardson: Both Yokosuka and Sasebo were very, very competent in rendering support.

Q: What do you remember about the reception on the part of the Japanese people to the recent victors?

Admiral Richardson: I remember when we headed west in September 1952, we went into Osaka. The night before we entered Osaka, I got the officers together and lectured them on the fact that the Japanese had so recently been our enemies. They had to conduct themselves ashore with great care. I wanted people to go in pairs, and this was to apply to all the crew. And as I looked around the room, I saw heads shaking. "All bad dope," they were signaling.

    The next day, why, several of us went ashore under the rules. What we found was totally different from what I had expected. Now, these officers had all been out before. They were returning for their second trip into Japan. They knew that it simply wasn't the way I expected it to be at all. We were well received. The general attitude of the people was not hostile. We had no problems at all.

Q: Of course, they liked the American income, and they were willing to do business.

---

* Com7thFlt--Commander Seventh Fleet.

Admiral Richardson: That's right. A Japanese pilot took our ship in and handled it very well, put it alongside the dock. I was bemused at the entire episode. It changed my ideas completely.

Q: And they were extremely industrious in their ship repair facilities.

Admiral Richardson: That's right, very, very good.

Q: How sophisticated were the electronics on board that ship?

Admiral Richardson: They weren't. Still in the early days of radio, and whatever else new we had electronically, I don't even recall. It was not of significance.

Q: So your job was just to get the planes there and launch every one of them.

Admiral Richardson: Well, as XO, I didn't do that. The air officer actually ran that. My job was mostly the care and feeding of the group aboard. I was chief housekeeper and then spun off of the skipper on operational control. Swede Ekstrom was our ASW cardiv commander at that time.*

In the course of our first three months out there, we went up to Hakodate in the northern end of Japan, and we were entertained by the mayor. A dozen or so of us were in the hotsi bath there, Swede in the nude, alongside him the Japanese mayor. Swede, who easily weighed 270 pounds and was about 6-4, was alongside this Japanese who did not weigh 90 pounds. Then in came women to scrub our backs. Most of us were sitting on the edge, because the water was too hot, and we quickly submerged. Oooh!

Q: In this housekeeping area, what do you remember about all the usual problems of dealing with masts and conducting inspections and VD concerns and all that business?

---

* Rear Admiral Clarence E. Ekstrom, USN, commanded Carrier Division 17 in 1952-53.

Admiral Richardson: Nothing of significance. The problem always was to prevent the ship's crew from encroaching into the air crew spaces, because when the air group was away and all this vacant space was there, those in the crowded areas tended to move in. And so the executive officer's job, in part, was to prevent the air group from suffering. There were occasions when I had to take strong action to make sure that the young pilots were sleeping comfortably. They were in their three tiers in the bunk rooms while our staff communicators were more comfortably set up. I made them move. So those sort of things we had to struggle with.

When a staff was aboard, then I saw that finding living quarters for the others was much more difficult, and that's when these problems would occur. I had to fight with the admiral's operations officer one time over who was entitled to what bunk space. I insisted and said, "All right, I'll take it to the admiral." He was insisting that his communicators all be kept together, which required our pilots in the ASW group having to sleep in cramped quarters beneath steam pipes--not a comfortable world, and they had night flights. But then he didn't want to go to his admiral. Joey counseled to give in, but I wouldn't.

Q: Was it generally an overcrowded ship?

Admiral Richardson: Not normally. But with a staff aboard, you had all the additional staff officers, and the ships simply were not big enough to handle that kind of a staff. There must have been 10 or 12 additional officers that came in with that staff. We couldn't handle them.

Q: Did you get as good quality officers and enlisted men as the big carriers did?

Admiral Richardson: We got good quality, yes. Also, I should tell you that when I was XO of Badoeng Strait, I had my first experience in control of NROTC officers.[*] We had at that time both Naval Academy graduates and NROTC graduates on board. I found the NROTC graduates were less inhibited, and that, in some ways, made them more effective.

---

[*] XO--executive officer. NROTC--Naval Reserve Officers' Training Corps.

Q: In what way more effective?

Admiral Richardson: Well, they didn't need to be told to do things quite as much as the Naval Academy graduates. The Naval Academy graduates wanted to be sure that they knew exactly what you wanted. The NROTC grads weren't quite so worried about that. And that's the way it should be. You shouldn't have to ensure you are "pleasing the old man." That is not always the best thing.

Q: I've just come from visiting Slade Cutter in San Antonio, and he made a similar point about his time as a submarine skipper in World War II.[*] He did not want Naval Academy graduates to come to his boat, because they were not inclined to react without approval from above, and he wanted people who would react and do what was needed right away.

What do you remember about morale in the Badoeng Strait?

Admiral Richardson: Morale was fine. No problem.

Q: Anything else about that ship?

Admiral Richardson: I don't think so. We went into the Navy yard when we came back. I left the ship, then went to ComAirPac, served for a year as assistant plans officer there. During that period of time, I met Jeanne Simonds, who became my wife. We were married in 1955.

In that assignment I was heavily engaged in planning the rotation of carriers into the Western Pacific. We were having to be helped by the East Coast carriers, and so we were interlocking with the East Coast and working out rotational plans. Our deployment schedule was completely out of whack in the sense that we were deploying people 10 and 11 months on a stretch and then returning them to the States for five to six months, then

---

[*] The oral history of Captain Slade D. Cutter, USN (Ret.), is in the Naval Institute collection.

another long deployment. The result of that was that our enlisted people were leaving as soon as their enlistments were up.

I remember in particular the difficulty in retaining radiomen and boiler tenders. Those two rates in particular were very short in numbers. Many of those young men would come back from a long deployment on one ship, then be transferred immediately to another ship and moved forward. We fought heavily against that sort of thing being done. One thing I wanted to do was leave them be.

Then when we sent people off to, say, radio school, which we had to do from time to time, we wanted the people we sent off to come back to the same ship and not simply go into some pool, and then go wherever. We couldn't get that done, but it's simple and clear to me that had they come back to the ship they left, and we knew that was going to happen, we would have sent our best, not the ones we could afford more easily to be rid of, which is what was being done. We should have been guaranteed that people we sent would come back. I think if that policy had been established throughout the fleet, we wouldn't have had anywhere near the trouble that we had with retaining people.

Q: You were penalizing the good people.

Admiral Richardson: Well, we were destroying the good people, forcing them out. We could not get it changed, and I have never understood why there was that adamancy at the top personnel levels. I'd have to say BuPers was the culprit. Their representative on the West Coast was the one who actually controlled the assignment of personnel, and presumably he had the authority to establish policies.

Our planning was heavily related to carrier readiness, carrier rotation, so that year that's what I spent doing.

Q: Why were those deployments so long?

Admiral Richardson: I don't know where the requirements were being set. They obviously were at least JCS requirements. We were required to keep a certain number of carriers on station, and to do that we couldn't do it within the resources of PacFlt.* We had to use both fleets and overly long deployments.

Q: The Korean War was over then, so presumably the need would have dropped off.

Admiral Richardson: This was in the fall of '53 and into '54.

Q: The armistice had been in July of 1953, so it sounds like there wasn't much of a standdown. Which admiral was the type commander then?

Admiral Richardson: Beauty Martin.† He was the brother-in-law to Admiral Sherman.

Q: I didn't know that.

Admiral Richardson: Admiral Sherman wanted Martin to come to Washington. Martin was a very fine aviator, very practical and down to earth, likable, a very able man, and Sherman felt that if he accepted Washington duty, there would be no question but that he'd be promoted to four stars. I watched him, attended meetings with him, attended as a member of his immediate staff in visits to CinCPacFlt when Felix Stump was PacFlt and Dave McDonald was operations officer out there, along with Rivero, who was assistant ops, and Martin was respected wherever he went.‡ But he refused duty in Washington, said it wasn't worth it.

Q: I've known other people who were just the opposite, that would do whatever they had to do to get that next star.

---

* PAcFlt--Pacific Fleet.
† Vice Admiral Harold M. Martin, USN, served as Commander Air Force Pacific Fleet from 1 April 1952 to 1 February 1956.
‡ Admiral Felix B. Stump, USN, served as Commander in Chief Pacific and Commander in Chief U.S. Pacific Fleet, 10 July 1953 to 14 January 1958. Captain David L. McDonald, USN. Captain Horacio Rivero, Jr., USN. Stump's oral history was done by Columbia University, those of McDonald and Rivero by the Naval Institute.

Admiral Richardson: Yes, that's right.

Q: Admiral Martin had been Com7thFlt when Sherman was CNO, so that was obviously a plum assignment. Any specific recollections on him, any incidents?

Admiral Richardson: Nothing noteworthy that I can recall.

Q: What else do you remember about that tour?

Admiral Richardson: It was a very busy time. I don't recall anything of lasting significance.

Q: Some of those carriers were starting to be pulled out of mothballs for modernization--the Lexington, for example. Was that an attempt to ameliorate this rotation setup?

Admiral Richardson: It would have been. I don't recall that that was being done.

Q: Well, then, let's move on. Where from there?

Admiral Richardson: Roy Johnson, my skipper for a month on the Badoeng Strait, wanted me to come work for him in Washington. He was air weapons analyst, OP-05W--officer in charge of that. So I came back on a conference with Beauty Martin one time, and I was leaving I saw Roy. He motioned me to come over. He said, "Well, you had orders to be commanding officer of the naval air station in Tucson, where we store planes and where the commanding officer's principal assignment is to play golf with different local authorities, but I wanted you back here. That assignment was no good for you, anyway."

    I thought to myself, "Thanks, but no thanks," but I didn't express that.
    Anyway, he said, "You're coming back to 05W to work for me."

He then got Jig Ramage and Mickey Weisner shortly after that, and the three of us worked in the air weapons analysis staff, while Noel Gayler was working over in OP-55 in the requirements.* We worked a lot with Noel and others at that time.

One of the first things that Roy assigned me was to prepare a study on the future of the carrier task forces, and I worked on that thing for a long time, the better part of a year. The feature of future operations that came through to me in the course of that time was the impact of a burgeoning electronics technology on carrier task forces.

There were a couple of incidents or anecdotes during that time that sort of highlight this. One was that it was quite apparent in doing this work that the Ship Characteristics Board was really not the way to go about creating ships for task forces, because there was an interdependency among the ships. Instead of putting all of the thought on making a destroyer a better destroyer, a cruiser a better cruiser, we needed to look at the task force as the basic entity and state the requirements for ships according to how they would be fitted into the task force and used as a member of the carrier task group, the battle group. Especially in electronics matters it later came into vogue. This later happened, but it was much later.

A second feature was the need for incorporation of electronics capabilities, but the particular office in OpNav that had to do with that was under Rear Admiral Red Ramage, who later became Com1stFlt.† Red Ramage had a small office of several people. I went around and spent a week with them. They worked in considerable secrecy, and my questions had to do with what the requirements were that they were working against, or deriving, and what the equipments were that were coming along, and how would they be fitted into the future carrier task force. And what they told me was that, "Well, the thing is technically driven. We are moved by technical opportunity to adopt this or that. We don't create a requirement based on a study of what the task group is supposed to be." In other words, the technical tail was wagging this operational dog.

---

* Commander James D. Ramage, USN; Commander Maurice F. Weisner, USN; Captain Noel A. M. Gayler, USN. The oral histories of Ramage and Gayler are in the Naval Institute collection.
† Rear Admiral Lawson P. Ramage, USN, served as Director of the Surface Type Warfare Division of OpNav from December 1956 to September 1958. His oral history is in the Naval Institute collection.

So I went back and wrote a memo to Captain Turner Caldwell. At this point in time, Roy Johnson had left to take over Forrestal as its first skipper, and Turner Caldwell was now the head of OP-05W. I wrote him a personal memo, describing in some detail my unhappiness with this particular approach.

Well, about a week or so later, I was out flying. When I got back, I learned that Admiral Ramage was very upset with me and wanted to see me immediately. I tried to get him. I didn't succeed, because he had gone to make a speech at the Air War College. Then I left about that time and went to Strike Force South, so I missed seeing him, but I tried to find him.

I learned later what happened. Turner Caldwell took my personal note and handed it to the DCNO (Air), who then took it and handed to the DCNO (Ops), OP-03. This was a naval aviator named Theda Combs, a vice admiral, who called Ramage in and read him the riot act.[*] He gave him the weekend to answer the questions I had posed in my memo.

Q: How to win friends and influence people.

Admiral Richardson: That's right. And so I jumped on Turner Caldwell. I said, "For God's sake, if you want to send my memo forward, don't leave my name tied to it." But anyway, that happened. I never did see Red Ramage about it, and he never said anything to me about it. Later, Roy Johnson told me Ramage was a good guy and to forget about it.

Q: What was the thrust of your difference with him?

Admiral Richardson: Well, the difference was that I had asked a number of questions in the memo. I said, "These are the kind of questions I think should be asked." This memo goes down, and Ramage is called in, "I want your section to work straight through to answer these questions for me." That took them about a week, and they worked through the weekend answering the questions that I had posed in this memo. That didn't make him happy.

---

[*] Vice Admiral Thomas S. Combs, USN.

I also recall another hassle I was involved in during that period. When I was in OP-05W, Don Felt, whom I'd known in the Saratoga, came into the OP-03 organization.* I wrote him a memo one day about some aviation details. I don't now recall the details, but it was professional, and I got notes back. Arleigh Burke was CNO. He wrote in red, blue, I forget which, but he had a color and Don Felt had a color. So back came my memo, and at the bottom he said, "Hereafter, if you mean something private for me, don't send it through the mail."

So I thought about it a few days, and I said, "Well, by God, I didn't send that thing through the mail, and I'm going to go tell him."

So I went into his office. He came in while I was in the outer office. He breezed by, looked at me disdainfully, and walked into his spaces. Captain Kinsella was his executive assistant, out of '34, a submariner.† Don chewed him out on two or three subjects, and then he looked at me, and to this day I can still see him leaning forward and saying, "What do you want?"

I said, "Well, Admiral, I just want you to know that that memo that you sent back to me, I didn't send through the mail. I brought it around here personally and I handed it to Captain Kinsella."

He looked at Kinsella and he said, "Did you open that?"

Kinsella said, "Yes, sir. [Don Felt's predecessor] always had me open his mail, everything he had."

Felt chewed Kinsella up one side and down the other for opening that memo. I felt, "My God, I've knifed that guy." But to me, giving it to Kinsella was just as good as giving it to him. And I thought, "Oh, my God, what have I done?"

Q: Did Kinsella ever come back to you on that?

---

* Rear Admiral Harry Don Felt, USN, served as Assistant Chief of Naval Operations (Fleet Readiness) from 1954 to 1956. His oral history is in the Naval Institute collection.
† Captain William T. Kinsella, USN.

Admiral Richardson: No. No. He left the Navy.* I think Don Felt drove him out. All I remember is how awful I felt that I had inadvertently knifed that man.

Mickey Weisner, Jig Ramage, and I had a bet about who the next Vice Chief would be. So the phone rang one day, and I was heard saying, "Yes, sir. Yes, sir. Yes, sir. Yes, sir. Aye-aye, sir."

Mickey, "Who was that?"

I replied, "That's our next Vice Chief." I said, "Well, that was Rear Admiral Don Felt, and he just called me and told me to go over and chew out Vice Admiral Combs." (Combs was then my boss.)† So I said, "That means but one thing. He's the next Vice Chief." [Laughter] So I made a bet. Mickey Weisner and I bet a bottle of Scotch. And so the first thing you know, Don Felt got ordered to Sixth Fleet.‡ I paid off the bet. In the meantime, the then-Vice Chief, Admiral Duncan, stayed.§ Then, a few months later, Don Felt came back as Vice Chief.** I said, "Okay, Maurice, two bottles." So Mickey had to pay me off with two bottles of Scotch.

The DCNO we had at that time was not the best of them. We had good ones normally, but Combs was so-so. He went from that job to OP-03, then disappeared. But he wasn't up to the standard, and Don Felt knew that.

Q: Felt had a meteoric rise that year.

Admiral Richardson: Well, Arleigh Burke thought the world and all of him. Then, of course, when we were out in Honolulu, when I was Deputy CinCPacFlt out there, Don Felt was there and we saw him a good bit. He and I always had a good relationship. [Laughter] I knew him very well.

---

* Kinsella retired from active duty on 30 September 1957 and received a tombstone promotion to rear admiral.
† Vice Admiral Combs served as Deputy Chief of Naval Operations (Air) from 11 April 1955 to 1 August 1956.
‡ As a vice admiral, Felt served as Commander Sixth Fleet from April to August of 1956.
§ Admiral Donald B. Duncan, USN, served as Vice Chief of Naval Operations from 10 August 1951 to 1 September 1956.
** As a four-star admiral, Felt served as Vice Chief of Naval Operations from 1 September 1956 to 28 July 1958. He and Admiral Arleigh Burke, USN, the Chief of Naval Operations, were both in the Naval Academy's class of 1923.

Q: What other recollections do you have of Weisner?

Admiral Richardson: Well, I have so many of them. Mickey was about my closest friend in the military. Our times go back to that time we were in OP-05W, where I first met him. Tex Guinn, who later became Chief of Naval Personnel, was a detailer at that time, and he said, "You're getting Commander Weisner into 05W. Do you know him?"[*]

I said, "No, never heard of him."

He said, "Well, if you want to keep him happy, keep him busy."

That was my first one, and I've had many, many involvements with him through the years.

Q: What was the overall business that 05W was trying to achieve?

Admiral Richardson: It was looking ahead in air capabilities. There was at that time an idea of a nuclear-powered patrol plane, that large Martin plane.

Q: P6M, the jet-powered seaplane.

Admiral Richardson: Yes.

Q: Was there also a plan for a nuclear-powered version?

Admiral Richardson: Yes, but radiation and weight killed it. The Assistant Secretary of the Navy for Air took a look at the study we completed, then sent it back to the DCNO (Air), describing this study as a perfect example of backward thinking. But we were right.

Fortunately, that program never got anywhere. We were dead right. It made no sense at all. We did a study on seaplane tenders with seaplanes armed with nuclear weapons operating from remote locations around the world that did make sense. At that

---

[*] Commander Dick H. Guinn, USN. As a vice admiral Guinn served as Chief of Naval Personnel, 1970-72.

time we were facing the prospect of surprise attack with nuclear weapons, and dispersal was attractive.

The three of us--Weisner, Ramage, and I--went out to St. Louis to see the mock-up of the F-4, then on down to Dallas to see the mock-up of the F-8.[*] Then we came back to make recommendations regarding those two. In many ways, we were sort of a double check on OP-55, who were the aircraft requirements people. But the air weapons analysis staff was itself an outgrowth of OP-23, which was the section that fought the B-36 battle.[†]

A number of analytical offices that were later created were headed up by graduates of our 05W group. It started out as the study group. Then, of course, some of these major studies migrated over to CNA at later times.[‡] But the genesis of much of that work was 05W, air weapons analysis, looking at not only individual systems, weapon systems, but looking at systems within systems, that is, total systems, such as carrier task groups and task forces, seaplane tenders, each with its bevy of seaplanes.

Q: The P6M's demise was speeded probably by the fact they had some crashes during their early tests. So that didn't make it look any more attractive.

Admiral Richardson: No. The trouble with the nuclear power thing was that you could get nowhere near the power you needed to run it. You had to have radial engines. Then, whenever you ran your nuclear power plants, the radiation simply would radiate their crew. So it did not make sense. It did not make sense as a practical matter, although the idea of being able to cruise around the world two or three times sounded great.

Q: If there was any reason you needed to do that.

---

[*] The F4H Phantom II was a jet fighter built by McDonnell. It first entered fleet squadrons in 1961. In 1962 the aircraft was redesignated F-4. The F8U Crusader was a jet fighter built by Chance Vought. It first entered fleet squadrons in 1957. In 1962 the aircraft was redesignated F-8.
[†] In the late 1940s, the Navy and Air Force were competing for scarce defense dollars. Secretary of Defense Louis Johnson accelerated production of the Air Force's B-36 bomber and canceled the aircraft carrier United States (CVA-58) soon after the beginning of construction. The Navy's organization to counter the Air Force was OP-23. For details, see Jeffrey G. Barlow, Revolt of the Admirals (Washington, D.C.: Naval Historical Center, 1994).
[‡] CNA--Center for Naval Analyses.

Admiral Richardson: If you needed to, yes. But we gave it a resounding down, and the office caught hell from the Assistant SecNav for Air. But we were right.

Q: What about the A-3 and the A-5 and some of those planes? Were they coming along then also?

Admiral Richardson: Yes, the A-3 was. The RA-5 came out of the A-5, which started out as a nuclear weapons delivery plane.[*]

Q: They both started out as heavy bombers, didn't they?

Admiral Richardson: They did. The A-3 was Douglas, and the A-5 was North American. Both of those planes started out as nuclear weapons carriers. I remember in the A-5 its twin weapons slipped out of tubes in the rear. The plane was not especially attractive. It didn't add a lot new that was worth the enormous cost. But its performance was quite good, and so it migrated into being a reconnaissance plane, not a nuclear weapons delivery plane.

The A-3, of course, migrated into being an electronic collector, the EA-3, and only within the last few years was it finally retired, because we never got around to developing its replacement, which originally was to be the TASES.[†] We were stopped on that by Congress, a great mistake. Ultimately it became BGPHEs--battle group horizon extender, meaning passive electronic collection while airborne, linked electronically to the ship, providing both information and receiving instructions. This plane would also be capable of intercept controlling, and certainly if a radar-equipped plane were in the area, then it would

---

[*] The North American A3J Vigilante first entered fleet squadrons in 1961 as a carrier-based heavy bomber. It was reclassified A-5 in 1962. The photo reconnaissance version, RA-5C, entered the fleet in 1964. That same year a number of the Navy began converting the attack planes to the recon version, which had considerable service in that role during the Vietnam War. The Douglas A3D Skywarrior first entered fleet squadrons in 1956 as a carrier-based heavy bomber. It was reclassified as the A-3 in 1962.
[†] TASES--Tactical Airborne Sigint [signals intelligence] Exploitation System.

pass to him. That plane is just now finally entering the inventory, but it's a derivative of the A-3 back in the '50s.

Q: What about air-to-air missiles? Were you looking at them?

Admiral Richardson: We did. Not in terms of the specific capabilities of the missiles. We didn't have to do with that. The work done on Sidewinder was itself technically driven, but its applicability was enormous.[*] And the Sparrow.[†]

Had there been a need for something like that that didn't already exist, we might have recognized it. That's what we basically did. But where it did exist, or where the technology was already moving along and functioning, we simply adopted what there was and incorporated that in our thinking as an aspect of the total force.

Q: That was a great success story for China Lake.[‡]

Admiral Richardson: Indeed it was. Tom Moorer was much involved in it.[§] The technical gent who did that Sidewinder development at China Lake was W. B. McLean, who died of throat cancer not too many years ago. He later became the technical director at the submarine lab here on Point Loma. It was he who said it could be done. There were 100 who said it couldn't.

Q: What about electronic countermeasures? Were you looking at that in that era?

---

[*] Sidewinder is an air-to-air infrared-homing missile with a speed of approximately Mach 2.5. It has been operational, in various forms, since 1956.
[†] Since the late 1950s the Sparrow has been the U.S. Navy's major long-range air defense missile. The Sparrow I version entered fleet service in 1956 on board F3H Demons and F7U Cutlasses.
[‡] China Lake is another name for the Naval Ordnance Test Station at Inyokern, California.
[§] Captain Thomas H. Moorer, USN, later CNO and Chairman of the Joint Chiefs of Staff. His oral history is in the Naval Institute collection.

Admiral Richardson: In a rudimentary way, yes. We simply didn't know enough about it to have any real good ideas about it. We didn't know signals technology then or signals behavior in atmospherics. We just simply recognized some broad principles.

We, or at least I, failed to translate the concept of the task force functioning electronically as a total system until I read a study by the PSAC--Presidential Scientific Advisory Commission--in early '72 that pointed out that the Russian Navy mandated that all task force electronics should be made to evolve compatibly and centrally controllable, a requirement for effective electronics countermeasures. This study also pointed out that the U.S. Navy simply added new on top of old, without being made to comply with an identified operational concept. Now, that was a perfectly logical extension of my OP-05W study of a future carrier task force operational concept.

The idea of C^3 countermeasures beyond countering specific weapons never occurred to me.* But from the time I read that report, I started referring to our naval operational patterns as "brute force Navy." That PSAC concept was the centerpiece of my address at the Armed Forces Communications and Electronics Association annual meeting at Dallas in the fall of 1972, not long after I retired. I was the principal Navy speaker there that year, and it is the basis for my being invited to join the Naval Research Advisory Group (special committee on electronics) in '73. In the Sixth Fleet we actually witnessed Soviet major task force central control of radars during Exercise Okean 70 and reported on it. Imagine broadly spaced ships, each periodically making a couple of sweeps with active radar, then radar silence, and you have the idea for one mode of operations.

Q: And another factor is that the surface-to-air missiles probably weren't a significant threat yet at that point in the 1950s.

Admiral Richardson: Well, we had at that point in time the early surface-to-air missiles. That section was under the DCNO (Air). It was OP-53. The early Terriers and the early Talos were being conceived in those time frames. I don't remember the specific missiles now that were engaged, but, yes, they were coming along.

---

* C^3--command, control, and communications.

We're talking '55 to '57. Now, in 1962, a mere five years later, I was the Navy planner. One of the projects that came before us was the EA-6B, which was an electronic jammer aircraft.* So I would say that the technology advancement was even then under way, and as things evolved, we learned more. My problem was that instead of laying out the requirements for guidance in the thing, we were simply adapting the old to new--updating.

Q: Anything else to mention about that job before moving on?

Admiral Richardson: No.

Q: From there you went over for duty in the Med with NATO.

Admiral Richardson: Yes, I have been involved in NATO now for a number of times. My first involvement was on the Silver Team and the Joint Staff '49 to '52. During the period '57 to '59, I was assistant chief of staff for operations and intelligence in the Commander Strike Force South office in Naples, Italy. The NATO counterpart to Commander Sixth Fleet was ComStrikForSouth. Commander Sixth Fleet was also ComStrikForSouth. His deputy, when I was there, was Rear Admiral Dale Harris.† He was Deputy Commander Strike Forces South, based in the Banoli compound in Naples, along with CinCSouth and ComAirSouth.

For those two years, I was directly involved with Greeks, Turks, and Italians, as well as Americans, in those command structures. Then later, as Com6thFlt, I had that same kind of involvement again. It was interesting that two of the Chiefs of Naval Operations of the Greek Navy had worked for me in Strike Force South. Stavros Pervenas was the Greek liaison and assistant to me in DepComStrikForSouth ashore, as was Margaritis, who relieved him in Naples.‡ My wife and I knew both of those families very well and had socialized with them a great deal. Later, when I became Commander Sixth Fleet, why, I

---

* The EA-6B Prowler was the electronic warfare version of the Grumman A-6 Intruder.
† Rear Admiral Dale A. Harris, USN.
‡ In the late 1960s Vice Admiral K. Margaritis became Commander in Chief of the Royal Hellenic Navy.

worked very closely with Stavros and subsequently with his successor, Margaritis. It made for a fine relationship.

We were very actively engaged in nuclear weapons employment planning during the period that I was in Strike Force South in Naples. Air South wanted to control all strikes inland, and Com6thFlt would have no part of that, and for very good reasons. And so there was the not-at-all-unusual battle on command and control of forces that went on between the Air Force and the Navy when air operations were involved. It was very intense. Admiral Briscoe did not take a stand and did not solve a coordination problem, and Admiral Cat Brown, who was then ComSixthFlt, complained to Admiral Burke.[*] Admiral Burke then retired Admiral Briscoe and put Cat Brown in as his relief.[†] So then Cat Brown had to solve that problem, which he quickly did.

Q: One of the people I interviewed recently is Vice Admiral Beetle Forbes, class of '45.[‡] He was an A-1 pilot during that period, and he said that some of that planning was so tightly held that the only people who would know his specific target list, for example, would be himself and somebody back in Washington.[§] It was very highly compartmented.

Admiral Richardson: There are two sets of plans in all of this. You've got the NATO plans, and you have our own unilateral plans, which are brought into coordination to a great degree, but not exclusively so, because what NATO was interested in had to do with the common good, but what Sixth Fleet was also interested in was its own survival. And so the combination resulted in strikes and priorities for strikes by Sixth Fleet forces that were not in the NATO plans.

Yes, there was a great deal of sensitivity on that. Alternate targets were used for practice runs. But on one occasion an Air Force pilot flew from a NATO base, delivered a

---

[*] Admiral Robert P. Briscoe, USN, served as Commander in Chief Allied Forces Southern Europe from July 1956 to January 1959. Vice Admiral Charles R. Brown, USN, commanded the Sixth Fleet from August 1956 to September 1958.

[†] As a four-star admiral, Brown served as CinCSouth from January 1959 to January 1962.

[‡] Vice Admiral Bernard B. Forbes, Jr., USN (Ret.)

[§] Douglas AD Skyraider propeller-driven attack planes first entered fleet squadrons in late 1946. The AD-2 version was 38 feet long, wing span of 50 feet, gross weight of 18,263 pounds, and top speed of 321 miles per hour. In September 1962 Skyraiders still in service were redesignated A-1s.

practice run right into the middle of Hungary, his real target, as I was informed, instead of going to the alternate target in NATO territory. There were a lot of practice runs being done those days, and so that sort of thing could happen.

We were in Naples for two years, and from that point, I came back to the West Coast. I took command of a fleet oiler, Cimarron, in Yokosuka Harbor.[*] When I took command, it was just completing its tour, and we left for the States the next day.[†] I went through the usual repair period back here, and then we deployed again. I took her through one deployment.

The Cimarron was really ancient. We had a terrible time keeping it operating. Things happened that were the consequences of age. Valves would separate from the valve stems, for example. In one occasion, we were refueling Com1stFlt in his carrier flagship when all of a sudden an oil hose went limp. There wasn't anything we could do to get the oil flowing again. We later learned that the valve plate had separated from the stem and closed off the flow. The admiral judged me incompetent. His golfing partner was Dale Harris, who saved the day for me, as I later learned.

When we went forward, I applied for an extra optar from ComServPac.[‡] We needed so much work. We had two boilers retubed while in San Diego. The rest of them needed to be done. The ship really needed a terrible amount of work, and the maintenance officer on ComServPac staff said, "Let's face it. You drew a lemon. My problem is, how much sugar does it take to make lemonade?" Well, it evidently didn't take much sugar, because I struck out. On my way out I saw Admiral Campbell, who was Commander Service Force Pacific Fleet.[§] He said, "I know what a terrible ship you inherited from your predecessor."

---

[*] USS Cimarron (AO-22) was commissioned on 20 March 1939. She was 553 feet long, 75 feet in the beam, had a draft of 32 feet, and displaced 25,425 tons fully loaded. She had a top speed of 18 knots and a cargo capacity of more than six million gallons of fuel oil.
[†] Captain Richardson commanded the ship from September 1959 to September 1960.
[‡] Optar--operating target--the amount of money allocated by the Navy for a unit to spend in a given period of time. ComServPac--Commander Service Force Pacific Fleet, the type commander for the underway replenishment ships.
[§] Rear Admiral Robert L. Campbell, USN, served as Commander Service Force Pacific Fleet from May 1958 to February 1961.

I had relieved Captain Monk Russell, and I told the admiral that it wasn't his fault.* I was grateful Russell had it when he did, because he had turned the ship around. I had very good officers aboard. When he himself had relieved, the skipper that he relieved had to be carried over the side. He was drunk. The ship was a total mess. I was very grateful Russell had it before me.

Russell had written BuPers and identified the personnel problems he had and had gotten a good response.† He had good officers aboard as a result and had done a lot to improve things. So I inherited a ship that was on the mend.

I said, "Well, we need more help, and we want a $10,000 addition to expend in our three weeks in Yokosuka." Three or four days later, while headed west, we got the $10,000. We did a lot of work when we were in Yokosuka. And the Japs were terrific. We cleaned out rust from spaces that had never been touched in all the years, just literally tons of rust out of some of the voids, fixed our boilers, etc. So we brought the ship up considerably from what it had been.

Years later, when I was Deputy CinCPacFlt, Admiral Campbell, who had long before retired, lived in Hawaii.‡ I saw him frequently during those two years there, and I guess he must have mentioned a half a dozen times, "You know, you didn't run your predecessor down." [Laughter] I guess that made quite an impression on him. Maybe that was worth $10,000.

Q: And that ship kept going after that for a while longer.

Admiral Richardson: It went on. I don't know when it finally gave up the ghost.§ But we used to--not entirely laughingly--caution any women who came aboard in high heels to walk on their toes. Their heels might go right through the decks.

---

* Captain Hawley Russell, USN, commanded the Cimarron from July 1958 to September 1959.
† BuPers--Bureau of Naval Personnel.
‡ Rear Admiral Campbell retired from active duty on 1 October 1964.
§ When the Cimarron was decommissioned on 30 September 1968, she was then the oldest U.S. Navy ship that had been in continuous active service.

Q: I saw that ship in Yokosuka in the late '60s, and she was still going.

Admiral Richardson: I was on Cimarron when this gentleman, Bob Dosé, who called a couple of hours back, was skipper of Mispillion.*

Q: He has been described to me as an aviator's aviator, a superb pilot.

Admiral Richardson: A great guy, a wonderful gent.

Q: What do you recall of the Cimarron's operations during that period when you had her?

Admiral Richardson: We deployed into WestPac and were really neither more nor less than a floating gas station.† We took position at sea and loitered until the carriers came there to get their drink of fuel, then away they went. So we journeyed in and out of port to load, deliver, and reload. Our reward was carrier-baked fat pills, i.e., cookies and rolls.

Q: Where did you get the oil, usually?

Admiral Richardson: In Tokyo Bay. We'd fill up there and go out and man a service station spot for two weeks or so.

Q: Any other interesting incidents you remember besides that fiasco with the First Fleet flag?

Admiral Richardson: No, I don't. Nothing else in particular. When I deployed forward, a member of the ComServRon 3 staff, a lieutenant commander, met me en route and rode the ship out. He was to report to Commander Service Squadron Three, who was Rear Admiral Andy Hill, regarding our operations.‡ So we did drills just shortly before we got into

---

* Captain Robert G. Dosé, USN.
† WestPac--Western Pacific.
‡ Rear Admiral Andrew J. Hill, Jr., USN.

Yokosuka. Another oiler came out and met us. We made approaches on the oiler to hook up and were graded.

The normal procedure for shifting from one side, working one set of rigs, to the other side, was to steam ahead and around. That was no problem with a carrier, but with an oiler it took 20 minutes to add another two or three knots on the doggone thing, and you'd get around an hour later to making an approach on the starboard side. I said to myself, "This is ridiculous." So when I finished, instead of pulling ahead, I just nosed out a little, then cut my speed. And as I was dropping back like this, I poured the soup to it and pulled across the stern of the other oiler and then came in on this side. I cut the time down by four. Perfectly safe. There's no way on earth the ships could have collided with me dropping back of him, then crossing through his wake. Even if both ships had a total failure, their momentum would continue and keep us apart.

The lieutenant commander was very upset because it wasn't normal procedure, so I found myself on the report at the other end. [Laughter] I explained to the admiral what I was doing and why I was doing it that way. He said, "Well, that's not the normal procedure, but the lieutenant commander is just simply trying to make sure." The last I ever heard of it. Thanks again to Norm Ellis and his direct approach to getting the job done.

Q: The purpose of that was to give you deep-draft command experience before going to a carrier. How well did it serve that purpose?

Admiral Richardson: I think it served it very well. It brought your thinking back to slow responses, whereas you had been conditioned to relative motion and high-speed responses.

Q: The right way is not always the best way.

Admiral Richardson: Yes, that's right.

Q: What about just the bigness of it? Certainly, this ship was bigger than the destroyer you'd last conned.

Admiral Richardson: Yes. Everything about it is so very slow, and you have to anticipate a lot because of it. It doesn't matter whether you're turning or whatever. But it's a whole area of activity. The slow speed and response reorient your thinking processes, and it's good to go through that.

From that, I went on to Hornet, which was an ASW carrier.[*] It was a super ship. It really was great. It had won three battle efficiency E's, and none of the other CVSs could touch it, although they tried. It won the fourth one when I had it, and it should have won the fifth one, but they were determined they weren't going to give it five. That was after I left. Hoyt Mann relieved me.[†] He was a classmate.

I relieved Captain Christensen, who was promoted to rear admiral not too much later.[‡] I took over the ship in Hong Kong. There was a rear admiral aboard, Bob Townsend, an ASW type.[§] Then we transited back to the States, went into overhaul in Bremerton.[**] When we came out, we began to build up toward deployment again. I was ordered away before I ever took Hornet into deployment. I operated it off the coast here for four or five months after coming out of overhaul, and I really got shortchanged on that particular assignment.

We operated, put on demonstration flight operations in Tacoma Bay, which isn't all that big to get that ship up to 25-plus knots. We would charge across the bay, launch, turn around, and come back again and recover. We really were creating waves on the beach. But they wanted to see it, so we did. It was incredible what you could do with that ship because it was so maneuverable. Took it down the Hood Canal to load ammunition. I'd swear the canal is narrower than the ship. It was a delight to handle. It just handled beautifully.

---

[*] USS Hornet (CV-12) was originally commissioned 29 November 1943 as an attack carrier, decommissioned in 1947. In the early 1950s she was modernized and recommissioned 11 September 1953 as CVA-12. In 1958 she was converted to an antisubmarine warfare carrier (CVS-12). In that role she had the following characteristics: standard displacement: 33,100 tons; length, 899 feet; beam, 101 feet; maximum width, 192 feet; top speed, 33 knots.
[†] Captain Hoyt D. Mann, USN, commanded the Hornet from 18 October 1961 to 24 September 1962.
[‡] Captain Ernest E. Christensen, USN, commanded the Hornet from 20 November 1959 to 2 November 1960.
[§] Rear Admiral Robert L. Townsend, USN, commanded Carrier Division 17 in 1960-61.
[**] Puget Sound Naval Shipyard, Bremerton, Washington.

Q: More power than the oiler, certainly.

Admiral Richardson: A lot more power, and you could do all sorts of things with it you couldn't do at all with the oiler. You'd go ahead on one engine in the oiler and back on the other. Then, if you'd come back the next day, she'd just begin to swing. Hornet was very responsive. It was like a sports car. It was a delight--a ship version of the Bearcat. I was sorry to leave it.

I also had an encounter with my friend Mickey Weisner during that period. He was skipper of an oiler when I had the Hornet and had come out of the Navy yard.[*] We were going through refresher training. So we were practicing approaches, hooking up for replenishment. Both I and my officers were making these runs. I inherited a technique on the Hornet from my predecessor that put that ship in place much faster than was called for. It worked beautifully. At certain relative positions you called up certain engine speeds, and you ended up right where you should be.

Mickey called over on the bridge-to-bridge interphone and said, "How about grading us on one of our competitive exercises?"

I said, "Well, better than that, we have the fleet training group aboard observing our operations. Why don't I get him to do it?"

He said, "Fine."

So we made two or three approaches like that, and he said, "How am I doing?"

I called the training group commander and I said, "Captain Weisner wants to know."

He said, "There's somebody back there with his helmet off and another with no glove. It really isn't too good. I see a couple of people sitting around."

I said, "Mickey, maybe we better not count this one, because the commander is not very happy with two or three little things, not big things."

Mickey said, "Let me talk to him."

---

[*] Captain Maurice F. Weisner, USN, commanded the fleet oiler Guadalupe (AO-32) in 1960-61.

So I'm sitting there. This conversation went, "Yeah. Oh. Oh, really? Where are you going? Yeah? Hmm. Yes, sir. Well, yeah, it looked very good. I think you've really done extremely well on this thing." Then the officer from the training group left.

I got on the phone with Mickey and asked, "What in the hell's going on here?"

Mickey was chuckling. He said, "Well, we had a little talk. I told him that a low grade didn't make much difference. I was being ordered away, so whatever the score, it didn't make any difference to me."

I said, "Oh? Where did you tell him you were going?"

"I told him I was going back to duty in BuPers."

I said, "Oh? And where?"

"I told him I was going to be the commander detail officer." [Laughter] Needless to say, he got this commander's attention.

Q: So Weisner was going back to be the commander detailer?

Admiral Richardson: So he said, but actually he had orders to command the Coral Sea.* There were a great many anecdotes in our professional and social lives together.

Q: What were the satisfactions for you in having a major command in the Hornet?

Admiral Richardson: There were a great many. One major satisfaction was the crew itself, and that was reflected in the general appearance and the functioning of the ship. When I relieved, Christensen said, "Well, we'll put on a general quarters for you. If the crew's feeling good, they'll do it between nine and ten minutes." Fifteen minutes was the requirement for excellence. That was the highest standard. He said, "If they're feeling good." The other measure, of course, is how many deficiencies are there, and there just were doggone few deficiencies, and they were small, very minor. Sure enough, they completed that thing in about nine and a half minutes. And their performance remained that way.

---

* Captain Weisner commanded the aircraft carrier Coral Sea (CVA-43) from 1961 to 1962.

The ship was incredibly clean, the best I had ever seen. We had few disciplinary problems. I don't recall any of significance. I'm sure there must have been some. But if there had been that were sufficiently noteworthy, I would remember.

Q: You must have had a good exec.

Admiral Richardson: Yes, I had a superb exec. In fact, all of the crew was good. And, sequentially, two super operations officers.

Later I was consulting up at Sanders Associates in Nashua, New Hampshire. When I first started up there in the fall of '73, Roy Sanders had two things he wanted me to look into. He said he had such a fine relationship with the Navy when Tom Connolly and I were in OP-05 back in '67, '68, and now his relationship was poisoned.[*] He was at odds with NavElex on a program.[†] And there was another problem, a production performance problem--would I look into them? So I did.

What I found out on the first one was that there were some minor problems that had risen between the project manager at Sanders and the project manager in the Navy. As this argument went up the line, it intensified. So my advice to him was, "Whenever Sanders wins a program, go down to the program manager and say, 'Here's my card. Here's my telephone number. If you've got any problems, call me directly, immediately.'"

The other one, I didn't know quite how to handle it. I said, "Well, I don't know. I can't tell you. But I can tell you how you win a battle efficiency pennant on a ship at sea. You do it by having your department heads feel free, and you help them do their jobs. Instead of having them look up to you to tell them this, that, and so forth, make them assume full responsibility, and then you back them up by finding out what they need or what their problems are with what you can do to help them. That's how you win a battle efficiency pennant." You decentralize down. That point that ought to be taught, taught,

---

[*] Vice Admiral Thomas F. Connolly, USN, served as Deputy Chief of Naval Operations (Air) from 1 November 1966 to 31 August 1971. Admiral Connolly's oral history is in the Naval Institute collection.
[†] NavElex--Naval Electronics Systems Command.

taught, taught, taught. Use McNamara as an example of what not to do.* You get these guys to working the problem, and the top guy's got to go around and say, "Okay, what do you need that I can give you?" and back them up. That was my advice to him.

That was the way the Hornet had been operating when I arrived and continued to operate. So the result was that I found I inherited darn good officers, and the ones who came in fitted into that mold. I mentioned earlier that a ship takes a certain air and a character about it which seems to persist. That's very true, but the reason is that somebody set it up right to start with. That man was Tom Connolly.†

Q: My guess is that you did not live on the bridge the way Roy Johnson had on Badoeng Strait.

Admiral Richardson: No, I didn't do that. It wasn't necessary, and I made a point of having as many officers as we could work in take their turn at the conn. Because you never know what you'll have to do, particularly in ASW, where you run three to four days in hunts to exhaustion. All of your people had to be good, or you'd have collisions. So you had to have them do it, unless you were going to stay up all the time. There aren't many people that have that capacity. Some of them ought to go to sleep. [Laughter]

Q: Right. [Laughter] And that person's judgment may be impaired without him realizing it after a certain period.

Admiral Richardson: That's exactly right.

Q: How much more sophisticated was the ASW capability then than it had been when you were in the Badoeng Strait?

---

* Robert S. McNamara served as Secretary of Defense from 21 January 1961 to 29 February 1968. He had a reputation as a micro-manager.
† Captain Thomas F. Connolly, USN, commanded the USS Hornet (CVA-12) from 12 August 1957 to 28 August 1958.

Admiral Richardson: Well, a great deal more, primarily because of the electronics we had, and also because now we had helicopters. But when one looks at the state that we then had in 1960-61, and then looked at the development of ASW aboard the Moskva, they moved ahead of us rapidly, and they conceptualized better than we did.* Of course, they built later and they could therefore do that. But when the Moskva ran an ASW exercise, their electronic link to their helicopter was both ways. It was a command and control link, as well as an information link from whatever sonobuoy signals they were getting. We didn't have anything like that at that time. So in an ASW sense, we still were rudimentary, even by Soviet standards.

I took over the Hornet in Hong Kong, and then we operated in and around the Philippines for a while before we came home. I must have relieved, say, midway into the cruise, roughly that, and we did do exercises in that area. I don't recall we did any exercises on the coast that way while I still had the ship, because we were in earlier phases of working back up to operational competence--ship handling, launching, recovering, handling the aircraft, supporting the aircraft, but not conducting ASW. I don't recall we ran a single ASW exercise after coming out of the yard before my detachment.

Q: Was it primarily the S2Fs that were flying?

Admiral Richardson: S2Fs and helicopters.†

Q: How capable a team was that?

Admiral Richardson: I can't say they were all that good. I didn't know that then. I've known it since that they really weren't very effective, and we were easily defeated by a reasonably smart submarine.

---

* Moskva was a Soviet cruiser with a stern flight deck for antisubmarine helicopters. She began operating on sea trials in July 1967.
† Grumman S2F Tracker propeller-driven antisubmarine planes first entered fleet squadrons in early 1954. In 1962 the Tracker was redesignated S-2. The S-2E version was 44 feet long, wing span of 72 feet, gross weight of 26,867 pounds, and top speed of 253 miles per hour.

Q: Did you work against nuclear boats?

Admiral Richardson: No, not then.

Q: So presumably you would have been even worse against those.

Admiral Richardson: Well, yes, I'm sure we would. In '60-61, they were just beginning to come around. I don't think we had too many. We still were nursing along World War II fleet subs. I'm not sure just when the nuclear boats came along.

Q: Well, the Nautilus had been commissioned back in '54 or '55, but they were not there in great numbers yet.[*]

Admiral Richardson: No, and they were running their own sort of thing at that time, doing their own type of work. The submarine, in my view, is by far the best counter-submarine, and the work they've done in recent years is incredible.

Q: Who was your admiral on board?

Admiral Richardson: I've forgotten. Forgotten the name. Very nice guy. I never knew him before and I don't think I ever saw him afterward. But he was a pleasant, genial, and competent gent.

Q: Did you feel a sense of disappointment in getting the Hornet at that point instead of a CVA?[†]

---

[*] The USS Nautilus (SSN-571), the Navy's first nuclear-powered submarine, was commissioned 30 September 1954.
[†] CVA--attack aircraft carrier.

Admiral Richardson: No, I didn't. I was delighted to get the <u>Hornet</u>. I wasn't inclined to fight the issue that I had a CVS and some others had CVAs. It didn't upset me. Maybe it should have, but it didn't.

Q: After that, you again went to Washington for duty.

Admiral Richardson: Once again, my friend Roy Johnson had put his finger on me, and I went back to OP-60 this time. He was a rear admiral, OP-06B.

Q: What was involved in that job?

Admiral Richardson: At that time, Admiral Oley Sharp was OP-06, vice admiral. Roy Johnson was his deputy, and Wally Wendt was OP-60.[*]

Q: You're talking about a lot of talent in those gents.

Admiral Richardson: That's right. So Roy put the finger on me, because certainly neither Oley Sharp nor Wally knew me at all. Wally and I, our families are very close now. But I then came to work for Wally as 60 Bravo--Bravo 1, I guess it was. There was a Bravo 1 at the time; he was Turner Caldwell. [Laughter] And when Turner left, why, I became 60 Bravo and Wally Wendt, OP-60.

My job was Navy planner. Whatever JCS item came up, I was the one that always went to cover that at planners' meetings. Then I or the specific action officer would brief OP-06 or the CNO before the three JCS meetings a week they had--Monday, Wednesday, and Friday. They had the agenda and the items that were in it, the action officers would do the briefing, and then the planner would be there to elucidate as required.

---

[*] Vice Admiral U. S. Grant Sharp, USN, served as Deputy Chief of Naval Operations (Plans and Policy) from August 1960 to August 1963. His oral history is in the Naval Institute collection. Rear Admiral Waldemar F. A. Wendt, USN, was Director, Strategy, Plans, and Policy.

Ricketts was Vice Chief one time, and in one of these meetings he threw away what I had won at the planners.* Everybody had a big laugh over that. He said, "The Army would never agree to that."

I said, "But the Army did agree to it." [Laughter]

Q: So did he fall off?

Admiral Richardson: No. The chiefs had been discussing it, and they had made up their own mind about it. But none of the planners had been in on it. They had already negotiated their settlement when this came up, and, of course, here was a paper that was an agreed paper that was right in line with what the Navy had wanted, but that was not now the case. And so the questions arose. It was just one of those funny things that will on occasion happen.

Q: Do you remember what the issue was?

Admiral Richardson: I don't remember what it was now. It was not of any great shakes, no major issue. It had to do probably with the military assistance program, or something like that.

Anyway, during those years from December of '61 until I was selected for flag and left the job in February of '64, I worked down there Saturdays, Sundays. It just was interminable, because there were always issues that had to be resolved within time frames. Even through Christmas holidays, I came back. There were a great many individual things that came up during that time. We often were all together in opposition to OSD.† At that point in time, there were people in systems analysis in OSD, who, in our views--and I say views, plural--were subversive.

Q: Was Alain Enthoven one on your list?

---

* Admiral Claude V. Ricketts, USN, served as Vice Chief of Naval Operations from 1 November 1961 until his death on 6 July 1964.
† OSD--Office of the Secretary of Defense.

Admiral Richardson: No. Alain Enthoven was a problem, but not in that sense.[*] There was a man named Dieter Schweb--I'm not sure of the spelling. They found him in Germany. He was brought in by Vance.[†] The intelligence people gave us reports that were suspicious of him.

Well anyway, President Kennedy had sent over a letter to SecDef questioning whether we were procuring enough fighter aircraft, and the Joint Chiefs made answer to it.[‡] The answer was that we were not procuring enough fighter aircraft. So that letter sat in OSD systems analysis for two or three months, didn't go over to the White House.

We planners were all in agreement. The chiefs bought what we said, without change. Then down came a proposed answer, sent for our concurrence. We went through it and tore it apart. We had the information on Soviet programs and capabilities, and we picked it to pieces, revised it, and sent it back up through the chiefs. It was Christmas time. Again for, I would say, a month the proposed answer sat in OSD. The President wanted an answer months back, but it just sat there.

So we were questioning the thing one day while it hadn't gone out of OSD yet. We understood that they were coming back with still another draft. I said, "I'll fix that." So I called the naval aide over in the White House, and I said, "How about getting a call from somebody over there to SecDef and say, 'President Kennedy wants to know where's that letter he asked for last October, giving him the answer to the fighter aircraft query.'"

Q: What was the upshot of that ploy?

Admiral Richardson: The upshot was that either SecDef or Deputy SecDef said, "Why has that thing not been answered?" And so there was an accounting. Dieter Schweb, the gentlemen specifically at fault in that, was fired. We were glad to see him go. He was

---

[*] Alain C. Enthoven served as Deputy Comptroller and Deputy Assistant Secretary of Defense, 1961-65, and as Assistant Secretary of Defense for Systems Analysis, 1965-69.
[†] Cyrus R. Vance served as Deputy Secretary of Defense, 1964-67.
[‡] John F. Kennedy served as President of the United States from 20 January 1960 until he was assassinated on 22 November 1963.

blocking the whole bloody business because he personally didn't happen to agree with the JCS.

Q: What do you remember about Wendt as somebody to work for?

Admiral Richardson: Wendt was great: easy individual, very competent, but very approachable on anything. He was agreeable to hearing whatever argument you might bring to him.

When I was ordered to Sixth Fleet, it was due to Wally Wendt wanting me. He was going as CinCUSNavEur, and he wanted me as Com6thFlt.[*] Tom Moorer was agreeable to that.[†] Tom Connolly had offered me the training command, which I refused, even though it meant three stars.

But when I went over, I went through London for three or four days before going down. Wally said, "Come into the briefing with me." I went into the morning briefing, and when we left, he said, "What did you think of the briefing?"

I said, "I don't know any more than I did when I went in. The reason I don't is because they gave a biopsy--'These are the things that are happening now.' But they didn't explain anything in the context of what was going on yesterday or the day before, then project out into what this means today and tomorrow, what we'll be looking for and that sort of thing. There was no depth in that sense. The essence of intelligence exploitation is to develop sequences of past activity that indicate certain things that are going to happen."

He changed his entire briefing setup. Now, there's a person, that instead of being upset about the thing, actually wanted to know what I thought.

Q: He took it constructively.

Admiral Richardson: Yes. Yes. But he's that way.

---

[*] Admiral Waldemar F. A. Wendt, USN, served as Commander in Chief U.S. Naval Forces Europe and Commander in Chief U.S. Naval Forces Eastern Atlantic from July 1968 to June 1971.
[†] Admiral Thomas H. Moorer, USN, served as Chief of Naval Operations from 1 August 1967 to 1 July 1970.

Q: What about Sharp? I suspect he was not as approachable as Wendt.

Admiral Richardson: No, he was not. But Sharp was a very competent guy, and he just was a totally different personality. We've always gotten along fine. His aide at that time was Rembrandt Robinson.[*] Rem and I had worked together in OP-60, and we knew each other well. When I wanted to get something across to Oley Sharp off Vietnam, I went to Rem Robinson. Rem was very effective with Oley Sharp. Rem would have been CNO had he not had an accident in a helicopter that killed him.[†] There wasn't anybody I knew but that knew that Rem Robinson would one day be CNO. My approach to Sharp was through Rem Robinson. That was easier and fruitful.

Q: Robinson carried a little baggage from the scandal that came out about messages going back and forth being filched from National Security Council and going to Admiral Moorer.[‡]

Admiral Richardson: Yes, that's right. He did. That was, as I recall, a little bit later.

Q: But it might have been thrown back at him if he'd gone up for CNO confirmation.

Admiral Richardson: Maybe. Memories are short. At this earlier time, though, any number of us who were involved in OpNav were of the view that he was so exceptional that some day he was likely to be CNO.

Q: What qualities did you admire in Sharp in running OP-06?

---

[*] Commander Rembrandt C. Robinson, USN.
[†] On 8 May 1972 Rear Admiral Robinson, then serving as Commander Cruiser-Destroyer Flotilla 11, was killed in a helicopter crash in the Tonkin Gulf.
[‡] Yeoman First Class Charles E. Radford, USN, claimed that he took NSC papers for use by Admiral Moorer during his tenure in the early 1970s as Chairman of the Joint Chiefs of Staff. For a detailed--albeit biased--account of the Moorer-Radford affair, see Len Colodny and Robert Gettlin, Silent Coup: The Removal of a President (New York: St. Martin's Press, 1991).

Admiral Richardson: I don't have an answer for that. He was a very competent individual.

One thing about Sharp that was standard operating procedure--and that I thought was absolutely the way it ought to be--was that an action officer, any one of the people in all of OP-06 who had an urgent problem, could go into Oley Sharp's office anytime, and be seen immediately, and his problem laid on the deck. Now, when he went out, he went back down the line and briefed his normal seniors. The normal procedure is go up through OP-60 and so forth. So he just sort of reversed that to cut everybody in on what had happened. But the shop was used to operating on the basis of individual responsibilities, and every individual had complete access to OP-06 to handle an urgent matter at any time. He didn't have to go through anybody. He then came back down, alerting the intermediaries. That procedure may have been standard a long time, I don't know. I became acquainted with it when Oley Sharp was OP-06.

Q: What do you remember about the Cuban Missile Crisis, which occurred during that period?[*]

Admiral Richardson: There were three of us--Turner Caldwell, myself, and one other--who were on around-the-clock watch as OP-60 in the several days before the fleet sailed from Norfolk.[†] The CNO was charged with developing the operational guidelines for CinCLantFlt.[‡] On that Sunday night, I had the midnight to 8:00 A.M. watch, and when I relieved, I was told that the guidelines that were to go out to CinCLantFlt had been reviewed by the Joint Chiefs, corrections made, and they had been returned to the Navy to make those corrections. They were to be delivered to the director of the Joint Staff and immediately sent to CinCLantFlt, who was awaiting them. He knew he was sailing at 8:00 A.M., but he had no instructions.

---

[*] In mid-October 1962, U.S. reconnaissance plane photographed a Soviet nuclear missile site in Cuba and the presence of Soviet bombers. On 22 October President John F. Kennedy went on national television to announce a naval quarantine of Cuba, to be implemented on 24 October. On 28 October Premier Nikita Khrushchev of the Soviet Union notified President Kennedy that he was ordering the withdrawal of Soviet bombers and missiles from Cuba.
[†] Rear Admiral Turner F. Caldwell, USN.
[‡] CinCLantFlt--Commander in Chief Atlantic Fleet. At the time it was Admiral Robert L. Dennison, USN, whose oral history is in the Naval Institute collection.

So I monitored the progress. About 2:00 o'clock, when the directive corrections had been made, I took them down to the director of the Joint Staff, who was Vice Admiral Riley, a naval aviator.[*] I cooled my heels outside for 30, 40 minutes, and finally said, "This is urgent. I've got to get in to see the director with this thing. I've been instructed to do so."

So I then was taken in, but I was dressed down with a look: "What are you doing here?"

I said, "I was directed to bring these revised instructions to you to be sent out immediately."

He said, "I had an agreement with Don Griffin that he would only send a flag officer down here to see me."[†]

I said, "I'm just doing what I was told." I then left. So I went back up to my office in OP-60. About an hour later I hadn't received a copy of that message. An hour and a half later, well, now it's about 4:30, 5:00 o'clock. I went back down to find out why it hadn't gone out, and I was informed that Admiral Riley had sent it to the Joint Staff team to work over. I said, "That is not what was supposed to happen."

So I went up to see the Vice Chief, who was Admiral Ricketts. I woke him up--he was sleeping near his office--and told him what had happened. He got on the phone, called Riley, chewed him out, and ordered, "Get that message out right away."

Well, it finally did get out. It was about 7:00 o'clock when it got out, and CinCLantFlt was sailing about 8:00. Not a typical OP-60 day.

Q: How much did you hear about the reverberations from the incident that led to Admiral Anderson being fired?[‡]

---

[*] Vice Admiral Herbert D. Riley, USN, served as Director of the Joint Staff from February 1962 to February 1964. His oral history is in the Naval Institute collection.

[†] Vice Admiral Charles D. Griffin, USN, served as OP-03, Deputy Chief of Naval Operations (Fleet Operations and Readiness) from January 1962 to June 1963. The oral history of Griffin, who retired as a four-star admiral, is in the Naval Institute collection.

[‡] Admiral George W. Anderson, Jr., USN, served as Chief of Naval Operations from 1 August 1961 to 1 August 1963. His oral history, including an account of his being relieved of duty as CNO, is in the Naval Institute collection.

Admiral Richardson: Well, we knew firsthand what was happening there because we were all more or less intimate with that operation. I was not a witness to it but immediately heard about it. Within minutes of the time it happened, we in OP-60 knew.

In that flag plot there were two portions, you know--the front part and the back part. Security then required that special intelligence was operated in back. McNamara came into that place to give rudder orders to the DD skipper.* Anderson made him stop. McNamara stormed out and several months later fired Anderson. Kennedy certainly didn't agree with it, but because he didn't want to embarrass his SecDef, he appointed George Anderson as ambassador to Portugal. George Anderson just died.†

Q: A couple of weeks ago.

Admiral Richardson: A few weeks ago, his seventh stroke or something like that.

Q: The submarine Thresher was lost in the spring of '63.‡ Did you get involved in that?

Admiral Richardson: No.

Q: That would be a technical matter rather than a planning matter, I take it.

Admiral Richardson: We knew it happened. It wasn't an issue that came into OP-60 at all.

Q: What about the continuing deterioration in Vietnam?

Admiral Richardson: That was the situation during Kennedy's time, and we were tracking a great deal of that, but I don't recall that we gave advice to the President as to the ramifications of this or that.

---

* DD--destroyer.
† Admiral Anderson died 20 March 1992.
‡ The attack submarine Thresher (SSN-593) was lost with all hands on 10 April 1963 while operating east of Cape Cod. The presumed cause was a reactor shut-down during a dive.

The one thing I recall was when a Marine general was sent down there to make an assessment. Several of us accompanied him to the State Department for the briefings he received. I think a man by the name of Cleveland, as I recall, was one of the people who briefed him. He then went down into Vietnam, and when he came back had a number of recommendations. When he got there, the French set about entertaining him, and that wasn't what he had in mind. He wanted to get out into the front, which he did, and came back with a report. It wasn't favorable.

Q: What other issues did you deal with in that job?

Admiral Richardson: Well, we dealt with military assistance. We dealt with policy and plans of all sorts. We dealt with command and control. OP-602 was command and control. 601 is the budgeting process. We had all of those things.

The one thing that OP-601 had to do was with the formulation of the budget, and he always--that was the area of involvement of his entire shop--and the senior officer there always did the planning in the Joint Staff on that. I handled OP-602, OP-603, OP-604, and OP-605. Mike Michaelis was OP-605 at the time, and I remember he had nuclear weapons problems, some of those sort of things that were coming along.[*] But they all came to me, other than the 601 people. They worked directly with Wendt and Sharp.

Q: The budgeting people had to shift to get into this new system that McNamara had imposed--the PPBS. Any impact you recall from that?

Admiral Richardson: I don't quite understand what you were saying.

Q: It was the economic or whatever statistics-type budget approach that McNamara brought in from business.

---

[*] Captain Frederick H. Michaelis, USN. The oral history of Michaelis, who retired as a four-star admiral, is in the Naval Institute collection.

David C. Richardson #2 - 185

Admiral Richardson: Oh, in the context of planning for force structure.

Q: Right.

Admiral Richardson: No, I didn't get into that in a specific way. I was involved in Polaris development.* Those things came into the Joint Staff. CinCLantFlt was the principal "inputer" that the Navy used in that when we were examining the relative merits of Minuteman I, II, and III and Polaris I and II and the relative accuracy of systems. That was an Air Force-Navy area of competition, budgetary competition, and I was in the middle of that, arguing in favor of Polaris. But as a general proposition, the force levels was handled by 601.

Q: Of course, when you get into that assessment of the various strategic weapon systems, your objectivity sometimes gets colored by the uniform you're wearing.

Admiral Richardson: Indeed it does, and the effectiveness of your presentation is the quality of data that you present. That's what will carry the day in the long run, and it did. The Air Force could not comprehend how we could have the accuracies we claimed. It had to be demonstrated. Submarine location accuracies were incredibly accurate, thanks to Dr. Draper.†

Q: Anything else from that job to remember?

Admiral Richardson: Well, there are a lot of things. I don't know of any particularly significant thing. We could go for weeks on this subject. For one example, Gene La Rocque was a very effective officer at that point in time, and I was quite pleased with him

---

* Polaris was a submarine-launched ballistic missile used as part of the nation's strategic deterrent. It had just entered the fleet a few years earlier.
† Dr. Stark Draper of the Massachusetts Institute of Technology had an important role in the development of the inertial navigation systems used in Polaris missiles and later in the space missions sent to the moon.

and his operation in 603.* He was a hard worker, very assiduous in attending to his duties. I had a good opinion of him then.

Q: Where did you go from your job in OP-60?

Admiral Richardson: I was selected for flag and was ordered to be Commander Fleet Air Norfolk and was in that job two years, until February 1966. There was nothing of historical significance that went on in that. I had charge of facilities, airfields, inspecting squadrons, and readying people to go forward to Vietnam in '65 and '66. I left in early '66, February.

The A-6 squadrons were going through.† We had the usual problems one has in connection with the introduction of new plane types, the A-6 being one in particular. That again was a question of scheduling facilities for bomb runs, nuclear weapons runs, gun-firing accuracies, and all that sort of stuff. I would not cite any significant item of general interest that developed during that time.

Q: You were sort of the naval aviation daddy in the area and had to deal with all the aviation matters.

Admiral Richardson: Well, you've got ComNavAirLant there, and he deals with a much broader scope of things.‡ These ComFAirs are subordinate to him for managing the facilities and training--in charge of training, that sort of thing. So there are delegated duties from ComNavAirLant, but he's really the champion. We spent a lot of time with ComNavAirLant in connection with maintenance, training, and inspections.

Q: What proportion of the carrier support in the Vietnam War was coming from AirPac as opposed to AirLant? Would you have an idea?

---

* Captain Gene R. La Rocque, USN. Following his retirement from active duty as a rear admiral, La Rocque became the head of the Center for Defense Information, an organization that presents views counter to those held by the Department of Defense.
† The Grumman-built A-6 Intruder was the Navy's principal carrier-based bomber from the early 1960s to the early 1990s.
‡ ComNavAirLant--Commander Naval Air Force Atlantic Fleet.

Admiral Richardson: AirLant provided somewhere around a third of it, no more than a third.

Q: Because you still had to support the Sixth Fleet deployments.

Admiral Richardson: Yes. Right.

Q: Did you notice an upturn in the tempo because of Vietnam during that two-year period?

Admiral Richardson: No. Pretty early in that game. I left in February of '66, and so I didn't, at that point in time. The buildup came soon after.

Q: Please tell me about the means by which you found out you'd been selected for flag rank. That had to be an enjoyable thing.

Admiral Richardson: I had a call from a woman who worked in the White House. It was about dawn. She said, "You'll be happy to know that your name is on the selection list that goes to the President today." And so I learned about it informally through a friend of a friend. I knew the board was meeting, but I didn't know whether they had concluded. That was how I heard.

Q: Great news after almost 30 years as a commissioned officer.

Admiral Richardson: That's right.

Q: Did you go through the usual charm school business to indoctrinate you?

Admiral Richardson: Yes.

Q: What was involved in that?

Admiral Richardson: Well, I was intrigued by George Anderson's insistence that you really have to consider carefully what the British tell you, because they often tell you what serves their interest, and, of course, I knew that to be true in spades. Back in my days in the Silver Team, we would sometimes get intelligence assessments from the Brits, and it soon became clear to us that this was a second-echelon assessment that we got, that the first one was the best they could produce for the British policy people. The second one was a revision of that to bring us into line with their views.

The other aspect of that was when functioning with them in connection with Standing Group matters, there would be quite frank discussions. Then, when an agreement had been reached, the Brits would propose a way to present it to the rest of the NATO nations so that if you lost your point, you wouldn't lose the battle. It would be an indirect something from which this other--the thing you really wanted--would follow automatically. They were extremely good at merchandising.

Q: But they've always been very smooth.

Admiral Richardson: Yes, indeed.

Q: Well, after that job, you were due for sea duty. What were your desires there?

Admiral Richardson: When I had been a rear admiral for two years, ComFAir Norfolk, my friend Mickey Weisner was then the flag officer detailer. He wanted to assign me to a CVS task group at the time, and I said, "Mickey, I don't want one."

"Well," he said, "if you don't do that, you'll never get a CVA division."

I said, "CVA or nothing. I don't want it."

He and Tex Guinn got together on the thing, and they decided among themselves. They were the two BuPers characters. They decided I was being unwise. My guess was that, given the number of CVAs and CVSs we had, they wouldn't keep putting us first in

CVSs, then into CVAs. I just didn't think it was going to happen, and I didn't care one bit for an ASW assignment.

Well, they did manage to get me assigned to a CVA cardiv.[*] I had commanded an air group in an attack carrier. I said, "I fought in wars with the CVs and CVSs. I don't see that I have to learn anything from a CVS to operate a CVA."

The upshot was that in late 1965 BuPers had me going to CarDiv 6, which would operate in the Atlantic. Al Fleming was the cardiv commander, and I was slated to relieve him.[†] Don Griffin, who was CinCUSNavEur, was someone I'd known since he was a lieutenant. He got the word that I would be coming over to relieve Fleming, unless he had objections. He told Fleming, who told me. So my name went in to Dave McDonald for approval, and he said no.[‡] He scratched it off and said, "I want him to be ComCarDiv 7 and then to be ComCarDiv 5 as the permanent commander out in the Gulf of Tonkin." So that's what sent me out there.

The detailer called and said, "You were slated for CarDiv 6, but this has happened."

I said, "Well, the first thing I want you to know is that I am delighted. But now having settled that, tell me what the hell went on."

He said, "Well, Dave McDonald changed it."

So I went in to see McDonald, and I said, "You probably had something in mind when you did that."

He said, "Yeah, one thing. Take care of the lads."

Q: That's all?

Admiral Richardson: That's all. The message was crystal clear: "Don't try to win the bloody war by heroics. Don't get carried away with it. Take care of the pilots." There was too damn much nonsense around then. He knew a lot more about the nonsense. I didn't

---

[*] Cardiv--carrier division.
[†] Rear Admiral Allan F. Fleming, USN, Commander Carrier Division Six.
[‡] Admiral David L. McDonald, USN, served as Chief of Naval Operations from 1 August 1963 to 1 August 1967. His oral history is in the Naval Institute collection.

understand the extent of it then, but I never forgot what he said. As time went on, I came to comprehend what he had in mind, and it was that first and foremost, you take care of those pilots.

Q: Do you think that his choosing you for that job traced back to your time with him in Florida in World War II?

Admiral Richardson: I'm sure that it traced back to the reputation that I had in the Operational Training Command. It had to, because I had not worked for him since. We had met subsequently. He and I went to Heidelberg, Germany, together once, a two-day junket. But I'd known him a long time, and I'm as certain as one can be, without knowing what's in another man's mind, that the reason I was sent there was because he thought I wouldn't put my professional ego, my ambition, or promotion interests above the pilots and the proper employment of the force. I'm convinced he thought that I wouldn't try to exploit the situation to make three or four stars.

Q: Can we read into that, perhaps, that he thought it was an unwinnable war at that point?

Admiral Richardson: He had witnessed so much of the McNamara nonsense that was going on. He later told me that he had complete faith in General Wheeler, the JCS Chairman.[*]

Q: What do you recall about taking up the job and getting started on it?

Admiral Richardson: Well, Jig Ramage was assigned as my chief of staff; I asked for him.[†] He and I had been at the war college together, adjacent rooms there. That's when I first knew him, and I respected him a great deal as an operator. So when I found myself headed out for the Gulf of Tonkin, why, I asked for him, and he gladly came. When I went out, I was assigned to ComCarDiv 7 in a make-you-learn period of about four months, after

---

[*] General Earle G. Wheeler, USA, served as Chairman of the Joint Chiefs of Staff from 3 July 1964 to 2 July 1970.
[†] Captain James D. Ramage, USN.

which I relieved Jim Reedy as ComCarDiv 5 and became the permanent on-station commander there for the balance of a year.[*]

Jig was ordered as chief of staff to ComCarDiv 5, so when I moved over, he had already been there for two or three months. Before that, he was on duty down at Albuquerque in the heavy attack wing doing analyses of--well, it had to do with the creation of improved capability in aircraft nuclear weaponry. It was a very fine job he was in, but the minute he had a chance to get out and into the war, he was very happy to go.

Q: What were your first activities?

Admiral Richardson: We flew west, and this was about six weeks after I relieved. We went aboard the Enterprise in the Philippines in April '66. I was very fortunate. The staff that I took over had made a previous deployment. Only the chief of staff was new. The operations officer was Bob Hunt, and his assistant was Dicky Wieland, both very competent.[†] Bob is the one who opened my eyes to the exploitation of intelligence, and this was after we got out west. I had gone down to see Ralph Cousins, and I wanted to know what the system was for target selection.[‡] What Ralph told me was, "Well, some Yankee team commanders are hipped on railroads, others on bridges. There really isn't a system."

Bob Hunt said, "If you want to screw up the other guy, you find out how he functions and you focus your attack on his weaknesses." He said, "I think I can develop a system for target selection that would make a lot of sense and not be quite so wasteful as what we've been doing."

Q: How much latitude did you have in doing that?

Admiral Richardson: Well, we had almost complete latitude in the interdiction campaign. We had no latitude in striking Alfa targets, which were the targets in and around Haiphong and Hanoi, the northern regions--none at all. But for the interdiction campaign, which was

---

[*] Rear Admiral James R. Reedy, USN.
[†] Captain Robert F. Hunt, USN; Captain Dicky Wieland, USN.
[‡] Rear Admiral Ralph W. Cousins, Commander Carrier Division Nine, 1965-66.

down in route packages three, two, and one, we had a great deal of freedom--not complete freedom, but a great deal of freedom. We received some guidance.

So I made Bob targeting officer, and he picked out an intelligence officer to work with him. Those two worked together in a map room with photography and air-strike records. Of course, Bob had a lot of clout on the staff, being the senior one next to the chief of staff. Dicky Wieland took over duties as ops officer. Bob started doing a careful sequential study of the past strike photography. He finally ascertained the scheme that the Vietnamese were using to move their supplies south.

When a railroad was cut, they would simply off-load at that point and put the stuff they had onto vehicles and continue a move south. Or if there were mountains nearby, they dug into the hillsides and created any number of supply storage areas, and they put supplies in there. They went to work repairing the railroad, and when they had that repaired, they moved farther down. But they really would "worry" their supplies south by rail, road, or barge, transshipping as necessary, but they kept the movement going. If you put a bridge out, why, they created a bypass to that bridge. They'd float it across or walk it across in shallow water and then reload on the other side.

Q: Very ingenious.

Admiral Richardson: Very ingenious. The end result of their effort across a period of several months was to create what amounted to a supply area that was 50 miles long, north of Vinh in that narrow coastal area. So when you made a cut further up, they simply started drawing down from the supplies that were below that cut. They then began to move in antiaircraft into the area. There was none at first.

Bob's explanation of that was, "Well, you have a choice. You can hit a large bridge in town, or you can knock out three small bridges, seemingly insignificant ones, out of town along the railroad or the road line." And he said, "Then they have to send people out and they have to send food out, and you're talking 10 or 20 miles out maybe. They have to repair the outer bridge before they get to the next bridge. You do a lot more damage, create a much bigger problem by destroying several small bridges in a sequence than knocking out some big, attractive-looking bridge in town where they all are, and where they can pull boats down into place and move across."

That was the general line of thinking, and at that time we had photographs of barges in their canals. An Olympic runner could run for 20 miles jumping from barge top to barge top. I've seen photographs of the waterway literally with barges touching barges for miles on end. And so I sent Bob down to Saigon. Barges were off limits. We might damage the countryside if we broke a levee or something like that, which we thought would be a hell of a good idea. We'd love to break it. But it was off limits.

So I sent Bob down to brief Westmoreland and his staff on barges and their significance in the moving of traffic south to get the constraints lifted from striking barges.[*] Well, that worked. They probably had to go back to JCS or maybe CinCPac. Anyway, we got the authority to strike barges, and in no time at all, the barges were out of the picture as logistical supply vehicles.

Q: You were working for Seventh Fleet, but MACV was making the rules of engagement?[†] Is that what you're saying?

Admiral Richardson: I was working for Com7thFlt, but CinCPac was in control of all that was being done, or thought he was, and he would set priorities. For example, one of his priorities was to destroy all oil supplies. Very wise generally, but that wasn't always the best thing to do. And one of the things we learned as time went on, and as more and more bypasses were being created and as the AA defenses were going up on a broader scale, we could see that our effectiveness was not such that we were going to win.

The thing that never registered in the thinking back in Washington was the adverse impact of the weather there on flight operations. They had surface-to-air missiles, the SA-2s. We declared, for our own purposes, an operable day as a day that had five miles of visibility and no overcast, because if you flew above an overcast, you were going to get hit by missiles. You couldn't avoid them. Without an overcast, 10,000-foot ceiling with five

---

[*] General William C. Westmoreland, USA, served as Commander U.S. Military Assistance Command Vietnam from 20 June 1964 to 2 July 1968.
[†] MACV--U.S. Military Assistance Command Vietnam.

miles' visibility was adequate to properly make a bombing run. If we got that kind of weather for a four-hour period, that was an operable day.

We kept a chart of how many operable days we had each month of the year, and during July, August, September, there would be 17, 18, or 19 operable days. October, November, December--ten, eight, six. January, February, March, April--two, three. The operable days in January, February, March, December maybe, were the days immediately following the passage of a typhoon--clear, crystal clear, and marvelous for air strike operations for about two, maybe three days. So we exploited that, because we were able on our radar to plot very accurately where a typhoon was, and we'd stay right up in there until the last minute. Then when we had to come out, out we'd come fast; and as it went by, we chased it and would go right in behind it. Radars made that easy--no problem at all.

But we were dealing with a situation wherein during November to late April we might get three or four days or five days a month at most when we could operate air strikes. And, of course, the point is when you damage an interdiction target system, you've got to be able to concentrate a lot of strikes from more than one carrier--two or three carriers--into a fairly narrow area, and get everything in that area, to really stop that flow. Then you're going to have to re-strike it within a fairly short period of time, because repairs are being made, and their system of a warehouse 45 miles long, a supply center 45 miles long, is very difficult to defeat.

Of course, other activity was taking place behind the mountains over in the Seventh Air Force areas, but we were concerned with our own area, working that problem. We didn't have access--nor knowledge, really--of what they were doing in the other area. I kept the air commander in Saigon informed about what I was doing. I made a visit and explained to him our whole process, so he'd know. Then we had exchange Air Force officers operating with us. They loved to operate with the Navy because they had freedom and they saw the naval aviators--the CAG and the squadron commanders, the strike leaders--had so much to say about what they did and how they did. In the Air Force it wasn't that way at all.

Anyway, out came the director of Defense Research and Engineering, Johnny Foster, and Dr. Herzfeld.* Dr. Herzfeld is a high-level official right now in OSD. Bob Hunt briefed them on the targeting system that he had developed, and I had adopted and implemented. Bob explained that if we put our talents on improving flight deck operations, we could perhaps have increased our effectiveness by 5%. But if we could choose targets wisely, we could multiply, we could double or triple our effectiveness. Herzfeld made the remark, "That's a force multiplier," and that's when that term was born. It was as a direct result of a briefing that Herzfeld received from Bob Hunt.

Then, in further implementation of Hunt's approach to target management, with Johnny Hyland's approval I required all carriers to participate.† Bush Bringle came out to learn about it.‡ He was then assistant chief of staff for operations at CinCPacFlt. We had one of these Seventh Fleet conferences. I made a presentation of this whole scheme there, and Bush wholeheartedly supported it. So, with his support, I converted the FICFPacFac, which is Fleet Intelligence Center Forward Facility in Subic Bay and which had been a photo distribution facility, into an analytical facility. I required all five of the carriers out there to have an operator and an intelligence officer in communion, working the problem of interdiction targeting, and always touching base in Subic with the analytical facility there. That was where we kept the records and where, for example, if a cardiv had made strikes and had success, the photography was also there. This photography was then available to oncoming carriers, and a date would be set which would indicate re-strike time.

Q: How soon after you got out there did you become CTF 77?

Admiral Richardson: Well, I got out there in late April of 1966. We went aboard Enterprise, and then we shifted to Oriskany. We were on Oriskany for a short while. In

---

* Dr. John S. Foster, Jr., served as Director of Defense Research and Engineering, 1965-73. Dr. Charles M. Herzfeld served as deputy director of the DoD Advanced Research Projects Agency, 1963-65, and as director, 1965-67.
† Vice Admiral John J. Hyland, USN, served as Commander Seventh Fleet from 13 December 1965 to 6 November 1967. The oral history of Hyland, who retired as a four-star admiral, is in the Naval Institute collection.
‡ Rear Admiral William F. Bringle, USN.

early August, I relieved Jim Reedy as CTF 77. But by virtue of my forthcoming assignment, I implemented all this stuff before I ever relieved Reedy. Jig Ramage was over there, he was my man, and Jim Reedy was perfectly agreeable to the whole thing. So the system was in effect by the time I took over.

Q: So your role didn't change all that much.

Admiral Richardson: That's right. As the oncoming CTF 77, these things that were different were being placed into effect without any loss of time.

Q: What do you remember about the Enterprise as flagship?

Admiral Richardson: Well, it was an interesting thing. I made Jim Holloway and his air officer very unhappy one time, because they had so much room on their hangar deck that they'd complain from time to time about being overcrowded.* I said, "Well, how about sending your air officer over to the Oriskany and let him take a look at a hangar deck that is really well managed?" The Oriskany was incredible, and it was so far more efficient than the Enterprise in its constrained spaces that it was pitiful.

Q: What do you remember about Holloway as a skipper?

Admiral Richardson: Jim was a fine guy. He knew his ship well, and he operated well. On one occasion, he had that radar that was a powerful emitter, and the Russian electronic collector ships--their version of a tattletail--were in the gulf, often near our flagship.†

One day I said, "Jim, let's go by that guy, and when we get right opposite, put every ounce of power into that radar that you can possibly put. Let's see what happens." (I

---

* Captain James L. Holloway III, USN, commanded the aircraft carrier Enterprise (CVN-65) from July 1965 to July 1967. He later served as Chief of Naval Operations, 1974-78.
† "Tattletail" was a nickname for small Soviet ships that steamed in proximity to American warships, observing their movements and, presumably, prepared to provide targeting information in the event the Soviets wanted to attack them.

think it was Don Issitt's idea; he was my chief of staff then.)* So that's what Jim did, and he passed the guy. He wasn't 100 yards at most away from him when he lit off that radar. [Laughter] The tattletail left. He went up into China someplace and was there in port for about three weeks before he came back. We must have blown out every radio tube he had on that thing.

I think the implementation of Hunt's target selection system was the major event of that time. The other very noteworthy experience is that whenever we talk about composing forces and employing them in some area, we better have studied the weather thoroughly. And, of course, for future McNamaras--never forget which end of the lance has the point.

Of course, the Alfa target selection was frequently ridiculous. On one occasion, we had a series of targets assigned to us that were described as "buried and dispersed POL."† We had the photography. It was in an area that was fairly heavy, with surface-to-air missile capability, SA-2s, and I refused to go. We would have consumed more fuel in half the strike group than we could possibly have destroyed if every drum had been full and we'd hit every drum, and there was also the danger. The risk-to-reward danger was cockeyed. I refused and protested to CinCPac. CinCPac backed me, and it died.

I learned later, after coming back to Washington, that the targets were sometimes being selected by LBJ and Walt Rostow on their knees in the Oval Office thumbing through the bombing encyclopedia.‡ If they saw something, POL or whatnot, that caught their attention, they would specify that as an Alfa target.

Q: Secretary McNamara was also involved in running the Vietnam War from Washington. What is your reaction to the whole McNamara approach in general?

Admiral Richardson: It was disastrous. His conduct of the Vietnam War was disgraceful. When I had CTF 77 and was filling out the OpRep system--1, 2, 3, 4, 5--half of my staff

---

* Captain Donald K. Issitt, USN.
† POL--petroleum, oil, and lubricants.
‡ LBJ--Lyndon B. Johnson served as President of the United States from 22 November 1963 to 20 January 1969. Walter W. Rostow served as a special assistant to the President from 1966 to 1969.

was engaged in reporting back to Washington and informing them of what we had done, were doing, and were going to do.[*]

The bombing shortage was indeed a shortage, especially in the context of the weather conditions that we had and the need to go all out when we had good weather. But we were McNamara-constrained to use only a few weapons, and we had to use up those big fat bombs instead of sleek new ones. The old bombs increased substantially the danger to the pilots, because they were forced to fly more slowly, and they couldn't turn as effectively in avoiding surface-to-air missiles.

He was, as SecDef, a complete disaster. His basic idea was that everything would be fed up to him, and he would then know how to manage all of it. The spear was pointed in the reverse direction. The entire thing was turned around. What should be the position of the SecDef, particularly when you have troops in combat, is to find out what they need and want and provide it to them. They have a hell of a lot better grasp on their needs and problems than anyone sitting back in a comfortable office in the Pentagon or the White House.

At one point in time when I had come back from the Gulf of Tonkin, Admiral Moorer was then the CNO. He required every OP-60 paper that dealt with the Vietnam War to be sent to me for my chop. I was OP-05 Bravo at the time. But, anyway, down all the OP-60 stuff would come on every Vietnam issue, and in the course of performing that way, I had occasion to review the JCS summary of recommendations over several years that they had made to the SecDef, his actions on them, and the dates when he took these actions. About half of them were just simply disapproved. A great many of the others, nearly all the others, had dates when they were enacted, partially approved, or approved, three months, six months later.

He had no respect at all for the people working the military problem. Oh, there were so many instances, many preceding Vietnam. Arleigh Burke could tell you some fascinating ones. One had to do with the firing of George Anderson the time when McNamara was giving squads left and squads right to this destroyer skipper who was intercepting the Soviet ship going into Cuba and suspected of carrying missiles.

---

[*] OpRep--Operational report.

I gave a briefing on Vietnam to a bunch of reserve Navy captains shortly after I came back. One of the reserve Navy captains, on his two weeks' active duty stint, was a high official in the Ford Motor Company, and he said, "Well, how do you like your SecDef?"[*]

I made some remark that I didn't want repeated around. I said, "Well, he wasn't my choice."

He said, "Well, your misfortune is our good luck." He had an enormous mental capability, but no wisdom.

Q: And also the feeling that everything could be and should be quantified.

Admiral Richardson: Yes.

Q: A disdain for professional experience.

Admiral Richardson: Oh, we saw a number of examples of that. I mentioned all these OpReps that were sent back. But systems analysis didn't know what they signified when they got them. The computer was filled with that sort of stuff, but they didn't know what it meant. They were always coming back to us for explanations, which we would do without the benefit of computer. We had copies of all our reports, so we'd go through and say, "This means so and so." We already knew what it meant.

When the surface-to-air defenses in North Vietnam had increased to the point that it simply was too dangerous for the A-1s to go in over land in the northern areas, I restricted them.[†] My flag lieutenant was an A-1 pilot, and he strenuously fought the restriction, but anyway, I did it, because it simply was getting too dangerous. So when that word got to Enthoven, I got a message back. It was a typical systems analysis. It pointed

---

[*] McNamara had been an executive with the Ford Motor Company from 1946 to 1961, serving as president, 1960-61.
[†] Douglas A-1 Skyraider propeller-driven attack planes first entered fleet squadrons in late 1946; at the time they carried the designation AD. The AD-7 version was 39 feet long, wing span of 51 feet, gross weight of 25,000 pounds, and top speed of 318 miles per hour. It could carry a bomb load of up to 8,000 pounds beneath the wings and fuselage. In 1962 Skyraiders still in service were redesignated A-1s.

out that the A-1 carried several times the bomb load of an A-4, there was one pilot in the A-4, the shootdowns in the A-4 were so and so.[*] The shootdowns in the A-1 was such and such.[†] This shows that the A-1 was three times more effective than the A-4 but lost only twice as many pilots. Therefore, why did we take the A-1 off the line? And I thought, "My God, I don't want any of our pilots ever to see this." That line of thinking, where they equated a pilot's life to the cost of a bomb was, to me, absolutely unbelievable. Nothing wrong with the mathematics, though.

Q: Really a callous approach.

Admiral Richardson: Well, I prefer the word "stupid." It was such a shame. But we saw so much of that sort of thing.

Q: Did you view pulling back on the use of A-1s to be part of your mandate from Admiral McDonald to take care of the pilots?

Admiral Richardson: I suppose so. I didn't specifically connect it with that. It just was apparent that there was too much AA, and it was increasingly dangerous to the A-1, so I decided just to keep it out of the more dangerous areas, especially where there were SAMs.[‡] We had quite a struggle over that for a couple of days while the staff fought one side, then the other. We had a lot of discussions about it, but the general feeling was that it was too dangerous. There were A-1 stalwarts who wanted the A-1 to stay on. They would have flown it through hell.

Q: They might have been forced to fly through hell had they stayed on.

Admiral Richardson: That's exactly right.

---

[*] The McDonnell Douglas-built A-4 Skyhawk was a jet bomber used at the time in Navy and Marine Corps light attack squadrons.
[†] The Vought A-7 Corsair II was another light attack plane flown from carriers in that period.
[‡] SAMs--surface-to-air missiles.

Q: What do you remember about the A-6s and A-7s and their roles?

Admiral Richardson: The A-6s were remarkable, and, of course, that's been written up since in book form.[*] They could fly low, and they were very, very effective in the long strikes with the heavy loads they could carry.[†]

But the unfortunate thing was that even while we were down there, the North Vietnamese were analyzing their own vulnerabilities and taking measures to reduce them. One thing that we noticed in short order was that everything we hit was either an orphanage or a hospital. After so many months, if you added up all the orphanages and hospitals, it must have exceeded the buildings they had in the entire country.

Let's go back a minute to the Oriskany. There were two people on the Oriskany. Gordon Smith and his very close friend Bill Smith were A-1 pilots.[‡] When they went in on strikes, they carried hand cameras with them, and they took pictures. They had a remarkable collection of pictures, both of them.

Bill Smith came over with this set of pictures--there must have been 200 or so slides--and showed them to me. It was by far the best photography that I had seen of the events taken while they were going on. You'd see two or three photos of an SA-2 missile out on the highway chugging along, and then the first thing you know, it was in a village where we could no longer attack it. It was out of bounds then. It was home safe, and here you see the picture of that. The photography was remarkable, and in color. It was so good, I had sent him up to Johnny Hyland. Johnny Hyland sent him back to Roy Johnson at CinCPacFlt, who sent him up to Oley Sharp.[§] He briefed Sharp, who sent him back to McNamara, and he briefed him with this photography. Then Smith came back out.

---

[*] See, for example, René Francillon, Tonkin Gulf Yacht Club: US Carrier Operations off Vietnam (Annapolis: Naval Institute Press, 1988) and Peter B. Mersky and Norman Polmar, The Naval Air War in Vietnam (Annapolis: Nautical and Aviation Publishing Company of America, 1981).
[†] The A-6 had a maximum bomb capacity of 17,280 pounds.
[‡] Commander Gordon H. Smith, USN, commanded Attack Squadron 152 from February 1966 to March 1967. Lieutenant Commander William Cody Smith, USN.
[§] Admiral Roy L. Johnson, USN, served as Commander in Chief Pacific Fleet, 30 March 1965 to 30 November 1967. Admiral Ulysses S. Grant Sharp, USN, served as Commander in Chief Pacific from 30 June 1964 to 31 July 1968.

Well, at that point in time, Bill Smith had something like 270 flights over in North Vietnam, and he went on to exceed 300. When I learned that, 200 was the rotational base figure for daily completion. We figured that they'd had their share of the danger in that number of flights. And so I called the skipper of the Oriskany and said, "Don't let him fly anymore. He's up to 300, and he's just pushing his luck. Don't let him fly." So he was grounded.

Well, Bill Smith talked the skipper into letting him go again. He finally got 306 flights, as I remember, before he got shipped out. So Gordon Smith and Bill Smith were the two that were doing this.

Years later, about 15 or so, over-the-horizon targeting was very much the subject--I went in to see Gordon Smith, who was now a rear admiral and Deputy NavElex, and we were talking about things. I was very concerned at this point in time as a member of the intelligence panel with the development of capability to counter SSN-3 missiles and technologies that go with that. He had in his office a Captain Smith, who was the over-the-horizon, OTH, targeting officer working that problem. Well, in comes Captain Smith, sporting a large mustache. I looked at him, he looked at me. He said, "You don't know me."

I said, "No."

He said, "I'm Bill Smith."

"For God's sake."

Bill Smith was enormously imaginative, really effective in that OTH targeting. He got Dr. Bob Hess, who was the technical director for the Navy space system, to work with him. They had a little cabal of maybe a half a dozen people, all of whom were of the same mind in this business of OTH targeting, struggling with that problem. They were providing, in effect, the targeting capability for Tomahawk missiles against moving targets. Not only is the target a matter of concern, but any other ships that might be in the general vicinity that you might encounter before you hit your target. So they were working that whole problem of OTH targeting to get moving targets, the effort led by Bill Smith.

Well, Bill Smith later had an automobile accident, and he was paralyzed from the neck down. He had just the use of his one hand. He continued working. He went through therapy. Mitre Corporation took him on. He was here at Naval Ocean Systems Center working the OTH problem. He invented a wheelchair that he could steer and manage, and the company bought the thing. They are now building wheelchairs using his electronic control. He bought a vehicle to move around in, one where he could get in and he could drive. A man with just one hand, now he's driving. Then he got a second vehicle.

I used to see him frequently at NOSC here, and he said, "How about coming riding with me one day? I want to show you how this van works."

I said, "I'd love to."

Well, about two weeks later, he was coming down the hill on Hawthorne Street in San Diego, directly toward the bay. Something happened. He went out of control. His vehicle went across Harbor Drive, over the bank, and into the bay. People dove in to pull him out. The vehicle was constructed so that its access was the rear. They didn't know. They couldn't open a door. The window was up. He was inside alive, in the water, helpless, and they literally watched him drown, trying to rescue him.

Gordon Smith and Bill Smith, I guess when Bill was injured, there wasn't a day that passed that Gordon didn't contact him by telephone, wherever he happened to be, one way or another, and give him support.

Q: Were they both in the Oriskany air group?

Admiral Richardson: They both were in the Oriskany air group. Both were flying A-1s. Then the Oriskany fire occurred.[*] I was awakened about 7:00 A.M. I usually worked till about 2:00 or 3:00 in the morning, then went to bed. I'd get up around 8:00 or 9:00 the next morning. I went up to the bridge and saw smoke pouring out of Oriskany. I decided to fly over and see what was taking place.

Q: What ship were you in then?

---

[*] On 26 October 1966, while the aircraft carrier Oriskany (CVA-34) was operating off Vietnam, a parachute flare ignited a fire in the ship's hangar deck. Fouty-four men were killed as a result of the fire.

Admiral Richardson: It was either the Constellation or the Kitty Hawk; I think it was the "Connie."

I took the public affairs officer with me, a commander, and we landed on deck. I wanted to see if the crew was fighting, how they were going. You could see what looked like a waterfall coming out the elevator opening at the port side of the hangar deck. And, yes, they were working like mad but no panic or anything like that. We had a couple of destroyers trailing behind to pick up anybody that dove overboard from a hot spot. So they were fighting it, and there wasn't anything we could do.

There was a Life magazine reporter aboard Oriskany at that time. He was busy taking photographs of this whole episode. A chief grabbed the camera and stopped him. I didn't see it, but my PAO saw it.[*] He went over, took the camera away from the chief, and gave it back to photographer and told him to take all the pictures he wanted. I learned about it afterward. So anyway, all those pictures that we saw in Life magazine came about because of that, and it was the proper thing to do.[†] Facts are less harmful than fiction. So after talking with the skipper and observing what was going on, it was clear they were doing everything possible. Then I flew on back.

We lost a number of people in the air group during that fire. I learned that a Mark 24 flare had been off-loaded from a plane, then dropped. Instead of ditching it into the ocean, a new crewman threw it into the ammunition locker. It triggered all the rest of the flares there. And, of course, fumes and everything went right up the starboard side of the ship and into the area where all the pilots lived. They were asleep, so we lost a lot of people. Bill Smith was away on a trip at that time. He hadn't returned from his long visit that went back as far as McNamara.

Q: Did you conduct an investigation?

---

[*] PAO--public affairs officer.
[†] Life, 25 November 1966, pages 104-119. Included with the spectacular photos in color, the coverage included an article by Don Moser titled, "Fire in Alpha 107 Mike!"

Admiral Richardson: Yes. We learned what the cause of it was, and, of course, the fix is better training of individuals. It was just a stupid act, throwing a lighted flare into an ammunition storage area.

Q: Why would anybody do that?

Admiral Richardson: It was a kid who was frightened, and that's what he did, threw it into the area right by the elevator well. But here he was, right next to the ocean. He could as easily have thrown it into the ocean.

There were a lot of anecdotes. I'm trying to recall what else might be of significance. We did get some Alfa targets. We had deep runs in against the steel mills. But what I said earlier was that the Vietnamese had learned to anticipate what would be happening. For one example, by the time we were allowed to strike the power plants, they had received so many portable generators that it didn't hurt them.

We had pilot recovery capability. When we lost a pilot and thought we could get him back, we called in to Saigon and got help from an organization in Tan Son Nhut.[*] We flew them out to the ship, inserted them ashore in North Vietnam, then pulled them back out. Rescue was, of course, a major endeavor that we were constantly engaged in. There are many stories.

One was about the CO of an attack squadron. He got hit over land and managed to fly out to the water, but he didn't realize that he'd lost his right forearm.[†] He couldn't stop the A-4 from rolling until he looked and saw his nearly severed forearm. He then flew using his left hand until over water and recovery. But anyway, he was returned to the States, hospitalized. He just did not want to stop his Navy career.

Later he appeared before medical examiners. I had a long letter from him explaining what had happened and would I support him? The medical board was going to retire him. I said, yes, I would. Roy Johnson did also. We all supported him. The medical people, of course, were of a different opinion. We all went to bat for him, and strongly. I

---

[*] Tan Son Nhut was the name of the U.S. Air Force base at Saigon, South Vietnam.
[†] This incident occurred on 23 July 1966.

pointed out that some of our most effective officers in World War II were crippled, and there's no reason on earth why he shouldn't continue. He wasn't a yeoman.

Q: We have a book coming out from that gent. I think Wynn Foster was his name.[*]

Admiral Richardson: Correct. I corresponded with him for several years during the time he was wanting support to fight the system.

Q: I'm interested in your feeling on whether that interdiction program was a viable strategy.

Admiral Richardson: Well, very shortly after I got back to Washington, I went to see Tom Moorer, who had relieved Dave McDonald as Chief of Naval Operations. I said, "I can tell you whether or not we're winning that war, the interdiction war, that is."

He said, "How are you going to do that?"

I said we had a target selection system, and because we had a system, we had photography associated timewise within that system. "We have the photography we took when I got out there. We have it six months later, and we have it a year later. If we look at that photography, compare the status of Vietnamese target choices then, at mid-term, then a year later, we can judge how successful we have been.

He said, "Go do it."

Several of my officers, when they were detached from CTF 77, were ordered back to Washington, including my intelligence officer, Verne Jennings.[†] So I had him put in charge of the effort, and I think three, four other officers. We sent for photography. There was a lot of it. We collected the necessary photography, and we showed that as time went on, each target was losing its significance as more and more bypasses were created. More and more systems were being created for bypassing damaged areas, using underwater

---

[*] Captain Wynn F. Foster, USN (Ret.), Captain Hook: A Pilot's Tragedy and Triumph in the Vietnam War (Annapolis: Naval Institute Press, 1992). In 1966, as a commander, Foster was commanding officer of Attack Squadron 163 in the Oriskany. Later, following his retirement, he was chairman of the Tailhook Association, an organization of carrier pilots.

[†] Commander Verne H. Jennings, Jr., USN. He was promoted to captain by the time of reporting to Washington. Later in the interview Admiral Richardson discusses the circumstances of the promotion.

pavement, rocks, boat bridges, what have you. Boats or floats stacked upstream were moved down at night, moved back the next morning. We couldn't get into the storehouses that were drilled into hillsides. Occasionally, we could lob a bomb in, but it was luck when we did.

It was apparent that there were more targets, each one becoming less significant, and more thoroughly defended as antiaircraft moved out into a broader area. More and more of the SA-2s came in, so the cost of doing business was going up in terms of losses. The benefits from air strikes were lessening. And there was that weather, that awful weather.

We simply were not winning. We were losing the interdiction campaign, because our improvements were not keeping up with the rate of improvement that the North Vietnamese were able to achieve as they created more and more means for bypassing. And so that said, we were losing the interdiction campaign, that we needed to reexamine our policies on the conduct of it. That's the report that went back to him, and I indicated personally that if we were to insert small amphibious forces in raids in the area along the coast, where the transit areas were only a few miles wide and flat, we could do much more damage using a battalion, or maybe even a company, of Marines, because it was then so lightly defended. We could really wreck things and do far more that way than we could with air wings because of the weather. So we really needed to get into insertion operations if we were going to win that interdiction war where we were.

I don't know what Tom did with it. I do know that not too long after that, the Joint Staff formed up a targeting section to do what we were doing, but it never got anywhere. They didn't understand it, perhaps. There wasn't the motivation, the urgency, yesterday, today, and tomorrow, any of that, and it dried up and disappeared in time. The important thing is not that specific target management system, but that a system--some system--be established that enables people to reason and to see what progress they're making.

Q: You may be able to rationalize that you're winning the battle, but you're losing the war, and, in effect, that's what eventually happened. And the other argument was that mining made so much more sense, because you knock out those ships before they could ever get in and unload, so you don't have to deal with all that product flowing down south.

Admiral Richardson: That's partially right. Some supplies came through China. We weren't allowed to strike the ships, and we finally started a mining campaign with A-3s. We at that point were mining the small rivers that entered the Gulf. One night an A-3 launched. We had a MOMAT, and they armed an A-3.[*] The pilot flew in and thought he dropped his mines. They were unarmed. He had failed to release the arming control. You have a device, and if a mine is released and this wire is not first pulled out, the mine will not explode. They can then land back aboard with mines that way.

Now, what the pilot had failed to do was to set a switch that locked that wire to the airplane, so he dropped unarmed mines. So the next night, the MOMAT warrant officer came to us when the A-3 failed to return. He told us what had happened. The pilot insisted that he wasn't going to let that happen again. He wanted the arming device modified slightly so that it didn't depend on him electrically arming them. So whenever a mine left, it would be armed. One of them must have gone off on impact and blown him up. But he broke the rules and the warrant officer allowed it, which he never should have done.

We did develop mining plans. We mined Haiphong Harbor at a later date with A-6s when I was Deputy CinCPacFlt.

Q: In '72, that happened.[†]

Admiral Richardson: Okay. I was trying to think what mining we did at that point in time. We were also interested in PT boats.

We were keen on the subject of MiGs. It took a Philadelphia lawyer to interpret the rules of engagement. There were two basic requirements. One, the MiG had to be

---

[*] MOMAT--mobile mine assembly team.
[†] In May 1972, confronted by North Vietnamese intransigence at the Paris peace talks and a North Vietnamese spring offensive against South Vietnam, President Nixon ordered the Navy to carry out existing plans for mining the harbors of North Vietnam. On 8 May, A-6 Intruders from U.S. carriers sowed mines at Haiphong, Hon Gai, Cam Pha, Thanh Hoa, Vinh, Quan Khe, and Dong Hoi. The flow of seaborne supplies in North Vietnam ceased immediately.

flown by Vietnamese, not Russians, and the second, it had to evidence hostile intent. Now, if they're flying from Hanoi to Vinh, that wasn't hostile intent. What they would do would be to fly to Vinh one day. Then, when the B-52s came over the next day, they'd launch and attack.[*] When they started up and we had B-52s coming, they were then fair game, but the rest of the time, we couldn't touch them. Then, of course, we had to listen in and be able to recognize the language that was being used to know that it was North Vietnamese and not Russian. So this whole process was itself an absurdity, but those were the sort of things that constrained us. There was many a time we could have shot down MiGs, but we weren't allowed to unless they exhibited hostile intent.

Q: What do you remember about the Ault report and the increase in effectiveness of fighters?[†]

Admiral Richardson: I don't. In '66-'67, we had cases where our pilots were not handling their Sparrows and Sidewinders properly. They were getting in too close or not close enough. We also were landing aboard repeatedly with these weapons, and we weren't sure whether or not the problem was caused by being banged around in carrier landings. That experience became the reason for the fighter weapons school. When we looked into it, we found a whole series of problems that focused on training. They were not technical problems. There were some, but they were minor compared to the training problems. And so we started providing a lot more emphasis on training pilots in employment of these weapons.

  I never saw the Ault report. I think it started and was completed after I left for Sixth Fleet.

---

[*] The Boeing B-52 Stratofortress is an eight-engine jet-propelled heavy bomber flown by the U.S. Air Force. The first B-52s were delivered to the Strategic Air Command in June 1955. The Stratofortresses built, the B-52H model, were delivered to the Air Force in October 1962. Some upgraded B-52s are in the active inventory in the 1990s.

[†] In early 1969 the Navy issed the Ault Report, which led to considerable change in fighting training procedures and maintenance. The author of the report was Captain Frank W. Ault, USN. For an account published 20 years afterward, see "The Ault Report Revisited," The Hook, spring 1989, pages 36-39.

Q: I'm confident that it was. What do you remember about logistic support? You were consuming a lot of bombs at that point.

Admiral Richardson: During the good weather, the summer of June, July, August, September of '66, we had a limit placed on us of how many "good" bombs we could use, and then I had to allocate a limit on each carrier. They were only permitted to drop so many bombs, and we had a lot of 250-pound bombs, which were next to worthless. The 500-pound bombs were better, but the 1,000-pound bomb was really the least size that was effective and created any real disturbance, and, of course, the 2,000-pound bombs. We had a great stack of those old fat bombs, World War II things, that we put on the A-1s as much as we could in the lower threat areas. They slowed down the A-4s and F-8s so much that we wouldn't use them except in limited fashion.

So we had to submit the OpReps--one, two, three, four, and five. And so when we couldn't get an alleviation of the bomb limit, I directed the staff to schedule flights as if we had all the bombs that we could possibly use, in whatever type we wanted. Then in the next day's OpRep, we would indicate "canceled for lack of weaponry." That way, we'd have a measure of the bomb shortage. So would Washington. [Laughter] We did that three or four days, and then I got a message from Roy Johnson at CinCPacFlt that just said three words: "Knock it off." So I don't know what flak he was getting while McNamara was distorting the truth by denying there was a bomb shortage. There were plenty of bombs you couldn't use, no lack of those. Washington was speeding up production, and there wasn't anything really you could do until production lines got moving, this being a long time after they started. War on the cheap!

Q: I interviewed Kent Lee, who relieved Holloway as skipper of the Enterprise.[*] Lee said the division of labor was that he, as the ship's captain, ran the tactical formation, and the admiral ran the targeting. Was it that way during your time?

---

[*] Captain Kent Lee, USN, commanded the Enterprise from 1967 to 1969. The oral history of Lee, who retired as a vice admiral, is in the Naval Institute collection.

David C. Richardson #2 - 211

Admiral Richardson: That's right. The Yankee Station commander was actually in charge of all the strike operations, and the CAGs, working with the intelligence officers and the ship's operations officers, worked the details out.* One CAG arrived. He was determined to go in at low altitude. He felt he could defeat the AA that way. We said no, but he insisted. We said, "Well, okay, give it a try." He lost people right away. We stopped that. They wanted to try it, and so they did. It didn't work, and we quickly choked it off. We shouldn't have permitted it. We really knew better. But on the other hand, we felt that, well, maybe there's something we don't know, and we allowed it.

Q: How much appreciation during this year did you have of how well the war as a whole was going?

Admiral Richardson: Well, it seemed to me a year in which I kept learning more and more and not liking what I saw. It also seemed to me that given the resources that we had and assuming that there was some bit of balance that the North Vietnamese would see how foolish it was and what enormous costs they were paying, they'd stop. They had their half of the country. They didn't need to assert themselves over the Roman Catholics in the South, who were there by choice, many of whom had come out of North Vietnam and moved south. We saw, certainly, evidences of their determination that were very, very impressive, but that was it.

Q: Any recollections on your relationship with the fleet commander, Admiral Hyland?

Admiral Richardson: He was a delight to work with. He'd come down and stay with us part of the time aboard his flagship, then sometimes aboard the carrier with me. Roy Johnson would come out from time to time and would witness the operations and the functioning of the staff and all that sort of thing. They both were pleased.

---

* During the initial stages of involvement in the Vietnam War, the U.S. Navy maintained aircraft carriers on two stations based on Civil War designations--Yankee Station off North Vietnam and Dixie Station off South Vietnam. The latter, which began on 16 May 1965, was dropped 15 months later once airfields were available ashore in South Vietnam.

Q: Hyland is one enthusiastic guy.

Admiral Richardson: A sweetheart. He's a wonderful gent. He's a man of principle.

Q: How much coordination did you have with the other division commander, the subordinate, when you were task force commander?

Admiral Richardson: We laid out the policies and supervised the target selection process, so the others simply implemented that system. They chose the individual targets for the day. We were often up in Yokosuka, Hong Kong, Manila, or somewhere else. We all were rotating onto the line. We'd be down 29, 30, 31 days, and we'd go off for about two weeks, then back again. Sometimes there were two of us up there, often one. Yankee Station command was rotated. But it was within the policies that were established, and we saw the work they were doing.

Q: How demanding was that physically? How much did it test your stamina?

Admiral Richardson: I don't think it bothered those of us in the staff. It certainly tested the stamina of the people in the planes, but not the rest of us.

Q: Well, and also the ship skippers.

Admiral Richardson: That wasn't a problem.

Q: Anything more on that tour of duty?

Admiral Richardson: I'm sure there are things I should be mentioning and have forgotten for the moment, but let's move on.

Q: So after that, you went back to Washington.

Admiral Richardson: As assistant to the DCNO (Air) for one year, during which time I made a number of talks to groups of people in different cities. Tom Moorer sent me out. He'd get requests from a congressman for someone to come out and "explain the war." And on one occasion, I ran into a very hostile crowd of about 600 people in Milwaukee. One of the gents at the head table was in Navy uniform, a reserve commander, but he was a local and a lawyer. He said, "If you get a real tough problem you don't want to answer, just pass it to me." [Laughter] I made my talk. One of the questions came back immediately, "My question is, if we finally get a proper President after this next election, are we going to have to retrain all our pilots?"

I had described how careful we were to not hit nonmilitary targets. These were some of the guidelines we had. We'd run an attack. If the first five or six planes got close hits, there was so much debris in the air, the last five or six in the strike group couldn't specifically see their targets, so they weren't allowed to drop. Those were the guidelines that were imposed on us because of the desire to avoid any civilian damage.

Well, there wasn't any civilian anything that you could damage; everything was military at that point in time. It didn't matter what it was. All the civilians and their activities had long since moved out. So that's what provoked this particular question.

Q: So how did you answer the question?

Admiral Richardson: I think I just sort of shook my head at it. Not my question.

Q: Let the lawyer handle that.

Admiral Richardson: I think--or maybe hope--I said, "Anybody want to volunteer an answer?" I don't really remember. One man got up and made it all very clear. He said, "Get in and get it over with, or get out." They were a very nice crowd. I thoroughly enjoyed it, but the questions were all critical of McNamara; oh, boy, they had no use for

McNamara and the way he was conducting the war. So they were asking questions, and there wasn't any way I could allow myself to join in a criticism of McNamara.

Q: As much as you would have wanted to.

Admiral Richardson: Much as I would have wanted to, I couldn't do that. All this nonsense about constraints. They weren't interested at all in that. They had one view: "Let's get in and get it over with or get out." It was very interesting to get the viewpoints and compare them against all these constraints we had.

We attacked the power plant in Haiphong after a long, long time and after, in fact, there was no power coming from it. It had been abandoned. They had gone to power generators that were portable. But it was still a power plant, and the North Vietnamese had learned not to depend on it, not to count on it. So we got it assigned, and we attacked it.

I got a message: highest authority wants to know, "Did you hit any civilians?"

I asked, "Who's seen this message? Tell any and everyone who's seen this message to say absolutely nothing to the pilots about it." The people in "highest authority" didn't ask how many pilots we lost. Instead, it was, "How many civilians did you hit?" So we got the photography and looked at it. The answer back was that all bombs landed within the target area, with the exception of one bomb which was outside in a culvert right alongside a bridge. No evidence of any civilians having been killed. And that's what went back to "highest authority."

That thing bypassed CinCPac and CinCPacFlt. They could have stopped it, but it went through from "highest authority." It wasn't stopped, and it should have been stopped. It never should have been allowed to get down to where the pilots were. Their commander-in-chief's concern is far more for the civilians in the hostile country than for his own pilots.

Q: Yesterday you mentioned Admiral Gene La Rocque. What do you remember about the time he accompanied the Under Secretary of the Navy on a visit to the Seventh Fleet?*

Admiral Richardson: After I returned to Washington from my year as CTF 77, La Rocque came to see me one day and requested that I go see the Under Secretary of the Navy.† He had recently escorted the Under Secretary out to WestPac. The secretary had spent some time on the carriers with Rear Admiral Roger Mehle, who had relieved me as CTF 77.‡ The Under Secretary was very unhappy with what he saw, said La Rocque, and would I mind going around and straightening him out?

I said, "Roger, what do you have in mind for me? Shall I go knock on the door and say, 'Mr. Secretary, I understand your views are all screwed up. I'm here to straighten you out'?" I said, "I'll be glad to talk to him if he sends for me, asks for me, but I don't feel I have any business inviting myself in to discuss with him what he saw out there."

Q: In what way did La Rocque think that the Secretary was off the track?

Admiral Richardson: Well, he just said the Under Secretary had a bad impression of what he had seen. What he had seen, I don't know. It was not at all clear to me at that point in time what it was that had made him unhappy, whether it was the conduct of operations, whether it was the way things were being done, whether it had to do with personalities or what. I later learned that it had to do with an event and maybe other events. I know of only one, and that was when Roger Mehle became very dramatic during a briefing that was being given the Under Secretary and said, "Well, why wasn't I told about that?" and began to chew out some people for having failed to let him know.

The chief of staff was Tex Conatser, and Tex is the source of this story.§ Tex was my chief of staff for several months after relieving Jig Ramage. Tex told me the story. He

---

* The trip was in the summer of 1967. At the time, Rear Admiral Gene R. La Rocque, USN, was serving as Assistant Director of the Strategic Plans Division in OpNav.
† Charles F. Baird served as Under Secretary of the Navy from 1 August 1967 to 20 January 1969.
‡ Rear Admiral Roger W. Mehle, Jr., USN.
§ Captain Charlie N. Conatser, USN.

said that when Mehle complained, he had responded, "Well, Admiral, I woke you up myself this morning about 3:00 A.M. and made this report to you." He said that the Secretary was very unhappy with Roger Mehle, as it turned out.

Well, later--shortly after La Rocque had been to see me--down came the CNO, Admiral Moorer, to see Tom Connolly to discuss this problem that he had with the Under Secretary regarding Roger Mehle.* It had to do with relieving Mehle as CTF 77. I was called in and listened to part of the discussion, but what was clear also was that in the CNO's mind La Rocque had done a poor job in handling the Under Secretary. I don't know what the Under Secretary told Moorer, but I suspect that was the major point--that he felt that Mehle was the wrong man for CTF 77. Ralph Cousins was sent out from CinCPac to relieve him.

Q: Part of it apparently was that the atmosphere was just very tense in the flag mess, that people were walking on eggs, and that situation completely changed when Admiral Cousins arrived. People could relax and do their jobs.

Admiral Richardson: That's exactly right. That tenseness was certainly brought about by Mehle's attitude. For example, my intelligence officer, Commander Verne Jennings, was a very good intelligence officer. He was studious, and when he said what he had to say, he stood by it. He made a presentation to Mehle about something which made Roger quite unhappy. I think it had to do with a report that Jennings prepared. Roger changed the report radically, and Jennings said, "This isn't correct. It's the other way around."

Well, Roger took a dislike to him and gave him an unsat fitness report. Well, there he was. His selection board for captain was about to meet. The flag secretary later told me this himself. The flag sec received this unsat fitness report to mail in, and he "lost" it in his bottom drawer, where it remained until after the board met. [Laughter]

Q: Imagine that. [Laughter]

---

* Vice Admiral Thomas F. Connolly, USN, served as Deputy Chief of Naval Operations (Air) from 1 November 1966 to 31 August 1971. Admiral Connolly's oral history is in the Naval Institute collection.

Admiral Richardson: And didn't mail it in until a month later, and Jennings was selected and promoted. [Laughter]

Q: What was the eventual outcome of the request that you straighten out the Under Secretary?

Admiral Richardson: As far as I was concerned, nothing.

Q: Did you talk to him at all?

Admiral Richardson: No.

Q: Well, it may have been just taken out of your hands by the fact that Admiral Moorer went ahead and took action.

Admiral Richardson: Well, I don't think the Under Secretary felt the need to send for anybody to advise him. I seriously doubt that. He was a very fine man, a very level-headed gent, and he was quite capable of arriving at his decisions without help from me.

Q: I may not be remembering exactly, but I think Admiral Hyland said that La Rocque was sort of provoking the situation and made Mehle appear even worse. And so maybe he was trying to ameliorate that a bit.*

Admiral Richardson: Could be Hyland felt Mehle had been railroaded.

Q: What do you recall about working with Admiral Connolly?

---

* See the Naval Institute oral history of Admiral John J. Hyland, USN (Ret.).

Admiral Richardson: I liked him. I worked intimately with him on the F-14 introduction.[*] Tom Moorer came down at some point and told Tom Connolly to keep me out of the F-14 thing. He said, "Because heads are going to roll, and we want a few left." And so I never got really intimate in the thing, except one time when Connally was on a long trip.

Mac Snowden was the project manager for the F-14.[†] We had--"we" meaning the Navy Department--had sent forward to SecDef a request for 30 TFX, the F-111.[‡] Enthoven and his crowd had cut this back to 21. We were now in the process of reclamaing the cuts, and we were "supposed" to reiterate that we wanted 30. It had all the earmarks of a deliberate scheme to trap us.

Snowden looked at that and said, "The truth is, we don't want any. We were stuck with having to put in 30 in the first place. Now they've cut us to 21, and that's a favorable move. But if we don't reclama this thing, we might have a problem with McNamara. If we do reclama it, then SecDef's got his perfect point to go before the Congress and say, 'Look, we cut the Navy from 30 to 21, but they've asked for 30. They wanted 30, so we have set that back up to 30. So how can you say that the Navy doesn't like it? When we cut them, they objected to it.'"

So then Mac and I sat down. We wrote out a statement which, in effect, said that we accepted the cut that had been imposed by OSD. There were so many competing needs for the relatively scarce dollars that we agreed we would spend those dollars saved from that cut in other much-needed areas.

So we took it in to Tom Moorer and said, "This is one you better go over carefully, because we see a fireworks display coming up." Tom had some changes to make on our draft reply. He spent an hour struggling with the thing, made several modifications, and sent it down.

Well, there was a lieutenant commander Navy supply officer in McNamara's office when this paper hit. He told us what happened. When McNamara saw that we had not

---

[*] The F-14 Tomcat fighter entered the fleet in the mid-1970s. For an article by Admiral Connolly on its development, see "Of Fighters and Facts," U.S. Naval Institute Proceedings, July 1972, pages 113-116.
[†] Captain Macon S. Snowden, USN.
[‡] The F-111--originally designated TFX, for tactical fighter experimental--was a controversial fighter plane that Secretary of Defense Robert McNamara tried to develop in the 1960s for use by both the Air Force and the Navy.

been suckered by that slick trick, he blew up. He said, "By God, I'm not going to stand for the Navy being this obstinate. I'm going to cut all of their EA-6 production. I want that stopped. They'll learn one of these days that they can't do this."

But here was this man who was guided solely by logic and who deplored the employment of emotion, but his response was totally emotional. He cut another program to injure us for having dared to do what we had done.

That whole saga has been written up. I won't go into it. It finally came to an end one night when Stennis had Moorer and Connolly and the Secretary of the Navy over.* Stennis was asking questions, and he wanted Moorer and Connally to answer these questions, but the Secretary of the Navy kept answering them. He was saying, "Mr. Senator, I'll answer that question."

So Stennis, after a couple of those, said, "Admiral Moorer, are you not the chief of all naval operations?"

"Yes, sir."

"And Admiral Connolly, are you not the senior naval aviator?"

"Yes."

"I want to hear your views. I'm not interested in what the Secretary thinks."

So he queried Tom Connolly, and one of the questions he asked Connally was, "What with this new engine?"

Connally's answer was, "Mr. Senator, with all the engines on earth put into that plane, it still would not be a good airplane."

Later, they were in an evening session with Senator Stennis, and a call came from a New York Times reporter to Senator Stennis. He said, "Senator, I understand that you're meeting on the TFX, and we would very much appreciate confirmation. We understand that you will be supporting the buy of the plane, and I just want to confirm that for tomorrow morning's edition." Stennis blew up.

---

* Senator John C. Stennis (Democrat-Mississippi). The aircraft carrier John C. Stennis (CVN-74) is named in his honor.

What had happened was that the McNamara group and Nitze, the people working this problem, had triggered this query.[*] They knew that Stennis had these people questioning them, so they went in from the newspaper side. Stennis would have no part of it. When he came back, that was the end of the TFX as far as Navy was concerned. "There will be none," said he. Yes, that story is absolutely fascinating. It's dramatic as all get-out.

Q: Jerry Miller said he believed that Admiral Connolly sacrificed his chance for a fourth star with that statement.[†] Do you believe that to be the case?

Admiral Richardson: I don't question that at all. It certainly blocked any move that Connolly might have made. Tom Connolly was very competent, but he had an adamancy about him that worried some people, like Wally Wendt. Tom Moorer was in Connolly's office frequently. Moorer was very close to him during those years.

Q: He was a classmate.[‡]

Admiral Richardson: Classmates, and either roomed adjacent to each other or very close, because I was a plebe at that time and I knew them there. I had a very high regard for Tom Connolly. Jerry Miller was Tom Connolly's very close buddy. Tom was really in love, practically, with Jerry Miller, he was so fond of him. They played golf a lot. Several Navy flag officers around the Pentagon were very upset with Jerry Miller. So I went in one day to see Tom and said, "Tom, you are ruining our very fine Jerry Miller. You are spoiling him." Tom was upset for a minute, and I said, "Well, I've had two or three flag officers come to me and say, 'Why don't you get Jerry Miller under control?' I don't control Jerry Miller, but his reputation is suffering, and it's your fault."

---

[*] Paul H. Nitze served as Deputy Secretary of Defense from 1967 to 1969. He had previously been Secretary of the Navy from 1963 to 1967.
[†] Rear Admiral Gerald E. Miller, USN, was then part of the OP-05 organization. He retired as a vice admiral; his oral history is in the Naval Institute collection.
[‡] Both were in the Naval Academy class of 1933, as was Wendt.

Q: Suffering in what sense?

Admiral Richardson: Jerry was being autocratic around the area, and there were several rear admirals that were bothered by him. He was very much Tom's favorite, and Tom needed to sit on him, calm him down a little bit. Jerry's a very competent guy, very attractive in so many ways, but he was getting a little out of hand. He'd been Rivero's executive assistant. He worked with Enthoven. God knows, Jerry didn't mind tangling with anybody. And he was a very gifted, a very, very gifted individual.

Q: Very likable, too.

Admiral Richardson: Yes. But he was riling the ranks, is probably the best way to put it. Flag officers, rear admirals who were senior to him by several years, who were of my time, said, "You ought to get him under control."

I said, "It's not my job. He works for Tom Connolly."

But I did, and Tom said, "Well, I guess you're right." Tom knew this too. "Well, I guess you're right," he said.

Q: That just brought it into focus.

Admiral Richardson: Yes, that's right.

Q: Did that prediction come true that heads would roll on that F-111B?

Admiral Richardson: Admiral Bill Schoech, who had previously commanded Seventh Fleet, was the Chief of Naval Material as the F-111 was coming along.[*] He was involved in the early phases of this plane, and there was an agreement drawn up between him and the

---

[*] Vice Admiral William E. Schoech, USN, served as Chief of Naval Material from 1 July 1963 to 30 April 1965.

Secretary of the Navy. The Secretary of the Navy said, "You write down what the minimum requirements are for this plane."

Bill told me, "There were only three copies of that understanding, and I have one in my safe. I laid out nine requirements that the plane should meet in order to be acceptable. The plane met only one of them." And he said, "It was implied to me that I would move to four stars if I approved the plane."

That meant the Secretary of the Navy found a way of expressing to him that if he withdrew his objection, he would then be rewarded with four stars. He left the Navy instead, so I suppose his head rolled because of that.

Q: So those are two potential four stars who didn't make it on that plane--Schoech and Connolly.

Admiral Richardson: I can't certify that that's true, but I can certify that what I stated about Bill Schoech is true, because he told me himself.

Q: Anything else you remember about that episode?

Admiral Richardson: No, I think not.

Q: What other issues did you deal with in that job?

Admiral Richardson: We spent a lot of time working the war problem. Tom Connolly told me he wanted me to concentrate on winning the war and that the rest of the business that was normal to 05, he would work directly with the people. So that's the way that worked out.

Q: What specifically was involved in that, in winning the war?

Admiral Richardson: Nothing specific about it. It was just that I was to consider that my primary involvement when I was there.

Q: But I mean, did that have to do with getting better weapons, different planes, or just what?

Admiral Richardson: It had to do with military force application and governing policies. It didn't have anything to do with weaponry or aircraft or equipment. It had to do with the targeting processes, the policy processes, talking to people, briefing about it, and that sort of stuff.

Q: Was there anything about personnel training that could be a factor?

Admiral Richardson: No. It was attitudinal, practically all of it. And it wasn't within the Navy that there was a problem; it was external to the Navy.

Q: What do you mean by that?

Admiral Richardson: Well, I mean it had to do with the policies of targeting; I was Moorer's JCS adviser, is what it amounted to. Whenever the JCS found themselves involved vis-à-vis SecDef and the President, I was the Navy "consultant" who was to figure out the solution to that problem. The fact that I couldn't do it was something else again. There's no way I could have solved the political problems and the McNamara mind-set, because it took leadership from the top of a type we did not have in either McNamara or LBJ.

Q: What do you remember about the bombing halts as part of that whole equation?

Admiral Richardson: The bombing halts were disastrous. Just about the time we'd get them really on their knees and where our losses, particularly with the big bombers, were suddenly negligible, there would be a halt. That was a technique that the other side was able to use effectively. Then that, of course, gave them time to regroup.

Q: Were POWs an issue at all when you were in OP-05?[*]

Admiral Richardson: We had a gentleman, a young pilot who was extremely proficient at escaping. He had twice escaped out of North Vietnam. I don't know that he'd been imprisoned and got out, but he escaped. And so we used him to assist in improving the quality of our training facilities for evasion and escape. We have one right over here near Warner Springs.

Q: Anything else about that tour of duty?

Admiral Richardson: I think not. We're going to have to be considering our time here. Why don't we get on into the Sixth Fleet thing. Do you want to continue tomorrow?

Q: Tomorrow I go to the decommissioning of the Missouri. I hope we can finish later in the week.

---

[*] POWs--prisoners of war.

Interview Number 3 with Vice Admiral David C. Richardson, U.S. Navy (Retired)

Place: Admiral Kidd Officers' Club, San Diego, California

Date: Thursday, 2 April 1992

Interviewer: Paul Stillwell

Q: Admiral, we're ready at this point to embark on the next phase of your career, which was taking command of the Sixth Fleet. That certainly was a capstone, being an operational commander at sea as a vice admiral. What do you remember about taking over that job?

Admiral Richardson: Well, the reason that I was sent there was to bring lessons learned in Southeast Asia. One of the most significant naval events of the decade was the creation of the Ocean Surveillance Information System. It started with us in Sixth Fleet. Actually, its genesis was a luncheon conversation with Vice Admiral William Schoech, of TFX fame, who had retired as the Chief of Naval Material. He'd also been Commander Seventh Fleet and was very much intelligence oriented--and William Holcomb, who was out of the Navy but had been Arleigh Burke's principal intelligence operator as a lieutenant commander. I say "operator" because a number of initiatives were taken during that time, and they were done at the instigation and desire of Admiral Burke, but they often were identified by and executed by Holcomb, who was also known as "Whispering Willie." The third person at the lunch was a Mr. Cunningham, who had run Air America in Southeast Asia at an earlier time.*

Back when I had Task Force 77, Schoech and Holcomb were sent out by CNO Dave McDonald to make an assessment. One of the things that they liked was the targeting system that Bob Hunt created and I had implemented. They were very favorably impressed by the briefings they received on that, by the accountability for air strike operations that we were able to give in that context, and by our exploitation of special intelligence in air strikes and rescues.

---

* Air America was an element of the Central Intelligence Agency.

When I was ordered to Com6thFlt, Schoech called and invited me out to lunch. Prior to that, I had gone to see the Director of Naval Intelligence, Fritz Harlfinger, and I asked him what was going on in Sixth Fleet.* He said he didn't know. Why didn't I go out to the CIA and then on out and spend a day with Ralph Cook at the Naval Security Group, then come back and he would see what he could dig up.†

Well, I did that. The three days at the CIA all had to do with SR-71 and were essentially a waste of time.‡ The one day with Ralph Cook at the Naval Security Group out on Nebraska Avenue was a very useful day. When I came back to Harlfinger, he had said he had found nothing, and that was therefore the end of my briefings before going over to Sixth Fleet.

During the course of the afternoon with Schoech, following the lunch, I mentioned this and said it was sad that no one in OpNav could brief me on what Sixth Fleet was doing. It wasn't until several months later that I learned what then happened. Schoech sent Holcomb to see Admiral Moorer, and Holcomb, with a finger waving and with the choice language that he was known for, assaulted the CNO: "You said you were going to straighten out this [expletive] mess, but here's the way. He recited my comment about no one in OpNav knowing what was going on in the Sixth Fleet. He said Moorer got halfway up out of his chair, sank slowly back down in, and sent for Harlfinger.

Harlfinger was instructed by the CNO to put one man directly under him, with his finger in every compartment. He wanted to know in detail what was going on in Sixth Fleet. That pick was Captain Bill Moffit, later rear admiral and one of the early heads of the National Reconnaissance Center in the JCS setup.§

I went to Europe through London, spent several days with Admiral Wendt there, and I've earlier recounted the circumstances of my visit to his morning intelligence briefing.** And then on down to Naples. I relieved on August 14, 1968. Immediately

---

* Rear Admiral Frederick J. Harlfinger II, USN, served as Director of Naval Intelligence from August 1968 to July 1971.
† Rear Admiral Ralph E. Cook, USN.
‡ The SR-71 was a high-flying intelligence aircraft operated by the CIA.
§ Captain Lloyd William Moffit, USN.
** Admiral Waldemar F. A. Wendt, USN, served as Commander in Chief U.S. Naval Forces Europe and Commander in Chief U.S. Naval Forces Eastern Atlantic from July 1968 to June 1971.

following the relief ceremonies, the cardiv commander, who was awaiting his own relief, invited me up to a change of command two weeks later in Nice. I accepted and said that when I got up there, I wanted to see the intelligence material that he had to work with.

Admiral Wendt was down for my change of command. I invited him to join me in the command change up in Nice and to go with me to see the intelligence resources that we had to work with. That took place two weeks later in Nice, following the change in command. We were taken into the carrier's IOIC, the integrated operational intelligence center, and shown Michelin's guides and an occasional picture of no significance. In other words, there was no available intelligence worthy of the name.

Q: Do you recall which aircraft carrier it was?

Admiral Richardson: One of the large carriers, but which one I don't remember. All carriers had IOICs.

Q: Had you gotten much of a turnover from Admiral Martin on the intelligence picture?[*]

Admiral Richardson: No. The Soviet fleet at that point in time was increasing rapidly in the Mediterranean area, and there was in place a NATO surveillance system. Unfortunately, the radars were maintained very poorly. They were located in Greece and Turkey. If we got reports at all, they were two to three hours late, long after the information was of any use.

To mention what was available, the Air Force ran peripheral reconnaissance, and the Navy had a role in peripheral reconnaissance, but we couldn't use the information for hours because there was not a secure circuit that existed between the reconnaissance aircraft and the fleet flagship. This was in the process of being corrected, and I knew when I relieved that within a short time spintcom would be installed.[†] But other than that, there simply was not a surveillance system. Very shortly after, I got myself oriented in current activities.

---

[*] Vice Admiral William I. Martin, USN, commanded the Sixth Fleet from April 1967 to August 1968. His oral history is in the Naval Institute collection.
[†] Spintcom--special intelligence communications.

Q: Did you bring in a new intelligence officer to help implement your program?

Admiral Richardson: No, I didn't. I had a superb intelligence officer by the name of Emory Sourbeer.* Emory died just about a year and a half ago, and, in my view, he was one of the greats in the intelligence community. I came to learn that soon in my tour.

Q: What attributes did he have that made him so valuable?

Admiral Richardson: Well, he was very forward-looking, well-informed, imaginative, and he had a very nice personality. He was uninhibited in working with people who were both junior and senior to him. Completely forthright and very knowledgeable and competent in his profession. He was assisted by two equally fine officers--one, Lieutenant Commander Robert Tolle, who left and went to the war college during 1970; and a second who was an intelligence subspecialist, a line officer named Mike Rodgers.† Mike Rodgers was commanding officer of the naval base at Guantanamo until this past summer, when he retired. He lives now in New England.

Mike Rodgers, incidentally, is the one who taught Tom Clancy how to get in the heads of submariners so he could write realistically about submarine functionings.‡ I've long maintained a relationship with Mike Rodgers. A defector and a prominent writer on Soviet intelligence subjects is a man with the pseudonym of Suvurov. Well, I became acquainted with his writings through Mike Rodgers. He and Mike corresponded. Suvurov was hiding somewhere in England under an assumed name, and I have no idea how Mike Rodgers got to know him, but he did, and they corresponded. I borrowed Suvurov's book. When I returned it, Rodgers was off on three weeks' leave. I called him a couple of weeks later and said, "I hope you got your book back all right. Where were you?"

---

* Captain Emory R. Sourbeer, USN.
† Lieutenant Commander Robert J. Tolle, USN; Lieutenant Commander John Michael Rodgers, USN.
‡ Thomas L. Clancy, Jr., author of The Hunt for Red October (Annapolis: Naval InstitutePress, 1984).

He said the Clancys had invited Peggy, his wife, and him to join them on their vacation, which was in a leased railroad car. They spent three weeks riding the rails in a private railroad car.

Q: It must be very nice.

Admiral Richardson: Mike's comment was, "I've lived high on the hog and I've lived low, and believe me, it's much better high."

Q: He also was involved in that Mayaguez operation in '75.

Admiral Richardson: He was, indeed. He was the skipper of the destroyer that was in that.[*] I went to his change of command that took place here in San Diego. The Marine general, Kenny Houghton, came down, was alternate speaker and delivered one of the most moving comments in a change of command that I've ever heard.[†] He extolled the performance of that ship during the rescue of the Marines that were involved in that operation.

So my two assistant intelligence officers were Bob Tolle and Mike Rodgers. Mike Rodgers, by the way, was a history buff, and when he briefed in the morning, he usually had some historic incident of interest that bore some resemblance to whatever, sometimes humorous, and that was always part of his briefing. He headed up subsequently one of the most sensitive spots in the Naval Intelligence Support Center. He had a team of about ten people that were working with him who were tasked with explaining the seemingly unexplainable.

---

[*] As a commander in May 1975, Rodgers was commanding officer of the destroyer Henry B. Wilson (DDG-7) during recovery of crewmen from the cargo ship Mayaguez, which had been captured by Cambodians. For Rodgers's account of the operation, see U.S. Naval Institute Proceedings, November 1976, pages 108-111.
[†] Major General Kenneth J. Houghton, USMC, was commanding general of the Marine Corps Recruit Depot in San Diego in the mid-1970s.

And then when he was ordered as engineer officer of the Saratoga, Bobby Inman and I both contacted him and said we would get him out of that.* We told him he didn't need to be an engineer on top of being a navigator, a commanding officer, and an intelligence specialist. But Mike said he'd go where they sent him. And he did, and the Saratoga performed magnificently. I'm told that on no occasion did the "Sara" have to operate on only two or three props during his tour. In my earlier associations with the Saratoga in the Med, she never, ever ran on four propellers, always two or three. Mike Rodgers is a very competent individual.

So this was a very high-quality intelligence group that I had, and I had an equally competent sigint group aboard.† The first thing I did was integrate the two of them. Up until that time, because of security regulations, the intelligence people would brief, the operators would brief, and then a very small group would hear the signal intelligence information. We weren't able to handle it as well as we should because it was not being integrated in our minds, although they, of course, had worked across between the 1610 and 1630 communities in the preparation of the brief.‡

I terminated that. We had a single briefing. The two organizations were fully integrated. I obtained additional clearances. It didn't require very many. The morning briefing became not just a once-a-day update on what was going on, but a comprehensive overview of what was going on, and through the rest of the day, the operations officer, chief of staff, and myself, the operations duty officer, were to be kept up to date on all events that took place. I'll come to that a little in just a minute at what that might be.

Now, this I'm getting into has to do with the Ocean Surveillance Information System and its creation, but I want to go back a minute and complete the comments that I made about Admiral Wendt and my visit into the IOIC and being briefed, being shown the intelligence resources, which, as I said, were nil, ridiculously poor.

So I instructed Bob Tolle to develop a message, and this I discussed with Admiral Wendt, and we would go for overhead photography. At that point in time, the

---

* Commander Bobby Ray Inman, USN, an intelligence specialist who later achieved four-star rank and served as deputy director of the CIA in the early 1980s.
† Sigint--signals intelligence.
‡ The officer designator for a cryptology specialist is 1610; for an intelligence specialist it is 1630.

photographic satellites--and it's ridiculous to hide the fact that they have existed. It's been published in books. The Soviets know all about it. So at this point in time in the summer of '68, overhead photography was reserved only for "strategic forces," and that, of course, meant SAC.*

Up to that time the photo systems requirements had been specifically written that they would not be used for tactical purposes, and so the requirements for the system specified architectural features that would prevent tactical forces from using not just photographic, but all of the space systems then in existence.

Q: Who did that, the Strategic Reconnaissance Office?

Admiral Richardson: No. I don't want to get into specifically who's in charge, because who was then still is, and it's still a classified subject.

Q: Somebody made the specification.

Admiral Richardson: Well, the specification was made at the very top level in the government. It had to involve the SecDef, and it had to involve the President or the National Security Council. It was at that level that that decision for strategic use only was made. Remember, the system replaced the U-2.†

Now, what is interesting is that later, in 1977, the Congress required that all space systems be exploited tactically, and they made an allocation of funds to the Air Force, Army, and Navy, and demanded in the appropriation bill that setups be created to bring that about. The organization within the Navy was--its acronym was TENCAP, tactical exploitation of satellites.‡ But this is quite a significant thing that the Congress did, because from that point on, the systems were modified, architectural features were modified to accommodate.

---

* SAC--Strategic Air Command.
† The U-2 is a high-flying photo reconnaissance aircraft.
‡ TENCAP--Tactical Exploitation of National Capabilities.

Systems updates that took place subsequent to 1977 have all highlighted the application of satellite systems for tactical purposes and, of course, they played a major role in the entire Desert Shield planning effort and Desert Storm operations. That's why I mention that and go astray for the moment.

But, anyway, when I got back to the flagship in Gaeta, I called Bob Tolle and said, "I want you to prepare a message we'll send to the CNO by way of CinCUSNavEur requesting overhead photography. We will point out that if we are given a week in which to become effective, we'll solve our own problem. But if they want us to be effective within the first 24 hours, they will have to provide us the intelligence support we need."

This would have been within two or three weeks after I took command. Several days later, the message went in. In December, Admiral George Anderson came over to see what this was all about, and then he left and went back.

Q: He was a part of the President's intelligence advisory committee.

Admiral Richardson: He was a member of the President's Foreign Intelligence Advisory Board at that time. And at some time in December, we received approval to obtain and store overhead photography. Well, immediately following that approval, CinCPacFlt shot in a similar request, which was approved, and, of course, that was much needed in coverage in the Northwestern Pacific.

Anyway, also in December a group from Washington arrived. Let me delay just a minute on that and come back to what happened during September, October, November.

We knew that the British down on Cyprus had a very large and efficient radar that covered the entire Eastern Mediterranean. We had circuitry that enabled us to interconnect with the Brits and exchange information of a highly classified nature in a very short period of time, information known as operational intelligence--the operational intelligence circuit.

I invited the British commanding officer of the station to visit with us on Sixth Fleet. He came up, and we proposed a tie-in. We wanted him to keep us informed on all information that would be of interest, especially Soviet Navy activity. We showed him around, what we were doing, what our interests were, the kind of information we needed.

He agreed. From that time on, we were receiving information updates on air and surface ship activity in time frames of three to five minutes from the time it occurred.

We set about getting a radar for Malta under Brit control, and we even toyed with the idea of getting one in Tunis, but decided that as sure as anything, if we put one in, that would bring the Soviets in, and we decided the best thing to do was to leave that out. We established liaison officers with the Central Intelligence Agency in Rome and in Athens, and they were able to update us on matters of interest. They were channels also to Greek, Turkish, and Italian military commands.

We were quite interested in Soviet air activity. At that point in time, Egypt was ruled by Nasser, and there was evidence that perhaps the Soviets might be putting some nuclear weapons into the Egyptian area, and we were concerned about that.[*] The Soviets often flew their reconnaissance aircraft over Yugoslavia, down the Adriatic, and into the Med. We got coverage on that, thanks to the Italian Air Force, via the CIA.

We were informed from Italian sources when the Soviet reconnaissance aircraft were approaching into the Mediterranean area, and were often able to get pictures because the Italian Air Force would fly up and photograph these planes from time to time at our request. We were interested in the specifics of the types of planes that came down. Some planes are capable of handling nuclear weapons and others are not, and we particularly were interested in whether or not any nuclear weapons were going into Egypt.

So we had major elements of a Mediterranean Ocean Surveillance Information System, thanks to the Brits on Cyprus. Our own resources and the Brits' combined gave us pretty thorough surveillance of the entire Mediterranean area and of the air activity over the northern part and the eastern part of the East Mediterranean.

So I then decided to test the efficiency of our surveillance by holding what we called National Week exercises. We started the first one, National Week One, within just two or three months after I took command. My operations officer wanted to also use this exercise to work the air wings, one against the other, and it fitted beautifully together with that. So we commenced the series of exercises known as National Weeks, and they're still carrying

---

[*] Gamal Abdel Nasser was head of Egypt--variously as President and Prime Minister--from 1954 until his death in 1970.

those out. Those evolved soon into developing tactical responses to the kinds of deployments and situational structures that the Soviets were using. As we monitored their patterns of operation, we then began on a perfectly normal, everyday basis of reacting to what we were learning in response to, you might say, the change in threat that would exist. Always the threat is changing up and down, and as the threat would increase, we would initiate movements to counter that.

To give an example of how these things come together, on one occasion as we monitored a Soviet exercise in the Med, we saw that they postulated a Sixth Fleet carrier group approaching them. They then dispatched a Kynda cruiser with SSN-3 missiles to get an attack off on their exercise ship that was simulating a Sixth Fleet carrier.

We noticed that in its approach to its hypothetical enemy, the Soviet cruiser hugged the shoreline. It was never more than five miles off the coast. The reason for that was that the effectiveness of surface ship radar, against a surface ship moving close to the shoreline, would be blanked. It would be in a void area. Well, we decided it was a pretty good technique. If it worked for them, probably it would work for us too. And so we would also, if need be, operate, emulating what we were learning from them.

Q: Where did all this information come together? Was that on the fleet flagship?

Admiral Richardson: It came together on the fleet flagship. Then, on the 16th of December, a group sent by Admiral Moorer came to visit us. The group was comprised of Captain Bill Moffit, the intelligence officer from CinCUSNavEur, three Air Force officers from USCinCEur, three CIA people, and there were two or three others.[*] I don't remember who they all were. The leader of the group was my friend Whispering Willie Holcomb.

We spent three to four days in and out of the flag cabin. I worked with them intimately as we planned how we could improve surveillance in various areas. During the course of that meeting, the CIA rep said, "We'll put a Mercedes on your masthead if that's what you want." Well, I couldn't quite think of what sort of Mercedes I needed on my masthead at that point in time, but several months later I did, and "Attsa My Boat" came

---

[*] USCinCEur--the joint-service commander in chief of U.S. forces in Europe.

into being as a direct result of that meeting. Attsa My Boat was a boat leased from Italians, manned by Italians. It moved around the Mediterranean. It had special collection equipment that was effective in several areas of considerable interest to us, and later it became still a different intelligence resource, but it wasn't always manned by foreign nationals.

But with this yacht we were able to sail in and around and through the various Soviet anchorages. There was a great deal of underwater activity in communications. We were very interested in getting assessments of the capabilities of their underwater communications. You know, one of the attack threats against Sixth Fleet was a tattletail moving in close vicinity to a carrier task force, but carrying out command and control information exchanges to a ship or submarine 50 to 60 miles away capable of firing a missile right into the middle of our force.

So this is just an example of the sort of information that we needed to monitor and understand. And we did come to understand a great deal about their underwater communications capabilities as a result of that. There were positive payoffs in at least three areas, and I've mentioned the one that is not sensitive--the others are sensitive--that we got from Attsa My Boat in its Italian-manned and American-manned versions.

The group from CNO brought with them a communications capability which enabled me to reach the CNO in a matter of minutes wherever he might be, home or at his office or any other time, and also reach Admiral Wendt. It was a three-way interconnection to ask for or provide intelligence support. It was to assure that whatever resource we needed that could be provided by the Navy would be provided and promptly. It didn't require great, long messages nor conferences nor anything else. It involved the Chief of Naval Operations, CinCUSNavEur, and myself. As I say, its purpose was also to exchange information should something specific occur. Remember Pearl Harbor?

The following summer, Admiral Moorer and Harlfinger came over to the Med for a visit, and we went through the things we were doing. It was the first time I'd had a chance to talk with Admiral Moorer, brief him in any detail about what we were doing, what our setup was, although he had received back much of this information from Holcomb. And so Harlfinger said, "We have been struggling for some time with the creation of an Ocean

Surveillance Information System to cover both oceans," and it looked like we had the answer to the start of that in what we were doing on the flagship. Would I agree to moving my intelligence unit to Rota, Spain?

There were a number of advantages in doing that. One is that the dissemination of intelligence information could take place from there without being hindered by radio silence. Then there were certain specific capabilities that were significant that could be made available in Rota. Harlfinger said that he would increase our resources, that he would put a commander in charge of the unit there. I had insisted that I had to have a nucleus unit aboard ship. I wasn't willing to let my intelligence officer or the two assistants go, but I was agreeable to setting up this structure and moving a portion of my people to Rota and to rotate the people who he sent in there through the flagship. They would have an understanding of what we needed and were interested in. The only requirement that I levied was that I retain tasking control, and that was agreed to.

Very soon, over came a commander and several brand-new intelligence officers as assistants. Several of my people moved over to Rota, and that unit was then established.

Q: When was that set up, do you recall?

Admiral Richardson: This was set up in the summer of '69. It was in place and operating during Okean-70 a year later.[*] We knew everything the Soviet Navy was doing in that exercise, wherever they were.

The new surveillance system immediately expanded into CinCUSNavEur headquarters, then CinCLant. Then, when I was deputy CinCPacFlt, I'd say in early '71, Harlfinger came out with a proposal to my boss, Admiral Clarey, that this system be expanded into the Pacific.[†] There would be an FOSIC at PacFlt headquarters, Fleet Operational Surveillance Information Center. Then there was a FOSIF, Fleet Operational Surveillance Intelligence Facility in Japan.

---

[*] Okean-70 was the name of a large-scale Soviet naval exercise held in 1970.
[†] Admiral Bernard A. Clarey, USN, served as Commander in Chief Pacific Fleet, 5 December 1970 to 30 September 1973.

So that system literally grew out of a chance comment made in a luncheon three years earlier. Many people played a significant role, and we ended up with an Ocean Surveillance Information System, headquartered in Suitland, Maryland.

Q: When and where was the luncheon? Who was involved in that?

Admiral Richardson: That was the one I mentioned earlier, with retired Vice Admiral William Schoech, Cunningham, and Whispering Willie Holcomb. Schoech invited me out. The lunch went from noon till 5:00 o'clock. It was in his office somewhere in downtown Washington. And in the course of that, I mentioned it was a hell of a note that nobody in Washington could tell me what was going on in Sixth Fleet. That was the comment relayed to the CNO via Whispering Willie Holcomb, whose normal talking voice sometimes we thought would wake up the dead in Arlington.

Q: Were there any reverberations when you took that job from the Liberty incident the year before?[*]

Admiral Richardson: Well, before going over, I had somehow come into possession of a paper describing the lapses in time that occurred associated with that, and suffice to say here, because I don't know what the clearance aspect of it is, that the JCS met shortly before midnight to consider what to do--why at that time, I don't know--and ordered the ship to move away from its location.

That message went over Army circuits and was mistakenly sent to the Philippines. Later it was readdressed to USCinCEur. It got to USCinCEur's headquarters somewhere around sunrise. It got to Sixth Fleet shortly before the Liberty was attacked, about 0730. Then it sat there for half an hour until the admiral arrived before anyone took action on it,

---

[*] On 8 June 1967, during the Six-Day War between Israel and Egypt, Israeli aircraft and torpedo boats made a number of attacks on the U.S. communications intelligence ship Liberty (AGTR-5). Of the ship's crew of 297, 34 were killed and 171 wounded. Israel claimed that the attack on the Liberty was a case of mistaken identity. Many in the ship's crew were skeptical of the claim.

and, of course, action should have been taken immediately. It may be that it would have made a difference if timely action had been taken, but the timing was then very tight.

I used the Liberty case in connection with an event that occurred after I took command of the Sixth Fleet. My antisubmarine warfare task force commander got upset because my staff duty officer preempted him by initiating an antisubmarine action at a time when his staff duty officer took no initiative. I had brought my staff up to know that they were expected to act. When something came up, if I was available, let me know. If a situation wasn't time-sensitive, then, of course, there was no problem. But if it was time-sensitive, then they were to initiate action.

My ASW task group admiral had been ashore, as was also his chief of staff. The staff duty officer was waiting until they got back before initiating an action. What happened then was that my staff duty officer, Ace Lyons, initiated action when the ASW command didn't.* His authority usurped, the admiral got mad, and he flew up to see me to complain. I took him in to have a cup of coffee. He asserted that he was in charge of ASW and didn't appreciate my staff duty officer stepping in.

I handed him my copy of the Liberty inquiry, a short thing, and said, "Read it." When he was done, I said, "Okay. You want to run your show. That's fine. You're expected to. But you have to do it so that it's done right away. Delegate to your watch officer all the authority he needs when you're not immediately available. Otherwise, we do it. It's that simple." And that was the end of it. The one whom he was mad at was then-Commander Ace Lyons, who went on to be CinCPacFlt. [Laughter] Ace was never noted for either diplomacy or patience.

Q: Who was the ASW task force commander?

Admiral Richardson: I think it's better left blank.

---

* Commander James A. Lyons, Jr., USN. Later, as a flag officer in the 1980s, Lyons served as Commander Second Fleet, OP-06, and Commander in Chief Pacific Fleet.

Q: Was there a perceived need for procedural changes to prevent something like the attack on the Liberty from happening again?

Admiral Richardson: Whatever changes were made, I'm not aware of.

Q: Was the length of Admiral Martin's tour in any sense shortened by that incident?

Admiral Richardson: I doubt it.

Q: How did the timing come about that you relieved him when you did, do you know?

Admiral Richardson: I don't know--just a normal rotation.

Q: Any more on intelligence?

Admiral Richardson: Yes. Dick Colbert was the head of the Naval War College when we created this Mediterranean surveillance net.* I invited Dick to send over some of his staff to see what we were doing in the Med in terms of keeping track of where the Soviets were, of learning what their patterns of operation were, and then taking measures in continuous response that would enable us to exploit that knowledge. He sent a captain, plus several others. I had promised that I would personally plan their exposures, so I did. We briefed them and we sent them around to other ships. They went back after being with us about a week. Near as I could tell, nothing happened.

After that, Bob Tolle, one of the assistant intelligence officers, was ordered to the Naval War College. I said, "Bob, I'm giving you an order. When you get there, you go see the president, and I'm going to write him a letter."

---

* Vice Admiral Richard G. Colbert, USN., served as president of the Naval War College from 30 August 1968 to 17 August 1971.

So I wrote Dick a letter and said, "Tolle can explain to you the details of our continuously functioning wide area surveillance system featuring special intelligence and how we respond operationally to revealed developments."

So Bob reported in at the war college and made himself known to the front office. He was put on the president's schedule a month or so later. The day of the appointment came, and he had 20 minutes. The outer office said, "Look, the admiral is busy as all get-out. If you cut it to ten, we'd sure appreciate it."

So in went Bob. He came out an hour and a half later. Dick Colbert told him, "Your primary duty here is to put in place for us a special intelligence capability."

So Bob worked the rest of his year identifying all of the actions required to be qualified to handle special intelligence. Can you imagine the Naval War College not training at all in special intelligence until 1971?

Q: It's difficult.

Admiral Richardson: That's the case. Later that capability was expanded to permit war gaming.

Now, there are other aspects of Sixth Fleet operations that I think are significant and I think that would be of interest. If I were a CNO, I really would require all selectees to captain to undergo some specific training in what I would call leadership. It's not quite the same sort of leadership training that we normally read about.

What I have in mind is case studies, just like we used in navigation, showing how, if you delay action or if you don't move on things promptly, you lose control. There are any number of incidents that can show how, across a broad span of events, if a senior naval officer in a command position fails to take action on something, then somebody else higher up does, or maybe events take control. The tendency is that the higher a situation goes for corrective action, the stronger the action taken. Then it takes a political flavor sometimes, and the reaction becomes disproportionate to the situation itself. That's one kind of item. Let me mention another.

In the entire field of intelligence, the exploitation of intelligence is so important. This was fully understood by Francis Marion. Back in the Revolutionary War he probably got greater returns for the number of people he had than any other general in that war. It's a remarkable story. Now, he was an attorney, a Frenchman, and he knew that you can't know too much about the enemy. On one occasion, he knew so much about British practices that he was able, with one other, to sneak into the fort, extract the number-two general, get him past the sentries, haul him out into the boondocks, and then trade him back for a number of his own people who had been captured. When you do that, you've got to know who's on watch, what their normal patterns are, whether some of them are drunk or not or who does get drunk or who you could manipulate in one way or another, and that requires a lot of detailed knowledge. It's a great example of exploiting intelligence.

The basic idea, as Bob hunt put it, "If you want to screw the other fellow up, you find out how he functions. Then you focus your efforts on his weaknesses." That is the basic idea in exploiting intelligence. Then there was Nathan Bedford Forrest in the Civil War. According to General Sherman, Forrest was the most impressive general in that war. His principle was "Get there fustest with the mostest." Where is there? When is fustest? How much is mostest?

There are other examples. When I had Sixth Fleet, I received orders directed by the JCS on several occasions. They came to USCinCEur. But as info addee, I was expected to move on them right away in the interest of time. They would order me to do certain things with a portion of my forces. Then the question would arise as to what to do with the remaining forces. I would then direct substantial redeployment in the remainder of our forces and take other actions to better assure the protection of a force that might have been required to move into an advanced position.

The tendency is that when you get instructions from high authority, you do precisely what they say--and no more. There's nothing in that guidance that says anything about the rest of your forces, and there's nothing in that guidance that relieves you from responsibility if your directed action has unanticipated consequences.

So you have to take the additional measures that you believe are appropriate in the circumstances of that time. Yet, strangely enough, that is a problem. You wonder if the next message will say, "If we had wanted to do that, we'd have said so!"

Another example was a case we had in Malta. This was during a time when there was a good bit of black unrest in the States. The amphib force, which we were watching very carefully at that particular point in time, was in Malta. They had liberty. A number of them were in the Gut.* A fistfight started in a local bar. In came the Marine captain on shore patrol with a Maltese policeman. The young Marine swung on the Marine captain, who ducked, so that he hit the Maltese policeman and knocked him down.

That started a riot. Bottles were flying. People in the saloon ran out into the street. A number of the Maltese, seeing the action, would pull American Marines into their doorway for safety. It was quite active until things settled down an hour or so later.

When I learned of it, which was almost immediately, I sent a message to the ambassador that I was sending a Navy flag officer down to investigate the thing right away. I sent a cruiser-destroyer flotilla commander, rear admiral, down to make an investigation. That was done immediately.

Then we contacted the Maltese Government through the ambassador and found that they really weren't all that upset about it, that the Gut had been resident to this sort of activity for 100 or so years. But by virtue of the fact that we had a Navy flag officer coming almost immediately--the next day he was there--that took pressure off a situation that might otherwise have worsened.

One of the duties and pleasures of being Commander Sixth Fleet was establishing relationships with the Spanish, Portuguese, Italians, Greeks, Turks, Moroccans, the Maltese--all the various naval and other military people around the Mediterranean. In the course of my tour, one of the first things I did was go to the Chief of Naval Operations of the Italian Navy, since the flagship was based in Gaeta. I told him that I had two bosses--CinCUSNavEur was one, and I considered him my other boss. We were guests living in his country, and if he were displeased with Sixth Fleet or if he desired anything, to please let me know directly, and I would take care of it. I said I hoped that if any

---

* The Gut is a section of town in the port of Valletta.

embarrassments of any sort came up that he would send for me. I'd come up and we'd have a look at it.

We had extremely good relations with the Italians. The Italian NATO commander was Roselli Lorenzini, a full admiral.[*] He and his wife lived in Malta and had his headquarters there. My wife and I visited with them in Malta. They visited with us. We established a good personal relationship and were often able to work out problems that within a total NATO context would be difficult. We enjoyed certain security levels of information that were on a bilateral basis and permitted us to work more closely with Italy sometimes than with some of the other countries.

Then the commanding admiral of the Italian fleet was Gino Birindelli.[†] Gino Birindelli spoke excellent English, Southern style. I asked him where he got his accent, and he said in a prisoner-of-war camp in Tennessee. He spent three years there. Gino was the most decorated Italian naval officer. He led the underwater group that penetrated Alexandria in World War II and planted mines on the British battleships that badly damaged them.[‡] He was captured, taken to Britain, was there for several months, and then shipped to a POW camp in this country in Tennessee.

We often saw Birindelli and his female friend, whom he later married. They were often at our quarters in Gaeta, and we were with them in Taranto from time to time. His flagship from time to time would swing into Gaeta, and we'd have meetings of the various officers. We had a very congenial relationship, which was a great pleasure.

The same was true in Greece. I indicated earlier that both CNOs, one there when I first arrived in the Med, my first year, was Stavros Pervanos. He had worked for me in NATO in Naples ten years earlier. And then he was relieved by Margaritas. I mentioned earlier a story about him. He was the CNO after Pervanos. We knew General Angelis, whom I regarded very highly, and was saddened when he was shipped off and kept in prison

---

[*] Ammiraglio di Squadra Giuseppe Roselli Lorenzini, Commander Allied Naval Forces Southern Europe.
[†] Ammiraglio di Squadra Gino Birindeli, Commander in Chief Italian Fleet.
[‡] The Italians used two-man "human torpedoes" as commando assault forces in the Mediterranean. On the night of 18-19 December 1941 Italian craft penetrated the harbor of Alexandria, Egypt, where they attached delayed-action mines to the British battleships Queen Elizabeth and Valiant. The resulting explosions put the ships out of action for several months.

following the overthrow of the "revolt of the colonels."* Angelis was a fine man, in my estimation. I enjoyed him and came to know him. Many times he was with Admiral Rivero in CinCSouth.†

The Turks, likewise, were very forthcoming. They were quite critical of the failure of the Sixth Fleet to intervene in a Nicosian event that had occurred in '66, so we had a little tough time over that specific incident.‡ But my point there to them was simply that President Johnson had directed the Sixth Fleet to intervene to prevent the Turks from invading Nicosia, and by virtue of preventing that, preventing an all-out war between Greece and Turkey--a situation of benefit only to the Soviet Union.

Q: They resented the fact they hadn't been able to have the war.

Admiral Richardson: They resented the fact they hadn't been able to insert their forces into Nicosia and counter the Greeks, because, as you know, that situation had been a tough one for a long, long time. They have a relatively small area there, and the Greeks are anything but hospitable to them, so you can certainly sympathize with them.

In Spain, we had a fine relationship with the Spanish Navy leadership. On one occasion, we had been to Gibraltar. As I said earlier, the four-star British admiral in command there had been my classmate at the Royal Navy Staff College back in '46, so we had a very pleasant time together for our several-day visit there. My wife went with me on these visits. In addition to offices, homes were opened, and the process of establishing relationships with other national authorities was definitely enhanced. The wives themselves relate.

---

* A junta of Greek military officers, led by Colonel George Papadopoulos, seized control of the government on 21 April 1967. The Papadopoulos regime was ousted on 25 November 1973.
† Admiral Horacio Rivero, USN, served as Commander in Chief Allied Forces Southern Europe from January 1968 to May 1972. His oral history is in the Naval Institute collection.
‡ In June 1966, the government of Cyprus imposed a blockade of the Turkish quarter of Nicosia in reprisal for explosions attributed to Turkish Cypriots. Cypriot President Makarios lifted the blockade after an appeal from U Thant, Secretary General of the United Nations.

Q: From my meeting of her a couple of days ago, your wife is a very gracious lady, so I'm sure that she was helpful.

Admiral Richardson: Yes, indeed she was. She's very gifted in getting along with people.

But anyway, when we left Gibraltar, we went to Barcelona. Then we immediately flew to Madrid so I could call on the Spanish admiral, whom I had not seen until then, and our Ambassador Hill.[*] He was busy saving the bases in Spain. The Spanish admiral was very critical that I had gone into Gibraltar and then came to Spain. He didn't see why I would . . .

Q: Why you would sully your flagship.

Admiral Richardson: Why I would sully my flagship by going into Gibraltar. If I had gone somewhere else and come back later, it might not have had quite the effect. But he was very displeased that I had come there directly from Gibraltar. I said, "Well, Admiral, our job in the Med has nothing to do with the argument over Gibraltar that the British and the Spanish are having. Our reason for being here is the Soviets. Please don't do anything that would create a problem that would pit us against either the Brits or the Spaniards, because that can't help at all."

The visit on the whole was very pleasant. The residue of good feeling toward the U.S. from the time of Sherman was very strong, so I wasn't particularly worried about that.[†] However, that evening, Ambassador Hill had a reception that had been set up for our visit. The ambassador and his wife were at the head of the receiving line, and my wife and I were next. In came the Spanish admiral and his wife. He came straight to me, and he said, "I've been thinking about what you said, and that's absolutely right." Then he turned to the ambassador to make his greeting.

---

[*] Robert C. Hill, U.S. ambassador to Spain.
[†] Vice Admiral Forrest P. Sherman, USN, commanded the Sixth Task Fleet from February 1948 until he became Chief of Naval Operations in November 1949.

The ambassador turned to me and asked, "Now, what was that all about?" [Laughter] I told him later that evening when things were over. We stayed with them for two or three days, then back to Barcelona.

But that's an example of the role that the Commander Sixth Fleet plays in the political sphere, and I mentioned earlier that NATO is a glue that holds those countries together by virtue of the fact that so many of their military people have had duty with one another through 40-plus years now. So they have come to respect one another and their way of thinking about things, and it is made much easier to work together. Wives' roles are understandably significant.

That, in my view, is perhaps the greatest contribution that the command structure in the NATO made, and it certainly wasn't thought about in advance. It just happened that simply by virtue of these people working together, from their different backgrounds, different nationalities, and being professional, came to know one another and respect one another, and it alleviated many, many problems that otherwise would occur. If a NATO defense agreement ever had to be implemented, it would be far more effective by virtue of this familiarity and trust that were only acquired with time.

Q: What do you recall of your dealings with the French? They had taken their military forces out of NATO by that point.

Admiral Richardson: Well, that's an interesting thing. The relationship between the French and the Americans, be it bilaterally or in a NATO context, couldn't have been better during my two years in Sixth Fleet. And I know that it was also that way, consistently so, before that time, because many of the people who I have known well and been involved with, we have talked about the relations with the French in the south of France.

I'll tell you a couple of anecdotes to give you a feel for the disparity between the French authorities in the south of France, both political and military, and French authority at the national level in Paris.

The Moskva came into the Med in '70.* That was the first of the helicopter carriers. So we met the Moskva with a destroyer, the Warrington, as she entered the Northern Aegean Sea. Our destroyer had a commanding officer who was an intelligence subspecialist, and it followed the Moskva throughout its tour in the Med as a tattletail.† We so often had Russian tattletails with us.

My flagship went into the south of France. The French admiral was Vice Admiral Philiponneau.‡ When I made my call on him, we were about to enter a major fleet exercise with the French, a bilateral exercise. Our Marines were to assault the French Foreign Legion on one of their islands. Then the Marines and the Foreign Legion, working together, would assault the French Army in the south of France. Our carriers were going to fight the French carriers. The two French carriers and our two carriers--with the Marines and the French Foreign Legion--were going to assault the south of France against the French Army and the French Air Force, so we would have had four carriers, two French and two American--a major exercise.

One of our officers spoke fluent French, and he had just finished briefing the French admiral about the Moskva. Then the French admiral said, "Well, I'm so sorry we can no longer have major exercises. Orders from Paris."

I said, "Well, I'm sorry to hear that. We'll get our staffs together and we'll scale this down."

"Oh, no, not necessary. We changed the name from major to minor." And that's what we did. Major exercises had to be referred to Paris, but minor exercises did not. So we could run a whole war. As long as we called it minor, it was all right.

You mentioned the fact that the French had withdrawn from NATO. On another occasion I met with a different French admiral. In the NATO plans the French Navy was responsible for escorting and defending our supply forces, our logistical forces. Of course,

---

* Moskva was a Soviet cruiser with a stern flight deck for antisubmarine helicopters. She began operating on sea trials in July 1967 in the Black Sea. Her first deployment in the Mediterranean lasted from 20 September to 4 November 1968. During that period the destroyer Basilone (DD-824) conducted continuous surface surveillance during much of her stay in the Med.
† This Mediterranean deployment by the Moskva began in early January 1970. The Warrington (DD-843) remained in close company with the Soviet ship during the remainder of January and into early February.
‡ Vice Admiral Pierre A. C. Philiponneau, French Navy.

our effectiveness depended heavily upon the logistics that were available to us. So I said, "Well, I guess we'll have to modify the NATO plans."

"Oh, no, not necessary at all." He said, "Instead of sending your message, 'Proceed promptly to so-and-so and do such and such,' just simply say, 'Would you be so kind as to . . .' We'll do it." [Laughter]

Q: It's gratifying when you can have that kind of a relationship.

Admiral Richardson: Yes, indeed. No problem at all.

Q: What else do you remember about the emergence of the Moskva?

Admiral Richardson: This all occurred shortly after the Christmas holidays. We had an EA-3 that was on peripheral reconnaissance in the Eastern Med.[*] Now, the Soviets would change their call signs when they went out of immediate home waters into an open ocean area. When we got a change in call sign, that was a tipoff that she was coming out. It had Topsail radar with its electronics characteristics, which were collectible. And so we sent the EA-3 up. This happened when my ubiquitous staff officer, Ace Lyons, was on duty. Ace diverted the EA-3 up into the Northern Aegean. He picked up Topsail radar emissions.

Ace immediately called around and located the fleet camera party. The flagship was anchored in Gaeta Harbor at this time. The fleet photo group was based in Naples. Ace rounded them up and got them out to Capodichino, got a pilot and a plane to fly them over to Athens, picked out a destroyer, the Warrington, that was in port in Athens that he knew had a skipper who was an intelligence subspecialist, sent that destroyer down to top off in fuel.[†] Then they came back, picked up the fleet photo group, and then went sailing on up into the Northern Aegean. They and were within 30 miles of the Straits of Dardanelles

---

[*] The EA-3B Skywarrior was the electronic warfare version of the former A-3 bomber. It was fitted with electronic and communications intercept equipment, comprising TASES (tactical airborne signal exploitation system).
[†] Commander Richard F. Rockwell, USN, commanded the Warrington at the time.

when they encountered the Moskva. That was a classic example of a staff duty officer taking an initiative. That had to tell the Soviets something.

Q: And this is the exception to that trend we talked about, about people who wait for higher approval.

Admiral Richardson: That's right. You don't do that. You can't do that with things moving as fast as they do in a modern world. They've got to have the authority at the scene to act when something occurs.

I had the policy that whenever a situation was seen to be evolving, we started counter operations. Our first operational response would be, "Cancel the cocktail party." That's an operational response. You'd start up the readiness ladder. You'd back back down the ladder many a time, but always as the threat changed. Events that were a little less benign even an hour or so earlier, as those events began to unfold, we also began to initiate a step-up in response. We would divert or initiate additional surveillance or whatever in order to avoid surprise.

Our surveillance of Soviet naval patterns of operations in the Med dealt with tattletails, submarines, Kresta and Kynda cruisers with their long-range surface-to-surface missiles, their Bear D surveillance and targeting aircraft, and their Badger long-range jet bombers. All this made clear to us then the substantial Soviet capability to mount a major surprise attack in a matter of hours.

Given continuous surveillance information by our VQ squadron, our radars, and our passive collection of electronics emissions of targets sources, including those from a Navy-developed satellite system that I've not previously mentioned, my intelligence staff identified Soviet threat system combinations.[*] Naval intelligence headquarters in Washington was intimately engaged in this, and I've not a clue as to whether their weapon systems identifications and definitions of their characteristics and capabilities was being done mostly in Little Rock, London, or Washington. Mostly likely, it was being done in

---

[*] VQ--fleet air reconnaissance.

Washington. The intelligence relationships were now much more focused because of Admiral Moorer's interests and assessments. Our interactions were intimate, constant.

It was years later that I came to know about--and to regard so highly--the genius of Soviet Admiral Gorshkov and his thesis of swift, sudden attack.* At the time it was our knowledge of the long-range SSN-3 missile capabilities of the Soviet naval units and their use of tattletails that alerted us in Sixth Fleet to the Soviet swift, sudden capability, and me as Sixth Fleet commander to the fleet mind-set that whenever we saw events proceeding that placed us within range of Soviet surface-to-surface missiles, we had to increase our readiness to react.

Of course, I'm not arguing the point that you would see this type of attack without all sorts of things going on elsewhere. That would certainly be the case. But within the area where I was and was responsible for, we were working against one- to two- to three-hour threat situations. We didn't sit back and wait for something to happen; we acted when we saw the possibility of things happening.

Q: Anything else on the French?

Admiral Richardson: As I mentioned, we were very gratified with the attitude of the people in the south of France. They were very pro-Sixth Fleet, very pro-American. They were a delight.

Monaco, the same way. We had a very good relationship. In fact, we visited with Prince Rainier and Princess Grace several times.† Our son Robert, who came over from Marion Military Institute for two or three weeks in the summer of '69, was with us and our other children in Monaco. We were put in a set of rooms in the hotel just opposite the

---

* Admiral of the Fleet of the Soviet Union S. G. Gorshkov served as Commander in Chief of the Soviet Navy from January 1956 to December 1985. He expressed his views in a series of articles on Navies in War and in Peace. They appeared in the book Red Star Rising at Sea, published in 1974 by the Naval Institute Press.
† Prince Rainier III has been head of state of the principality of Monaco since 1949. His wife was the former Grace Kelly, who had been an American movie star before her marriage in 1956.

casino, a room that Churchill used to occupy.* The price I had to pay was piddling. It normally went for hundreds of dollars. Maybe I paid $60.00 for a large suite.

Q: We should all be so lucky.

Admiral Richardson: We were having dinner with Princess Grace and Rainier and another couple when the remark was made that my son was having his birthday while we were there. Princess Grace was having a party for Stephanie, and she said, "Well, we'd love to have your son."† She converted the whole thing to a party for him on his birthday. Of course, I had to go out and buy him a jacket and a pair of shoes, because he didn't have any presentable clothes with him. Anyway, that's where he spent his birthday.

Later, I had a message from Prince Rainier. He wanted to bring his young son out to visit an aircraft carrier.‡ So I flew up and met them. They came out to an island in a yacht, then got into a COD and flew aboard.§ They were there with me for about three days. This young man was a very fine young man; I haven't heard anything of him in the tabloids in recent years. Unfortunately, Stephanie certainly has been a problem, but I've never heard anything about him.

Q: Any impressions of Grace and Rainier from your associations?

Admiral Richardson: Well, she ran a tight shop. She watched her husband closely. If he showed any particular attraction towards somebody, why, she'd fire an eye arrow at him. One of them went past me one day. [Laughter]

One time David Niven and his new wife were at dinner, and David Niven's wife was a living doll.** She was a beauty. As we were proceeding out to go into the court, to

---

* Winston S. Churchill, British Prime Minister in the 1940s and 1950s, had a fondness for the south of France.
† Stephanie is the daughter of Rainier and Princess Grace.
‡ The son is Prince Albert.
§ COD--carrier on-board delivery, an aircraft configured for carrier takeoffs and landings, dedicated to transporting personnel and cargo between ship and shore.
** David Niven was an American movie actor.

go into the stands for an evening performance that was going to be given, and since both Rainier and I were quite taken, our eyes often ventured toward Niven's wife. Princess Grace led the way out with Rainier in the rear. Her arrow shot past me and landed squarely on Ranier. [Laughter]

Q: I hope you weren't wounded by any ricochets.

Admiral Richardson: No, not at all. But I came to know a bit about that young man, the son. Of course, his grandfather was the one who created that marvelous aquarium they have there. Often when we were up there, we'd have parties on the flagship, cocktails on the barge before going aboard. One time there was a rumor that Jacques Cousteau and the Rainiers were at odds.* So the question was should we invite Jacques Cousteau and his wife and the Rainiers to dinner at the same time. So we made delicate inquiries, and there was no problem. We had both couples out to the ship together. They got along fine.

There was some jealously or some sort of a problem between Prince Rainier and Cousteau, and it probably had to do with funding arrangements in that aquarium that was so elaborate. But they were fine, no problem, and I was glad of that. The first time I ever saw ceiling-to-ceiling carpet was when we had dinner with the Cousteaus. The carpet went to the wall and went right on up to the ceiling. [Laughter]

Well, there were many interesting anecdotes. The things that are significant are the fact that when you're on a first-name basis or at least have achieved some social interaction with other people in high places, when problems arrive, they can be handled more easily.

Let me give you just one. The skipper of a destroyer going into Barcelona would not allow the Spanish pilot to pilot his ship. He was proud of his ship handling and his competence, and he just wouldn't do it. The pilot was very upset, and it was illegal for the American to do that. So when the pilot got off, he went in and reported it. It got to the

---

* Jacques-Yves Cousteau (1910-1997) was a French author, oceanographer, and motion picture producer. He developed many techniques for undersea exploration, including helping to invent the aqualung.

Spanish admiral, and the Spanish admiral ordered the destroyer out. Also, there were not to be any more naval ships coming into Barcelona. That was the action of the moment.

I knew the Spanish admiral and had visited with him several times. So I sent him a message that said, "From what I understand of this situation, my skipper was completely off base. I'll look into this and take whatever corrective action needs to be taken." Immediately, the ban was lifted, and entry back into the port was okay. But by virtue of the fact that he knew me and I knew him, I could go to him with a message of that type, and that's all he needed. Their pride and sensitivities are noteworthy. The Spanish have to be handled carefully.

Q: And he could count on you to follow through on your pledge to take care of it.

Admiral Richardson: He knew very well that I would do just what I had said I would do. That wouldn't happen again.

Q: You talked about all the procedures involved in setting up this enhanced intelligence capability. What was the payback that you got from setting that up? What were the results?

Admiral Richardson: The results were that we began to discern typical patterns of operations for the Soviet Navy's missile strike system. The Soviet Navy at that point in time was developing tactics for using aircraft with submarines, with the aircraft--or a tattletail--providing targeting data, and a surface ship/submarine combination. By knowing their patterns, we could predict what to look for, where, and when.

So if you look in terms of time at events that are taking place early in an attack cycle, you can predict what is coming, where it will be, when it will be, because of your knowledge of your own forces and where they are. We had lots of overflights, you know. We had tattletails with us constantly.

In that <u>Moskva</u> incident, for instance, we were specifically able to initiate action because we knew their communications patterns of operations. We knew the sequence of things that took place as a normal measure, and relying on the normality of it, why, we were able to do that. Of course, one of the things you know is that if you do things in a normal way, then you've set up a line of thought. You've conditioned someone else to expect you to do it that way, and therefore maybe you will do it differently. Any change in the normal is itself significant. But that's the kind of payoff that we had.

From another view, there has long been a gap between operations and intelligence. It has been engendered in part by security considerations, but in large part by the fact that the intelligence community likes to publish. The sequence of getting books out is a long, drawn-out matter, and often by the time they get there, why, some aspects of it are out of date, particularly in its electronics aspects. With change so rapid and radical, documents too often are not operationally useful. By making intelligence interactive with operations in real time, that gap is closed.

Q: Mike Rodgers, as a top-notch operator, would appreciate those qualities. Was Sourbeer equally adept on operational things?

Admiral Richardson: Oh, yes. Sourbeer was superb, by any measure, and so were his successors. He had one successor who was a problem, and I couldn't keep him. And then he was replaced by another who was very competent. I was very well served by them, very happy with them.

Now I'm off my track of a particular point.

Q: You were talking about the ability to get information when it's timely so you can use it before it gets stale.

Admiral Richardson: Yes. Oh, I know. We were talking about the gap between intelligence and its presentation and the exploitation by operators. I had worked that previously by putting an intelligence officer and an operational officer together in the Gulf of Tonkin in '66-'67. Each was expert in his own realm, and they worked in close coordination to produce a product that was operationally useful and immediately available.

We ended up translating intelligence about weapons into intelligence describing activity sequences in total weapon systems--as revealed by operational patterns.

Now, what did we do when we got the overhead photography? The ops officer was Jerry O'Rourke, whom you may know.[*]

Q: Oh, yes.

Admiral Richardson: Jerry assigned Ace Lyons the task of identifying targets of interest, which we had to do in order to task the overhead photography people. Well, that list of targets I then sent to ComNavAirLant, who was Vice Admiral Bob Townsend.[†] Townsend had been AirSysCom head when the TFX/F-111 came along.[‡] He and Connolly had often met in connection with that, and I was frequently with them. But anyway, Townsend supported me beautifully.

So with the list of targets and with the information on ingress/egress that we were able to get and some electronic information, at the secret level, they arrived in theater with strike plans. Now, these pilots had long done this in Southeast Asia, and they all knew how. It was duck soup for them to route plan or strike plan. All they needed to know was, what are the targets, then have the adequate intelligence support. So the relieving carrier arrived in theater with that. We were in a position where within a matter of hours we, too, could initiate attacks against whatever target.

These are the main things. Since you know Jerry O'Rourke, I might mention that when that intelligence group came to the Med in mid-December of '68, led by Whispering Willie Holcomb, of course, they hit the chief of staff and the ops officer right away, and Holcomb said, "I've got to go see Admiral Richardson."

Jerry said, "Well, no, you don't want to bother him." [Laughter]

---

[*] Captain Gerald G. O'Rourke, USN.
[†] Vice Admiral Robert L. Townsend, USN, served as Commander Naval Air Force Atlantic Fleet from 1 March 1969 to 29 February 1972.
[‡] As a rear admiral, Townsend served as Commander Naval Air Systems Command from 1 September 1966 to 20 February 1969.

Holcomb marched out of the room to my cabin, and the Marine orderly stopped him there. He said, "Get out of my way." Rapped on the door, you know. He barged in, in effect. Of course, I was delighted to see him--Whispering Willie! So everything moved into the flag mess from that point on. Jerry just didn't have any of that background. He didn't know that I had even heard of Whispering Willie. That always gave me a chuckle.

Q: Holcomb was not to be denied.

Admiral Richardson: Holcomb wasn't to be denied by anybody at any time.

Q: What did you have in the way of a Soviet language capability to try to exploit the Soviet communications?

Admiral Richardson: I didn't. The information that we got from that came from shore stations. We didn't have it on the ship. We do, you know, deploy teams. In the Sixth Fleet setup, we had a submarine command ashore. My submarine commander was Hap Perry, and then he was relieved by Chuck Grojean, who is down now at the Nimitz Foundation.[*]

Q: Whom I just saw last week.

Admiral Richardson: Yes. And Chuck, both of them are great. But submarine operations in those days were pretty much controlled out of Washington, and I didn't know what they were doing or where they were. So I had an understanding with both Grojean and Hap Perry that I considered them responsible for informing me whenever anything arose that I ought to know about that would be of concern to me, and that was covered. I think ComSubLant actually pretty much controlled the details of their operation at that time.[†] So that was all right. I didn't object to that. We had incidents which I won't go into, but I was well served by both of them.

---

[*] Captain Oliver Hazard Perry, Jr., USN; Captain Charles D. Grojean, USN. As a retired rear admiral Grojean heads the Admiral Nimitz Foundation, which runs the Nimitz Museum in Fredericksburg, Texas.
[†] ComSubLant--Commander Submarine Force Atlantic Fleet.

When I went down to brief Admiral Rivero right after New Year's on the fact that the Moskva had come into the Med, he said, "Well, no. It was a Soviet cruiser." And he started digging through stacks of papers. The Turks had informed him it was a cruiser. Well, of course, it was a cruiser in the sense that that's what the Soviets had declared to the Turks for clearance, and that's what they continued to call it.[*] I said, "We have a ship on it. We know it's the Moskva."

Also, on some occasions I got some orders from Rivero that I would have had to protest had it been a real situation. It occurred to me then that Admiral Rivero, although he had an Army major who handled special intelligence for him, was not getting anywhere near the quality of information that was available to me or he wouldn't have said some of these things.

So I set up with Grojean and Admiral Rivero. Grojean would go over and see Admiral Rivero, and he was given carte blanche to enter at any time. If he said he had an urgent matter, why, he went right in. Then Rivero would walk with him over to the submarine space to be briefed. That was done on several occasions. He had to go and get the admiral and bring him over into an all-source center and brief him on it. Years later, when different people would go over there to CinCSouth, I'd point out that there did exist an all-source center right on the Banjoli area there in the submarine headquarters. This arrangement had certainly saved some embarrassment to Bill Crowe and others who were over there later.[†]

Q: What are your impressions of Admiral Rivero?

Admiral Richardson: We're in a luncheon club together now. He's a very competent individual.

---

[*] Signed at Montreux, Switzerland, on 20 July 1936, the multinational Montreux Convention restored to Turkey control over the Turkish straits, the Dardanelles and the Bosporus. Control had been taken away by the Lausanne Conference of 1922-23. The 1936 convention also placed limits on the armament of warships passing through the straits while passing between the Mediterranean and the Black Sea. Passaage by a cruiser was acceptable under the terms of the convention.

[†] Admiral William J. Crowe, Jr., USN, served as Commander in Chief Allied Forces Southern Europe from May 1980 to May 1983.

Q: Apparently very popular over in that area, also.

Admiral Richardson: I wasn't aware of that. Ambassador Hill recommended him to be the ambassador since he spoke Spanish--Puerto Rican Spanish.

Q: This was a time of U.S. and Soviet incidents at sea, leading to a treaty later to try to put a damper on that. Did you see any of that unpleasantness in the Mediterranean ships shouldering each other or not following the rules of the road?

Admiral Richardson: Yes, there were a number of instances when one of our ships or one of their ships would attempt to intimidate the other. And, of course, there were the flyovers, and our fighters would be right on the wing tip of the others and things of that nature. There were any number of those. On one occasion, we knocked off a section of wing of one of the Soviet jet aircraft, long-range jet aircraft--not the Bear, but the Badger. So the treaty arrangements that were made were good.

This area was not without mutual respect, Soviets for us and vice versa. When the Warrington, the destroyer trailing the Moskva, was in position, and the Moskva was off Egypt, Egyptian destroyers came out and tried to shoulder the Warrington away. The skipper of the Warrington very casually kept to the inside of the curve. They'd charge at high speed and come around here, and then, of course, they'd overshoot, and he'd easily resume position. He essentially maintained the usual position, which was comfortably astern and off the quarter of the Moskva.

This thing went on for a couple of hours. Finally, the Egyptians gave up and went back into port. Then Warrington got a flashing light message from the skipper of the Moskva: "G-U-E-D-E-S-H-E-W."

Q: Good show. [Laughter]

Admiral Richardson: Yes. [Laughter]

Q: Well, there's an inherent respect among seafaring men of different nations.

Admiral Richardson: That's right. Sure there is.

Q: How adequately did the <u>Little Rock</u> serve as fleet flagship?

Admiral Richardson: It served very well. I had no complaints.

Q: What sorts of facilities did you have on board?

Admiral Richardson: Well, our spaces and communications capabilities were quite adequate. It had been in service in that role for a long time. I had no problems.

Q: Did she ever perform in a combatant-type role? Did she shoot her guns?

Admiral Richardson: Oh, yes. Yes, indeed. We often would function as a member of a carrier task group, and her instructions in all cases came from the task group commander. When we rode into formation, why, we chopped control to him for flagship operations.[*] Com6thFlt continued to operate on their own, but it was above and beyond what the ship was doing.

Q: What do you recall about the substantive planning, as in, "If so-and-so contingency happens, we will react in this way"?

Admiral Richardson: There were theater plans that were developed by SACEur and SACLant. They had major plans, and then they had contingency plans. They extolled joint task forces, then driven by interservice rivalry, and this, in my view, was a political thing. I ran into it as Com6thFlt. When General Goodpaster came down to see us, we briefed him

---

[*] "Chop" is short for change operational control.

on how unrealistic the contingency plan that involved Sixth Fleet was.* The briefer was Commander Ace Lyons, and he was leaning over the table at General Goodpaster, waving his finger and saying, "When the joint task force is implemented, who will furnish the typewriters? Where are the secretaries coming from? Who has the communications equipment to communicate with? Who's got Jeeps, and where will they come from?"

Q: How did the general react to all that?

Admiral Richardson: In his comment to me at lunch afterward, he said, "Your Commander Lyons, he's a very intense fellow." [Laughter] But the point was perfectly taken, and I had said that whenever a contingency plan was developed, a commander should be designated then, and the arrangements that permit command and control to be established should be designated at that point in time. There simply is no way you could put together a command structure without the commander knowing his chief of staff or the chief of staff knowing anybody on the staff. If they later want to shift to a joint command setup, fine, but at the outset it had to be an existing command.

Q: What can you remember about the Sixth Fleet operations? Specifically, what was the normal pattern?

Admiral Richardson: Well, we were constrained by the amount of money available to us. Since the resources were going primarily to Southeast Asia, the difficulty we had was in getting enough optar, operating funds, to fly to keep our minimum standards up and to keep our ships at sea. We wanted to be at sea at least 15 days out of the 30. At times we were cut back to 11 to 12 days, and by the time you add getting out and getting into an operation and back, that doesn't give you too much time to run night operations, things of that nature, and to keep your pilot proficiency up. So we had difficulties from that point of view, but it was a funding limitation.

---

* General Andrew J. Goodpaster, USA, served as U.S. Commander in Chief Europe and NATO Supreme Allied Commander Europe from 1969 to 1974.

Q: What do you remember about the interaction with other nations? Did you have NATO exercises as part of this?

Admiral Richardson: Oh, yes. We had a number of NATO exercises, and these were developed ahead of time and actually carried out. They were generally well conceived. But the thing that was deficient, and we all knew it, was submarine detection in the Mediterranean. We tried various ways of collecting some of that information. We knew in general how many were there and when they left and when they came in and things like that. But where they were when they were in there, it was awfully hard to keep track of, and that would have been our major problem.

We were not as worried about air attacks. We conceived a wartime placement for each of our two carrier task groups. Then years later, I was fascinated to see in <u>Okean-75</u> that the Soviets reckoned that's exactly where we would be, and so they had missile cruisers operating specifically in those areas. During <u>Okean-70</u>, we saw that starting, building. We had a complete picture of their movements throughout that operation. We had the information on the forces coming down from up north. We were aware of their operational patterns, the business of shifting the radars around the force, which wasn't particularly significant, but it had a certain confusing element in their employment of electronic warfare. At no time were we not in touch with everything that they had in the Med, where it was, where it was going, what it was doing, and we were sending reports back on that. Except for submarines, the surveillance system in the North Atlantic and in the Med worked perfectly. [Tape recorder turned off.]

Admiral Richardson: Some of the intelligence, I simply can't talk to you about.

Q: I understand.

Admiral Richardson: But there was a substantial augmentation of intelligence resources that came in various forms. There was a humint task force that later came on hard times.[*] We became a testing laboratory for some new technologies. Collectively, they enabled us to be so effective in keeping track of what the Soviets were doing in <u>Okean-70</u>. And Jerry O'Rourke was excellent. I couldn't have asked for a better ops officer. I was disappointed that he didn't get selected for admiral, but he and Ike Kidd didn't hit it off.[†]

Q: Did you institute any tactical innovations as a result of the enhanced intelligence pictures?

Admiral Richardson: Yes, as I mentioned, we structured planned responses to those patternized Soviet missile force combinations.

Q: What about deceptive measures?

Admiral Richardson: Yes, electronic warfare. Plus, we used open--or spread--formations. That type of employment became widespread in the Pacific Fleet under Admiral William Ramsey back in the early '80s.[‡] But we did use "open" formations, and we would have our ships with missile capabilities emulating a carrier electronically. We changed magnetrons, did things to make the electronic characteristics different--jamming, that sort of stuff.

    We were not nearly as sophisticated as we later became, and we didn't have those resources in the late '60s. Also, we were in a tight little area, and we often had tattletails on us. So we had often to dislodge a tattletail, which we sometimes did, which was itself a forcing measure. But, yes, we did some things, mostly in the deceptive field, using electronics. Electronic emission control came later, in the late '70s.

Q: What do you recall about logistics and materiel maintenance of the fleet?

---

[*] Humint--human intelligence.
[†] Vice Admiral Isaac C. Kidd, Jr., USN, commanded the Sixth Fleet from 29 August 1970 to 1 October 1971.
[‡] Rear Admiral William E. Ramsey, USN.

Admiral Richardson: It was good. The destroyers had fine service force support. That was seldom a problem. One thing I haven't talked about was Dom Mintoff.* Since you mentioned logistics support, Malta was very useful to us as an area to dock or to have repairs made. On one occasion, we had a collision with a Greek ship.† It knocked me out of my bunk, as a matter of fact, about 3:00 or so in the morning, and it was the Greeks' fault. Wow! [Laughter] And so we went in to have our bow repaired, into Malta.

Prior to that, on two occasions I had, at the request of our ambassador, met with Dom Mintoff in Malta. The first occasion, the ambassador asked me to pay a call on him, but Mintoff was not in power. He was just the opposition. And I objected to it. I said I thought it was improper for the Commander Sixth Fleet to deal with an out-of-power element of the government. The ambassador said, "Oh, no, that's not a problem. The government of Malta wants you to do it."

I said, "Well, I'll be glad to do it."

At that point in time, I had a reserve officer aboard on two weeks' active duty; his name was Bill Mailliard.‡ He's in Washington now. He was in the Congress.§ He came from South San Francisco as a Republican in a heavily Democratic area. He was the ranking Republican on the House Armed Services Committee. So I said, "Bill, you've got to go with me on this one."

So he did. We called. When we walked in, I thought Mintoff's house was the dreariest place. The walls were dirty, faded, orange-yellow. There were no pictures anywhere. It was dismal. The furniture looked like hell. There was a model of a ship on the mantle, quite an elegant little ship, the sole thing to look at in that living room. I thought that his wife, who was an Englishwoman, was wearing "mod" stockings. I looked again. Just ripped and torn.

---

* Dom Mintoff was head of the Malta Labor Party.
† On 13 June 1970 the USS Little Rock (CLG-4) collided with the Greek Navy destroyer Lonchi in the Gulf of Lakonia, off the southern coast of Greece. There was no casualties, and damage to both ships was light.
‡ Rear Admiral William S. Mailliard, USNR. He served on active duty as a reservist in World War II, including duty from 1943 to 1946 as flag lieutenant to Vice Admiral Daniel E. Barbey, USN, amphibious commander in the Southwest Pacific theater.
§ Mailliard served in the U.S. House of Representatives from 1953 to 1974.

He seemed to love misery, and he was very, very critical of everything the Sixth Fleet was doing. We went through an hour and half of sparring with him about this or that. So when we left, his wife said to Bill and me as we were going out, "Don't take it too harshly. He's a good man."

So as we got in the car, I said to Bill, "That guy is Commie through and through."

Bill said, "No. He's a politician. I deal with them all the time. I know them."

[Laughter]

And the second time was when Pritzlaff was our ambassador, and he was having Mintoff for lunch, and he wanted me to come down and join them.* I didn't know until I got there that Mintoff was dying to get an invitation over to the U.S. He wanted to be invited and to call on the President and all that. And they do that in Britain, you know, but this country doesn't do that. We don't deal with out-of-power politicians, the leader of the opposition in this case. He was riding Pritzlaff on that score, and Pritzlaff was defending the position. But we'd had some pretty hard words when I'd been with him before, and so he lit into me. He was very upset because the Sixth Fleet went into Athens often. He said, "You're supporting the colonels."

I said, "No. We're invited. We go in where we're invited. We like to go there. We have a very pleasant time when we're there. It isn't up to us to tell the Greek government what kind of government it ought to have."

His complaint to me had been that we were not welcome in Malta, and I said, well, we wouldn't come if we weren't welcome, that his government invited us and we invariably came in on an invitation. "But if we're not wanted, if we're really not wanted, we won't come."

He said, "You interfere in our political . . ."

I said, "No, that's the point. We don't interfere. You're complaining about how we're going into Greece. It is none of Sixth Fleet's business to interfere in who runs Greece, and it's none of Sixth Fleet's business to interfere in who runs Malta. We'll go where we're invited and we won't go where we aren't invited. It's that simple."

---

* John C. Pritzlaff, Jr., U.S. ambassador to Malta.

He would put forth a series of complaints, and the minute he'd get blocked on one, he'd shift to something else. He had a bag of half a dozen complaints that he could call up at will, and then he'd sort of work right around. But the minute he got blocked on a particular approach, he'd move to the next. He was a very unpleasant man.

Q: Was his objection in the belief that you were supporting his opposition? Was that why he didn't like you coming?

Admiral Richardson: Essentially, that's what he said. On the other hand, as I pointed out, I said, "We have ships that come in here that are worked on in your shipyard, and your people in the shipyard are benefiting from our presence here in the repair work."

I suppose what he may have had in mind--those guys scheme a lot. We did a lot of work in Naples, and we had a support ship that did a lot of work on destroyers and so forth. He would have liked for us to increase the amount of work that we had done in Malta. London worried about that more than I did.* In our quarterly schedules and annual schedules, we maintained a level of repair work in Malta specifically to maintain a good relationship there.

Q: What do you recall of your quarters in Italy and that being a home for your family?

Admiral Richardson: Well, very nice. Like so many things Italian, you have a choice, but you learn later that you really didn't have a choice at all. It just seemed like you did.

Q: What do you mean by that?

Admiral Richardson: We ended up in a very nice marble home with five bedrooms and seven baths, marble floors, which was typical. I had a large family there. I had my wife and

---

* This is a reference to Commander in Chief U.S. Naval Forces Europe, based in London. CinCUSNavEur was the reporting senior for Com6thFlt.

four children, and then from time to time we had a fifth child there, boys and girls, so four bedrooms was about the minimum size that could accommodate us.

The home we were in had been built by an Italian movie magnate. I don't remember his name. It had been decided by the Italians before I got there that that's where we were going to be. But we went through the process of house hunting here and there. Of course, we could have insisted on someplace else, but that one was in Formia, within two miles of the flagship. See, the bay is--Gaeta is over here. Formia is on this side.

But the people were very hospitable. At that point in time, there were a number of Communists in Rome, and from time to time they'd set up some sort of a march down in Gaeta, and we'd be concerned about whether or not this would turn into a problem. We always had the carabinieri, and then they were alert to it.[*] They weren't always at our house, but anytime there was any problem, and often we didn't know that there was any potential problem, we'd look out and there'd be a couple of carabinieri out in the front. It had to do with information they had but I didn't have.

But anyway, on one occasion, when the biggest march of Communist sympathizers out of Rome came to Gaeta, they came in a parade down the street there. All the Gaetani were out with their American flags waving. We had a good relationship. I don't know a single incident of trouble between our people and the Gaetani and Formians.

Q: Did you get to travel with your family at all?

Admiral Richardson: I took leave on one occasion, I think. I took my family up to Garmisch, Germany. We went to London a number of times, but not on leave status. And then up to Stuttgart with USCinCEur. We traveled a lot.

I had a wonderful chief of staff.

Q: Who was he?

---

[*] Carabinieri are Italian policemen.

Admiral Richardson: The last one was Fred Kelley, and he was very, very fine.[*] His predecessor, Alden Whitney, was equally good.[†]

Well, why don't we move to . . .

Q: One final question. Were you relieved before the Jordanian crisis came up in 1970?[‡]

Admiral Richardson: I was relieved the end of August 1970, before that happened.

Q: Just before that.

Admiral Richardson: Yes, immediately before that. And then I flew to Norfolk, then to San Diego, and then flew on CinCPacFlt's plane out to Honolulu. So my family, including two little dogs, flew all the way from Italy to Hawaii over a period of about a month.

Q: And you reported in, at least temporarily, with your old friend John Hyland.[§]

Admiral Richardson: Yes, indeed. I was with Johnny for about three months, and he's always one of the nicest people I've ever known and very firm in what he thinks is right or wrong. He's an ideal.

Q: Did he at that point express a sense of bitterness that he, in fact, had been fired from that job?

---

[*] Captain Frederick J. Kelley, USN.
[†] Captain Alden W. Whitney, USN.
[‡] In September 1970 commandos of the Popular Front for the Liberation of Palestine (PFLP) blew up three airliners--U.S., British, and Swiss--at Amman, Jordan and took the passengers as hostages. On 18 September the Pentagon announced that additional ships and aircraft had been ordered to the eastern Mediterranean because of U.S. concern for the safety of an estimated 450 Jordanians threatened by fighting there.
[§] Admiral John H. Hyland, USN, served as Commander in Chief Pacific Fleet, 30 November 1967 to 5 December 1970.

Admiral Richardson: He isn't given to that. He had his views and made known what they were vis-à-vis Zumwalt, and, of course, he was relieved from duty when Zumwalt came in.[*]

Bud Nance came to me.[†] I just saw an item in the paper here a month or two ago. Helms recruited Nance to head up his senatorial staff.[‡] He was getting into trouble of some sort with other congressmen. He sent for Bud Nance to head up his staff. Well, Bud Nance was on the watch list in the JCS as a new flag officer. He and the Air Force people were together down there, and they would stand the duty. One day, an Air Force brigadier general came to Bud and said, "You'd better come in and listen to what's on this tape." At that point in time, we were heavily engaged with North Vietnam. And the tape recorded a telephone conversation between Zumwalt, who had been told he would be the next CNO, and one of his close friends who was working preliminary problems for him back in Washington.

I was Deputy CinCPacFlt, and Bud Nance came in to see me about that tape when he was on a trip. He was troubled, and he said that when he listened to this tape, Bud Zumwalt had outlined to the vice admiral who was working the problem for him all of the people in aviation he was going to get rid of. Bud Nance said this, in his mind, was gross, and was wondering what to do about it.[§]

I said, "Well, go see Admiral Schoech. If you see him, you've got Admiral Radford, and you've got Admiral Anderson."[**]

So Nance, when he got back to Washington, went to see Bill Schoech, and in a meeting with Schoech, Radford, and Anderson, he outlined the information from this tape.

I've often wondered how much that intercession accomplished. Anderson was probably the only one in a position who could do something, because he was at that time on the President's Foreign Intelligence Advisory Board. I wondered to what degree that may have constrained what later happened. I have no idea. But that occurred.

---

[*] Admiral Elmo R. Zumwalt, Jr., USN, served as Chief of Naval Operations from 1 July 1970 to 29 June 1974. Hyland discussed this relief in his Naval Institute oral history.
[†] At the time Rear Admiral James W. Nance, USN, was Chief, Studies, Analysis, and Gaming Agency, Joint Chiefs of Staff.
[‡] Senator Jesse Helms (Republican-North Carolina).
[§] Nance was a naval aviator.
[**] Admiral Arthur W. Radford, USN, served as Chairman of the Joint Chiefs of Staff from 15 August 1953 to 14 August 1957.

Q: Did it turn out that some of the men on the hit list did not get hit?

Admiral Richardson: I don't know. I don't know who they were. I just know of the event itself, and Bud came to me with this story and questioned me on what to do about it.

When Zumwalt sent out a message to the four-stars, the fleet commanders, about eliminating parochialism in the Navy, he indicated he was going to put 1100 admirals in charge of aircraft carrier forces, and he was going to put aviator admirals in charge of crudesflots and so forth.[*] I read the answers that came back. The only one I didn't see was the one my boss, Clarey, sent.[†] Clarey was away when it came.

I wrote a letter to Bud Zumwalt and pointed out that professionalism at the top level was so important, that the chief of staff cannot function as the top man, and if he is so functioning, he ought to be the top man. It was a very critical letter of the basic idea and pointed out that at the end of World War II naval aviators had set up a screening board to ascertain which of its officers were more likely to be suitable as commanding officers on the basis of reviewing their record and their past performance in command, and that the 1100s had also done the same thing later. This was an attempt to improve professionalism in these top jobs. It was a long letter, five- or six-page letter. I have it. And I had many favorable comments.

Ralph Cousins wrote me and he said it was well received.[‡] And I got a very fine reply from Zumwalt on it, and from others to whom I sent copies. Bill Martin and others were praiseworthy that I had dared buck the thing. So anyway, the only message from Duncan or any of the other CinCs that came back to Zumwalt that took exception to the idea was from Rivero.[§] Rivero's comment was, "Don't mix up parochialism with professionalism." There was more to it, but the punch line was, "Don't confuse

---

[*] Crudesflot--cruiser-destroyer flotilla. The designator for surface warfare officers was 1100 at the time.
[†] Admiral Bernard A. Clarey, USN, served as Commander in Chief Pacific Fleet, 5 December 1970 to 30 September 1973. Clarey, a submariner, had relieved aviator Hyland of the fleet command.
[‡] Admiral Ralph W. Cousins, USN, served as Vice Chief of Naval Operations from 30 October 1970 to 1 September 1972.
[§] Admiral Charles K. Duncan, USN, served as Supreme Allied Commander Atlantic, Commander in Chief Atlantic, and Commander in Chief Atlantic Fleet from 29 September 1970 to 31 October 1972. His oral history is in the Naval Institute collection.

parochialism with professionalism." But it was the only one that went back that didn't indicate . . .

Q: Didn't indicate, "Aye, aye, sir."

Admiral Richardson: Aye, aye, sir, that's right. Except for Chick Clarey's, and I don't know what he sent. Before I sent mine in, I showed it to Clarey. I said, "I won't send it if you object to it, because it could reflect on you. I'm your deputy."

He said, "No, that's all right, send it." But he said, "My advice is, don't send it. They'll just eat you up."

I said, "Well, I feel strongly about it, and I think it's worth that risk." So I sent it.

Then Ralph Cousins, as I said, told me later that Zumwalt took it very well. However, I still got my letter that my services were no longer needed.

Q: Do you think your letter had any useful effect?

Admiral Richardson: I have no idea whether it did. He never did fully implement it. He started it, and then he stopped. There was a naval aviator put in charge of a crudesflot. So far as I know, it was the only one; it died at least. I don't know what happened later.

Q: One change that came about is that carrier group commanders started getting surface officers as chiefs of staff. I'm not sure if it was right as a result of that, but that's something that happened.

Admiral Richardson: Well, a carrier task group commander should have as his chief of staff an 1100, that's right. What had already happened--well, maybe it came with Zumwalt. The Com6thFlt who relieved me, Ike Kidd, was a surface officer, appointed by Zumwalt.

Q: That was a first.

Admiral Richardson: And that was about the first. Now, Ike had been Com1stFlt, and in the two years that I commanded Sixth Fleet, I reviewed what was being done in the other areas. We had meetings with Second Fleet. B. J. Semmes was Com2ndFlt, and we had a meeting once while our two flagships were together.* I couldn't see that Second Fleet did anything at all that was of any use to me, but Ike Kidd's work in First Fleet was very useful to me. I read the work that he was doing in surveillance, in readiness, and command and control generally, and I adopted some of the ideas that he had. This was fairly late in the game, sometime during 1970, but the work that he was doing in First Fleet was very interesting. For that reason, I wasn't at all sorry to see him coming as my relief.

But one of the problems that surfaced right out was that the crudesflot commanders were largely ineffective when they came. In talking with Wally Wendt about it, I said, "Well, for one thing, they have inadequate supporting staffs." And I wanted an intelligence officer for them. They had either a chief or a first class who functioned in intelligence, but they were just out of the picture. They were not SI-cleared.† They didn't have any of that information or resources. And so Wally went to work on it.

I wanted an intelligence officer as a minimum on every crudesflot that deployed to the Med. I got the word from Com2ndFlt that he only had three in his whole command. But Wally went to work on that one, and then we did build up the staffs of the crudesflot commanders so that they came to be more nearly on a par in their support qualities with the carrier group commanders who were well set up.

Q: Readiness was always very high on Admiral Kidd's agenda.

Admiral Richardson: Yes, that's right.

---

* Vice Admiral Benedict J. Semmes, Jr., USN, commanded the Second Fleet from April 1968 to September 1970. His oral history is in the Naval Institute collection. The meeting took place 22-23 October 1968 when the respective fleet flagships, the Springfield (CLG-7) and Little Rock (CLG-4) were at Rota, Spain.
† SI--special intelligence.

Q: Another change was that Jerry Miller became Com2ndFlt.* That then went to an aviator, where that had traditionally been a black-shoe command.

Admiral Richardson: For whatever the reason, I never had a feel for what he did there as Com2ndFlt. Probably timing--I departed Sixth Fleet in August '70.

Q: Please tell me what you did in your role with Admiral Clarey.

Admiral Richardson: Well, as deputy to him, we were heavily involved in the Vietnam War. This is '70 to '72. At that time, a lot of Navy thought was being diverted from what goes under the title of operational readiness into what goes into the Z-grams that were flooding the place and, collectively speaking, having a rather disastrous effect.†

Those whom I have known, such as Tex Guinn, who was Chief of BuPers to Bud Zumwalt, complained that thousands of people were being used in assignments for which there were no billets.‡ They were just being used there, and billets were going unfilled because of that. But he also said that Bud's ideas were very sophisticated. The unfortunate thing was that the people who were the supposed beneficiaries of the Z-gram ideas simply took advantage of it and got sloppy and dirty, instead of understanding them.

I have never heard any favorable comments regarding them. I should say that when Rivero was Vice Chief and I was ComFAirNorfolk, Rivero was doing everything he could to improve the lot of enlisted men. One of my involvements in Norfolk was with the barracks, inspecting the barracks and recommending needed things. There was just so much we needed. When Zumwalt came along, with his face on the front of Time, I had

---

* Vice Admiral Gerald E. Miller, USN, commanded the Second Fleet from September 1970 to August 1971. His oral history is in the Naval Institute collection.
† Z-grams were consecutively numbered policy directives from Chief of Naval Operations Zumwalt that attempted to deal with such issues as enlisted rights and privileges, equal opportunity, and Navy families. Junior personnel viewed them much more favorably than did their seniors. See U.S. Naval Institute Proceedings, May 1971, pages 291-298.
‡ Vice Admiral Dick H. Guinn, USN, served as Chief of Naval Personnel from 21 August 1970 to 1 February 1972.

high hopes that, by gosh, here at last we've got somebody who has the clout with Congress who can really do things for enlisted personnel."

To some extent he did improve the lot of enlisted men. He required more attentiveness of senior officers toward them and a lot more focus on their problems, and that's to his credit. But unfortunately, that was sullied by the unfortunate implementation of some of his ideas where he lost control of the quarterdeck, and the chiefs were undermined and lost their authority--that sort of thing. That was very unfortunate.

It is just such a shame that Zumwalt, who is enormously competent, was moved into that spot without having first had a fleet or even a major numbered fleet command, where he could have had a chance to gain experience with at-sea operations. He really never had much of that. His operational experience was ashore, down in Vietnam as a flag officer. And I think we blew the chance to have an exceptional CNO. It was blown by the Secretary of the Navy, Chafee, now the senator from Rhode Island.†

I have been told that Moorer recommended Clarey to be CNO and me to be VCNO. Chafee had Nitze's recommendation for Zumwalt, and Chafee bought that. Moorer interceded with SecDef; he was then Chairman, JCS.‡ But SecDef said SecNav could have who he wanted, as far as he was concerned. So that fell by the wayside. It's unfortunate, because had Zumwalt been given two, three, or four years in command of operational forces, he could easily have become one of the best CNOs we've known.

Q: It's fascinating to contemplate the possibility of yourself being VCNO also.

Admiral Richardson: Well, I don't think anybody in his right mind would really want to be VCNO.

Q: Why do you say that?

---

* A portrait painting of Zumwalt appeared on the front cover of the 21 December 1970 issue of Time. The accompanying article, "Humanizing the U.S. Military," was on pages 16-22.
† John H. Chafee served as Secretary of the Navy from 31 January 1969 to 4 May 1972.
‡ Admiral Thomas H. Moorer, USN, served as Chairman of the Joint Chiefs of Staff from 3 July 1970 to 30 June 1974. His oral history is in the Naval Institute collection.

Admiral Richardson: Oh, it's pure drudgery. Remember that anecdote I told about Arleigh Burke instructing me, "Don't call me tonight unless the building burns down. Then call me." It's that sort of thing. No, I have never wasted any time being upset or sorry about that.

Q: What do you recall about the racial unrest that was coming up at that time, the Kitty Hawk, the Constellation, the Hassayampa, and so forth?[*]

Admiral Richardson: There were some congressmen who made an investigation. These were two representatives on the House Armed Services Committee, and they were very critical of the impact of Zumwalt on Navy discipline. This was one of the consequences. Before they turned in their report, they gave it to Admiral Jim Russell to look over up in Washington state.[†] Jim's advice back to them was, "Well, if you want to get rid of the CNO now, turn this report in. If you don't want to do that, then you better soften your report." They softened their report.

I think that pretty much covers the whole topic. It was literally brought on, in a large part, by the degradation in authority of the commanding officer and his officers and the senior enlisted people. But it was also a part of the time, because we all know what went on in '68 in Baltimore and places like that. It was part and parcel of that, as well, but it was exacerbated by the degradation in authority, and that's very unfortunate.

Q: It's sort of an unknowable thing. One argument is that Zumwalt's changes made the situation worse. The other argument is that there was that pressure anyway, and he perhaps relieved some of that pressure with his reforms, and it might even have been worse. We'll never know.

---

[*] See Captain Paul B. Ryan, USN (Ret.), "USS Constellation Flare-up: Was it Mutiny?" U.S. Naval Institute Proceedings, January 1976, pages 46-53.
[†] Admiral James S. Russell, USN (Ret.), had been Vice Chief of Naval Operations when Burke was CNO.

Admiral Richardson: Well, that could be, but I think if anyone looks at the specifics of the case, and I did back at that time because it came through CinCPacFlt, you'd say things got out of hand. There weren't many people involved. They got out of hand because the authority of the master-at-arms had been pretty much undermined, and it need not have happened. I think that had the magnitude of the specific events been greater, it would have been a very serious problem.

Now, back in my Sixth Fleet days, there had been a murder at Camp Lejeune, a black/white confrontation thing.* And then over came the battalion in which this had occurred. That was a very touchy time. I got word the day before the battalion arrived in Spain, at Rota, that a plane was coming over, bringing Naval Investigative Service authorities and some others. They were going to find and take back for trial some personnel that were in that battalion. They had to identify who they were.

So I went over to Rota. I wanted to be there when this outfit landed, because I was afraid there would be further trouble. The troops were lined up on the dock, and an individual, whose face was covered, walked down the line and pointed out several individuals. They were taken aboard the plane and flown back to the States, to Camp Lejeune. I never heard any more about it. But there were a number of people in that group that got fingered that day and were taken away.

It was a very touchy time, and I wanted to be in Rota, because I was afraid there might be some outbreak ashore. But it all settled down. The battalion next went to the south of France. And once again I was really concerned, but there was no problem. That sort of ended it.

Now, that was before Zumwalt. I don't remember the exact date on it, but my recollection is that was six months to a year before he took over. So it was not a new problem. It wasn't of his creation.

Q: What do you recall about the prosecution of the war in Vietnam during that two-year period? By then, it was a very unpopular thing in this country.

---

* Camp Lejeune, located in North Carolina, is the major base for the U.S. Marine Corps on the East Coast.

Admiral Richardson: It had become very unpopular. The President was under a great deal of pressure.[*] When he did things that needed to be done, such as the attacks in Cambodia, he took a political beating.[†] The information was so obvious that Cambodia provided the main access route for supplies into South Vietnam for the Viet Cong and the North Vietnamese, and we knew where they were. There were huge stockpiles of material just over the border that we couldn't touch. So finally we did bomb it. Of course, that brought the house down.

At a later time, in about April of '72, CinCPac directed CinCPacFlt to develop the plans for Air Force/Navy strikes into Hanoi, Haiphong. Instead of passing it on down to CTF 77, who was Hutch Cooper at that time and who was heavily involved in developing three or four other plans passed to him, I decided we'd do it in CinCPacFlt headquarters.[‡] It wasn't all that difficult to do. I'd been doing it for a year down there and knew the processes, and we had a very fine rear admiral who had just returned from down there with his cardiv staff.

So I called CinCSAC and proposed a meeting in CinCPacFlt headquarters to do this planning.[§] Would they send representatives? Very happy to. So they sent a planeload of people out to do the planning. We sent for Rear Admiral Christiansen from San Diego to come and assist us as a recent commander there, familiar with the new types of planes that we had, and with current Air Force and Navy procedures for cooperation.[**] The Seventh Air Force sent somebody up to coordinate their actions. And so we developed in a three-day period the entire "Linebacker" strike plan.

Now, the whole thing was focused on B-52s making repeated strikes, with

---

[*] Richard M. Nixon served as President of the United States from 20 January 1969 until his resignation on 9 August 1974.
[†] Beginning on 29 April 1970, U.S. and South Vietnamese troops launched attacks into Communist staging areas in Cambodia. The invasion sparked widespread antiwar demonstrations throughout the United States. At Kent State University, Kent, Ohio, a detachment of Ohio National Guardsmen opened fire on a group of protesters and killed four students.
[‡] Rear Admiral Damon W. Cooper, USN, Commander Carrier Striking Force Seventh Fleet and Commander Carrier Division Five.
[§] CinCSAC--Commander in Chief Strategic Air Command.
[**] Rear Admiral John S. Christiansen, USN, Commander Carrier Division Seven.

suppression and coordination by both Seventh Air Force and our carrier aircraft.* That plan was developed and implemented, and it was pulverizing the North Vietnamese. The B-52s had their heaviest losses that first day. After that, it was essentially a free ride.

But that had to be stopped because of political pressure, and the Vietnamese were then able to negotiate their way out of it and succeed. They snatched victory from the jaws of defeat; then they broke the treaty that was later concluded. They'd been in violation of that, but there wasn't a doggone thing we were going to do about it, and they knew it.

Q: You talked the other day about Walt Rostow and President Johnson picking the targets for the Alfa strikes. What was the method for targeting during this period, during the Nixon administration?

Admiral Richardson: I don't know.

Q: But did you see such a heavy-handed approach from Washington?

Admiral Richardson: No, I didn't. That went through CinCPac and out to Seventh Fleet. We were on the fringes of the target assignment thing, but I have no specific recollections of that. We certainly were aware of what they were doing, and I would often get on a back-channel circuit and talk to CTF 77, who was Hutch Cooper at that time, about this or that.

We had on one occasion a long strike with three carriers into one target area in North Vietnam, and the Air Force was coming in the other side. The Air Force dropped out of it for some reason, so I called the Chairman of the JCS, Tom Moorer, and said this was a high-threat area and did they really want us to carry it out alone. He said, "If the others aren't there, yes, we do." So we did. Cooper didn't mind. We had no losses, it turned out. I was afraid we were going to have heavy losses on it, but we didn't. And I think we had only two carriers in it instead of three, for some reason.

---

* The Boeing B-52 Stratofortress is an eight-engine jet-propelled heavy bomber flown by the U.S. Air Force. The first B-52s were delivered to the Strategic Air Command in June 1955. The last Stratofortresses built, the B-52H model, were delivered to the Air Force in October 1962.

But we needed to do those things early in the war. When we didn't do them early and when the other people adapted, adjusted, and so forth, why, it just was too late. Their supplies were coming from abroad. They weren't supplying themselves from within their own resources, and everything at that point was really interdiction. So I don't know that destroying a cement plant or the steel plant or any of these things made a doggone bit of difference at that point in time.

Q: One thing that did have a dramatic effect was the mining of Haiphong. What do you remember about that operation?

Admiral Richardson: Well, I don't now recall the responses. When we got instructions, or authorization to do that, we sent for Rear Admiral Bill Moran, who was at that time at China Lake.[*] Bill was an authority in that area and came out, and we drew up plans for the mining, aided by a MOMAT team. I don't remember whether we used A-3s or not, but we did use A-6s to drop the mines in the channels up there.[†] My recollection is that it simply stopped the Soviet ships from coming in, but it didn't stop the supplies that were coming down from China itself. An awful lot of this stuff was coming down from China. It again is something that had we resolutely pursued early in the game, it would have had an effect, but by the time we got around to it, why, the other supply source, China, was adequate. Furthermore, their warehouses were loaded all the way down through Vinh and that area and the hills had been burrowed out. They had supplies, quantities of supplies from Cambodia, and it just didn't have the effect it could so easily have had earlier in the game.

Q: What do you remember about the response to the North Vietnamese Easter Offensive in 1972?

---

[*] Rear Admiral William J. Moran, USN, Commander Naval Weapons Center China Lake.
[†] In May 1972, confronted by North Vietnamese intransigence at the Paris peace talks and a North Vietnamese spring offensive against South Vietnam, President Nixon ordered the Navy to carry out existing plans for mining the harbors of North Vietnam. On 8 May, A-6 Intruders from U.S. carriers sowed mines at Haiphong, Hon Gai, Cam Pha, Thanh Hoa, Vinh, Quan Khe, and Dong Hoi. The flow of seaborne supplies in North Vietnam ceased immediately.

David C. Richardson #3 - 279

Admiral Richardson: I don't recall anything specific.

Q: What about the U.S. involvement or monitoring, or however you might describe it, of the Indo-Pakistani War in late '71, when the <u>Enterprise</u> task force went around to the Indian Ocean?

Admiral Richardson: I don't know. I just don't remember.

Q: What are your recollections of Admiral Clarey as a CinC and your working relationship with him?

Admiral Richardson: Well, Clarey is a very nice, very pleasant individual. He's slow to take action on some things. Very cautious, very, very cautious, and he didn't respond nearly as rapidly as I would like to see him respond in operational matters. He seemed afraid of making mistakes.

Q: Do you want to mention any examples?

Admiral Richardson: I suppose so. Once we learned that several missile-capable submarines were departing Vladivostok-Petropavlosk. We then had five carriers off Vietnam. I sent for Paul Lacy, ComSubPac, to prepare pronto a plan to send some nuclear boats to defend the carriers if events so evolved.* He responded within hours. I took the plan to Clarey. As often happened, he postponed taking action. Lacy called and said the plan would be impossible of implementation if not started within hours.

    I called my friend Mickey Weisner in Washington; he was then Deputy CNO for Air. I referenced the source of our basic information and asked that he go see Admiral Moorer, who was then Chairman of the JCS. In less than an hour, a call came to headquarters from Moorer, asking what we were going to do about that information. The

---

* Rear Admiral Paul L. Lacy, Jr., USN, served as Commander Submarine Force Pacific Fleet from 1970 to 1972.

answer: "We have a plan. We are implementing it immediately." And so we did. Clarey sought certainty and was reluctant to move until he felt he had it. On more than one occasion we had to take initiatives on less than complete information.

Q: What do you recall about living out in Hawaii? That must have been very pleasant.

Admiral Richardson: It was. It was a very busy time, but it was certainly pleasant, too, because we had a lot of friends. The local authorities were very, very considerate. There were many retired people there, including Admiral Felt, whom I'm always happy to be with, and Johnny Hyland and his wife. She died recently. So it was quite a pleasant time, but I get rock fever. I couldn't retire in Hawaii.

Q: What else?

Admiral Richardson: One day the commanding officer of the Pearl Harbor Naval Shipyard came to see me with a Greek rear admiral in tow. The Greek rear admiral had come out to inspect a destroyer that was offered to Greece by our Navy Department, and the commanding officer of the shipyard wanted to make the point that this destroyer was in very poor shape. It had to have a lot of work done on it, and he thought it was unwise to dump this on the Greek Navy. But the Greek admiral had his instructions, and they do not deviate from what they're told to do. I said, "Well, I'll call Admiral Margaritis and see if we can do something better."

So I did. I called him. In the meantime, I had checked with our Commander Cruiser-Destroyer Force in San Diego. At that time we still had a Commander Cruiser-Destroyer Force. He said that he had several destroyers that were being transferred to the reserves. One of the destroyers had just completed overhaul and was in very good shape. It would be just as easy for him to release that one to the Greeks and put another equally good destroyer into the reserves about two or three months later.

So I told Margaritis that we could do better if he left it to me. I knew from my previous duty, when I'd been aboard Greek ships, that the last thing on earth that navy needed was a troubled ship with a lot of maintenance problems, because it would never get fixed in the Greek Navy.

So Margaritis said, "Well, that's fine." He appreciated it very much. "Would you instruct Admiral [I've forgotten his name] So-and-so what to do."

So I sent him back to San Diego to get in touch with ComCruDesPac. Then that arrangement was made.

Well, about a year later, in early 1972, I got a message from the Secretary of the Navy. He said that I was wanted in Washington to receive an award. My wife and I flew back. Warner was Under Secretary at the time.[*] I don't know where the Secretary was. But, anyway, he was the presiding gent there, and who did I want to join us at the reception and dinner by the Greek ambassador? I said, "Vice Admiral and Mrs. Weisner and Rear Admiral and Mrs. Tom Hawyard."[†] Mickey Weisner and I were close friends for many years.

So we flew back, and we went to the Greek Embassy for an evening. I was awarded the Medal of St. George. I asked him, "What does this entitle me to?"

He said, "It entitles you to stand next to the prime minister during parades." [Laughter] That followed the initiative to get a proper ship in their hands, not a bucket of bolts.

Q: Anything else about your time in PacFlt?

Admiral Richardson: I think we've probably pretty well covered that period. I don't have any other noteworthy things to talk about. There are all sorts of events, social and otherwise, but I don't think that they would be significant to anyone looking back.

Q: Did you feel any pangs when you got this letter asking that you retire? You'd been in uniform for 40 years at that point.

---

[*] John W. Warner served as Under Secretary of the Navy from 11 February 1969 to 4 May 1972.
[†] Rear Admiral Thomas B. Hayard, USN, was Director of the Office of Program Appraisal in the officer of the Secretary of the Navy. As a four-star admiral he later served as Chief of Naval Operations, 1978-82.

Admiral Richardson: No, I don't really think I did. I wasn't surprised. I had no strong feeling of disappointment, no. I had no particular job that I had set my cap for, so to speak, and I just took it and didn't worry about it.

Q: So what did you settle into then after you retired?

Admiral Richardson: We came to the coast. I retired effective 1 July of '72. ComNavAirPac administered the retirement ceremony. As a matter of fact, I deliberately retired on the coast rather than in Honolulu. I didn't want Chick Clarey to feel pressured to give me an award, that he might have felt had I been there. So I just decided that I didn't want any pressure on him at all on that. I was surprised later to get a Distinguished Service Medal as a result of Chick. That was my third one, actually.

So back to the coast. I was asked to be the principal Navy speaker at an AFCEA conference.* The East, West Coast, the whole AFCEA was together in Dallas at that convention, and I spoke on "Brute Force Navy," pointing out that we really needed to develop deceptive capabilities, electronic warfare capabilities, and the capability to control the emission activity of our ships. If we can't control it, then we can't create false targets or create the sort of portrayals that we want. The speech was well received. I mentioned it earlier.

The following spring, I received an invitation. I think it really was triggered as a result of a retired vice admiral who was with the NRAC, getting in touch with the head of the NRAC, who then was director of research at Stanford University. He was a member of the NRAC, Naval Research Advisory Committee, SCOE--Special Committee on Electronics. This committee had been charged with assessing the effectiveness of the Naval Security Group in supporting fleet operating forces. What more should they do? What weren't they doing? We met at the Naval Security Group headquarters on Nebraska Avenue.

I was invited to join the group. This particular panel was headed up by Dr. Jim Wakelin, who had been Assistant SecNav earlier, and was a very competent individual, a

---

* AFCEA--Armed Forces Communications and Electronics Association.

very likable person.* I served on that committee and its successor for 18 years. We completed a study assessing the effectiveness of the Naval Security Group in supporting the fleet.

We transformed under Inman to a group called the Exploitation Advisory Board. Of the NRAC committees, we were the only one that had essentially any clearance required for us to do our work. We had all of the general clearances and some of the very special clearances that bore in certain areas that we were involved in. But, of course, to work with the Naval Security Group, you had to have the highest level clearances, and that's outside of secret and top secret. You're in the special intelligence area.

Our study was very well received. The director of research at the Naval Security Group was with us throughout that study, working with us, and was part and parcel of it, so the Naval Security Group people were an intimate part of our study. It wasn't done at arm's length; it was done in collaboration with them.

Then two other studies were done. One was the adequacy of intelligence support to the operating forces, and I traveled at that time out into the Pacific in '75 and '76. That study was a very good study. I had the part having to do with amphibious warfare. I worked in the others, but this was a specific charge.

In my visits out at CinCPacFlt and up to Pendleton, I ran into a lot of criticism of the functioning of intelligence within the Marine Corps, one complaint derived from the fact that these people were committed under NATO planning to move "somewhere," and they had no information from USCinCEur pertinent to "somewhere."† They had no information about the problems they would encounter after they got there. The intelligence void was enormous. So I made very critical comments having to do with this aspect of Marine Corps intelligence functioning.

I went to Jim Wakelin and said, "I think we'd better go brief the Commandant of the Marine Corps before publishing our criticisms."

He said, "Fine." And we did.

---

* Dr. James H. Wakelin, Jr., served as Assistant Secretary of the Navy (Research and Development) from 1959 to 1964. From 1970 to 1973 he was a member of the board of advisers to the president of the Naval War College.
† Camp Pendleton, near Oceanside, California, is the major Marine Corps base on the West Coast.

I set the meeting up. I knew the Commandant at the time, and over we went.* As we walked in the building, we saw a big purple slab there, "Commandant Marine Corps." Then go down, assistant to this and so forth, and down at the very bottom, "Assistant Intelligence, Colonel." I said, "There's the problem. No rank, no attention."

The Commandant listened for an hour to what we had to say. Then he got the Assistant Commandant and said, "I want a general officer to be the intelligence officer here."

There was also at that time a developmental program that would have fed a lot of passively collected information--in other words, electronics activity on the beach--using an airplane and back into a Marine headquarters afloat. If the Marine landing force commander didn't have a special intelligence capability in his headquarters and if he didn't have the capability to exploit this same kind of information when they transitioned control to the shore, he was working with a lot less information than he needed, and it would be costly in lives. The Marines just weren't with that program.

As a result of this particular briefing, the Marine Corps made a lot of changes in their intelligence functioning. Their thought had been, and the then setup was, that in the Marine Corps the integration of Marine intelligence takes place at the CinCPacFlt/CinCLantFlt level. Fine, they had integration of information there, but in the entire area of capability development, which is done in Washington, they weren't in that, or if they were in it, they were in at low levels.

The headquarters of the Marine Corps, which was the one who had to take care of closing that gap between Camp Pendleton-based MarDiv and whoever was to be in charge of them once they deployed overseas was the one to establish the liaison and start building up their intelligence resources. That arrangement had to be set up by the Commandant Marine Corps. So that study had a great deal of impact, especially in the Marine Corps. I think it was not all that startling in various aspects to the Navy. It was being worked in conjunction with naval officers who were implementing some of the arrangements immediately following our discussions with them.

---

* General Louis H. Wilson, Jr., USMC, served as Commandant of the Marine Corps from 1975 to 1979.

The third one had to do with the function of intelligence in the Navy lab setup--how well was intelligence integrated into the Navy lab system. We found China Lake was way above anybody else, and we found that Naval Ocean Systems Center (NOSC) was next, but some things needed to be done there to improve that. Now, the Naval Ocean Systems Center is at the very focal point of any and everything having to do in the field of intelligence exploitation and command and control. They required special intelligence capability above what they had heretofore had. So that study also was a very good, useful study.

That takes us up to about '79. But I want to go back. In the fall of '75, I had a telephone call up in Mammoth, Lakes, California. I was invited to join a panel to find out why the intelligence community failed to predict the October '73 War.[*] The panel was convened by SecDef. There were three military on it, all retired. Bennett was a four-star Army general, retired, who had been the former head of DIA.[†] Holloway was the former CinCSAC, Air Force.[‡] And then I was the Navy guy.

Jim Holloway put me on that panel.[§] He was the CNO. He wanted me to do it, and so I did. We met over a six-month period. Colby briefed us, as did many others.[**] What we found out was that basically our people relied much too heavily on Israeli intelligence. And the Mossad had said no, the Egyptians aren't going to attack.[††]

What was happening was that the Egyptians would go charging down, get all set, get their bridges up to cross, and then they'd stop and come back. It was a drill. The Mossad had decided this was another drill. NSA, on the other hand, went to wartime

---

[*] On 6 October 1973 Egyptian and Syrian forces began major coordinated ground offensives against Israeli positions, seeking to improve territorial claims in the wake of the Six-Day War of 1967. Supported in part by weapons supplied by the United States, Israeli forces counterattacked and drove back the Arabs. A cease-fire finally took effect on 25 October.
[†] General Donald V. Bennett, USA (Ret.). He was Director of the Defense Intelligence Agency, 1969-72.
[‡] General Bruce K. Holloway, USAF, served as Commander in Chief of the Strategic Air Command from 29 July 1968 to 30 April 1972.
[§] Admiral James L. Holloway III, USN, served as Chief of Naval Operations from 29 June 1974 to 1 July 1978.
[**] William E. Colby served as Director of Central Intelligence/Director of the Central Intelligence Agency from 4 September 1973 to 30 January 1976.
[††] Mossad is Israel's secret intelligence service.

coverage a week before the thing broke out.[*] The intelligence community did not agree that this time there would be a war.

I don't know how much of this has been written up, but it's intriguing, and again it shows how intelligence can play such an enormous role and save lots of lives. During the course of the war itself, there were very heavy surface-to-air missile activity. This was destroying the aircraft on both sides. But up north, a small Jewish force of maybe 20,000 approached Port Said, went across, headed down toward Cairo. The Soviets had a good many photographic satellites. They started one satellite after another each day. Instead of letting them run their full time, they'd make one or two orbits and they'd drop, and then more would come. They wanted photographs of where this small Israeli force was going.

When this particular activity was going on, I was a member of the intelligence panel and was at Suitland at the Naval Intelligence Support Center when Nixon went to a low level of alert. The Soviets had initiated an air train of a number of their transport aircraft, fully loaded with troops, into Cairo. They had an air train going in. They'd land, they'd gas up, and they'd fly out, still loaded. The Soviets approached Sadat to get permission to off-load "to defend Cairo."[†] They wanted to protect Cairo from the Israelis, and Sadat didn't agree. I don't have definite knowledge, but I was told Kissinger had a good bit to do with his not agreeing.[‡]

What we saw actually happening was the result of an electronics collection system that had only been in service a few months. This system told us was that instead of going to Cairo, this Israeli column headed down into the desert, east of Cairo. What they then did was go down to where the oil and water lines were, from Cairo to the troops, and they closed the valves. That ended the war. You knew that, I take it. Did you not?

Q: No, I hadn't heard that one.

Admiral Richardson: Well, that's what happened.

---

[*] NSA--National Security Agency.
[†] Anwar el-Sadat served as President of Egypt from 1970 until he was assassinated in 1981.
[‡] Henry A. Kissinger was the President's national security adviser, 1969-73 and later served as Secretary of State, 1973-77.

Q: That is intriguing.

Admiral Richardson: And I think what a shame that there isn't more known on that. But we knew what was happening as it happened. We didn't know what the objective was until later, but we knew where the Israelis were. We knew within 30 minutes the position of these forces from this new collection capability.

So, anyway, when the panel met, what was obvious is that nobody should expect intelligence officers to be mind readers. That's not their business. What they can do is collect and tell you what's going on. But the assessment of the significance of that information is an operational responsibility, assisted, obviously, by intelligence, but don't expect the intelligence people to make that operational decision. It's up to the operators. In this case it was SecState and SecDef who should have taken initiatives.

I have talked frequently about the need to take initiatives based on indications that something might happen. Now, what could have happened was that as SecDef and SecState saw these evidences of an increasingly dangerous situation, they could have done several things. They could, for example, have contacted three, four, or five attachés and said, "Go over and see your counterpart, the Egyptian, and ask him what's cooking, that your people think that this is for real this time. Throw some uncertainty into their minds, ask "Is that true?" That sort of initiative you could take. There are others, but that's an obvious one. But as evidence comes in of an increasing threat, you start reacting to it at the time, using the resources you've got.

I understand the President--I know the intelligence agencies expected the invasion of Kuwait a substantial time ahead, on the order of a week, and it's entirely likely that the President did a lot of thinking during that time and probably was able to move more rapidly by virtue of that likelihood.

Earlier, in my explanation to my panel members, I said, "What strikes me about it is that SecDef people act like a doctor who, when a patient came in to him with a fever of 101, said, 'Go home, and if it gets up to 104, come back, and I'll do something about it,' when he should start treating the guy right then. Don't wait till the last minute."

That panel went on for about six months. A lot of facts were found in it and so forth, but the main story was that you exploit intelligence when you get it, and don't expect your people to be mind readers.

Q: The obvious value of that kind of post mortem is to learn something for the next time, and I hope that was realized.

Admiral Richardson: I doubt it seriously.

Q: You were about to talk about 1979, you said.

Admiral Richardson: I was on several Defense Science Board panels. Also I consulted with Sanders Associates. I went with them in the summer of '73. About a year later, at the instigation of Whispering Willie Holcomb, I went with Lockheed Missiles and Space, and I especially enjoyed working with them. They were an absolute delight.

Their area of major interest where the Navy is concerned was in command and control, specifically in the flag tactical command center. Gus Kinnear in '75 on the Kitty Hawk had come in to NavElex and wanted computer-aided information management.[*] Julian Lake was the deputy at NavElex, later head of NavElex.[†]

Q: "Mr. ECM."

Admiral Richardson: Yes. He spent about five million bucks packing Kitty Hawk full of all sorts of computers, only a little bit of which was useful, but it started in motion two projects, one called Outlaw Hawk, followed by Outlaw Shark. Outlaw was because it was outside the normal procurement, and it was an evolution in which the command capability augmentation by information management was worked hand in hand with the people who were going to use it. In other words, it wasn't the way you normally produced airplanes or

---

[*] Rear Admiral George E. R. Kinnear II, USN, served as Commander Carrier Group One from April 1974 to May 1975.
[†] Rear Admiral Julian S. Lake, USN, Vice Commander, Naval Electronic Systems Command.

things or tanks. This was being developed in an intimate interrelationship with the customer, with things being modified all the time to better suit the customer and also to better exploit what the technical people were capable of doing as they came to understand the command problem better.

Q: The sermon you've been preaching all along.

Admiral Richardson: That's right. And so Outlaw Hawk shifted into Outlaw Shark, and Outlaw Shark was really a remarkable system. It provided integrated information derived from space systems along with HF/DF.[*] It integrated all of the information and presented it at highly secure levels that's in special intelligence field, using tactical circuitry as the network to do this. This was in the period '78, '79, '80. When Inman was the director of NSA and following the fracas in the desert, he knew of this system and installed that capability in NSA.[†]

At that time Tom Hayward was CNO, and Bob Long had gone out to CinCPac.[‡] Inman went to Hayward and Long and said, "I want to put a unit aboard Midway. We are creating in NSA the capability to integrate various informational inputs we get, having to do with position, identity, movement, that sort of thing, and we want to provide it directly to the Midway, bypassing the chain of command, because by the time you run it through all the nodes, it's too late for use."[§]

Of course, we had Tomahawk, where a missile that's going to be fired against a moving target, if it doesn't know a direction of movement and if the information that's in that is, say, more than 30 minutes old, you're not going to hit the target, except by dumb

---

[*] HF/DF--high frequency direction finding.
[†] In an effort to rescue American hostages held in Iran, on 26 April 1980 six Air Force C-130 cargo planes and eight Navy RH-53D helicopters flew to Iran with a joint-service commando team embarked. The aircraft rendezvoused at Desert One, a site 200 miles from the Iranian capital of Teheran. Because of helicopter problems, the mission was canceled. Several servicemen were killed in the futile rescue attempt. Vice Admiral Bobby R. Inman, USN, was Director of the National Security Agency.
[‡] Admiral Thomas B. Hayward, USN, served as Chief of Naval Operations from 1 July 1978 to 30 June 1982. Admiral Robert L. J. Long, USN, served as Commander in Chief Pacific from 31 October 1979 to 1 July 1983. Admiral Long's oral history is in the Naval Institute collection.
[§] The aircraft carrier Midway (CV-41) was then home-ported in Japan.

luck.* And so it requires almost direct output from a satellite system to the gunsight operator, whoever it is that cranks up the guidance mechanism in Tomahawk. So they agreed, and Inman's promise was that, "If anything real happens, I will cut you in. I'll be sure you're informed," and on that basis it went ahead.

Well, that general approach has worked a number of times since. It was the start of getting highly sensitive information directly to the commander who needed that information without the losses that were inherent in going through a lot of nodal points, but at the same time, taking precautions to keep the others fully informed so that they could interject should they need to do so.

Q: There was a story you told me a couple of days ago that's fascinating and worth putting on the record. It had to do with getting in touch with the war college.

Admiral Richardson: I had read an article when Jim Stockdale was the president up at the Naval War College.† The article was by Tom Weschler, a retired vice admiral who was working the problem there, but they simply were out of touch with current intelligence that was highly classified.‡ As I read the article, I thought, "Oh, oh. It's way off base."

It struck me that there was information that they didn't have about new Soviet capabilities to move their forces undetected by electronic means. Of course, when they're sighted by ships at sea, that's not what we're talking about. But then there are ways, of course, to avoid that by using spread formations and by being alerted so that what is seen is not a total force, but just an out-of-area ship. There are all sorts of ways. And by using space systems, you can quite easily avoid contact with other surface ships, so it's possible to move undetected.

---

* Tomahawk is a long-range cruise missile that entered the fleet in the early 1980s, capable of delivering either conventional or nuclear warheads. Originally conceived to have both antiship and land-attack versions, the antiship type is no longer in service. For details see Miles A. Libbey III, "Tomahawk," U.S. Naval Institute Proceedings, May 1984, pages 150-163.

† Vice Admiral James B. Stockdale, USN, served as president of the Naval War College from 13 October 1977 to 22 August 1979.

‡ The oral history of Vice Admiral Thomas R. Weschler, USN (Ret.), is in the Naval Institute collection. He taught an elective course at the war college for a number of years following his retirement from active duty in 1975.

So I wrote a letter to Jim Stockdale. I couldn't tell him exactly why I was critical. I don't remember the classification of my letter, but I said, "What if I told you that it's entirely possible for a Soviet force to leave a Soviet port and transit the Atlantic, and we would not even know they were here unless we detected them visually? And I had one or two other "what ifs."

Q: Did Admiral Stockdale know you?

Admiral Richardson: Yes. So Jim said, "Well, why don't you come up here and we'll show you what we're doing in this area."

So I set up a date, but before I did, I called the head of the Naval Security Group, then Rear Admiral Pat March, and said, "I've got to go up to the war college. There's some things that the war college doesn't know that they damn well ought to know. How about letting me take Don Jermann with me?"* He said fine, he would.

Q: Who is Don Jermann?

Admiral Richardson: Don Jermann is a naval officer, now retired, who did research work in signal technology that was extremely useful.† He is a very gifted individual. Don Germann was the head "cryppie" in the research section of NSG. Don once received an award with so damn many code words on it that nobody but him and Commander Naval Security Group knew what he had done! [Laughter] We laughed over it. Bobby Inman was the one who made that award.

Don had done work that was absolutely fabulous in analyzing new Soviet naval capability in communications. I was at that time on the Naval Research Advisory Committee, Special Committee on Electronics. We met at the Naval Security Group. We were keeping abreast of what Don was doing even as he was doing this work.

---

* Rear Admiral George P. March, USN, Director, Electronic Warfare and Cryptology Division, OpNav, and Commander Naval Security Group Command.
† Captain Donald R. Jermann, USN, as of the late 1970s.

At that time Bob Long was still the Vice Chief.[*] A CinCs' conference was coming to Washington. Shapiro was the DNI.[†] Somehow I learned that Shapiro was on the CinCs' agenda for a ten-minute presentation of this very thing. So I went to Bob Long and said, "Bob, there's no way in God's earth that Shappy can even begin to get this new capability described in ten minutes. Furthermore, he doesn't really know it. Why don't you get it from the horse's mouth?"

He said, "Well, who's that?"

I said, "Captain Don Jermann."

Jimmy Flatley, who was Long's executive assistant, was there, and Flatley wrote the name down.[‡] I later ran into Bob in the corridor. I knew from Don Jermann that Long had sent for him, and he briefed Long for an hour and a half. Then I ran into Bob Long in the corridor one day, and he said, "I want you to know that I set this up for the CNO," who was Tom Hayward at that time.

Well, that's the background. I met Don Jermann at the war college, and we went in to see Jim Stockdale. I said, "Well, we have to talk to you because what Jermann has to say he can't say except to you." Then Don Germann started explaining this new Soviet naval capability. This went on for about an hour or so, and then Jim Stockdale stopped him. "How do you know these things?"

Don said, well, 32 years ago he took the Russian language as a young man and he'd been in either the Naval Security Group or NSA all these years. So Jim Stockdale then went down to see the director of the CIA, Admiral Turner, to get the requisite clearances for the war college.[§] The point of it was that designated people on the war college staff who had to do with the course instruction should know these things so that they wouldn't teach the wrong things. They didn't have to teach this specific information. So Jim Stockdale charged down to see Stansfield Turner, and Turner threw him out. He said,

---

[*] Admiral Long served as Vice Chief of Naval Operations from July 1977 to September 1979.
[†] Rear Admiral Sumner Shapiro, USN, served as Director of Naval Intelligence from August 1978 to August 1982.
[‡] Captain James H. Flatley III, USN.
[§] Admiral Stansfield Turner, USN (Ret.), served as Director of Central Intelligence/Director of the Central Intelligence Agency from 9 March 1977 to 20 January 1981. The first part of his tenure was on active duty, prior to his Navy retirement on 1 January 1979.

"They don't need to know that stuff up there." Stockdale had made the point that they wanted their instruction to reflect the knowledge. Stansfield Turner threw him out.

Q: So was that the end of it?

Admiral Richardson: As time went on, like everything the Soviets do, it migrated more broadly out and became more broadly known.

Q: How could this force get across the Atlantic without being detected?

Admiral Richardson: They could communicate with one another, and we couldn't detect the signal activity.

Q: Not from electronic countermeasures, but we hope we would have other methods.

Admiral Richardson: There are other ways to do it, but the Japanese crossed to Hawaii, and we didn't pick them up.[*] If we had reason to think they were coming, we could put out large patrol plane searches and all like that, but this was in the context of electronic activity.

Q: You're saying strictly from that. Maybe SOSUS would have picked them up or something else.[†]

Admiral Richardson: SOSUS may have picked them up, but not likely. The Soviets knew how to avoid SOSUS.

Q: Did any changes come about at the war college as a result of this propagation of Don Jermann's knowledge?

---

[*] This is a reference to the November-December 1941 when the Japanese carrier task force crossed the North Pacific in radio silence to attack Pearl Harbor, Hawaii.
[†] SOSUS--sound surveillance system, a seafloor network of listening devices used by the U.S. Navy to detect noises from transiting ships.

Admiral Richardson: I don't know. At this point in time, they had a special intelligence facility there, had had since '72 when it was finally installed. I don't know in what form that exposure took, but I'm sure that where Jim Stockdale was concerned and while he was there, that he and Weschler went over their instructions and modified them where necessary in the light of Jim's knowledge.

Q: Now here's the question that I have. How did you know these things?

Admiral Richardson: Because I was involved in them.

Q: You were involved in what context?

Admiral Richardson: My main mission in those years was to nurture a desire for intelligence among senior naval officers. Inman, Studeman, Butts, Shapiro, Brooks, and the many heads of the Naval Security Group during those 18 years all knew my aim and supported it wholeheartedly. I knew most fleet commanders and was able to access them with really no trouble. Julian Lake, Gordon Smith, Dr. Robert Hess, Gene Mullins, and Dr. Red Shepard at Lockheed Missiles and Space Corporation--we all worked hard, individually and collectively, to get the word out. Hawk and Shark, for example, were Lockheed missiles conceived in full collaboration with the Navy, both technically and operationally, in developing the TFCC, tactical flag command center.

It was all driven by the need to exploit computer capabilities for command decision-making, and it was more likely to be correct and timely. One of our converts was Vice Admiral J. O. Tuttle, an extraordinarily capable and imaginative head of Navy command and control development in the late '80s and early '90s.[*] To these I had the members of the outside intelligence group, especially under the leadership of Ray Tate. All of them were assiduous in getting the intelligence message across.

---

[*] Beginning in May 1989, Vice Admiral Jerry O. Tuttle, USN, served as Director, Space, Command and Control, OP-094, which was subsequently retitled Director, Space and C4 Systems Requirements, N6, OpNav. He retired on 1 January 1994.

But all of the then foremost signals technology has now been eclipsed by digital technology. What was once highly classified is now old stuff. Its value is now derived from its historical content that emphasizes the essentiality of not getting behind the technological and intelligence power curves. We benefited enormously from the many years of effort in Desert Shield/Desert Storm.[*]

Q: Any other topics to explore?

Admiral Richardson: You remember I talked earlier about trying to optimize task forces rather than just individual ships. For example, the reason it's important to lay out the requirements is that if you want a task force to be able to move without emitting electronically--or to assume a false electronics profile--you've got to create that capability in whatever electronics come along. We never got around to that until after I retired. But had we had the electronics requirement problem under conceptual control, then we could have guided electronics development so that a sum total of new electronics capability wouldn't be harmful from one system to another; they would be compatible--no mutual interference. Their development could be done in ways that recognized the imposition of external influences on the way it was developed. The need to be able to move forces without emitting electronically all over the face of the earth was just simply not recognized at that time. Well, except for the Soviet Navy.

Q: I think it was the North Vietnamese SAM threat in the '60s that really focused the attention on electronic warfare and brought it up to GQ status.

Admiral Richardson: Perhaps. The response to that threat was recognition that multiple technological expertise was required to identify a solution, then fast response capability to design and field electronics capabilities that could effectively counter that system. This was

---

[*] In January 1991 U.S. and Allied Coalition forces attacked Iraq to get it to retreat following its August 1990 invasion of neighboring Kuwait. The holding action in the meantime was Operation Desert Shield. The conflict itself became known variously as Operation Desert Storm and the Gulf War. Coalition forces won the war in February 1991.

done. An organization was formed of appropriate experts from the services and industry, and the response was quick reaction. The ALQ-55 was one result. Side Saddle was another. Without going into details, the one confused missile terminal guidance, and the other provided timely warning for avoidance by maneuver. But it was an electronics response to a specific hostile weapon system. It did not treat electronics as a rapidly evolving technology, almost impossible to keep up with up-to-date products, and with applications that covered the entire fleet.

Now, while on this point, a presidential scientific advisory committee did a top secret study in about 1971. When I retired, I took a copy of this report with me, not out of channels. I had it shipped to ComNavAirPac, and then when I later had a space provided for me at the Naval Ocean Systems Center (NOSC) in their vault to handle very highly classified material. I had it transferred over there.

This study described the Soviet electronics evolutionary development as a systematized matter in which the requirements of the whole force were in mind when each individual electronic system was created for whatever it was to do. The U.S. Navy, on the other hand, had simply put new electronics on old without ever having an all-encompassing concept for the employment of electronics. The report was very critical of the U.S. Navy development in that direction. That was in '71.

It wasn't until 1979 that a panel was established, and I was on that panel. It really made a major change in the naval operations. That panel was started by Gordon Smith, rear admiral, who was then Deputy NavElex, who felt exactly as I did and who had a tight tie-in with intelligence, was deeply involved with them. He was a very competent technical man, and he put together a panel. It was thought amongst JCS that this should be an Air Force, Army, and Navy panel to do this. Well, they all thought they needed to get their individual houses in order first. The Defense Science Board took on the job of Air Force/Army. The Defense Science Board, working with the Navy, also took on the job of electronic warfare in the Navy.

The people on the board were a combination of insiders and outsiders, active duty, retired, and outside electronics experts. One, a very high official in NSA, was with us on that board. The head of the board was Bert Fowler, who a few years later was the head of

Mitre Corporation.* He has headed up the Defense Science Board at least twice. So I came to know Bert Fowler and have a very high regard for him. But when that study was completed, it was very highly classified. I kept a copy down at NOSC and made it available to all of the intelligence people and to the new Navy tactical school. They couldn't teach it, but their people, their instructors who had the requisite clearances, used it and studied it. I wrote CinCLantFlt--Vice Admiral Ron Hays was deputy--and sent him a copy of that report.† I listed half a dozen documents that bore on the subject. LantFlt didn't at that time have a tactical training school. They were sending their people out here to San Diego. But these were books that should be available for all their flag officers. They should read these things and be familiar with them. Ron Hays established that requirement in the Atlantic Fleet.

A briefing was given to the CNO, Admiral Holloway. He bought it wholeheartedly and declared that it would be called electronic warfare. He saw no reason why it shouldn't be called that. A great many of the recommendations were implemented. The study's impact since has been enormous, and the entire fleet operational pattern today is totally different from what it was 12 years earlier.

For example, as I mentioned, Admiral Ramsey, who later became Deputy CinCSpace, ran the task force against the red forces or orange forces, in a major fleet exercise. His entire plan highlighted space and electronics in wide-area surveillance, in electronics response, and in creating false targets.

One intriguing thing about it was that there was a space system that had been developed by the Air Force and functioned up in Sunnyvale, California. I was asked to come up and take a two-day briefing of that system. I asked, "What's this got to do with me? I've been retired for many years now." This was about '81 or '82, somewhere in there.

They said, "Well, we want you to get in touch with Com3rdFlt and have them use this system. We can set up a direct connection with them and can provide them very timely information from space."

---

* Charles Albert Fowler was vice president and general manager of operations for Mitre from 1976 to 1985.
† Vice Admiral Ronald J. Hays, USN.

So I did. Vice Admiral Ed Waller was Com3rdFlt at the time.* I wrote him a letter. He sent his intelligence officer back for briefings and to establish arrangements and communications to make the interconnection. So that exercise was fed from a space system that was especially effective over the Central and Eastern Pacific, and it was judged very useful. It was declared the single most significant source of information during that exercise.

A feature that was especially intriguing about that exercise was that they created an enemy force using simulators. These are emitters that we place aboard that have characteristics of hostile emitters. In other words, the Soviets have a Topsail radar. Well, we'll make a piece of equipment that emits the same as the Topsail so that any space system will identify its emissions as a Topsail and report it in that way. Well, these systems were planted on ships functioning as enemy ships. The Navy space system rejected them as false. [Laughter] Its measurements were more precise, and it knew the simulators weren't the real thing. So because of its discrimination, it lost the accolade of being the single most significant source of intelligence information.

The electronics characteristics of U.S. naval task forces changed very slowly, but it certainly has been a radical change. And while it started slowly, and I happened to be involved with it all along the way, it took an enormous change when the Navy leadership in Washington bought the recommendations of the Defense Science Board report on electronic warfare. That then became the Bible. Things changed rapidly as we moved into still more advanced electronics states of readiness. Rear Admiral Gordon Smith and Rear Admiral Julian Lake were prime movers in these changes, as were Whispering Willie Holcomb, Bill Smith, and Bob Hess, and the Directors of Naval Intelligence.

Q: Was this tied in with the creation of the Office of Naval Warfare to try to integrate all these things?

---

* Vice Admiral Edward C. Waller III, USN, served as Commander Third Fleet from October 1979 to August 1981.

Admiral Richardson: When the director of naval warfare was created, not much happened. I wrote Tom Hayward letters complaining about that. He said, "Well, come back and let us brief you on what we're doing." Vice Admiral McKee at that time occupied the directorate of naval warfare.[*] I spent two days being briefed by five different heads of groups there on the functional warfare areas, and I really wasn't very impressed. I wrote up my views and gave them to Tom Hayward.

The one group that was doing good work, exceptional work, was the group that was working the problem of the outer air battle. Their thinking, their initatives, and the scope of engagement that they envisioned--all of it was first rate. The other four were weak, especially in their interest in electronics. They just weren't good.

Q: Would you have an explanation for that?

Admiral Richardson: No, I don't. I could speculate that they probably were denied the clearances needed to become educated. But I'll add this. That entire atmosphere changed significantly when Vice Admiral Lee Baggett came into that job.[†] He was able to focus the totality of that effort in a very proper direction, and he brought, really, for the first--and one of the things he did was bring the Division of Electronic Warfare out of OP-094 and put it under him in 095. It could work in either place, but the 094s, until Jerry Tuttle came, were not that good. They simply have not been very good as bureaucrats and as conceptualizers. Jerry Tuttle is tremendous. When Tom Brooks was DNI, he said to me, "I pray every day that the good Lord will release me from active duty before Jerry Tuttle goes."[‡] [Laughter]

Q: [Laughter] Well, he got his wish.

---

[*] Vice Admiral Kinnaird R. McKee, USN, served as Director, Naval Warfare, OP-095, from 1979 to 1982.
[†] Vice Admiral Lee Baggett, Jr., USN, served as Director, Naval Warfare, OP-095, from August 1982 to April 1985.
[‡] Rear Admiral Thomas A. Brooks, USN, served as Director of Naval Intelligence July 1988 to August 1991. He retired on 1 September 1991. Tuttle retired on 1 January 1994.

Admiral Richardson: He did. But Lee Baggett really made major changes in the application of electronic warfare in naval operations. When he had been ordered into that job, I wrote him a long letter on electronic warfare. He called me, and we set up a meeting at NOSC. He said, "I'll be out and meet with you at NOSC on a Saturday morning." Then I got two or three people that were very much up on electronics technicalities, Dick Cook being one, an absolutely remarkable guy. He's got more sea time than most naval officers. He's an electronics technician working at Naval Oceans System Center. Dick was there and two or three others that I knew who were very keen on EW. We spent the whole Saturday going into aspects of electronic warfare.

One of the points that I made with him at the outset was that when we get into what we call maritime strategy, I said, "Strategy comes in levels." When you get down to operational strategy, there are just two things the U.S. Navy has to do. If we just focus heavily on that, all others will come as a byproduct. One, is <u>sink submarines</u>; and two, is <u>shoot down aircraft</u>. So those two requirements are the compelling ones. Now, we have to take forces overseas. But when it comes around to letting the strategists develop whatever strategies they want, then fine. As long as we can sink submarines and shoot down aircraft, we'll be able to carry out the mission assigned to us." And then in that context, the electronics aspect of things could be fitted.

One of the things I recommended was that Baggett go back and review Ladislas Farrago's book on the Tenth Fleet.[*] The Tenth Fleet was created during World War II. It was somewhat like Room 40 in the British Navy. It worked the sigint problem. The Tenth Fleet was a notional fleet, without a commander and without any ships.

Q: Except E. J. King, of course.[†]

---

[*] Ladislas Farago, <u>The Tenth Fleet</u> (New York: Ivan Obolensky, Inc., 1962). The so-called Tenth Fleet was essentially the U.S. antisubmarine warfare force in the Atlantic in World War II.
[†] Admiral Ernest J. King, USN, served as Chief of Naval Operations from 26 March 1942 to 15 December 1945 and as Commander in Chief U.S. Fleet from 20 December 1941 to 2 September 1945; he was promoted to the rank of fleet admiral in December 1944.

Admiral Richardson: That's right. You probably remember the story about Ingersoll.* When he said to King, "We need a commander," King replied, "You don't need a commander. I'll be it." I mentioned Farrago's book as one source of information that could be widely read. The other was Very Special Intelligence by Sir Patrick Beesly, a Brit.† Bill Studeman thought that Beesly's book was the best book ever written on the subject of exploiting special intelligence.‡ A friend of mine, who I'd been on a panel with for a long time, had Tenth Fleet. That was Frank Lehan, who lives up in Santa Barbara.

Well, I was back in Washington maybe three or four weeks later. The rear admiral in charge of electronic warfare was trying to find me. He said, "Where can I get a copy of Tenth Fleet?"

I said, "I don't know, but my guess is that there's one in the library that the Director of Naval Intelligence has, and I know that Very Special Intelligence is in that library." They've got a shelf of books in there.

Q: That was his homework assignment.

Admiral Richardson: That was his homework assignment, that's right. [Laughter] But Lee Baggett brought an enormous change. Then, of course, he went down to CinCLant, SACLant from there, and he retired. He's out here now, and I see him quite often.

Q: When we were discussing the '50s, you talked about the air-to-air missile as an example of technology driving a change. Did you have examples the other way, in which you had a concept and then tried to get the hardware to serve that concept?

Admiral Richardson: No, I don't.

---

* Admiral Royal E. Ingersoll, USN, served as Commander in Chief Atlantic Fleet from 1 January 1942 to 15 November 1944. He was promoted to four-star rank in July 1942.
† Patrick Beesly, Very Special Intelligence: the Story of the Admiralty's Operational Intelligence Centre 1939-1945, (London: Hamish Hamilton, 1977).
‡ Rear Admiral William O. Studeman, USN, served as Director of Naval Intelligence from September 1985 to July 1988.

Q: So frequently, it would sound like, technology was the driver.

Admiral Richardson: It was certainly the driver during those days. What was becoming increasingly apparent was that we were simply emulating the carrier operations of the last half of '44 and 1945, ranging up and down, going wherever we pleased, whenever we wanted, simply overpowering whatever got in our way. But there was really no basic change in the patterns of operation until much, much later. Almost 40 years later. It was in the '80s that these patterns really did begin to change.

Weisner set up the tactical training unit here in San Diego for admirals and their staffs.* He had in mind the same sort of thing several years later. I talked with the skipper there, and I had set up a library for his staff in the vault at Naval Oceans System Center with six or eight volumes of books that had to do with EW, including this new very highly classified electronic warfare Defense Science Board study. He couldn't teach it specifically. His teaching could reflect it, but he couldn't teach any of it because those people weren't cleared SI. Then one day, maybe a year later, he saw me. It was at a red-tie luncheon. He said, "Good news. I have authority at long last to indoctrinate the entire student body into special intelligence, and we can teach them for one day. Then we read them all out."

When Ace Lyons was CinCPacFlt, the Ranger was to make a crossing with ComCarGru 1, and it was desired to cross the Pacific Ocean and fool the Soviets, so that they could not find it.† He set up a "Red Cell," and the Red Cell was headed by Dick Cook, but it actually was staffed by the Center for Naval Analyses.

There were several intelligence types who were retired who were with companies who worked in these areas who volunteered. They were involved as members of the red team. CinCPacFlt went to NSA and tasked our entire surveillance system to work against us. The Ranger departed San Diego and went across the Pacific, employing countermeasures. Ace Lyons asked me if I would look in on the carrier plans to accomplish the crossing. There was one very special program, which I won't identify, that was

---

* Admiral Maurice F. Weisner, USN, served as Commander in Chief Pacific Fleet, 30 September 1973 to 12 August 1976.
† Admiral James A. Lyons, Jr., USN, served as Commander in Chief Pacific Fleet from September 1985 to September 1987. ComCarGru 1--Commander Carrier Group One.

extremely useful in determining whether or not you were suspect, whether a targeting interest was being placed on you.

Everything we had for surveillance was employed in that specific exercise. There's been a number of them since. In fact, Lyons ran five of them. But in every case, the force crossed the ocean without being found by Soviet aircraft. We were able to know that.

So Ace wanted me to look in on the plans at this end, then come out and watch the functioning of the Red Cell and let him know if he'd missed anything. So I did. Well, ComCarGru 1 briefed me on what their plans were. There were about eight people of his staff, all of whom had been cleared into every bit of this sensitive program, engaged in the briefing. Usually what had been happening was that you'll find one or two people who had been cleared, but no broad clearances, just a few here or there. The intelligence officer, yes. Sometimes the admiral only. That kind of nonsense. Here this entire group were cleared into the totality of that program. I was absolutely delighted to see that scope of clearance that now applied.

So then I went out and watched the operations of the Red Cell in Honolulu, but a problem erupted because everything worked. When the Ranger task group got to the other end, there were none of the patternized responses that we had always experienced. Previously, there was always a submarine exercise against whatever ship went out as it entered a specific area. Not this time.

There were changes in the operational patterns of the Bear Deltas that made clear to us that they didn't know where we were, and they were looking for us. The satellite that fell in Canada the other day, the Soviet radar satellite that's powered by a nuclear engine. When it goes on, it emits and you know when it's on. It was never able to collect against the Ranger. They were trying hard to collect, but they could not find it. There were deceptive measures that led the Soviets to believe that they'd taken a very far northern route. In the course of these transits, there were at least five of them, in every one at the far end it was intriguing to examine the Soviet responses and see how far off the mark they were.

For example, the Soviets would reason that certainly a nuclear cruiser with its radar capabilities would be between the carrier and the Soviet threat. They were allowed to find that, but then when the carrier wasn't anywhere near it, then where the devil was the carrier? Several hundred miles away. Their reaction to those sorts of things, to extra long-range A-6 strikes appearing someplace, all operation deceptions, not all electronic, but with total control of electronic operations. Yes, by every measure we were quite capable of arriving in theater in surprise.

Q: So the Ranger succeeded in this transit?

Admiral Richardson: It succeeded completely, yes.

Q: Do you remember what year that was?

Admiral Richardson: Well, it would have been about roughly '85, '86 maybe. These times, I can't be precise on them.

Q: What else were you involved in during those years after you left active duty?

Admiral Richardson: In the period following my retirement and over the next years, I consulted with Sanders Associates from '73 to about '86 or '87; with Lockheed Missiles from about '75 to about '87; with Aerospace for one year; Systems Development Corporation for five years; and about that same time with E Systems.

Decisions and Designs was a very interesting outfit. I consulted with them for a couple of years. It had to do with the employment of decision analysis techniques, Basian theories and things of that nature, about which I knew nothing. Decision analysis focuses primarily on the probability of making a correct decision in the context of informational inputs. It relies heavily upon artificial intelligence, and it is inherent in Navy command and control but rudimentary.

It's an area where in trying to improve the quality of decision-making, one goes into the guts of things, finding out what's actually going on, then finding candidate solutions to those kind of problems. It has to do with weighing the impact of a decision that's to be made for its possible significance politically, as well as militarily. It's still in its infancy, but in the years ahead, we'll see more about it. Decision analysis, by Decisions and Design, was an aspect of flag tactical command and control development. This was done under the Office of Naval Research. I was with them for two or three years.

Then I worked with Systems Development Corporation as a consultant. They had the contract to bring into the Naval Intelligence Support Center the Integrated Automated Intelligence Processing System, and there are a great many complexities that are inherent in that. One is inputting information into the system from which it will be extracted only by those who qualified to handle that kind of information. In other words, your database is comparable to what you now have in NISC in separate rooms, where only people with certain clearances can go into this area. Therefore, only analysts with those clearances can be allowed to access the various data bases in the system. That's the nature of it.

The Navy was very poorly set up to do that job. I worked with two naval officers--Captain Larry Wright for quite a long time and Ted Sheafer, who's the current DNI.[*] But I couldn't get them to realize that the first thing they had to do was to take the design engineers from Systems Development Corporation and let them sit and work for weeks or months in the doggone office with the people who were there until they knew their procedures, their processes for managing the information they had. Computer processes should match the analytical processes--the logic--already in place. You don't get the hands-on feel from reading a book that you get working with someone. I don't care how detailed the criteria are, and I doubt seriously that the criteria are even accurate enough to do it. But I couldn't get them to do that.

I did set up and took through the facility at Naval Intelligence Support Center the new project manager that Systems Development put in charge. I caused the former one to be fired. SDC's work was being quite unsatisfactory. They were going to lose their contract, and I told that to the company president and the chairman. I took the president of the company and the new head of the Washington office, Don Biggar, through the Intelligence Support Center. I took them through the whole facility so they could see what

---

[*] Captain Lawrence T. Wright, USN. Rear Admiral Edward D. Sheafer, Jr., USN, served as Director of Naval Intelligence from August 1991 to September 1994.

these people were actually doing, and I hoped that somehow they could then get several people working in the different sections to see firsthand the processes being used by the Navy analysts.

However, soon thereafter, the Naval Intelligence Support Center got a very good project man from NSA to head up the effort. While they themselves had no knowledge or experience in procuring a system, they got people in who did, and were ultimately able to do a good job. But they went from three people up to about 60 when I last touched base with them.

Then I consulted with E Systems for about five years and Comptec Research for a year. All of these had to do with command and control and related specifically to their particular area of naval warfare and contract interest. Occasionally I'd be asked to work on something, but I'd have to say, "Well, I'm sorry. I'm working that problem with Lockheed," or, "I'm working with Sanders," and that was fine.

I never experienced a lack of integrity in any of the people that I worked with, and I knew doggone well that if I ever evidenced an exploitation of the information I had from one company to the benefit of another, that the company that benefited from that would have no respect for me, and I would certainly be cut off. Integrity is essential. I suppose I could have been in conflict of interest half a dozen times.

I was initially hesitant about working for Systems Development Corporation. I was talking with the Director of Naval Intelligence, John Butts, in connection with other matters.[*] I mentioned that this had come up, but that I had turned them down because I was a member of the intelligence panel, and our intelligence panel was also advising him on this support system for the Naval Intelligence Support Center.

The panel was chaired by Dr. Ruth Davis, who was in DoD at one time and is one of the top computer people in the country. She is very active in intelligence circles. John Butts then said, "I wish you would take that job. You could be an honest broker. You can tell us where we're screwing up and you can tell them where they're screwing up."

So I said, "All right, I'll do it."

---

[*] Rear Admiral John L. Butts, USN, served as Director of Naval Intelligence from August 1982 to September 1985.

I took a contract with them. I worked with them several years, and in the course of that time found fault, that is, found things that I thought ought to be done on the part of the company that they weren't doing, and also things that the Navy should do but wasn't.

On one occasion, I called the head of SDC's Washington office and said, "You people have got to get together with Admiral Butts and get to the root of these problems that you're having. You're going to lose your contract if you don't sort this thing out and improve the responsiveness of your organization. That improvement can only come when you've had a meeting of the minds across the top as to what it is they expect and what you plan to do in order to meet those requirements."

Nothing happened. So a week later I called Frank Lehan, also a consultant with SDC. Frank developed the command and control system for the deep space probe. He's a Cal Tech graduate and very highly regarded as one of the maybe two or three top people in the entire country on signals technology.

Frank called the president of the company. The next thing I knew, George Miller, who was chairman of the board, set up a conference call. He asked me what the problem was. He said he was very proud when they won that contract. He thought that it was very important, and he wanted to be sure that they succeeded in it. "Where's the problem?"

I said, "The problem's in your Washington office. The problem is that your people back there are not getting together with the Navy at proper levels, and you need to clear the air."

So he said he would. Then he went to see John Butts, and they had a conversation about it. Then he fired his Washington office head and put in Don Biggar, who was about three or four in this setup out in Santa Monica.

Well, UNISYS bought out Systems Development at a later date, and shortly after that happened, why, I terminated my contract with them. I wasn't very active in the last two or three months of it, and so I terminated. I didn't want to adjust myself to a whole new setup.

Then the other outfit that I've been with, and am today, is with SWL, Special Warfare Lab. SWL is a subordinate company to General Research Corporation. They have long had a contract for providing support to the Navy space program. A number of the people that worked at the Naval Research Lab are SWL employees. The one who wanted me was Dr. Robert Hess. There was then a Navy captain working with Bob Hess on Navy space systems activities. I've been with SWL assisting Bob Hess since 1977. Then later in the '80s another retired Navy captain, a "SigInter," also an SWL employee, I've been assisting him.

All of this work takes place at the Navy Research Lab. I never go to--I think I've been out to SWL headquarters once, when Al Gallotta, who had been the head of the Navy's electronic warfare office in OpNav for a while, was president of SWL.* I went out to visit with him because I'd known and worked with him a long time.

In the early '80s, we began to see major changes in the way the fleet operated. It moved into spread formation. It began to use deception. It began to exploit quiet modes of movement. It began to take any number of steps to negate the effectiveness of Soviet surveillance systems, including their satellites and their radar satellite and all the rest of that, and many of these are not hard at all to do. All space systems have to be cued on to some target, and if you deny the cue or give false cues, they can't collect information. These applications are controlled in flag tactical command centers, outgrowths of Outlaw Shark.

Then my last involvement began in 1989 and wound up maybe early this past year. That was with the Institute for Defense Analyses (IDA). They were charged by SecDef with examining into competing technologies for a wide area space surveillance system. Both the Navy and the Air Force had recommendations in that area. When I asked why I was on the panel, since I'm not technical, the IDA gent in charge, Dr. Rosenberg, said, "Well, your job is to see that the Navy gets a square deal."

Well, that's an OP-60-type job. I said, "Okay, I'll take it on that basis."

I already was very familiar with the Navy system and its architectural aspects, which get into philosophies on command and control, specifically, whether you're going to permit nodal systems to intervene or whether you're going direct in getting information for targeting moving targets in time to be able to release a weapon with a terminal guidance system sufficiently accurately to destroy that target. That means no loss in time from beginning to end.

---

* Rear Admiral Albert A. Gallotta, Jr., USN (Ret.).

If you look at the system for exploiting the Patriot missile against Scuds, you find that the reason there were so many false alarms was because a space system had to trigger Patriot, and there are any number of things that could trigger that space system.[*] When you consider the turnaround time that's required from event to exploitation of same, you're talking two or three or four minutes.

But you can readily see how these things back up deeply into command and control philosophies. The command and control policies have to be such that the architectural features of a space system, meaning how it processes information and delivers it to the people who need it, by what routes and in what time frames, do not impose delays that reduce weapons accuracies. I envision moving targets.

I guess my principal point I would make in connection with that IDA study was that I was the only one on that panel--there was one other military, a retired Air Force Lieutenant General Brown, who was a Naval Academy graduate in '52, but I was the only one on that panel that had any understanding of how the fleet CinCs exploited information tactically that was derived from space systems.[†]

I also found that J-6 in the joint staff was incapable of translating the CinCs' requirements as to what they wanted in new space systems into a melded product that would represent the requirements of all of them. They were quite incapable of doing it, and it isn't surprising, because I'll bet not one single officer in J-6 had ever been in a position on a CinC staff where he was privy to that kind of information which is highly compartmented, and certainly neither Dr. Soper nor Dr. Pierce, in their OSD offices, had the remotest idea of any of this.[‡] They did not know that the architectural aspects of a space surveillance system was a major factor in any development, that the classification of that was very high, and that they couldn't sensibly discuss the systems that were proposed at the level of security that they specified, because that excluded all of the architectural features.

The architectural features have to do with how the satellite operates, how long it can stay on, how long it's required to be on, whether its recuperative ability to function can be accommodated in the short time that it's exposed to the sun again. These things are

---

[*] Scud is a missile used by the Iraqis in the 1991 Gulf War; Patriot was a missile used against the Scud.
[†] Lieutenant General Bruce K. Brown, USAF (Ret.)
[‡] Gordon K. Soper, Bruce Pierce.

powered by sun rays, and their batteries are recharged. So obviously a system that uses less electricity has attractions that permit it to be much more broadly used than one that's highly expensive in its use of electric power. One commander might exhaust its total capability within his area, and it would be out of use for another couple of hours till it could recuperate.

So I took the head of our panel, Dr. John Allen, who was head of the Air Force Scientific Advisory Board, out to Suitland. We were talking one day, and he made the complaint that he would like to know how the CinCs use information tactically that came from space systems.

I said, "Okay, I'll set up a series of briefings. You'll have to give me a whole morning, and we will explain to you exactly how the CinCs use information tactically that they get from satellites."

So I called Tom Brooks, the DNI, and told him that I'd made this commitment. I wanted Captain Jack Frost, recently CinCPacFlt's intelligence officer; Captain Hammer, recently CinCPacFlt's "cryppie;" and several others in his office. Also Federici from the Center for Naval Analyses--all with hands-on experience in satellite information.[*]

We started in the morning at about 8:30, and we went through till noon briefing Dr. John Allen. We went through the whole thing--all the various compartmented channels, the exploitation, some of the things that Ace Lyons had done as CinCPacFlt. Tom Brooks came down and talked for a few minutes, then went on.

When it was all done, John Allen said to me, "I wish OSD understood this." But anyway, that did help, because he wrote the final report that came out, and the whole thing was much more favorable to the Navy's case in command and control than would have been the case had he not had this exposure.

I'm still signed up with those people, but there hasn't been any activity for a year, and I consider it dead. I probably will terminate my contract with SWL at its expiration this April or May, at which point in time I'll be fully retired.

---

[*] Captain John A. Frost, USN; Captain George C. Hammer, USN.

Q: At lunch you were providing an assessment on Admiral Lyons as CinCPacFlt. I'd appreciate it if you could put that on the tape, please.

Admiral Richardson: Well, I've spent a lot of time with different CinCPacFlts, not all of them, but I know what's been going on out there by virtue of my involvement with the intelligence panel and the Naval Intelligence Support Center. Also, I've been out there, as I said, and was out in particular with Tom Hayward once and Ace Lyons on two or three occasions.

It was quite clear to me that no CinC has been as forward-looking or done as much to initiate a more modern employment of fleet assets than has Ace Lyons. He's head and shoulders beyond anybody else in exploiting intelligence. He sent for commanding officers of ships who went through and questioned them on intelligence. Seldom, if ever, did they get to go to see the CinC in the past. Yet Ace sent for them. He wanted them to come up to see him, and then he started asking a lot of questions on intelligence to find out what they knew. Then, when they went back, they had become "sensitized."

The skipper of the Enterprise was one. Ace asked him a number of questions and didn't get answers. So after a few choice words, why, the skipper of the Enterprise left, knowing there was some aspect of Navy employment that he had simply not gotten up to date on. I'm sure he went back and chewed out his intelligence officer.

But he did things in terms of exploiting, and I could cite things that are quite sensitive in the area of submarine warfare. He did them to substantially increase the extracting of information collected by satellites but not yet exploited. In the mission ground sites of satellites, he had additional people put in to look out for the sort of information that he needed and wanted. He had them trained, and then in tactical ways he created a number of exercise exploitations based on operational patterns. Most impressively, he created the Red Cell and ran several major forces across the Pacific into the northwestern region, measuring the amount of information that the Soviets were able to pick up, using our own space systems to simulate what Soviet space systems could do. He's done all that sort of stuff.

He definitely moved the fleet's competence well forward in the general area of modern warfare. Fortunately, we may not have to test that.

Q: You said you felt a need to come to his support because there was opposition to him. What did that entail?

Admiral Richardson: You know that he worked for me in Sixth Fleet. In the '80s, there were people in Honolulu in high places who were bad-mouthing Admiral Lyons. These were Navy retired people who were bad-mouthing him because he was the choice of the Secretary of the Navy and not the choice of the Chief of Naval Operations.[*]

This came to my attention from Admirals Mickey Weisner and Bobby Inman. Both he and Bobby Inman were very upset. On my first visit out there, I said to Ace that I had come out for three things. I wanted to show my support, and I wanted to make sure that he knew some of the leading locals who could then be in a position to counteract some of this unfortunate talk. And I wanted to see what the members of his staff were doing under his leadership. Third, I wanted to find out how he and his staff were getting along. I said, "I know you very well, Ace, and you're not the easiest guy to live with, and I'd like to know how your staff reacts to you."

He said, "Fine, go ahead."

I said, "If you have no objection."

He said, "Go ahead." He said, "As a matter of fact, I have a problem with one officer. Maybe you can help me with him."

So I did. I visited with that officer. In fact, I worked with him part of the time. I told him how to handle Ace Lyons. I said that one had to really dig his heels in, stand up and take whatever guff that he might get, but hold his ground, deliver his message, and not be buffaloed.

---

[*] John F. Lehman, Jr., served as Secretary of the Navy from 1981 to 1987. The ties between Lehman and Lyons are discussed at length in Gregory L. Vistica, Fall from Glory: The Men Who Sank the U.S. Navy (New York: Simon & Schuster, 1995).

So when I came back, I talked to one of the people high up in intelligence back here, either the DNI or the deputy DNI--I won't be specific who--and pointed out this problem. He said, "I'll send him goodies to get him into the front office more often."

That did clear up. He was self-effacing, and that was a personality problem that had to be overcome. So that was my first visit.

My second visit was in connection with his first running of the Red Cell, and we've discussed that already. And my third visit was when he was relieved. I went out for that. Bobby Inman made the address. I knew that Ace had been canned, and I thought it most unfortunate. But I knew both CinCs. Ace had been my assistant ops officer in Sixth Fleet, and I had worked with him when he commanded Second Fleet. Ron Hays, who was CinCPac, had been my CAG on Kitty Hawk when I was the task force commander off Vietnam in '66.[*] So I knew both of them very well, and it really does take a genius to not get along with Ron Hays. He's easy to get along with. But Ace couldn't do it. As Bobby Inman one day remarked, he said, "I can't understand why anybody can't accommodate with Ron Hays." But Ron became upset with him, and not without reason.

But I later was talking with Chick Clarey at this same time. Chick Clarey told me, "I heard so many bad things about Ace Lyons, I decided to find out for myself. So I went out and introduced myself, got to know him. We play golf together now. What I found out is exactly the opposite of what I had been hearing."

Q: What was your connection with Admiral Lyons in Second Fleet?

Admiral Richardson: In the early '80s he was ordered as Com2ndFlt. I sent him a message. I said, "Dear Ace, Can't recall anything Second Fleet ever did. Don't remember any Commander Second Fleet ever got promoted. Congratulations on your new assignment." [Laughter]

Q: And he did get promoted.

---

[*] Admiral Ronald J. Hays, USN, served as Commander in Chief Pacific from September 1985 to September 1988.

Admiral Richardson: Then I started sending a group of people down to brief him. For example, I sent Don Jermann down. At that time, the naval intelligence expert on space activity was a good-looking blonde female who was quite large.

Q: Well endowed?

Admiral Richardson: Very well endowed. Well, I mean amply endowed everywhere.

Q: Big all over.

Admiral Richardson: A lot of her. So Don and she got together and went down, drove down together. And Don, of course, is the one who's out of this world in the business of signal intelligence. So Ace's staff stupidly put her on first, and Ace wouldn't let her leave. The two hours they had there, she was on the stage an hour and three-quarters. Then Don came up for about 15 minutes. And so Ace didn't get a lot out of him.

Bob Hess, Dr. Robert Hess, was at that point the technical director of the Navy's space program, which was designed for tactical purposes. The only space system ever designed specifically for tactical exploitation. Bob Hess went down and spent time with him. I arranged for the head of the outside advisory group to the NSA to go down. Mickey Weisner's been a member of that for a long time. I sent about half a dozen people down to bring Ace Lyons up to speed in the exotic world of TKSI.

So anyway, then I went down to visit with him and his intelligence officer. He's very domineering, and you're never quite sure how his staff would react to him. It's important that they assert themselves and stand their ground. And so I was interested in seeing how his staff worked, whether they were being cowed or not, and I thought they were being. I talked to different ones of them. I said, "You've got to stand up to that guy. You can't let him do that." But his intelligence officer was a commander, and he said, "It sure is exciting being here." He said, "Things were so doggone dull till he got here. Now they're . . ." He loved it, the intelligence officer.

Q: Do you have any observations on last year's war over in the Persian Gulf?

Admiral Richardson: One of the things done in Desert Shield was by an organization in Suitland. The air Navy has gone very heavily into strike planning, using intelligence. When Desert Shield came along, this intelligence group in Suitland had been working two months on the setup and structure within Iraq of air defenses and air capabilities. They completed this in the ensuing two to three months. The minute the Kuwait invasion started up, I immediately rejoined my intelligence panel. I was in emeritus status, so I got right back in it.

This intelligence unit briefed us, and it was an overview. But it had all of the detailed information on weapons control radars, their location, the whole air-defense system, so that a pilot planning ingress/egress would have all the detailed information immediately available to plan it, including the signal characteristics of the batteries, the missile batteries, their vulnerabilities, both to electronic jamming and to direct impact of weapons. Everything that he needed was in the form he needed so that he could plan ingress/egress in hours, not days.

This applied to everybody in the air strike community, be they EA-6B operators who were concerned with jamming or whether they were route planning or escape innovating, the whole thing. They could take this single document, which was in the form of a briefing, with charts and with additional information on all of the electronic details, the signals characteristics and all that, and do the entire planning job.

But I had questions: "Where are the targets? What targets are you going after? They couldn't answer that in the Naval Intelligence Support Center. I have written articles about the crucial importance of choosing the right targets. A point is, why do you go in in the first place? You have to have a target of value, and it has to make sense in the context of what you did yesterday and last week and what you plan to do tomorrow and the next day, and that wasn't being worked. They said, "Well, somebody somewhere else is working the target problem."

But as far as further closing that gap that always exists between intelligence and operations with the detailed planning information for air strike, they knew exactly where all of the Iraqi aircraft were by types, by the competence of the Iraqi pilots, and by the weapons they carried. You knew, for whatever your specific purpose might be, exactly what you had to contend with. Well, this is exactly what they needed, and it was handed to them on a silver platter. That's what I call one perfect example of closing a gap between ops and intelligence. That's so important. The Air Force picked that up, and I'm told they're doing the same thing. I'm delighted.

Q: Well, thank you for that benediction, and let me add one of my own, Admiral. It has been a delight to get to know you, and I much appreciate all that you've put on the record. This will be extremely valuable to people of future generations. So thank you very much.

Admiral Richardson: You're very welcome. I'm happy to have been involved in it. I feel very strongly about some of these things, as you well know, or I wouldn't have persisted with it for so long.

Q: Thank you.

Index To

Reminiscences of

Vice Admiral David C. Richardson

U.S. Navy (Retired)

AD/A-1 Skyraider
Commander Bruce Simonds, CO of VA-702, was killed in an AD-4 accident off the carrier Kearsarge (CVA-33) in 1952, 52; vulnerable during bombing operations against North Vietnam in the mid-1960s, 199-201, 210

AF Guardian
Flown from the escort carrier Badoeng Strait (CVE-116) in 1952 during ASW exercises in the Pacific, 145

A3D/A-3 Skywarrior
Developed in the mid-1950s as a carrier-based nuclear bomber, 160; used for the dropping of mines against North Vietnam, 208

A3J/A-5 Vigilante
Developed in the late 1950s as a carrier-based nuclear bomber, 160

A-4 Skyhawk
Use against North Vietnam during bombing operations in the mid-1960s, 199-200, 205, 210; Commander Wynn Foster, CO of VA-163, lost his right hand when his plane was hit while on a bombing mission against North Vietnam in July 1966, 205-206

A6M Zero (Japanese Fighter Plane)
Operations in late 1942 against U.S. forces on Guadalcanal, 64, 67-68

Accidents
Grounding of the battleship Tennessee (BB-43) at San Francisco in June 1937 as the result of poor navigation, 22-25, 28-29; Commander Bruce Simonds, CO of VA-702, was killed in an AD-4 accident off the carrier Kearsarge (CVA-33) in 1952, 52; loss of a scout plane from the carrier Wasp (CV-7) early in World War II, 57-58; plane crashes during the course of fighter plane operational training in Florida during World War II, 83-85; the aircraft carrier Oriskany (CVA-34) suffered a disastrous fire on 26 October 1966, 203-205

Aircraft Carriers
The staff of Commander Air Force Pacific Fleet conducted carrier air group type training in Hawaii in 1945, 88-95; busy deployment schedules for Pacific Fleet aircraft carriers in the mid-1950s, 150-152; OP-05 studies in the mid-1950s on the future of carrier task forces, 154

See also specific ships: Badoeng Strait (CVE-116), Cowpens (CVL-25), Enterprise (CV-6), Enterprise, (CVAN-65/CVN-65), Hornet (CVS-12), Kearsarge (CVA-33), Kitty Hawk (CVA-63), Midway (CVB-41/CV-41), Oriskany (CVA-34), Princeton (CV-37), Ranger (CV-4), Ranger (CV-61), Saratoga (CV-3), Saratoga (CV-60), Wasp (CV-7), Yorktown (CV-5)

Air Force Pacific Fleet
Conducted carrier air group type training in Hawaii in 1945, 88-95; responsible after the end of World War II for getting servicemen home from overseas, 96; concern in the mid-1950s about busy deployment schedules for Pacific Fleet aircraft carriers, 150-152

Air Force, U.S.
Comparison of the Polaris ballistic missiles with Air Force weapon systems in the early 1960s, 185; bombing operations in the mid-1960s during the Vietnam War, 194; B-52 bombing of North Vietnam in the early 1970s, 209, 276-277

Air Group 13
As air group commander on board the carrier Princeton (CV-37) in the late 1940s, Richardson urged squadron skippers to land aboard ship quickly, 53, 114; deployed to the Western Pacific in late 1948, 114-121; comparison of the role of air group commanders in the 1940s and in later years, 116-117, 123-124; makeup of the air group in the late 1940s, 117, 120; relationship with the officers of the Princeton ship's company, 122-123

Air Warfare
Shore-based aircraft operations from the island of Guadalcanal in late 1942, 62-64, 66, 74-75; in the Battle of the Eastern Solomons in August 1942, 65, 67-68, 77; role of the Operational Training Command in 1943-44 in preparing fighter pilots for combat duty, 79-87; mock dogfight in 1945 between a Navy F8F and Army Air Forces P-47s, 88-89; carrier-launched bombing operations against North Vietnam in the mid-1960s, 191-195, 197-202, 205-207, 210-214, 223-224; rules of engagement for U.S. fighters against North Vietnamese aircraft during the Vietnam War, 208-209; bombing of North Vietnam in the early 1970s, 276-278

AFCEA
See Armed Forces Communications and Electronics Association

Allied Forces Southern Europe (CinCSouth)
Role in nuclear weapons delivery plans in the late 1950s, 164-165

Anderson, Admiral George W., Jr., USN (USNA, 1927)
Was relieved as CNO in 1963, in part because of his actions in the Cuban Missile Crisis the year before, 182-183; advice to Richardson on dealing with the British, 188; visit to the Sixth Fleet in the late 1960s as a member of the President's Foreign Intelligence Advisory Board, 232; was approached in 1970 concerning a plan by Admiral Elmo Zumwalt to get rid of a number of naval aviators once he became CNO, 268

Antiair Warfare
The capability of the battleship Tennessee (BB-43) in the late 1930s was rudimentary to the point of being useless, 21; the North Vietnamese mounted formidable surface-to-air missiles against U.S. attack aircraft in the mid-1960s, 199-201, 207

Antisubmarine Warfare
   In 1952 the escort carrier Badoeng Strait (CVE-116) took part in ASW exercises in the Pacific, 144-146; capability of the aircraft carrier Hornet (CVS-12) was enhanced by electronics and helicopters, 174-175; in the Sixth Fleet in the late 1960s, 238, 261; role of the Tenth Fleet in the Atlantic in World War II, 300-301

Armed Forces Communications and Electronics Association
   Conference in 1972 addressed Navy electronic warfare needs, 162, 282

Army Air Forces, U.S.
   In 1945 a group of P-47s had a mock dogfight with a Navy F8F Bearcat, 88-89

Arnold, Captain Murr E., USN (USNA, 1923)
   Commanded the aircraft carrier Princeton (CV-37) in the late 1940s when she collided with an oiler, 120-122

Austria
   Discussion by the Joint Staff in the late 1940s of the matter of equipping the Austrian Army, 126-127

Awards
   see Medals and Decorations

B-52 Stratofortress
   Air Force aircraft used in the bombing of North Vietnam in the early 1970s, 209, 276-277

Badger, Vice Admiral Oscar C., USN (USNA, 1911)
   Tried to get some newly commissioned ensigns to go with him in 1936 when he transferred from the Naval Academy to a cruiser on the West Coast, 19-20; served in the late 1940s as Commander U.S. Naval Forces Western Pacific, 118-119

Badoeng Strait, USS (CVE-116)
   A Marine Corsair squadron on board provided close air support to ground troops during the Korean War, 141-144; in 1952 took part in antisubmarine exercises, 144-146; liberty in Japan in 1953, 147-148; space allocations between ship's company and air group, 149; NROTC officers were effective in ship's company, 149-150

Baggett, Vice Admiral Lee, Jr., USN (USNA, 1950)
   Did an effective job as Director of Naval Warfare in the early 1980s, 299-301

Bailey, Midshipman Claude F., USN (USNA, 1934)
   Took seven years to complete the Naval Academy's four-year program, 14

Baird, Charles F.
   As Under Secretary of the Navy in 1967, took a trip to the Western Pacific that resulted in the relief of Rear Admiral Roger Mehle as CTF 77, 215-217

Barcelona, Spain
  Misunderstanding in the late 1960s over a U.S. destroyer skipper refusing to take a Spanish pilot, 252-253

Bates, Rear Admiral Richard W., USN (Ret.) (USNA, 1915)
  Egotistical officer who led a team that in the late 1940s did analyses of World War II battles, 102-107, 111-113; got caught in an awkward social situation when he wanted to attend conflicting events, 105; combat experience, 105

Beakley, Vice Admiral Wallace M., USN (Ret.) (USNA, 1924)
  Commanded VF-5 in the Wasp (CV-7) in 1941, 56, 61; as a retired officer, visited Lisbon in the late 1960s, 57

"Betty"
  See G4M "Betty" (Japanese Torpedo Bomber)

Birindeli, Admiral Gino
  Served as Commander in Chief of the Italian Fleet in the late 1960s, 243

Bode, Captain Howard D., USN (USNA, 1911)
  Commanded the heavy cruiser Chicago (CA-29) during the ill-fated Battle of Savo Island in August 1942 and subsequently killed himself, 111-112

Bombing
  Carrier-launched bombing operations against North Vietnam in the mid-1960s and early 1970s, 191-195, 197-202, 205-207, 210-214, 223-224, 276-278; use of Air Force B-52s against North Vietnam in the early 1970s, 209, 276-277

Borie, USS (DD-215)
  Lieutenant Commander Charles Hutchins, the destroyer's skipper when she was sunk during action against a U-boat in 1943, had been kicked out of the Navy in the 1930s, 17

Bradley, General of the Army Omar N., USA (USMA, 1915)
  Intelligent, down-to-earth officer who served 1949-53 as Chairman of the Joint Chiefs of Staff, 125-128; recommended Admiral Forrest Sherman as his relief, 128; involved in the early 1950s in the question of rearming West Germany within the NATO structure, 140

Bringle, Rear Admiral William F., USN, (USNA, 1937)
  As a football player at the Naval Academy in the 1930s, 13; had a good relationship with Captain Tom Hamilton, 90; commanded Carrier Air Group One in the late 1940s, 114-115, 117; dealt with the bombing of Vietnam while serving as Pacific Fleet operations officer in the mid-1960s, 195

Brooks, Rear Admiral Thomas A., USN
Served as Director of Naval Intelligence in the late 1980s and early 1990s, 299, 310

Brown, Admiral Charles R., USN (USNA, 1921)
Served as a guest speaker at the Naval War College in the late 1940s, 109; concern in the late 1950s about command and control of NATO air forces, 164

Burke, Admiral Arleigh A., USN (USNA, 1923)
As CNO in the late 1950s was interested in the process of sending aviators to command fleet auxiliaries, 27-28

Butts, Rear Admiral John L., USN (USNA, 1951)
As Director of Naval Intelligence in the early 1980s, encouraged Richardson to work with the Systems Development Corporation concerning installation of integrated automated intelligence processing at the Naval Intelligence Support Center in Suitland, Maryland, 305-307

Caldwell, Rear Admiral Turner F., USN (USNA, 1935)
Flew SBDs in support of the Guadalcanal campaign in the autumn of 1942, 62; headed the aviation requirements section of OpNav in the mid-1950s during a study on future carrier task forces, 155; stood watches in OpNav during the 1962 Cuban Missile Crisis, 181

Campbell, Rear Admiral Robert L., USN (USNA, 1924)
As ComServPac in the late 1950s, was sympathetic with Richardson's plight in taking command of the fleet oiler Cimarron (AO-22), which was in poor material condition, 165-166

Camp Lejeune, North Carolina
A murder there in the late 1960s sparked racial unrest when a Marine battalion subsequently arrived in Spain, 275

Carrier Air Group 13
See Air Group 13

Central Intelligence Agency
Links with the U.S. Sixth Fleet in the late 1960s, 233-234

Chafee John H.
As Secretary of the Navy, selected Admiral Elmo Zumwalt to become CNO in 1970, 273

Chicago, USS (CA-29)
Role in the ill-fated Battle of Savo Island in August 1942, 111-112

China
U.S. aircraft carriers visited Tsingtao in the autumn of 1948, 104, 118-119

Christensen, Captain Ernest E., Jr., USN (USNA, 1934)
The aircraft carrier Hornet (CVS-12) performed well under his command in 1959-60, 169, 171

Christiansen, Rear Admiral John S., USN
Assisted in CinCPacFlt's planning of bombing strikes against North Vietnam in the early 1970s, 276

Cimarron, USS (AO-22)
Was in poor material condition in 1959 when Richardson took command, 165-166; Western Pacific deployment in 1960, 167-169

CinCSouth
See Allied Forces Southern Europe (CinCSouth)

Clancy, Thomas L., Jr.
Author who received help from Captain John M. Rodgers in creating his novels in the 1980s, 228-229

Clarey, Admiral Bernard A., USN (USNA, 1934)
Service in the early 1970s as Commander in Chief Pacific Fleet, 269-270, 279-280, 282; observations in the mid-1980s concerning Admiral James Lyons, 313

Clark, General Mark W., USA (USMA, 1917)
Involvement in plans to equip the newly created Austrian Army in the late 1940s, 126-127

Clifton, Rear Admiral Joseph C., USN (USNA, 1930)
Was in an awkward position in 1945 while serving as executive officer under a poor carrier skipper, 91-92; commanded Carrier Division Seven in the early 1960s, 93

Coffin, Commander Albert P., USN (USNA, 1934)
Late in World War II commanded a squadron of F8F Bearcats, 93

Colbert, Vice Admiral Richard G., USN (USNA, 1937)
As president of the Naval War College in the early 1970s, picked up on the idea of teaching about operational intelligence, 239-240

Collisions
The aircraft carrier Princeton (CV-37) collided with an oiler during a deployment in late 1948, 121-122; between the Sixth Fleet flagship Little Rock (CLG-4) and a Greek Navy destroyer in June 1970, 263

Combs, Vice Admiral Thomas S., USN (USNA, 1920)
As OP-03 in the mid-1950s was concerned about electronic warfare in connection with future carrier task forces, 155; was OP-05 in 1955-56, 157

Command and Control
Experiments in the aircraft carrier Kitty Hawk (CVA-63) in the mid-1970s, 288-289

Communications
Were rudimentary in the late 1930s in the destroyer Downes (DD-375), 38-39; role of signals intelligence in the Sixth Fleet staff in the late 1960s, 230; in the late 1960s Italy provided a boat to the U.S. Sixth Fleet for communications surveillance in the Mediterranean, 235; excellent communications in the late 1960s for exchanging Sixth Fleet intelligence information, 235; fiasco regarding message transmission in the Liberty (AGTR-5) incident in June 1967, 237-239; command and control experiments in the aircraft carrier Kitty Hawk (CVA-63) in the mid-1970s, 288-289

Conatser, Captain Charlie N., USN
Served as chief of staff to Commander Task Force 77 during bombing operations against North Vietnam in 1967, 215-216

Congress, U.S.
Richardson was appointed to the Naval Academy in 1932 by a Pennsylvania representative, even though Richardson lived in Mississippi, 5-6; involvement in the F-111 fiasco in the late 1960s, 218-220; required in 1977 that satellite reconnaissance systems be used for tactical purposes, 231; reserve Rear Admiral William S. Mailliard served a short period of active duty with the Sixth Fleet while a congressman in the late 1960s, 263-265; conducted an investigation of racial unrest on board various Navy ships in the early 1970s, 274

Connolly, Vice Admiral Thomas F., USN (USNA, 1933)
Service as OP-05 in the late 1960s, 172, 216; the aircraft carrier Hornet (CVA-12) performed well under his command in 1957-58, 173; involvement in the F-111's cancellation as a Navy aircraft in the late 1960s, 218-220; close relationship with Rear Admiral Gerald Miller in the OP-05 organization, 220-221

Cooper, Rear Admiral Damon W., USN (USNA, 1941)
Was Commander Task Force 77 during carrier-launched bombing attacks on North Vietnam in the early 1970s, 276-277

Cook, Rear Admiral Ralph E., USN
As Director of the Naval Security Group in 1968, was helpful in giving Richardson up-to-date information on the Sixth Fleet, 226

Cotton, Captain Clement F., USN (USNA, 1921)
In 1945 was relieved of command of an air base because of devoting too much attention to fixing up his quarters, 90

Cousins, Admiral Ralph W., USN (USNA, 1937)
Was a carrier division commander during bombing operations against North Vietnam in the mid-1960s, 191; was sent to relieve Rear Admiral Roger Mehle as CTF 77 in 1967, 216; as Vice Chief of Naval Operations in the early 1970s, 269-270

Cousteau, Jacques-Yves
French oceanographer who visited the Sixth Fleet flagship in the late 1960s, 252

Cowpens, USS (CVL-25)
Used in 1945 to ferry cattle to Guam, 96

Craig, Lieutenant Kenneth, USN (USNA, 1926)
Served as executive officer of Fighting Squadron Five shortly before World War II, 61-62

Crommelin, Commander John G., Jr., USN (USNA, 1923)
As operations officer of the carrier Enterprise (CV-6) during the Battle of the Eastern Solomons in August 1942, 67-68

Crommelin, Lieutenant Commander Quentin C., USN (USNA, 1941)
Commanded VF-132 in the aircraft carrier Princeton (CV-37) in the late 1940s, 88, 120, 122-123

Crutchfield, Ensign Jack R., USN (USNA, 1936)
Dated in Hawaii while serving in the battleship Tennessee (BB-43) in 1936, 34

Cuban Missile Crisis
Actions in OpNav and the Joint Staff during the crisis in October 1962, 181-183

Cyprus
In the late 1960s the British used a highly effective radar on Cyprus to cover the Eastern Mediterranean, 232-233; unpleasant incident involving Greeks at Turks in Nicosia in 1966, 244

Damage Control
Reaction on board ship when the aircraft carrier Oriskany (CVA-34) suffered a disastrous fire on 26 October 1966, 203-205

Defense Science Board
Work on electronic warfare in the late 1970s, 296-297, 302

Desert Storm
See Persian Gulf War

Downes, USS (DD-375)
Ship handling by the ship's junior officers in the late 1930s, 35-36; participation in fleet exercises, 37, 39; communications were rudimentary, 38-39

EA-3 Skywarrior
Developed as an electronic warfare plane after its original design in the 1950s as a bomber, 160-161; monitored the Soviet helicopter cruiser Moskva in the Mediterranean in early 1970, 248

Eastern Solomons, Battle of
Air action on 24 August 1942 against Japanese carrier-based planes, 65, 67-68, 77

Egypt
Intelligence surveillance of in the late 1960s because of a concern over Egypt's possible acquisition of nuclear weapons, 233; intelligence failed to predict the 1973 Yom Kippur War against Israel, 285-287

Eisenhower, General of the Army Dwight D., USA (USMA, 1915)
Was considered by Joint Staff members as the ideal choice to head the newly forming NATO military establishment in the early 1950s, 129, 137

Ekstrom, Rear Admiral Clarence E., USN (USNA, 1924)
As Commander Carrier Division 17 in 1953, took a hot bath while on liberty in Japan, 148; his staff officers had trouble fitting in on board the escort carrier Badoeng Strait (CVE-116), 149

Electronic Warfare
Was an element considered during OpNav studies in the mid-1950s, 154-155, 160-161; work in the 1970s to make task force electronics compatible, 162, 295-296; development in the 1960s of the EA-6 jammer aircraft, 163; monitoring of Soviet signals in the Mediterranean in the late 1960s and early 1970s, 248-249, 261; use of by U.S. forces in the 1970s and 1980s, 262; an AFCEA conference in 1972 addressed Navy electronic warfare needs, 282; work of the Defense Science Board in the late 1970s, 296-298; use of in a Third Fleet exercise in the early 1980s, 297-298

Ellis, Lieutenant Commander Norman W., USN (USNA, 1924)
Was a sharp operator as commanding officer of Fighting Squadron Five in the early 1940s, 46, 53; helped Richardson with family problems in 1940, 50

Enlisted Personnel
Hardships imposed on crew members of Pacific Fleet aircraft carriers because of difficult deployment schedules in the mid-1950s, 151; changes implemented by Admiral Elmo Zumwalt in the early 1970s to improve the lot of enlisted personnel, 272-273

Enterprise, USS (CV-6)
Took aboard planes from the carrier Saratoga (CV-3) during the Battle of the Eastern Solomons in August 1942, 67

Enterprise, USS (CVAN-65/CVN-65)
   During bombing operations against North Vietnam in the mid-1960s, 196-197; in the mid-1980s the ship's commanding officer was embarrassed when quizzed about his knowledge of intelligence, 311

Enthoven, Alain C.
   As a Defense Department systems analyst in the 1960s, 177-178, 199-200, 218

F3F
   Grumman-built biplane that operated in Fighting Squadron Five in the late 1930s, 40; landing on board the carrier Ranger (CV-4) in 1941, 54; flown to San Diego in June 1941 for disposal, 55; comparison with the F4F, 69-70

F4F Wildcat
   Operations in Fighting Squadron Five in the Atlantic in 1941-42, 55, 58; shore-based aircraft operations from the island of Guadalcanal in late 1942, 62-64, 74-75; in the August 1942 Battle of the Eastern Solomons, 65, 67-68; comparison with the F3F, 69-70; comparison of the F4F-3 and F4F-4 models, 76-77

F4U Corsair
   Fighter plane that was difficult to fly when it was first introduced to the fleet in World War II, 80; a division of Corsairs leapfrogged carriers from the West Coast to Hawaii in late 1948, 115; Marine Corsair pilots from the escort carrier Badoeng Strait (CVE-116) provided close air support to ground troops in Korea in 1952-53, 141-144

F6F Hellcat
   Characteristics of in World War II, 87

F8F Bearcat
   Highly maneuverable fighter plane that had a successful mock dogfight in 1945 against Army Air Forces P-47s, 88-89; flown from the carrier Princeton (CV-37) in 1948, 114-115

F-14 Tomcat
   Entered the fleet in the 1970s after a squabble in the 1960s over the suitability of the F-111 for carrier use, 218-219

F-111
   Was the subject of a squabble in the 1960s as Secretary of Defense Robert McNamara tried to make a carrier plane of it, 218-219, 221-222

Felt, Admiral Harry D., USN (USNA, 1923)
   Commanded the air group in the carrier Saratoga (CV-3) during support of the Guadalcanal operation in the summer of 1942, 68-69; was difficult to work for while in the OP-03 organization of OpNav in the mid-1950s, 156-157; had a quick rise to become VCNO in 1956, 157

Fernandez, Arturo
Worked for many years, 1905-38, as a professor of the Spanish language for the Naval Academy, 2

Fighting Squadron Five (VF-5)
Operated Grumman F3Fs in the late 1930s, 40; Lieutenant Commander Norman Ellis was a top-notch skipper in 1940, 47, 53; assigned to the carrier Yorktown (CV-5) in 1940-41, 47-48, 54; transition to F4F Wildcats in 1941, 55; operations from the carrier Wasp (CV-7) in 1941-42, 55-57; operations from the carrier Saratoga (CV-3) in support of the Guadalcanal operation in the latter part of 1942, 59-61, 65, 67-68; operations while based ashore on Guadalcanal, 62-64, 74-75; living conditions for squadron personnel on the island of Guadalcanal in late 1942, 71-73; withdrawn from Guadalcanal in October 1942, 75-76

Fighting Squadron One (VF-1)
Training in 1944 for deployment to the Pacific, 87

Fire Control
Achieved by the Ford range keeper, a primitive computer, in the battleship Tennessee (BB-43) in the late 1930s, 22

Fires
The aircraft carrier Oriskany (CVA-34) suffered a disastrous fire on 26 October 1966, 203-205

Fitness Reports
An unsatisfactory fitness report on Commander Verne Jennings was "lost" for a while to permit his selection to captain in the late 1960s, 216-217

Fletcher, Vice Admiral Frank Jack, USN (USNA, 1906)
Was a man of indecision during the Guadalcanal operation in August 1942, 59-61

Flight Training
Various phases at Pensacola in 1939-40, 42-46

Football
At the Naval Academy in the mid-1930s, 14

Foster, Commander Wynn F., USN
As CO of VA-163, lost his right hand when his A-4 was hit while on a bombing mission against North Vietnam in July 1966, 205-206

France
In the early 1950s argued within the NATO structure against the rearmament of West Germany, 138-140

French Navy
    In the early 1970s had a harmonious relationship with the U.S. Sixth at the working level, despite official government policy, 246-248

G4M "Betty" (Japanese Torpedo Bomber)
    Operations in late 1942 against U.S. forces on Guadalcanal, 63-64, 77

Gayler, Captain Noel A. M., USN (USNA, 1935)
    Work in the aviation requirements section of OpNav in the mid-1950s, 154

Germany
    Dispute within NATO in the early 1950s over the rearmament of West Germany, 138-140

Gill, Lieutenant Cecil B., USN (USNA, 1925)
    Was a fine officer of the deck on board the battleship Tennessee (BB-43) in the late 1930s, 26-27

Ginder, Rear Admiral Samuel P., USN (USNA, 1916)
    Commanded Carrier Division Two when the Princeton (CV-37) and Tarawa (CV-40) deployed to the Western Pacific in late 1948, 118, 121

Goodpaster, General Andrew J., USA (USMA, 1939)
    Was briefed on Sixth Fleet plans while serving as SACEur in the late 1960s and early 1970s, 260-261

Grace, Princess
    Former film actress who provided hospitality in Monaco to Commander Sixth Fleet in the late 1960s, 250-252

Gray, Lieutenant James S., USN (USNA, 1936)
    Was disappointing but not cowardly as CO of VF-6 during the June 1942 Battle of Midway, 102-103

Gray, Lieutenant Richard, USN (USNA, 1936)
    As a fighter pilot in VF-5 during the 1942 Guadalcanal campaign, 67

Great Britain
    Richardson's experience in early 1946 as a student at the Royal Navy Staff College in England, 95-100; Admiral George Anderson's advice to Richardson on dealings with the British, 188; had a highly effective radar on Cyprus that covered the Eastern Mediterranean in the late 1960s, 232-233

Greece
    Has had a long-standing antipathy toward Turkey, 137-138; had a poor radar surveillance system of the Mediterranean in the late 1960s, 227; involvement in an unpleasant incident in Cyprus in 1966, 244

Greek Navy
Richardson made friendships in the 1950s with Greek naval officers with whom he later worked in different capacities, 163-164; harmonious relationship with the U.S. Sixth Fleet in the late 1960s, 243-244; collision between the Sixth Fleet flagship Little Rock (CLG-4) and a Greek Navy destroyer in June 1970, 263; received a U.S. destroyer in good condition in the early 1970s, 280-281

Grojean, Captain Charles D., USN (USNA, 1946)
Served in the late 1960s as commander of Sixth Fleet submarines, 256-257

Guadalcanal, Solomon Islands
The disastrous Battle of Savo Island that sank four Allied cruisers in August 1942 was the result of the rigid prewar way of thinking, 18, 60-61; invasion of in August 1942 was supported by the aircraft carrier Saratoga (CV-3), 59-61; shore-based aircraft operations from the island in late 1942, 62-64, 74-75; action in the August 1942 Battle of the Eastern Solomons, 65, 67-68; living conditions for U.S. personnel on the island in late 1942, 71-73

Guadalupe, USS (AO-32)
Incident involved in the refueling of the aircraft carrier Hornet (CVS-12) in the early 1960s, 170-171

Guinn, Vice Admiral Dick H., USN (USNA, 1941)
As a detailer in the Bureau of Personnel in the 1950s and 1960s, was involved in various officer assignments, 158, 188-189; served as Chief of Naval Personnel in the early 1970s, 272

Gunnery-Naval
In the battleship Tennessee (BB-43) in the late 1930s, 20-22; Japanese surface ship bombardment of Guadalcanal in October 1942, 71-72

Guns
Effectiveness of .50-caliber machine guns in the F4F Wildcat in late 1942, 63-65, 76

Hamilton, Captain Thomas J., USN (USNA, 1927)
Was a fine role model as head football coach at the Naval Academy in the mid-1930s, 13; supervised type training while serving in 1945 on the staff of Commander Air Force Pacific Fleet in Hawaii, 88-89, 91-92; exemplified fine leadership, 89-90

Harlfinger, Rear Admiral Frederick J. II, USN (USNA, 1935)
As Director of Naval Intelligence in 1968, was not helpful in giving Richardson up-to-date information on the Sixth Fleet, 226; asked Richardson to move his Ocean Surveillance Information System to Rota, Spain, in 1969, 235-236; similar setup in the Pacific in the early 1970s, 236-237

Hawaii
Social life for officers from the visiting battleship Tennessee (BB-43) in 1936, 33-35

Hayward, Admiral Thomas B., USN (USNA, 1948)
Was CNO in the late 1970s when the Office of Naval Warfare was established, 299

Hays, Admiral Ronald J., USN (USNA, 1950)
As Deputy CinCLantFlt in the late 1970s, received Richardson's report on electronic intelligence, 297; as CinCPac in the mid-1980s had a poor relationship with CinCPacFlt, Admiral James Lyons, 313

Helicopters
Value of in antisubmarine warfare operations in the 1960s, 174

Henry B. Wilson, USS (DDG-7)
Role in helping to recover the crew of the U.S. merchant ship Mayaguez, which had been seized in May 1975 by Cambodia, 229

Hess, Dr. Robert
Civilian official who worked in the 1980s on over-the-horizon targeting of cruise missiles and Navy space programs, 202, 298, 314

Hill, Rear Admiral Andrew J., Jr., USN (USNA, 1931)
Was Commander Service Squadron Three during underway replenishment operations in the Western Pacific around 1960, 167-168

Hill, Robert C.
Served as U.S. ambassador to Spain in the late 1960s, 245-246

Hoffman, Lieutenant Commander Melvin C., USN
Former enlisted pilot who served as executive officer of VF-1 in 1944, 87

Holcomb, William
Role in the late 1960s in the creation of the Ocean Surveillance Information System in the Sixth Fleet, 225-226, 234-235, 237, 255-256; suggested Richardson work for Lockheed after retirement, 288

Holloway, Admiral James L. III, USN (USNA, 1943)
Commanded the carrier Enterprise (CVAN-65) off Vietnam in the mid-1960s, 196-197; as CNO in the mid-1970s put Richardson on a panel to determine why intelligence failed to predict the 1973 Yom Kippur War, 285-287; interest in electronic warfare, 297

Houghton, Major General Kenneth L., USMC
Delivered a moving change of command speech about the rescue of Marines in the 1975 Mayaguez operation, 229

Hornet, USS (CVS-12)
Had an excellent record in battle efficiency competition in the late 1950s and early 1960s, 169, 172-173; West Coast operations in the early 1960s, 169-171; antisubmarine warfare capability in the early 1960s, 174-175

Hunt, Captain Robert F., USN
Did a superb job as targeting officer for Task Force 77 during Vietnam War bombing operations in the mid-1960s, 191-193, 195, 197, 225, 241

Hutchins, Lieutenant Commander Charles H., USNR (USNA, 1936)
Was kicked out of the Navy as an ensign in the late 1930s but came back to serve well in World War II as commanding officer of the destroyer Borie (DD-215), 17

Hyland, Admiral John J., USN (USNA, 1934)
As Commander Seventh Fleet during bombing operations against North Vietnam in the mid-1960s, 195, 201, 211-212, 217; retired from CinCPacFlt in 1970, soon after Admiral Elmo Zumwalt became CNO, 267-268; retirement in Hawaii, 280

Inman, Admiral Bobby R., USN
As director of the National Security Agency in the early 1980s, 289-291; alerted Richardson in the mid-1980s about opposition to Admiral James A. Lyons, 312-313

Intelligence
Role of photo reconnaissance in the targeting of carrier-launched bombing operations against North Vietnam in the mid-1960s, 191-193, 195, 197, 201; use of photos to assess the effectiveness of the bombing of North Vietnam, 206-207; creation of the Ocean Surveillance Information System in the Sixth Fleet in the late 1960s, 225-227, 230-236, 239; role of signals intelligence in the Sixth Fleet staff, 230; tactical photo reconnaissance by satellites in the late 1960s and early 1970s, 230-232, 255, 286; in the late 1960s Italy provided a boat to the U.S. Sixth Fleet for communications surveillance in the Mediterranean, 235; expansion of the Ocean Surveillance Information Center into the Pacific in the early 1970s, 236-237; the importance of prompt action in response to intelligence, 240-241, 254-255; the Soviet helicopter cruiser Moskva was kept under surveillance while in the Mediterranean in early 1970, 247-249, 253-254, 257-259; upgrading of intelligence capabilities of cruiser-destroyer flotillas deploying to the Mediterranean in the late 1960s, 271; mid-1970s study on intelligence support of the operating forces, including the Marine Corps, 283-284; failed to predict the 1973 Yom Kippur War, 285-287; the Outlaw Hawk and Outlaw Shark programs were initiated in the 1970s to provide integrated intelligence information, 289-289; attempts in the late 1970s to upgrade the Naval War College's teaching on intelligence, 290-294; use of satellites in the early 1980s, 297-298, 308-310; role in antisubmarine warfare in the Atlantic in World War II, 300-301; the aircraft carrier Ranger (CV-61) managed to elude surveillance during an exercise in the Pacific in the mid-1980s, 302-304; installation in the early 1980s of integrated automated intelligence processing at the Naval Intelligence Support Center, Suitland Maryland, 305-307, 311; in the early 1980s the U.S. Navy began operating in spread formations to thwart Soviet satellite surveillance systems, 308; emphasis on intelligence by CinCPacFlt in the mid-1980s,

311; the Naval Intelligence Support Center provided targeting information in the 1991 Persian Gulf War, 315-316

Iraq
Iraqi soldiers endured intense bombardment during the 1991 Persian Gulf War, 71-73; role of satellite reconnaissance, 232, 309; use of Scud missiles in the war, 309; targeting information provided by the Naval Intelligence Support Center, Suitland, Maryland, 315-316

Israel
Intelligence failed to predict the 1973 Yom Kippur War against Egypt, 285-287

Italian Navy
In the late 1960s provided a boat to the U.S. Sixth Fleet for surveillance in the Mediterranean, 235; harmonious relationship with the U.S. Sixth Fleet in the late 1960s, 242-243

Italy
Comfortable living quarters in Formia in the late 1960s for Commander Sixth Fleet and his family, 265-266

Jacksonville Naval Air Station, Florida
This station and satellite fields elsewhere in Florida provided a great deal of operational training to fighter pilots in 1943-44, 79-87

Japan
U.S. plans for the invasion of the island of Kyushu in late 1945, 94; the Japanese people were quite receptive in 1953 when crewmen from the escort carrier <u>Badoeng Strait</u> (CVE-116) were ashore on liberty in Osaka, 147-148

Japanese Navy
Air operations against Guadalcanal in late 1942, 63-68, 74-75, 77; surface ship bombardment of Guadalcanal in October 1942, 71-73; in the late 1940s Commodore Richard W. Bates led a Naval War College team that did analytical studies of World War II battles between U.S. and Japanese forces, 99-100, 102-107, 111-113

Jennings, Captain Verne H., Jr., USN (USNA, 1947)
Served as intelligence officer on the staff of Commander Task Force 77 during bombing operations against North Vietnam in the mid-1960s, 206, 216-217

Jensen, Lieutenant (j.g.) Hayden M., USN
Flew the F4F Wildcat while serving in 1942 as a pilot in Fighting Five, 63; return to the United States in the autumn of 1942, 78

Jermann, Captain Donald R., USN
Delivered briefings in the late 1970s on the Soviet Navy's ability to transit undetected, 291-294; briefing of Commander Second Fleet in the early 1980s, 314

Johnson, Admiral Roy L., USN (USNA, 1929)
Demonstrated great stamina as skipper of the escort carrier <u>Badoeng Strait</u> (CVE-116) in 1951-52, 143-144; in 1954 brought Richardson into the air weapons analysis section of OpNav, 153-155; recruited Richardson in 1961 for duty in OP-06, 176; as CinCPacFlt in the mid-1960s, was briefed on bombing operations against North Vietnam, 201, 211; supported the efforts of Commander Wynn Foster to remain on active duty after losing his right hand during a bombing run, 205; directed Richardson not to send operational reports that indicated a bomb shortage, 210

Joint Chiefs of Staff
Assessment of the various chiefs in 1949-50, 125-126

Joint Staff
Description of staff members working various problems in the late 1940s-early 1950s, 126-127, 133; involvement in planning for the NATO military establishment, 127-129, 133-140; work in relation to the Korean War, 129-130, 133; as director of the Joint Staff during the Cuban Missile Crisis in 1962, Vice Admiral Herbert Riley slowed down an urgent message, 181-182; had an ineffective targeting system for the bombing of North Vietnam in the mid-1960s, 207, 223

<u>Kearsarge</u>, USS (CVA-33)
Commander Bruce Simonds, CO of VA-702, was killed in an AD-4 accident off the ship in 1952, 52

Kidd, Vice Admiral Isaac C., Jr., USN (USNA, 1942)
As Commander First Fleet in 1969-70, 2, 271; as Commander Sixth Fleet in 1970-71, 262, 270

Kinnear, Rear Admiral George E. R. II, USN
Involvement with command and control experiments in the aircraft carrier <u>Kitty Hawk</u> (CVA-63) in the mid-1970s, 288-289

Kinsella, Captain William T., USN (USNA, 1934)
Had a run-in with Rear Admiral Don Felt while serving in OpNav in the mid-1950s and retired soon afterward, 156-157

Kirkpatrick, Lieutenant Commander Raleigh C., Jr., USN (USNA, 1935)
Monitored pilot performance during operational training in Florida in World War II, 84-85

<u>Kitty Hawk</u>, USS (CVA-63)
Conducted command and control experiments in the mid-1970s, 288-289

Korean War
President Harry S. Truman's involvement in negotiations with the North Koreans, 129-130; the firing of General Douglas MacArthur in 1951 for insubordination, 130-131;

possibility of using nuclear weapons, 131; in 1950, early in the war, Marines and Turks appeared to do much of the fighting, 133-134; Marine Corsair pilots from the escort carrier Badoeng Strait (CVE-116) provided close air support to ground troops in 1952-53, 141-144

Lacy, Rear Admiral Paul L., Jr., USN (USNA, 1943)
As ComSubPac in the early 1970s, prepared a plan for dealing with out-of-area Soviet submarines, 279

La Rocque, Rear Admiral Gene R., USN
Was a very effective officer while serving in the OP-06 organization in the early 1960s, 185-186; accompanied the Under Secretary of the Navy Charles Baird on a trip to the Western Pacific in 1967, 215-217

Leave and Liberty
Junior officers from the battleship Tennessee (BB-43) had an active social life while visiting Hawaii in 1936, 34-35; the Japanese people were quite receptive in 1953 when crewmen from the escort carrier Badoeng Strait (CVE-116) were ashore on liberty in Osaka, 147-148; fighting involving U.S. personnel on liberty on the island of Malta in the late 1960s, 242

Liberty, USS (AGTR-5)
Intelligence ship that was the victim of poor communications in connection with a warning to move away from the Mediterranean coast in June 1967, 237-239

Little Rock, USS (CLG-4)
Service as Sixth Fleet flagship in the late 1960s and early 1970s, 249, 259, 271; collision with a Greek ship in 1970, 263

Logistics
Support of U.S. operations on Guadalcanal in the latter part of 1942, 75-76; subject of study at the Naval War College in the late 1940s, 107-108; shortage of the right kind of bombs for use against North Vietnam in the mid-1960s, 210

Long, Admiral Robert L. J., USN (USNA, 1944)
Was CinCPac in the early 1980s during the installation of enhanced intelligence capability in the aircraft carrier Midway (CV-41), 289; as VCNO in the late 1970s, 292

Lorenzini, Admiral Giuseppe Roselli
Italian officer who commanded NATO naval forces in the late 1960s, 243

Lovelace, Lieutenant Commander Paul C., USN (USNA, 1938)
Commanded Attack Squadron 135 in the aircraft carrier Princeton (CV-37) in the late 1940s and filed a report when a ship collision damaged one of his airplanes, 120-121

Luckey, Lieutenant Colonel Robert B., USMC
Was stationed on Guadalcanal in late 1942, 71-72

Lyons, Admiral James A., Jr., USN (USNA, 1952)
Was an aggressive, take-charge individual in the late 1960s-early 1970s while serving on the Sixth Fleet staff, 238, 248, 255, 259-260; was Commander in Chief Pacific Fleet during ocean transit exercises in the mid-1980s, 302-304; emphasis on intelligence in his tenure as CinCPacFlt, 311; engendered opposition on the part of some retired naval personnel in the Hawaii area, 312; poor relationship with CinCPac, Admiral Ronald Hays, 313; as Commander Second Fleet in the early 1980s, 313-314

MacArthur, General of the Army Douglas, USA (USMA, 1903)
Fired by President Harry S. Truman in 1951 for insubordination, 130-131

Mailliard, Rear Admiral William S., USNR
Served a short period of active duty with the Sixth Fleet while a congressman in the late 1960s, 263-265

Maintenance
A decentralized setup worked well for aircraft overhaul and repair at Sanford, Florida, in World War II, 81-82

Malta
U.S. personnel on liberty on the island in the late 1960s were involved in a riot, 242; Maltese politician Dom Mintoff had contacts with Commander Sixth Fleet in the late 1960s and early 1970s, 263-265

Margaritas, Vice Admiral K.
Served in the late 1960s and early 1970s as Commander in Chief of the Greek Navy, 163-164, 243, 280-281

Marine Corps, U.S.
Air operations from Guadalcanal in the autumn of 1942, 62-63; living conditions ashore on Guadalcanal in late 1942, 71-73; Marine Corsair pilots from the escort carrier Badoeng Strait (CVE-116) provided close air support to ground troops in Korea in 1952-53, 141-144; fighting involving U.S. Marine Corps personnel on liberty on the island of Malta in the late 1960s, 242; racial unrest in Rota, Spain, in the late 1960s, 275; deficiencies in the 1970s in the service's intelligence function, 283-284

Marion Institute, Marion, Alabama
Served as a feeder school for the Naval Academy in the 1930s, 4

Martin, Vice Admiral Harold M., USN (USNA, 1919)
Highly respected officer who hurt his chances for promotion in the 1950s by declining duty in Washington, D.C., 152-153

Martin, Vice Admiral William I., USN (USNA, 1934)
Service in 1967-68 as Commander Sixth Fleet, 227, 239; comments on a letter Richardson wrote in 1970 to criticize a plan designed to reduce parochialism in the Navy, 269

Mayaguez (U.S. Merchant Ship)
Seized by Cambodians in May 1975, when her civilian crew was recovered at considerable cost, 229

McDonald, Admiral David L., USN (USNA, 1928)
Served in the headquarters of the Operational Training Command in Florida in World War II, 83-84; as CNO in the mid-1960s, picked Richardson to serve as Commander Task Force 77 and gave him direction concerning the Vietnam War, 188-190, 200; as CNO directed an assessment of the Task Force 77 targeting system for the bombing of North Vietnam, 225

McKee, Vice Admiral Kinnaird R., USN (USNA, 1951)
Served as Director of Naval Warfare in the early 1980s, 299

McNamara, Robert S.
As Secretary of Defense in the early 1960s, 183-185, 198; disastrous conduct of the Vietnam War, 197-199, 201, 210, 223; was not held in high repute by a civilian audience Richardson addressed after returning from the Western Pacific, 213-214; unsuccessful attempt in the 1960s to make a carrier plane of the TFX/F-111, 218-219, 221-222

Medals and Decorations
Inequity of awards to personnel of different services in World War II, 74

Medical Problems
Richardson was operated on for appendicitis in the late 1930s, 42; Richardson's first wife had mental problems throughout their marriage, 49-51; Richardson was wounded in the legs by enemy gunfire when his plane was shot down near Guadalcanal on 12 September 1942, 63, 65-66; Commander Wynn Foster, CO of VA-163, lost his right hand when his A-4 was hit while on a bombing mission against North Vietnam in July 1966, 205-206

Mehle, Rear Admiral Roger W., Jr., USN (USNA, 1937)
In 1967, Under Secretary of the Navy Charles F. Baird made a trip to the Western Pacific that resulted in the relief of Mehle as CTF 77, 215-217

Midway, Battle of
Postwar analysis of the battle by a team at the Naval War College, 102-104

Midway, USS (CVB-41/CV-41)
The air group commander was killed in an aircraft accident in 1949, 56; the ship received enhanced operational intelligence capabilities in the early 1980s, 289

Miller, Rear Admiral Gerald E., USN (USNA, 1942)
Close relationship in the late 1960s with Vice Admiral Thomas Connolly in the OP-05 organization, 220-221

Mine Warfare
Use of air-dropped mines against North Vietnam in the 1970s, 208, 278

Mintoff, Dom
Maltese politician who had contacts with Commander Sixth Fleet in the late 1960s and early 1970s, 263-265

Missiles
Role of the long-range Tomahawk in the 1980s and 1990s, 45, 202, 289-290; development of Sidewinder and Sparrow in the 1950s, 161; the North Vietnamese mounted formidable surface-to-air missiles against U.S. attack aircraft in the mid-1960s, 199-201, 207; concern in the 1980s on over-the-horizon targeting of cruise missiles, 202; improper use of air-to-air missiles in the Vietnam War, 209; use of Scud and Patriot missiles in the 1991 Persian Gulf War, 309

Moffit, Captain Lloyd William, USN
Role in the late 1960s in monitoring intelligence developments connected with the Sixth Fleet, 226, 234

Monaco
Prince Rainier and Princess Grace provided hospitality to Commander Sixth Fleet in the late 1960s, 250-252

Moorer, Admiral Thomas H., USN (USNA, 1933)
As Chief of Naval Operations in 1967, discussed with Richardson the use of photography to assess the effectiveness of the U.S. bombing of North Vietnam, 206-207; sent Richardson out to talk to civilian audiences about the Vietnam War, 213; directed the relief of Rear Admiral Roger Mehle as CTF 77 in 1967, 216-217; involvement in the F-111 fiasco in the late 1960s, 218-220; role in the JCS, 223; reaction in 1968 when he heard that the Office of Naval Intelligence did not have sufficient up-to-date information on the Sixth Fleet, 226; monitoring of Sixth Fleet intelligence concerns, 234-235; recommendation of Admiral Bernard Clarey to be his successor as CNO, 273; as Chairman of the JCS in the early 1970s, 277, 279-280

Moran, Rear Admiral William J., USN
As Commander of the Naval Weapons Center at China Lake, was involved in the planning for the mining of North Vietnam in 1972, 278

Morison, Rear Admiral Samuel Eliot, USNR
Spent time at the Naval War College in the course of writing the operational history of the U.S. Navy in World War II, 102, 111

Moskva (Soviet Cruiser)
ASW capabilities in the late 1960s as a result of carrying helicopters, 174; was kept under surveillance while in the Mediterranean in early 1970, 247-249, 253-254, 257-259

N3N "Yellow Peril"
Biplane used for students in flight training at Pensacola in 1939, 43-44

Nance, Rear Admiral James W., USN (USNA, 1945)
Approached Richardson in 1970 and told him of tape-recorded telephone call in which Admiral Elmo Zumwalt outlined plans to get rid of a number of naval aviators after he became CNO, 268-269

NATO
See North Atlantic Treaty Organization

Naval Academy, Annapolis, Maryland
Academic studies in the mid-1930s, 2, 9-10; hazing in the mid-1930s, 7-9, 14; leadership structure among midshipmen, 10-11; role of the commissioned officers on the academy staff, 12-13; football team, 13; summer training cruises in the mid-1930s, 15-16; restrictions on midshipmen, 16-17; social life for midshipmen, 18

Naval Intelligence Support Center, Suitland, Maryland
Installation in the early 1980s of the integrated automated intelligence processing system, 305-307, 311; provided targeting information in the 1991 Persian Gulf War, 315-316

Naval Ocean Systems Center, San Diego, California
Work in the 1980s on over-the-horizon targeting of cruise missiles, 202-203; intelligence exploitation in the 1970s and 1980s, 285, 300, 302

Naval Reserve Officer Training Corps
In 1952-53 NROTC officers were more effective than Naval Academy counterparts in the crew of the escort carrier Badoeng Strait (CVE-116), 149-150

Naval Security Group
Assessment of its work in the 1970s in supporting the fleet, 282-283, 291

Naval War College, Newport, Rhode Island
In the late 1940s Commodore Richard W. Bates led a team that did analytical studies of World War II operations, 99-100, 102-107, 111-113; basic philosophy that students are there to improve themselves and imagination is welcome, 101; curriculum of the course in the late 1940s, 107-108; distinguished guest speakers, 109; contacts among classmates, 110; in 1971 added a course in operational intelligence to the curriculum, 239-240; attempts in the late 1970s to upgrade the college's teaching on intelligence, 290-294

Navigation
Grounding of the battleship Tennessee (BB-43) at San Francisco in June 1937 as the result of poor navigation, 22-25, 28-29

Nevada, USS (BB-36)
Several of the ship's junior officers in the late 1930s were kicked out of the Navy for misbehaving, 17

News Media
A photographer from Life magazine took a series of photos when the aircraft carrier Oriskany (CVA-34) suffered a disastrous fire on 26 October 1966, 203-204

North Atlantic Treaty Organization
Planning in the late 1940s and early 1950s for the NATO military establishment, 127-129, 133-140; role in the early 1950s in containment of Communism, 134; the Sixth Fleet did much to hold NATO together in the early years, 137; value in building cooperation among member nations, 138; dispute over rearmament of West Germany in the 1950s, 138-140; cooperation with the Greek Navy, 163-164; CinCSouth role in nuclear weapons delivery plans in the late 1950s, 164-165; Admiral George Anderson's advice to Richardson on dealings with the British, 188; had a poor radar surveillance system of the Mediterranean in the late 1960s, 227; maintained a naval headquarters on Malta in the late 1960s, 243; role of the command structure in holding the various nations together, 242-247

North Vietnam
See Vietnam, North

NROTC
See Naval Reserve Officer Training Corps

Nuclear Propulsion
Studies in the mid-1950s on nuclear-powered seaplanes for the Navy, 158-159

Nuclear Weapons
Possibility of use in the Korean War, 131; study in the mid-1950s of seaplanes armed with nuclear weapons, 158-159; the A3J and A3D were developed in the late 1950s and early 1960s to deliver nuclear bombs, 160; CinCSouth role in nuclear weapons delivery plans in the late 1950s, 164-165; comparison of Polaris with Air Force weapon systems in the early 1960s, 185; U.S. concern in the late 1960s about the possibility of nuclear weapons going into Egypt, 233

Ocean Surveillance Information System
Creation of in the Sixth Fleet in the late 1960s, 225-227, 230-236, 239; movement of to Rota, Spain, in the summer of 1969, 235-236; similar setup in the Pacific in the early 1970s, 236-237

Office of the Secretary of Defense
Difficulties in the early 1960s between Secretary Robert McNamara's systems analysis people and OpNav, 177-178; involvement in the F-111 fiasco in the late 1960s, 218-219

O'Grady, Vice Admiral James W., USN (Ret.) (USNA, 1936)
As a Naval Academy midshipman in the mid-1930s, 6; shut down the ship's engineering plant when the battleship Tennessee (BB-43) went aground in June 1927, 23; was executive officer of the aircraft carrier Kearsarge (CVA-33) during an AD-4 accident in 1952, 52

Operational Training Command
Role in 1943-44 in preparing fighter pilots for combat duty, 79-87

OpNav
OP-05 studies in the mid-1950s on the future of carrier task forces, 154-156, studies of seaplanes with nuclear power and nuclear weapons, 158-160; planning role of the OP-06 organization in the early 1960s, 176-186; activities in OP-05 in 1967-68, 212-214

Oriskany, USS (CVA-34)
Served as a platform for U.S. bombing operations against North Vietnam in 1966, 196, 201-202; suffered a disastrous fire on 26 October 1966, 203-204

O'Rourke, Captain Gerald G., USN (USNA, 1945)
Duty in the late 1960s as operations officer on the Sixth Fleet staff, 255-256, 262

Outlaw Hawk\Outlaw Shark
Programs initiated in the 1970s to provide integrated intelligence information, 289-289

P-47 Thunderbolt
Mock dogfight in 1945 against a Navy F8F Bearcat, 88-89

Panama Canal
"Secret" passage through the canal by the aircraft carrier Yorktown (CV-5) in May 1941, 48-49

Paré, Lieutenant Commander Edward E., USN (USNA, 1920)
Commanded the destroyer Downes (DD-375) when Richardson left for flight training in 1939, 41-42

Patton, Lieutenant Colonel George S., USA
Family life while serving in Hawaii in the mid-1930s, 34-35

Perry, Captain Oliver Hazard, Jr,. USN (USNA, 1944)
Served in the late 1960s as commander of Sixth Fleet submarines, 256

Persian Gulf War
   Iraqi soldiers endured intense bombardment during the 1991 war, 71-73; role of satellite reconnaissance, 232, 309; targeting information provided by the Naval Intelligence Support Center, Suitland, Maryland, 315-316

Philiponneau, Vice Admiral Pierre A. C.
   French officer who maintained good working relations with the U.S. Navy in the Mediterranean in the late 1960s and early 1970s, 247

Photography
   Role of photo reconnaissance in targeting of carrier-launched bombing operations against North Vietnam in the mid-1960s, 191-193, 195, 197, 201; a photographer from Life magazine took a series of photos when the aircraft carrier Oriskany (CVA-34) suffered a disastrous fire on 26 October 1966, 203-204; use of photography to assess the effectiveness of the bombing of North Vietnam, 206-207; tactical photo reconnaissance by satellites in the late 1960s and early 1970s, 230-232, 255, 286; satellites in the 1980s, 297-298, 308-310; in the early 1980s the U.S. Navy began operating in spread formations to thwart Soviet satellite surveillance systems, 308

Pineau, Lieutenant Roger, USNR
   His interrogations of Japanese naval officers after World War II were used in the Naval War College's analyses of various battles, 102, 111

Pirie, Vice Admiral Robert B., USN (USNA, 1926)
   As DCNO (Air) in the late 1950s, was involved in the process of sending naval aviators to command fleet auxiliaries, 27-28

Planning
   U.S. plans for the invasion of the Japanese island of Kyushu in late 1945, 94; planning in the late 1940s and early 1950s for the NATO military establishment, 127-129, 133-140; CinCSouth role in nuclear weapons delivery plans in the late 1950s, 164-165; theater plans involving the Sixth Fleet in the late 1960s, 259-260; CinCPacFlt's planning of bombing strikes against North Vietnam in the early 1970s, 276

Polaris Program
   Comparisons with Air Force nuclear weapons systems in the early 1960s, 185

Princeton, USS (CV-37)
   As air group commander in the late 1940s, Richardson urged squadron skippers to land aboard ship quickly, 53; visit to Tsingtao, China, in the autumn of 1948, 104, 118-119; deployed to the Western Pacific in late 1948, 114-122; collision with an oiler during the WestPac deployment, 121-122; relations between the ship's officers and the air group, 122-123; operations off the West Coast in early 1949, 124-125

Prisoners of War
   One pilot was proficient in escaping during the Vietnam War, so he was involved in improving training for others, 224

Pritzlaff, John C., Jr.
Served as the U.S. ambassador to Malta in the late 1960s, 263-265

Promotion of Officers
An unsatisfactory fitness report on Commander Verne Jennings was "lost" for a while to permit his selection to captain in the late 1960s, 216-217

Public Affairs
A Navy public affairs officer permitted a photographer from Life magazine to take a series of photos when the aircraft carrier Oriskany (CVA-34) suffered a disastrous fire on 26 October 1966, 203-204

Puget Sound Navy Yard, Bremerton, Washington
Overhaul work on the battleship Tennessee (BB-43) in the late 1930s, 29-31

Racial Unrest
On board various Navy ships in the early 1970s, 274; at Rota, Spain, in the late 1970s, 275

Radar
Use of in the latter part of 1942 during the Guadalcanal operation, 75-76; role in fighter director operations in World War II, 95; the carrier Enterprise (CVAN-65) gave a Soviet trawler a heavy dose of radar energy in 1966 in the Gulf of Tonkin, 196-197; NATO had a poor radar surveillance system of the Mediterranean in the late 1960s, 227; during that same period, the British had a highly effective radar on Cyprus that covered the Eastern Mediterranean, 232-233; use of electronic warfare in a Third Fleet exercise in the early 1980s, 297-298

Radford, Admiral Arthur W., USN (USNA, 1916)
Was approached in 1970 concerning a plan by Admiral Elmo Zumwalt to get rid of a number of naval aviators once he became CNO, 268

Radio
Communications by the destroyer Downes (DD-375) in the late 1930s, 38-39

Rainier III, Prince
Monaco head of state who provided hospitality for Commander Sixth Fleet in the late 1960s, 250

Ramage, Captain James D., USN (USNA, 1939)
Served in the air weapons analysis section of OpNav in the mid-1950s, 154, 157; role as Task Force 77 chief of staff in the mid-1960s, 190-196

Ramage, Rear Admiral Lawson P., USN (USNA, 1931)
In the mid-1950s headed a group studying future requirements in the area of electronic warfare, 154-155

Ramsey, Rear Admiral William E., USN (USNA, 1953)
In the early 1980s ran Pacific Fleet exercises with deceptive electronics, 262, 297-298

Ranger, USS (CV-4)
Richardson had a difficult landing aboard with an F3F in 1941

Ranger, USS (CV-61)
Was used in an ocean surveillance exercise in the Pacific in the mid-1980s, 302-304

Ray, Captain Herman L., USN (USNA, 1929)
Did an excellent job of commanding the escort carrier Badoeng Strait (CVE-116) during the Korean War, 143-144, 149

Reedy, Rear Admiral James R., USN (USNA, 1933)
Served as operations officer in the aircraft carrier Princeton (CV-37) in the late 1940s, 122-123; served as Commander Task Force 77 during bombing operations against North Vietnam in the mid-1960s, 190-191, 195-195

Reeves, Captain John W. Jr., USN (USNA, 1911)
Was demanding and difficult as commanding officer of the aircraft carrier Wasp (CV-7) in 1941-42, 56-58, 61

Refueling at Sea
Difficult for the fleet oiler Cimarron (AO-22) in 1959-60 because of the ship's poor material condition, 165-169; incident in the early 1960s when the oiler Guadalupe (AO-32) refueled the aircraft carrier Hornet (CVS-12), 170-171

Richardson, Vice Admiral David C., USN (Ret.) (USNA, 1936)
Ancestors of, 1; parents of, 1-3, 5, 51; boyhood in Mississippi in the 1920s and 1930s, 1, 3; education of, 2, 4; children of, 4, 44, 50-51, 250-251, 265-266; as a midshipman from 1932 to 1936 at the Naval Academy, 7-19; service from 1936 to 1938 in the battleship Tennessee (BB-43), 20-35; service in 1938-39 in the destroyer Downes (DD-375), 35-42; flight training in 1939-40 at Pensacola, 42-46; duty in 1940-42 in Fighting Squadron Five, 46-78; first marriage to wife Dorothy House, 49-51; second marriage to Jeanne Simonds McHugh, 51-52, 150, 245-246, 265-266; duty in the Operational Training Command in Florida in 1943-44, 79-87; while on the Air Force Pacific Fleet in 1945, conducted carrier type training in Hawaii, 88-95; duty in early 1946 as a student at the Royal Navy Staff College in England, 95-100; at the U.S. Naval War College, 1946-48 as a student and then a staff member, 99-113; served in 1948-49 as Commander Carrier Air Group 13, 113-125; as a member of the Joint Staff, 1949-52, 125-141; as executive officer in 1952-53 of the escort carrier Badoeng Strait (CVE-116), 141-150; served 1953-54 on the staff of Commander Air Force Pacific Fleet, 150-153; duty from 1954 to 1957 in the OP-05 organization in Washington, 153-163; service in the late 1950s on the CinCSouth staff in Naples, Italy, 163-165; commanded the fleet oiler Cimarron (AO-22) in 1959-60, 165-169; commanded the aircraft carrier Hornet (CVS-12) in 1960-61, 169-176; duty from 1961 to 1964 in

OP-06 in Washington, 176-186; selection in 1964 for rear admiral, 186-188; served from 1964 to 1966 as Commander Fleet Air Norfolk, 186-187; as cardiv commander and Commander Task Force 77 in 1966-67, 188-214; served in 1967-68 as Assistant Deputy CNO for Air, 212-224; service from 1968 to 1970 as Commander Sixth Fleet, 225-267, 271; as Deputy CinCPacFlt from 1970 to 1972, 267-282; activities following retirement in 1972 from active naval service, 282-316

Richardson, Commander David W., USNR (USNA, 1966)
Joined the reserve after service as a naval aviator, 50

Richardson, Lieutenant Samuel B., USN
As an instructor in the early 1990s at the Top Gun school, 44

Ricketts, Admiral Claude V., USN (USNA, 1929)
As Vice Chief of Naval Operations in the early 1960s, was involved in discussions with the other services, 177; intervened when an urgent message was delayed during the 1962 Cuban Missile Crisis, 181-182

Riley, Vice Admiral Herbert D., USN (USNA, 1927)
As director of the Joint Staff during the Cuban Missile Crisis in 1962, Riley slowed down an urgent message, 181-182

Rivero, Admiral Horacio, Jr., USN (USNA, 1931)
While serving as CinCSouth in early 1970 received a briefing on the Soviet helicopter cruiser Moskva, 257; served as an ambassador following retirement, 258; comments on a plan suggested by Admiral Elmo Zumwalt in 1970 to reduce parochialism in the Navy, 269; as VCNO in the mid-1960s, worked to improve the lot of enlisted personnel, 272

Robinson, Commander Rembrandt C., USN
While serving as aide to OP-06 in the early 1960s, was seen by some as a potential Chief of Naval Operations, 180

Rodgers, Captain John Michael, USN
Did a fine job as assistant intelligence officer on the Sixth Fleet staff in the late 1960s, 228-229; assistance to writer Tom Clancy, 228-229; served in the 1970s as chief engineer of the aircraft carrier Saratoga (CV-60), 230

Rooney, Commander Carl W., USN (USNA, 1934)
Flew in VF-71 in the carrier Wasp (CV-7) in 1942, later was ineffectual as air officer in the Princeton (CV-37) in the late 1940s, 122-123

Rota, Spain
In the summer of 1969 acquired the Sixth Fleet's Ocean Surveillance Information System for reasons of communication security, 235-236; site of Marine Corps racial unrest in the late 1960s, 275

Royal Navy
A British carrier operated in the Yellow Sea in 1952-53 to provide close air support to ground troops in Korea, 142

Royal Navy Staff College, Greenwich, England
In 1946 provided training that was a British counterpart to that offered in the U.S. Naval War College, 95-100

Russell, Captain Hawley, USN
The fleet oiler Cimarron (AO-22) was in poor material condition when he commanded the ship in the late 1950s, 165-166

Russell, Admiral James S., USN (Ret.) (USNA, 1926)
Advice concerning a congressional report on racial unrest in the Navy in the early 1970s, 274

Sanford, Florida
Site of Navy fighter plane operational training in World War II, 81-82, 84-85, 87

San Francisco, California
Grounding of the battleship Tennessee (BB-43) in June 1937 as the result of poor navigation, 22-25, 28-29

Saratoga, USS (CV-3)
Was too late to take part in the Battle of Midway in June 1942, 59; support of the invasion of Guadalcanal in August 1942, 59-61, 65-68, 77; torpedoed on 31 August 1942, 66; high degree of compartmentation made travel difficult below decks, 70

Saratoga, USS (CV-60)
Was well served by having Commander Mike Rodgers as chief engineer in the 1970s, 230

Satellites
Use of for tactical photo reconnaissance in the late 1960s and early 1970s, 230-232, 255, 286; in the early 1980s, 297-298, 308-310; in the early 1980s the U.S. Navy began operating in spread formations to thwart Soviet satellite surveillance systems, 308

Savo Island, Battle of
The disastrous battle that sank four Allied cruisers in August 1942 was the result of the rigid prewar way of thinking, 18, 60-61, 75; postwar analysis of the battle by a team at the Naval War College, 102, 111-113

Schoech, Vice Admiral William E., USN (Ret.) (USNA, 1928)
As Chief of Naval Material in the mid-1960s refused to support the F-111 as a carrier plane, 221-222; role in the late 1960s in the creation of the Ocean Surveillance

Information System in the Sixth Fleet, 225-226, 237; was approached in 1970 concerning a plan by Admiral Elmo Zumwalt to get rid of a number of naval aviators once he became CNO, 268

Second Fleet, U.S.
Vice Admiral B. J. Semmes, Jr., as fleet commander in the late 1960s, 271; Vice Admiral James Lyons as fleet commander in the early 1980s, 313-314

Semmes, Vice Admiral Benedict J., Jr., USN (USNA, 1934)
Served as Commander Second Fleet in the late 1960s, 271

Service Force Pacific Fleet
In the late 1950s and early 1960s ran the force of fleet auxiliaries that supplied logistic support in the Pacific, 165-169

Seventh Fleet, U.S.
Carrier air operations in the mid-1960s, during the Vietnam War, 190-212

Sexton, Midshipman Ormond Griffith III, USN (USNA, 1936)
After graduating as president of his Naval Academy class, joined several classmates in reporting to the battleship Tennessee (BB-43), 19

Sharp, Admiral Ulysses S. Grant, USN (USNA, 1927)
Working style as OP-06 in the early 1960s, 176, 180-181; as CinCPac in the mid-1960s, was briefed on bombing operations against North Vietnam, 201

Sherman, Admiral Forrest P., USN (USNA, 1918)
As CNO from 1949 to 1952, displayed a powerful intellect, 125-126; recommended as relief for General Omar Bradley as JCS Chairman but died before he could take over, 128, 131-132; recommended in vain that his brother-in-law, Vice Admiral Harold Martin, seek Washington duty, 152

Ship Handling
By junior officers in the destroyer Downes (DD-375) in the late 1930s, 35-36

Shore Patrol
Action in policing prostitution in Washington and Florida in the late 1930s, 29

Simonds, Commander Bruce T., USN (USNA, 1941)
As commanding officer of VA-702, was killed in an AD-4 accident off the carrier Kearsarge (CVA-33) in 1952, 52

Simpler, Lieutenant (j.g.) Leroy C., USN (USNA, 1929)
Served as commanding officer of Fighting Squadron Five during air action against the Japanese in the autumn of 1942, 61-63, 74, 76

Sixth Fleet, U.S.
Did much in the 1950s to hold the Mediterranean region together in the NATO alliance, 137; CinCSouth role in Sixth Fleet nuclear weapons delivery plans in the late 1950s, 164-165; Admiral Waldemar Wendt, as CinCUSNavEur, in 1968 asked for Richardson as Com6thFlt, 179; role of Richardson, as fleet commander in the late 1960s, in the creation of the Ocean Surveillance Information System, 225-227, 230-236, 239; monitoring of Soviet naval activity in the Mediterranean in the late 1960s and early 1970s, 227, 232-235, 239, 247-250, 253-259, 261-262; staff officers in the late 1960s and early 1970s, 228-230, 238, 248, 254; links with the Central Intelligence Agency, 233-234; National Week exercises in late 1968, 233-234; the intelligence ship Liberty (AGTR-5) was the victim of poor communications in connection with a warning to move away from the Mediterranean coast in June 1967, 237-239; relations in the late 1960s with various foreign governments and their navies, 242-253, 263-265; theater plans developed in conjunction with NATO, 259-260; operations limited by funding during the Vietnam War, 260; comfortable living quarters in Italy for the fleet commander and his family, 265-266; racial unrest at Rota, Spain, in the late 1960s, 275

Smith, Rear Admiral Gordon H., USN
Served as an attack pilot flying on strikes in late 1966 from the aircraft carrier Oriskany (CVA-34) against North Vietnam, 201; served as deputy commander of the Naval Electronic Systems Command in the late 1970s, 202, 296, 298; was on board the Oriskany during a disastrous fire in October 1966, 203

Smith, Captain William Cody, USN (Ret.)
Used aerial photography to advantage while serving as an attack pilot flying on strikes in late 1966 from the aircraft carrier Oriskany (CVA-34) against North Vietnam, 201-202; was an expert on over-the-horizon targeting in the 1980s, 202-203, 298; paralyzed and later killed in auto accidents, 202-203

Snowden, Captain Macon S., USN (USNA, 1946)
Was project manager in the late 1960s for the F-111, which was canceled in favor of the later F-14, 218

Sourbeer, Captain Emory R., USN
Did a superb job as Sixth Fleet intelligence officer in the late 1960s, 228, 254

Southerland, Commander James J. II, USN (USNA, 1936)
As air group commander in the Midway (CVB-41), was killed in an aircraft accident in 1949, 56; as a junior officer in VF-5 in the early 1940s, 56, 61

Soviet Navy
Emphasis in the 1970s and 1980s on the compatibility of task force electronics, 162, 296; ASW capabilities of the cruiser Moskva in the late 1960s as a result of carrying helicopters, 174; the carrier Enterprise (CVAN-65) gave a Soviet trawler a heavy dose of radar energy in 1966 in the Gulf of Tonkin, 196-197; heavy Mediterranean presence in the late 1960s and early 1970s, 227, 232-235, 239, 247-250, 253-259, 261-262; deployment of submarines out of Vladivostok in the early 1970s, 279-280; methods in

the late 1970s of avoiding detection while transiting, 291-294; unable to track the aircraft carrier Ranger (CV-61) and her battle group during an exercise in the Pacific in the mid-1980s, 302-304

Spain
In the summer of 1969 Rota acquired the Sixth Fleet's Ocean Surveillance Information System for reasons of communication security, 235-236; relationship with the Sixth Fleet in the late 1960s, 245-246; misunderstanding in the late 1960s over a U.S. destroyer skipper refusing to take a Spanish pilot in Barcelona, 252-253; Rota was the site of Marine Corps racial unrest in the late 1960s, 275

Special Warfare Laboratory
Support for the Navy space program in the 1980s and 1990s, 307-310

Spruance, Admiral Raymond A., USN (USNA, 1907)
Much admired as president of the Naval War College from 1946 to 1948, 101-102, 107

Stapler, Captain John T. G., USN (USNA, 1906)
Was the commanding officer of the battleship Tennessee (BB-43) when she went aground at San Francisco in June 1937 as the result of poor navigation, 22-25, 28-29

Stennis, Senator John C.
Involvement in the F-111 fiasco in the late 1960s, 218-220

Stockdale, Vice Admiral James B., USN (USNA, 1947)
As president of the Naval War College in the late 1970s, discussed attempts to upgrade the college's teaching on intelligence, 290-294

Strategy
Subject of study at the Naval War College in the late 1940s, 107-108

Sutherland, Lieutenant William A., Jr., USN (USNA, 1927)
Made an impressive appearance as a junior officer in the late 1920s, 4; service in the aviation training command in 1940, 47

Systems Analysis
Difficulties in the early 1960s between Secretary Robert McNamara's systems analysis people and OpNav, 177-178; shortcomings of in relation to the U.S. carrier-launched bombing operations against North Vietnam in the mid-1960s, 199-200

Systems Development Corporation
Installation in the early 1980s of the integrated automated intelligence processing at the Naval Intelligence Support Center, Suitland Maryland, 305-307, 311

TFX
See F-111

Tactics

Lieutenant Commander John S. Thach made great contributions to fighter plane tactics before World War II, 46, 69; Soviet tactical patterns while operating in the Mediterranean in the late 1960s and early 1970s, 234, 253-254, 261-262; in the mid-1970s CinCPacFlt set up a tactical training unit in San Diego, 302; in the early 1980s the U.S. Navy began operating in spread formations to thwart Soviet satellite surveillance systems, 308

Tennessee, USS (BB-43)

Gunnery in the late 1930s, 20-22; grounding at San Francisco in June 1937 as the result of poor navigation, 22-25, 28-29; boat operations, 25-26; formation steaming, 26-27; overhaul work at the Puget Sound Navy Yard, 29-31; feeding of junior officers, 30-31; calls on senior officers, 31-32; great fellowship among the crew in the late 1930s, 32; fleet operations, 32-34

Tenth Fleet, U.S.

Role in antisubmarine warfare in the Atlantic in World War II, 300-301

Thach, Lieutenant Commander John S., USN (USNA, 1927)

Made great contributions to fighter plane tactics before World War II, 46, 69

Tolle, Lieutenant Commander Robert J., USN

Did a fine job as assistant intelligence officer on the Sixth Fleet staff in the late 1960s, 228-230, 232; went to the Naval War College in the early 1970s to heighten awareness of operational intelligence, 239-240

Tomahawk Missile

Role of the long-range missile in the 1980s and 1990s, 45, 202, 289-290

Townsend, Vice Admiral Robert L., USN (USNA, 1934)

Served as a cardiv commander in the Hornet (CVS-12) in the early 1960s, 169; as ComNavAirLant in the late 1960s and early 1970s, was supportive of aerial photo reconnaissance, 255

Training

Summer cruises in the mid-1930s for Naval Academy midshipmen, 15-16; various phases of flight training at Pensacola in 1939-40, 42-46; role of the Operational Training Command in 1943-44 in preparing fighter pilots for combat duty, 79-87; in 1945 Air Force Pacific Fleet supervised type training for carrier air groups going through Hawaii, 88-95; schools for enlisted personnel in the mid-1950s disrupted aircraft carrier crew stability, 151; one pilot was proficient in escaping during the Vietnam War, so he was involved in improving training for others, 224; in the mid-1970s CinCPacFlt set up a tactical training unit in San Diego, 302

Truman, President Harry S.

Involvement in negotiations with the North Koreans in 1952, 129; the firing of General Douglas MacArthur in 1951 for insubordination, 130-131

Tsingtao, China
Visited by U.S. aircraft carriers in the autumn of 1948, 104, 118-119

Turkey
Has had a long-standing antipathy toward Greece, 137-138; had a poor radar surveillance system of the Mediterranean in the late 1960s, 227; involvement in an unpleasant incident in Cyprus in 1966, 244

Turner, Admiral Stansfield, USN (USNA, 1947)
As head of the Central Intelligence Agency in the late 1970s, would not grant clearances for increased intelligence instruction at the Naval War College, 292-293

Tuttle, Vice Admiral Jerry O., USN
Was extraordinarily capable as head of the Navy's command and control programs in the late 1980s and early 1990s, 294, 299

VF-5
See Fighting Squadron Five (VF-5)

Vietnam, North
Carrier-launched bombing operations against North Vietnam in the mid-1960s and early 1970s, 191-195, 197-202, 205-207, 210-214, 223-224, 276-278; the North Vietnamese mounted formidable surface-to-air missiles against U.S. attack aircraft in the mid-1960s, 199-201, 207; precautions to minimize bomb damage, 201, 205-207, 214; U.S. mine warfare against, 208, 278; rules of engagement for U.S. fighters against North Vietnamese aircraft during the Vietnam War, 208-209; bombing by Air Force B-52s, 209, 276-277

Vietnam War
Vietnam was of limited concern to OpNav in the early part of the 1960s, 183-184; support provided in the mid-1960s by Commander Fleet Air Norfolk, 186-187; as CNO in the mid-1960s, Admiral David McDonald picked Richardson to serve as Commander Task Force 77 and gave him direction concerning pilots, 188-190; carrier-launched bombing operations against North Vietnam in the mid-1960s, 191-195, 197-202, 205-207, 210-214, 223-224, 276-277; U.S. mine warfare against North Vietnam, 208, 278; rules of engagement for U.S. fighters against North Vietnamese aircraft during the Vietnam War, 208-209; bombing by Air Force B-52s, 209; after his return to Washington in 1967, Richardson went out to discuss the war with civilian audiences, 213-214; prisoners of war, 224

Wakelin, Dr. James
In the early 1970s headed a panel dealing with Navy intelligence support of operating forces, 282-283

Wallace, Captain Richard W., USMC (USNA, 1936)
Was stationed on Guadalcanal in late 1942, 71-72

War Games
At Britain's Royal Navy Staff College in 1946, 97-98

Warrington, USS (DD-843)
Shadowed the Soviet helicopter cruiser Moskva during operations in the Mediterranean in early 1970, 247-249, 258-259

Wasp, USS (CV-7)
Took aboard VF-5 in the autumn of 1941 because VF-71 was deficient, 55; operations in the North Atlantic in early 1942, 56-58

Weather
Impact on carrier-launched bombing operations against North Vietnam in the mid-1960s, 193-194, 197

Weisner, Admiral Maurice F., USN (USNA, 1941)
Hard-working officer who served in the air weapons analysis section of OpNav in the mid-1950s, 154, 157; commanded the Guadalupe (AO-32) during a refueling exercise with the aircraft carrier Hornet (CVS-12) in the early 1960s, 170-171; involvement in 1966 in detailing Richardson to a carrier division, 188-189; duty in Washington in the early 1970s, 279, 281; as CinCPacFlt in the mid-1970s set up a tactical training unit in San Diego, 302; alerted Richardson in the mid-1980s about opposition to Admiral James A. Lyons, 312

Wendt, Admiral Waldemar F. A., USN (USNA, 1933)
As CinCUSNavEur in the late 1960s invited Richardson to critique one of his briefings, 179, 226, 230; interest in Sixth Fleet intelligence concerns, 227, 235, 271

Wieland, Captain Dicky, USN
Did a fine job as Task Force 77 operations officer during bombing operations against North Vietnam in the mid-1960s, 191-192

Wilson, General Louis H., Jr., USMC
As Commandant in the late 1970s, addressed the Marine Corps intelligence function, 283-284

Wyoming, USS (AG-17)
Used for Naval Academy midshipman training cruises to Europe in the mid-1930s, 15-16

Yom Kippur War
A panel met in the mid-1970s to determine why intelligence failed to predict the 1973 war between Egypt and Israel, 285-287

Yorktown, USS (CV-5)
In 1940-41 she was a fine ship with excellent officers, 47-48; "secret" passage through the Panama Canal in May 1941 as part of being transferred from Pacific to Atlantic, 48-49

Zero
See A6M Zero (Japanese Fighter Plane)

Zumwalt, Admiral Elmo R., Jr., USN (USNA, 1943)
As prospective CNO in 1970, was recorded discussing plans to get rid of a number of naval aviators, 268-269; plan to eliminate parochialism by instituting non-traditional flag officer assignments, 269-270; instituted a series of Z-grams to promulgate changes in the Navy, 272-273; would have been a better CNO later, with more experience, 273; and the racial situation in the early 1970s, 274

www.ingramcontent.com/pod-product-compliance
Lightning Source LLC
Chambersburg PA
CBHW082149070526
44585CB00020B/2151